OFF THE RECORD

The *New* Music Business
Guide & Workbook
For
The Digital World

SECOND EDITION

Larry E. Wacholtz Ph.D.

Editing-*Brandon Michael Gaesser*
&
Tammy Talmadge

Thumbs Up Publishing

3803-a Woodmont Lane
Nashville, TN 37215
615-269-3383
www.thumbsuppublishing.com

—Off The Record—

The New Music Business
Guide & Workbook
For the Digital World
Second Edition
By

Larry E. Wacholtz, Ph.D.

Thumbs Up Publishing/Nashville
3803-a Woodmont Lane
Nashville, TN 37215
615-269-3383
www.thumbsuppublishing.com
lwacholtz@mac.com

LightningSource
www.lightningsource.com

ISBN- 978-0-9840572-0-7

Author- Larry E. Wacholtz, Ph.D.
Edited -Brandon Michael Gaesser & Tammy Talmadge
Cover Photo and Design-Cameron Powell
www.riverrockmediagroup.com/

Library of Congress
© 2009 Thumbs Up Publishing. All copyrights claimed in all chapter exclusive of U.S. government Library of Congress, Copyright Office material claimed including Chapter 2 (Protecting Creativity) and Chapter 3 (Copyright Registration), Chapter 4 (The Song Business), and Chapter 6 (Music Publishing). In addition, the contracts in Chapter 5 (a sample of a Single Song Agreement), Chapter 8 (a sample of a Recording Contract), and Chapter 11 (a sample of a Management Deal) are the sole property of attorney Rush Hicks, Attorney at Law, Nashville, TN.

All rights reserved. No part of this publication exclusive of United States material may be reproduced or used in any form or by any means, including photocopying, recording or information storage and retrieval without the written permission of the publisher. All United States government sources are not claimed as part of this copyright and may be used as provided by the United States Library of Congress.

Printed in the United States and England

TABLE OF CONTENTS

1-TALENT

- CREATIVITY-14
- CREATIVE SYSTEM-15
  - Songwriters-15
  - Artists and Vocalists-15
  - Musicians-16
  - Record Producers-16
  - Audio Engineers-16
- BUSINESS SYSTEMS-17
  - Music Publishers-17
  - Recording Studios-17
  - Labels-17
  - Promotions-17
  - Publicists-17
  - Artist Managers-18
  - Booking Agents-18
  - Concert Promoters-18
  - Mass Media-18
  - Click Media-18

ASSOCIATED CAREER-19
TYPES OF BUSINESS-19
    Sole Proprietorship-19
    Partnerships-Joint Ventures-19
    Corporations-19
ENTREPRENEURSHIP-20
REVENUE STREAMS-20
    Songwriting/Music Publishing Revenue Stream-20
        Songwriting Revenue Chart-21
    Record Label Revenue Stream-22
        Label Revenue Chart-23
    The Management /Touring Revenue Stream-24
        Management/Touring Revenue Chart-25
FINANCIALS-24
CAPTURING EMOTIONS AS SELLABLE PRODUCTS-26
LAUNCHING THE PRODUCTS-26
EVENT MARKETING-27
THE NEW MUSIC BUSINESS-27
SUMMARY-27
STUDY GUIDE-29
LECTURE POINTS-32
CHAPTER NOTES-35

2-PROTECTING CREATIVITY

- COPYRIGHTS-37
- HISTORICAL PERSPECTIVE-39
- STATUTE OF ANNE-39
- CONSTITUTION (ARTICLE-1, SECTION 8)-40
- EXCLUSIVE RIGHTS-41
  - Reproduction-copies-41
  - Derivative Works-41
  - Distribution-41
  - Public Performance-41
  - Public Display-41
  - Digital Transmission (Audio-Public Performance by Digital Transmission)-41
- TYPES OF COPYRIGHT OWNERSHIP-41
- PHONORECORDS-41
- SOUND RECORDINGS-42
- ACT OF 1790-42
- ACT OF 1831-42
- ACT OF 1909-43
- ACT OF 1976-43
- ACT OF 1992-44
- ACT OF 1993-44
- ACT OF 1995-45
- ACT OF 1997-45
- THE DMC-45
- ACTS OF 1998-45
- SONNY BONO-46
- P2P EFFECTS ON COPYRIGHT OWNERS-46
- SUPREME COURT DECISION ON PEER-TO-PEER FILE-SHARING-47
- ACT OF 2004-48
- NOTICE OF INTENTION-48
- NEIGHBORING RIGHTS-48
- GENEVA (1)-49
- GENEVA (2) (PHONOGRAMS CONVENTION)-49
- PARIS-49
- BRUSSELS-49
- THE BERN CONVENTION-49
- THE WTO AND WIPO-50
- NOT PROTECTED-50
- SUMMARY-51
- STUDY GUIDE-52
- LECTURE POINTS-57
- CHAPTER NOTES-59

3-COPYRIGHT REGISTRATION

- POOR MAN'S COPYRIGHT-61
- COPYRIGHT REGISTRATION-61

- A WORK-FOR-HIRE-61
- AUTHORSHIP-61
- FIXATION PROCESS-61
- PUBLICATION-62
- THE UNITED STATES COPYRIGHT OFFICE-62
- CERTIFICATE OF REGISTRATION-62
- REGISTRATION PROCESS-62
- ELECTRONIC REGISTRATION-63
- COPYRIGHT REGISTRATION FORMS-64
- MUSICAL ARRANGEMENTS-68
- SAMPLING-68
- FAIR USE RIGHTS-68
- COMPULSORY (MECHANICAL) LICENSE-68
- RECAPTURING ASSIGNED COPYRIGHTS-69
- KEY DEFINITIONS 69
- STUDY GUIDE-COPYRIGHTS-71
- LECTURE POINTS-73
- CHAPTER NOTES-75

4-THE SONG BUSINESS

- THE SONG BUSINESS-77
- ENTERTAINMENT AS EMOTIONAL COMMUNICATION-77
    - Stimulus-Response Relationship-78
    - Cognition-78
    - Expression of Creativity-78
- CONSTRUCT THEORY-79
- HISTORICAL PERSPECTIVE-80
- SONGWRITING AS A PROFESSION-81
- CAREER SONG-82
- WHAT TO "LOOK FOR" IN A MUSIC PUBLISHER-82
- PROFESSIONAL SONGWRITING ORGANIZATIONS-82
- WHAT PUBLISHERS "LOOK FOR" IN SONGWRITERS-82
- LECTURE POINTS-84
- CHAPTER NOTES-88

5-SINGLE SONG AGREEMENT

- SINGLE SONG AGREEMENT-SAMPLE CONTRACT-90
- WRITER-90
- PUBLISHER-90
- ROYALTIES-91
- NAME & LIKENESS-92
- ROYALTY PAYMENTS-93
- INDEMNIFICATION-94
- NOTICES-94
- SEPARABILLITY-95
- NOTICE OF BREACH-95
- CONTROLLING LAW-98
- SINGLE SONG AGREEMENT CONTRACT NEGOTIATION POINTS-98
- ADDITIONAL TERMS-100

6

- STUDY GUIDE-THE SONG BUSINESS-101
- LECTURE POINTS-103
- CHAPTER NOTES-104

6-MUSIC PUBLISHING

- PITCHING SONGS TO PUBLISHERS-107
- THE BUSINESS OF MUSIC PUBLISHERS-108
  - Major Publishers-108
  - Independent Publishers-108
  - Specialty Publishers-108
  - Foreign Publishers-108
  - Vanity Publishers-108
- DEPARTMENTS-109
  - Acquisitions-109
  - Legal-109
  - Administration-109
  - Payroll or the Royalty Department-109
  - Creative-109
- THE NATIONAL MUSIC PUBLISHERS ASSOCIATION (NMPA)-109
- SONGCASTING-109
- SPLITS AND SHARES-110
- VALUE OF COPYRIGHT OWNERSHIP-110
- BUSINESS EQUITY OF THE COPYRIGHT-111
- SINGLE SONG CONTRACTS-111
- TYPES OF DEALS-111
  - Work for Hire-111
  - Staff Writer-112
  - Co-Publishing-113
  - Administrative Publishing-115
  - Shark Deal-115
- CERTIFICATE OF REGISTRATION-116
- CERTIFICATE OF RECORDATION-116
- ARTIST LINE-116
- ROYALTIES/SPLITS/OWNERSHIP CHART-117
- LICENSES-118
  - Mechanicals-118
  - Sync (Synchronization)-118
  - Blanket (Public Performance)-118
  - Print-118
  - Transcription-118
- THE HARRY FOX AGENCY-118
- MECHANICAL LICENSES-118
- HOLDS AND FIRST USE RIGHTS-118
- THE STATUTORY RATE FOR MECHANICAL LICENSES-119
- THE CONTROLLED COMPOSITION CLAUSE-119
- COVER TUNE MECHANICALS COMPULSORY LICENSE-119
- FOREIGN MECHANICAL ROYALTIES-120
- INDIRECT ROYALTY "SPLITS"-121
- RECOUPMENT-121

- MEMORANDUM OPINION ON RINGTONES-1121
- SOUNDSCAN-121
- SYNC (SYNCHRONIZATION) LICENSE-122
- PERFORMANCE RIGHTS ORGANIZATIONS (PRO'S)-122
  - ASCAP-122
  - BMI-122
  - SESAC-122
- AFFILIATION/MEMBERSHIP-123
- BLANKET LICENSE-123
- BLANKET LICENSE FEES-104
- DIRECT PAYMENTS-123
- COLLECTIONS-123
- THE FAIRNESS IN MUSIC LICENSING ACT-124
- IN THE PIPELINE-124
- PAYMENT RATES AND SCHEDULES-124
- PRINT LICENSE-124
- TRANSCRIPTION LICENSE-125
- BEST EFFORTS-125
- TERMINATION OF CONTRACT-125
- REASSIGNMENT PROCESS-125
- SUMMARY-126
- STUDY GUIDE-MUSIC PUBLISHING-127
- LECTURE POINTS-132
- CHAPTER NOTES-135

7-LABELS

- MEGA ENTERTAINMENT INDUSTRY-137
- HISTORICAL PERSPECTIVES-138
- TRADITIONAL MEGA'S-138
  - Bertelsmann, AG-138
  - The Walt Disney Company-138
  - EMI Group, PLC-139
  - Sony Entertainment-139
  - TimeWarner-140
  - Vivendi/Universal-141
- MEGA ENTERTAINMENT-DIVISIONS-141
- MEDIA-ENTERTAINMENT DISTRIBUTION-142
  - News Corp-142
  - Comcast-142
  - Viacom-142
- 360-MUSIC -ENTERTAINMENT CORPORATIONS-142
  - LiveNation-143
- TYPES OF LABELS-144
  - Major Labels-144
  - Affiliate Labels-144
  - Independent Labels-144
  - Vanity labels-144
  - Specialty and Virtual Reality Labels-144
  - Promotion Branding Labels (PBL's)-144
- IMPORTANT HISTORICAL RECORD LABELS-144

- Columbia Records-144
- RCA Records-145
- Capitol Records-145
- Warner Bros. Records-145
- Motown Records-145
- A&M Records-145
- CREATIVE BUSINESS MILIEU-145
- FIVE FUNCTIONS OF SUCCESSFUL LABELS-146
  - Finding and Signing Talent-146
  - Creating a Product-146
  - Distribution-146
  - Promotion-146
  - Publicity-146
- FOUR P'S OF MARKETING-147
- WHAT ARTISTS LOOK FOR IN LABELS-147
- WHAT LABELS LOOK FOR IN ARTISTS-147
- GETTING NOTICED-148
- DIGITAL DISCOVERY-148
- SHOWCASES-148
- PITCH MEMO-148
- DEAL MEMO-149
- TYPES OF DEALS-149
  - The 360 Deal-149
  - Traditional Major Deals-150
  - Development Deals-150
  - Indie Label Deals-150
  - Vanity Label Deals-150
  - Shark Deals-150
- ROYALTY POINTS AND PACKAGING FEES-151
- RECORDING LABEL-RECOUPMENT-151
- RECORD LABEL-BREAKEVEN POINTS-152
- RECORD LABEL-PROFITS-152
- MARKETING PLANS-153
  - Marketing Plans-Product Platforms-153
  - Marketing Plan-Price-153
  - Marketing Plan-Promotion-154
    - Radio-154
      - Clear Channel-155
      - Cox Radio-155
      - NPR-155
    - Advertisment-156
    - Music Videos-156
    - Internet and Cell Phones-156
  - Marketing Plan-Publicity-156
    - Stories and Interviews-156
    - Appearances-156
    - Tour support-156
    - Internet and Cell Phones-156
  - Marketing Plan-Placement/Distribution-156
    - Traditional-157

- One-Stops-157
  - Mass Merchandisers-157
  - Rack Jobbers-157
  - Record Clubs-157
  - Television-PI (Per Inquiry)-157
- Digital Music Distribution-157
- Internet Websites-157
  - Cell Phones-157
  - Satellite Direct Distribution-157
- TOP RETAIL OUTLETS-158
- DIGITAL RIGHTS MANAGEMENT (DRM)-158
- SYNERGY OF SOCIAL WEBSITE DISTRIBUTION-158
  - www.myspace.com-158
  - www.facebook.com-158
- SYNERGY OF DIGITAL DISTRIBUTION-CELL PHONES-158
  - Apple's iPhone-159
  - Rhapsody-159
  - SYNERGY OF LEGAL & FREE DIGITAL DISTRIBUTION-159
  - www.Spiral Frog.com-159
  - www.qtrax.com-159
- LABEL ADMINISTRATION-159
  - Chairperson of the Board or C.E.O.-159
  - President-159
  - Vice-Presidents-159
  - Administrators-159
- DEPARTMENTS-159
  - The Legal Department-160
  - Personnel/Payroll/Royalty-160
  - Artists and Repertoire (A&R)-160
  - Development-161
    - Creative Development-161
    - Artist Development-161
    - Product Development-161
  - Marketing & Sales-161
    - Free Goods-161
    - Promotional Copies-161
- RECORDING INDUSTRY ASSOCIATION OF AMERICA (RIAA)-161
- THE INTERNATIONAL FEDERATION OF THE PHONOGRAPHIC INDUSTRY (IFPI)-162
- PIRACY-162
- SUMMARY 163
- STUDY GUIDE-LABELS-165
- LECTURE POINTS-170
- CHAPTER NOTES-177

8-THE RECORDING DEAL

- SAMPLE RECORDING CONTRACT-180
  - Exclusive Services-180
  - Term-180
  - Recording Commitment/Delivery-181

- Recording Procedure-182
- Grant of Rights-183
- Marketing Restrictions-185
- Advances-185
- Recording Fund-185
- Royalties-187
- Accounting-189
- Notices-190
- Licenses for Musical Compositions-190
- Events of Default-191
- Injunctive Relief-192
- Collective Bargaining Agreements-192
- Warranties and Representations:Indemnities-193
- Approvals-195
- Videos-195
- Marketing & Publicity-196
- Group Provisions-196
- Definitions-197
- Assignment-200
- Assignment of Publishing Interest in Recorded Songs-200
- Merchandising-200
- Confidentiality-201
- Miscellaneous-201
- CONTRACT TERMS-203
- WORLD CHARTING COMPANIES-205
- CONTRACT STUDY POINTS-207
- LECTURE POINTS-209

9-THE RECORDING BUSINESS

- CREATING MAGIC-214
- RECORDING VARIABLES-214
  - The Recording Team-214
  - Type of Session-214
  - Stages of Sessions-214
- THE RECORDING TEAM-214
  - Producers-216
    - Independent-216
    - Label Staff-216
    - Major Artist Producer-216
  - Musicians-216
    - Garage/Jam Band Musicians-216
    - Working Musicians-216
    - Road and Event Musicians/Artists-216
    - Studio Musicians-216
  - Audio Engineers-217
    - Entry-Level-217
    - Second Engineers-217
    - Staff Engineers-217
    - Major Artist/Independent Engineers-217
  - Signal Flow-218

- - Basic Tracks/Tracking-218
  - Overdubbing-218
  - Mix-Down-218
- RECORDING ARTISTS-218
  - Royalty/Label Artist-218
  - Virtuosos-219
  - BGV's (Background Vocals)-219
- TYPES OF RECORDING STUDIOS-219
  - Master Studios-219
  - Project Studios-219
  - Demo Studios-219
  - Post-Production Studios-219
  - Computer Based Studios--220
- SCHEDULING SESSIONS-220
- UNIONS-220
  - The American Federation of Television and Radio Artist (AFTRA)-220
  - The American Federation of Musicians (AF of M)-220
- TYPES OF SESSIONS-221
  - Master-221
  - Low Budget-221
  - Limited Pressing-221
  - Demo-221
  - Non-Union-221
- A.F. OF M. RECORDING SCALES -221
- THE AF OF M TRUST FUND-222
- AFTRA RECORDING SCALES-222
- NON -UNION RECORDING SESSIONS-223
- STAGES OF A RECORDING SESSION-224
  - Pre-Production-224
  - Basic Tracks-224
  - Overdubbing-224
  - Mixdown-225
  - Mastering-225
- RECORDING BUDGET-225
  - The Recording Budget Chart-226
- PRODUCTION BUDGET-227
- PROMOTION BUDGET-227
- PUBLICITY BUDGET-227
- BREAK-EVEN POINTS-227
- LOWERING THE COST OF PRODUCTION-228
- COMPUTER BASED RECORDING BUDGET-228
- STUDIO TERMS AND EQUIPMENT-229
- SUMMARY--234
- STUDY GUIDE-THE RECORDING BUSINESS-235
- LECTURE POINTS-241
- CHAPTER NOTES-249

10-ARTIST MANAGEMENT

- MARKETING CULTURAL ICONS-252
- NON-LABEL ARTISTS-252

- FAME-253
- IMAGE-253
- SHAMELESS SELF-PROMOTION-253
- SELECTING A MANAGER-254
- TYPES OF MANAGERS-255
    - Heavyweight/Heavy Hitter-255
    - Middleweight-255
    - Lightweight-256
- SELECTING A MANAGER-256
- MANAGEMENT DUTIES-256
- NON-MANAGEMENT DUTIES-257
- ARTIST MANAGEMENT RELATIONSHIP-257
- POWER OF ATTORNEY-257
- COMMISSIONS-258
- TERMINATION OF CONTRACT-258
- MANAGEMENT TEAM-258
- BOOKING AGENTS-259
- TALENT BUYER-259
- ATTORNEYS-259
- BUSINESS FINANCIAL MANAGERS-259
- ROAD MANAGERS-260
- STAGE MANAGER-260
- PROMOTION-ARTIST PERSPECTIVE-260
- PUBLICITY-ARTIST PERSPECTIVE-260
- PUBLIC RELATIONS-261
- ELECTRONIC PRESS KITS AND BIO'S-261
- TV APPEARANCES-261
- PUBLICITY BUDGETS-261
- STAGE NAMES-262
- TOUR SUPPORT-262
- SUMMARY-263
- STUDY GUIDE FOR ARTIST MANAGEMENT-262
- LECTURE POINTS-266
- CHAPTER NOTES-270

11-THE ARTIST MANAGEMENT DEAL

- SAMPLE PERSONAL MANAGEMENT AGREEMENT-272
- TERM-272
- MANAGER'S SERVICES-273
- NON-EXCLUSIVITY-273
- AGENCIES & PUBLICITY-274
- MANAGER'S AUTHORITY-274
- RECEIPT OF ARTIST'S COMPENSATION-274
- MANAGER'S COMPENSATION-275
- EXPENSES, LOANS & ADVANCES-276
- OFFERS OF EMPLOYMENT-277
- NOTICE OF BREACH-277
- BUSINESS ENTITIES-277
- MANAGER'S OTHER BUSINESSES-278

- BINDING EFFECT-278
- ARTIST MANAGEMENT CONTRACT TERMS-280
- STUDY GUIDE-282
- LECTURE POINTS-284
- CHAPTER NOTES-288

12-CONCERT PROMOTION

- PROMOTERS-290
- SELECTING A PROMOTER-290
- SELECTING AN ACT-290
- TOUR QUESTION LIST-291
- TYPES OF CONCERT PROMOTION/ARTIST DEALS-292
    - Straight Guarantee-292
    - Guarantee Plus a Percentage of the Net (Gate)-292
    - Guarantee Versus a Percentage of the Net-292
    - Guarantee Plus a Bonus-292
- CONCERT PROMOTION PROCESS-292
- VIRTUAL CORPORATIONS-292
- DEPOSITS-293
- PROFIT MARGINS-293
- BID SHEETS-293
- BID SHEET EXAMPLE-294
- SPONSORING RADIO STATION-295
- MERCHANDISE-295
- RIDER-295
- I.A.T.S.E.-295
- ROADIES-206
- TICKETMASTER-296
- THE NON-PROFIT MUSIC MARKET-296
- POLLSTAR & SOUNDSCAN-296
- BILLBOARD MAGAZINE-297
- SUMMARY-298
- CONCERT PROMOTION TERMS-299
- STUDY GUIDE-300
- LECTURE POINTS-304
- CHAPTER NOTES-310

13-THE RIDER

- SAMPLE EAST COAST RIDER-313-329
- LECTURE POINTS-330

14-THE CREATIVE DESTRUCTION OF THE MUSIC & ENTERTAINMENT INDUSTRY

- CREATIVE DESTRUCTION-332
- THE NEW DIGITAL MUSIC INDUSTRY-333
- NEW BUSINESS MODELS-333
- SUMMARY-335

TALENT

THE CREATIVE AND BUSINESS SYSTEMS
THE THREE REVENUE STREAMS

"I wish there had been a music business 101 course I could have taken."
—**Kurt Cobain**[1]

"The hardest thing in the world to do in this business is start a band nobody's heard of."
—**Tom Whalley, Interscope Records**[2]

We've always loved being hated and the rebel aspect of never being in the right place at the right time. That's how we started... Anger still fuels my fire.

—**James Hetfield of Metallica**[3]

"If you're going to play an acoustic instrument, you have to be a really good player to work."

—**Branford Marsalis, Recording Artist**[4]

Talent is a famous old unit of weight and value. The Hebrews, Babylonians, Greeks, and Romans used it. No coin of this denomination was ever struck (made), because such a coin would be too large. Instead, a certain number of other coins equaled a talent. The Hebrew silver talent equaled 3,000 shekels in silver. The gold talent had different weights and values in different places. The present use of the word talent, meaning special ability, may come symbolically from a Bible story (Matthew 25: 14-30).[5]

Artists in the music and entertainment business are responsible for much of their own success. Instead of waiting to be discovered, young artists need to pro-actively pursue their career. Being able to sing well, knowing someone in the business and going to school is a good start. Developing creative and analytical mental talents, grabbing an understanding of the serious and popular cultures of society is helpful, gaining business and industry specific knowledge is useful, networking is necessary and having a personal passion for success is absolutely essential.

It is the placement of the artist's sellable talents and products, based on an image, released through recordings, concert tickets, and the public's use of live and recorded music through the mass media and digital "click media" (personal devices such as iPods, iPhones, mp3 players, cell phones, and ring/master tones) that establishes revenue streams and profits for the industry. Thus, sometimes it is hard to understand and accept the reality that the music and entertainment is not based on pure artistic talent but on the profit and loss statements generated from artist's sellable products. So if this industry is just like every other one based on money, how can you become successful? Learn the business!

CREATIVITY

Start with creativity and figure out what makes you special. *Creative talent is the beginning, not the end to stardom or industry related career success.* As an artist, producer, manager, label executive, what makes you valuable to the industry? What makes you special? What unique knowledge or creative skills can you provide to help an artist become rich and famous or successful? As an artist or performer what

1 http://www.barryrudolph.com/utilities/quotes.html
2 Ibid.
3 The Recording Industry Career Handbook by the NARAS Foundation (1995)
4 Ibid
5 Burton H. Hobson, B.A., President and Editorial Director, Sterling Publishing Company, World book (2006).

messages are you trying to say through your lyrics, image or essence that connects with the emotional needs of consumers? Yet, we are talking about more than just the musicians, singers and recording artists here. If you are a businessman or woman what do you provide to the business side of the industry that helps it generate sales and profits? Thus, creativity is required in the "suits" as well as in the songwriters and performers.

CREATIVE SYSTEM

The traditional music and entertainment business is a complex industry. It is a collection of artists, entrepreneurs, mega entertainment organizations, record labels, consumers, and the mass media (radio, television, print), cell phone networks, and Internet portals that together form the industry. The creative side (*creative system*) is typically composed of songwriters, musicians, producers, recording artists, singers, audio engineers, graphic artists, actors, film directors, union members, and computer technicians. They create the digital downloads, albums, concerts, movies, videos, computer games, and other entertainment products we use, listen to, rent, or buy. The supporting business side (business system) generally consists of the traditional and independent labels and companies who finance and manage the artists, their recordings and other entertainment products. Others provide management, promotion and distribution of images, products, events and artists. Entrepreneurs and corporations create concert events and management opportunities that generate product based income such as tours, merchandise sales, and corporate sponsorships for various media and communication outlets.

Talent defined as creativity is present in the products provided through the business side of the music and entertainment industry. Thus, it has many different meanings to various entities. For instance:

- **Songwriters** create the most vital part of the industry, a great song, which is truly the foundation of the communicative link between the artists and consumers. The business is built on the shoulders of a great song; yet, the writers who create the songs are often the last to be paid. Songwriters are customarily creative and energetic, as they appear to be consistently seeking a better way to express a catchy idea or hook. They are poets who use music to ingeniously combine words (lyrics) and music (chords and melody) to create emotionally charged messages (songs).[6]

Concerns about the *emotional power of music* include the Greek philosophers. *Plato* demanded "a strict censorship of modes and tunes, least citizens be tempted by weak or voluptuous aires to indulge demoralizing emotions" (Republic bk iii). "The legend of the sirens is based on a belief in the narcotic and toxic effects of music, as is Terpander's preventing civil war in *Sparta*, or of the *Danish King Eric*, committing murder as a result of the harpist's deliberate experiment in mood-production" (Die Musik XXIX-Part II). It's amazing how few things really change. "Mobilizing Against Pop Music and Other Horrors" by Chris Hedges of The New York Times International states that in Iran, "the Bassij are an army of volunteers formed by Islamic clerics to monitor and seize western popular entertainment products in an attempt to prevent western entertainment from corrupting the youth of their nation."[7] Additional creative system people include:

- **Successful Artists and Vocalists** breathe life into a song by conveying the song's emotional message to potential listeners. They infuse energy into lyrics and vitality into the notes printed on the sheet music. Session musicians and vocalists are considered recording artists. Performances must be believable, sellable, and true to the communicative message in the song and the persona of the artists.

---

6 Webster's New World Dictionary, p894 (1986).
7 Philosophy in a New Key by Susanne Langer (1951). Langer cites stories from "Von sonderbahrer Wilrchung und Krafft der Music:" Die Musik XXIX (1937), part 11, pages 625-630. & "Mobilizing Against Pop Music and Other Horrors" by Chris Hedges of The New York Times International (July 21, 1993)..

- *Background Singers* (BGV's) are the "oohs" and "aahs" of the industry. They provide the vocal supporting harmony parts for major recording artists, sing live at theme parks, in night clubs, on concert tours and cruise ships, often becoming the voice on popular radio jingles and television commercials.

- *Musicians* are the great interpreters of songs. They reveal their emotions and personalities through their musical instruments and performances. They are the backbone of the recording process, supporting both the lyrics of the song and the performance of the vocalists. Working in the "arts" is often a part-time gig as there are fewer recording studio positions available than players. However, there are plenty of opportunities for musicians to work in bands, orchestras, churches, theaters and other various types of venues.

- *Record Producers* have the ability to intelligently and creatively combine artists, talented background singers, studio musicians, and audio engineers to create potential hit recordings. In pre-production, producers, recording artists, managers, and record companies search to find the types of songs that will best fit the images and vocal capabilities of the artists. In the studio, producers are in charge of the actual recording session and responsible for the budget of the final product.

- *Audio Engineers* are considered electronic creative artists because they use the studio's acoustics, microphones, consoles, tape machines, computers, and special effects outboard equipment to enhance the quality of the recording. Audio engineers are responsible for the technical quality of the recording, just as the producers are responsible for the creative quality of the recording. Their job is to make the artists and musicians sound as good as technically possible. Accordingly, they work with the recording artists, musicians, and producer to capture the artists' and musicians' best creative efforts on tape or computer hard disk. Additional professional opportunities for audio engineers include audio production for movies, videos, television shows, radio broadcasts, jingles, and commercials. Entry-level jobs are often found in nightclubs, hotels, amusement parks, on cruise ships, convention performance art centers, as well as government and military installations.

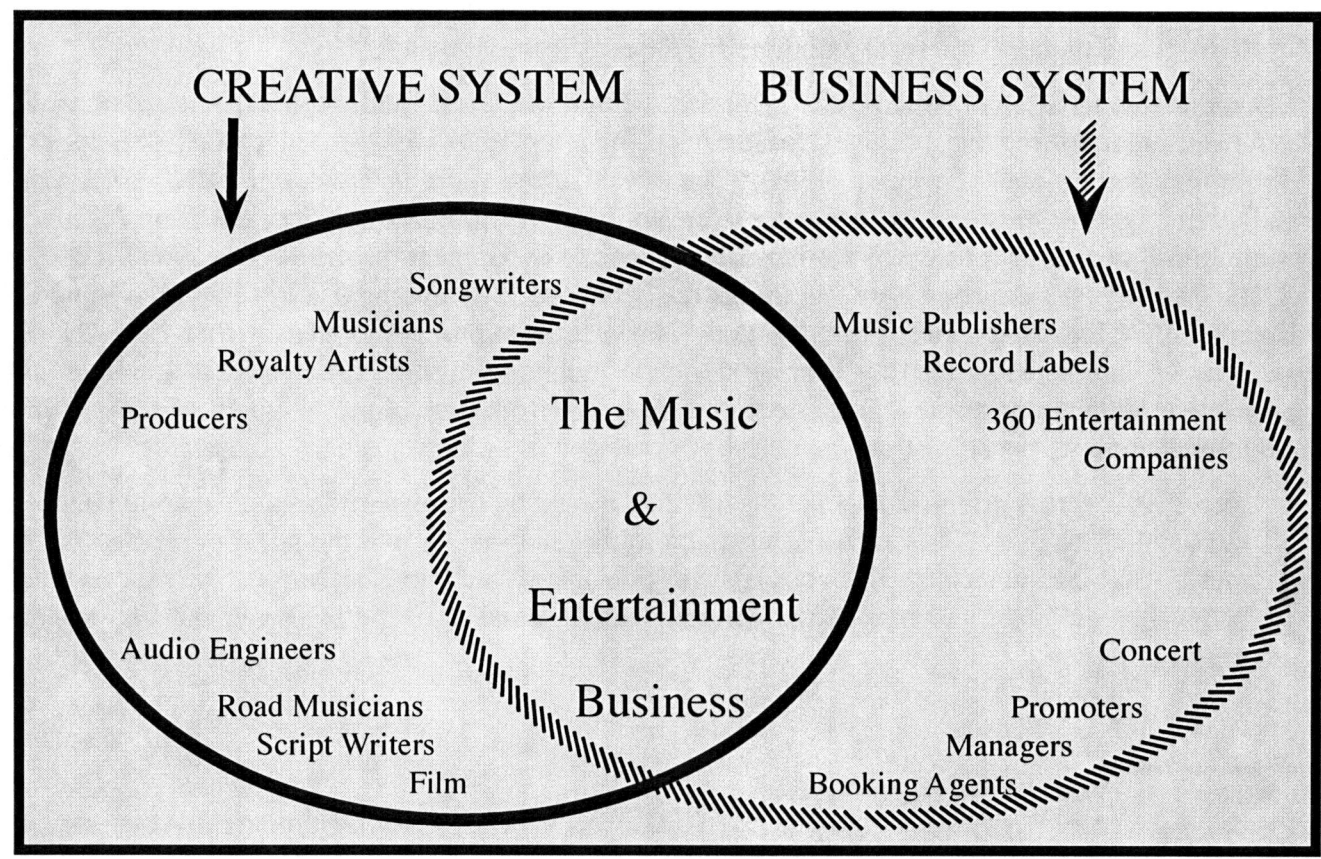

BUSINESS SYSTEM

Accordingly, the *traditional business side* (***business system***) consists of entrepreneurs and business minded individuals who publish songs, fund the development of films, computer and internet related programs and games, finance artists, their recordings, shows, and concerts, and distribute, promote and market the entertainment products through traditional retail outlets, the media and click media to various consumer markets. It is the purchasing of the recordings, DVDs, CDs, downloads, concert tickets, merchandise, and the public and private use of music by the media that provides the revenues and profits required by the creative and business sides of the industry to exist.

- *Music Publishers* bridge the creative and business systems. On the creative side, they screen new songs from independent songwriters, hire staff writers to write new songs, demo record accepted songs, print or have sheet music printed, and pitch the songs to artists, record labels, managers, and producers. They also operate as part of the business system by registering copyrights, issuing licenses, marketing songs, collecting song royalties and paying writers.

- *Recording Studios* often cost more than a million dollars to own and operate. The studio is where the two industry systems (creative and business) meet. The performance studio and control room can easily account for a couple hundred thousand dollars when designed and constructed by the best consultants and contractors in the business. Consoles, digital tape machines, computers, special effects equipment, Pro Tools software, microphones, and monitor speakers quickly add up to between $300,000 and $700,000. Add offices, operational personnel, and a cup of coffee and you have a million-dollar business. Major studios rent for $1,000 to $1,500 a day to cover the cost of their initial investments. It also explains why record labels routinely rent studios instead of owning them. However, computer technology has shifted the recording studio's importance to labels and artists to a much lower standard. Computer programs such as Pro-Tools and many others now provide quality recordings for a very limited cost.

- *Labels* tend to define talent by the original meaning of an old unit of weight and value.[19] Thus, from the label's perspective, the amount of talent an artist has is defined by how much money/profits their recordings/image generate. An act with limited musical or vocal talent is as important to a label as any of their other acts due to their ability to creatively connect with consumers and sell millions of units of recordings. A *unit* is the term labels use to describe the CD, digital downloads, and old vinyl recordings they sell. Labels want to make the most profit possible for the least amount of investment. The need to use an expensive recording studio and sessions that often add hundreds of thousands of dollars to the debt of an artist is now in doubt as computer programs provide quality recordings that lower the cost and quickly make new artists more profitable.

- The purpose of *Promotion* is to alert the public to the artist's new products (which are for sale) and to create a buzz, a conversation or topic consumers get excited about and discuss. Giving consumers a free sample through radio station airplay, 30 second samples on internet web sites such as iTunes, and free cell phone downloads provide consumers a chance to discover the act and their recordings. *The buzz is really word-of-mouth advertising, which is commonly considered by the labels to be one of the best forms of promotion.* Younger consumers tend to hype each other about the artists and their recordings, which ultimately increases unit sales. *Radio stations broadcast recordings to attract audiences in order to sell airtime to businesses.* The larger the audience, the more stations charge for their commercial airtime. Thus, all forms of Promotion generate record sale propensity for recording artists and album purchases. Independent producers and production houses produce music videos to create public awareness of artists, their images, and their recordings. Labels also view concert tours as promotion for the artist and their new recordings. Thus, tour support (money) is provided by the label to encourage a successful concert tour to increase radio station airplay, media publicity, and bottom-line profits.

- *Publicists* provide consumers an opportunity to discover the artist's life story that is hopefully tied to their image of a hero, rebel, lover, good guy, bad guy, cowboy, teen idol, or ideal partner.

Television talk shows book celebrities to gain larger audiences in order to sell commercial airtime. Radio and television stations and businesses contract "star" voices to promote their products and stations. In addition, labels also consider concert appearances as publicity as a great show often increases unit sales. Lastly, live radio interviews, store signings, and Internet web pages are used to increase public awareness of the act.

- *Artist Managers* bring representation, administrative supervision, and surrogate control to a recording artist's complex image and long-term career. A business plan tied to a marketing plan for the business side of the artist's career is regularly developed. Career plans and goals are established based on the perceived commercialization of the artist's image and talents. Managers approve the artist's personal appearances and concert tours. They use the albums distributed and marketed by record labels and promoted by radio stations to emphasize the image of their artist that, in turn, provide the artist's manager many opportunities to make money. Artist managers hire accountants to balance the books, financial advisors to invest the profits in long-term investments, stocks and money markets, and attorneys to negotiate, draft and oversee the process of executing contractual agreements. Event coordinators, security, merchandisers, union stagehands, road managers, roadies, arts managers, and thousands of other niche occupations are available on the business side of the industry to anyone who has the knowledge and the desire to make positive and profitable things happen.

- If the label's marketing and promotional efforts are working, the artist's representation, **Booking Agents/Talent Agents**, encourage *promoters* to produce concerts in various markets. Agents with an *American Federation of Musicians* booking license generally book union musicians for concerts, nightclubs, and other types of personal appearances and tours. A.F. of M. contracts provide protection to the union musicians who are playing the gig. Non-union musicians and booking agents do not usually have the protection of union attorneys if the promoter or club owner fails to fulfill their contractual obligations. Agents work as part of the management team to generate revenues for the act based on the act's fame and consumers need to relate to the artist's image, essence, and recordings the consumers "discovered" through promotion and publicity as defined and described previously.

- **Concert Promoters** provide the money required to fund concerts and tours. They are the industry's high rollers betting big money on the popularity of an act to sell seats in local venues and arenas. Booking agents representing specific acts call the promoters to set up concert tours. A retainer of 50% or more of the band's payment is customarily required to secure the date for the promoter. The promoter is also required to fulfill the obligations of the rider, which is the musician's/act's instructions to the promoter about their needs for the concert. A *rider* is an addition to the contract between the management company/booking agent and the concert promoter. It details specific additional requirements that must be satisfied before the artist will perform and thus becomes part of the contract. Examples of many artist's riders may be found at the website *www.thesmokinggun. com*. As an example, the size of the stage, lighting, sound requirements, dressing room and dining preferences are listed. Promoters pay for radio advertisements, media promotion, the venue, security, and stagehands. They usually need 80% of all tickets sold to break-even at an event. Successful recording artists often act as their own concert promoters. For example, they set up virtual reality companies in a hotel, hire the people they need to run the business and then disband as soon as the tour has been completed.

- **The Mass Media** consists of radio, broadcast television and cable, the print media, Internet, billboards and advertisement placed on everything from the side of trucks to shopping carts. Thus, success in the mass media is based on the number of impressions tied to the success of and amount of product(s) sold.

Click Media consists of interactive use of the Internet, cell phones, and PDA's/other devices that are used to download specific entertainment free/promotional samples and purchased products. The mass media are dependent on free recordings from the labels to draw an audience. Thus, the mass media are not in the music business or film business as they make their profits from selling airtime and space to advertisers. However, a distribution revolution is currently in progress as the beforehand "passive" mass media is now competing with the interactive digital entertainment product sites such as *iTunes, Google, Netflix, iPhone* and other digital product suppliers. Unlike the traditional *mass media*, the *click media* allows consumers to interact with their selected media sources to enjoy and purchase entertainment products quickly.

ASSOCIATED CAREERS

There are many additional professional creative/business careers available in the music and entertainment industry. *Computer graphic artists* create computer-generated movies, television shows, images, posters, computer games and album covers. *Music video scriptwriters, producers, directors, actors, and actresses* are involved in music videos, TV commercials and advertisements are used by record labels to market, promote, and publicize artists and album releases. As digital technology continues to inspire the ability of artists to create new forms of entertainment and as businesses evolve to meet the consumer's desire for click media products, many new careers will evolve and be created. Corporate sponsors often financially support artists, musicians, and orchestras in exchange for community service, product awareness, and increased product sales. Retail outlets sell and rent the industry's books, recordings, movies, and merchandise. Computer and software experts develop Internet based web pages, movies, games, and music videos.

Consumers, without whom the music and entertainment industry would not exist, support both the creative and business systems by buying and using traditional recorded and live presentations, plus the digital downloads. Consumer purchases and use of music and entertainment products made by the creative system and financed, marketed, and promoted by the business system, usually compensate the artists for their creative efforts and provide profits to the labels, entertainment production companies, networks, mass media and click media for their financial and creative risks.

TYPES OF BUSINESSES

- A *sole proprietorship* is a business owned by one person and, as an example most songwriters and music producers are in business for themselves. In addition, great *studio musicians* work as independent contractors represented by the AF of M, (The American Federation of Musicians). Label artists form their own companies and then hire a *manager, producer, road musicians*, etc., to work for them. They become employers, not employees.

- *Partnerships, joint ventures, and limited partnerships* are defined as businesses owned by more than one person. Many bands, small record companies, and publishing companies are legal partnerships.

- *Corporations* bind the artists and business people together and, just as in any business, they bring their culture of artifacts, perspectives, values and assumptions. Corporations are a separate entity apart from the owners and stockholders. Legal action can usually be filed only against the corporation's assets not the owners, who are typically record labels, artists, and stockholders. Thus, the corporation's business structure gives successful recording artists and entertainers a way to protect their personal assets from unjust claims.

"If you don't own the master, the master owns you."

— **Rapper Chuck D.**[8]

---

[8] "Steal This Industry", mp3 Central.

ENTREPRENEURSHIP

Entrepreneurship appears to illustrate the business psychology of the music industry. There is often an entrepreneur behind the success of a star or public personality that helps keep the entertainment industry engine running. Entrepreneurs write the songs and screenplays, finance recordings, manage the images and careers of artists, promote, publicize and market the products to consumers. It is often these individuals and their small businesses that make the industry's profits soar. Relying on their own creative and business decisions they work within the industry without the security of a corporate net to fall back on during negative sales periods. Once you have worked your way into the industry, networking with other industry professionals and entrepreneurs enhances mutually profitable opportunities. Joining together with others who have similar interests and talents is a common practice among industry professional entrepreneurs. As an example, if you are a songwriter, start a legitimate publishing company. This is a great way to introduce yourself to industry insiders who can help your career and your business, while at the same time, increase bottom lines.

Elvis Presley made it happen by having the talent to sing, a passion to entertain, the initiative to learn from others through listening, watching, and asking questions, and, most importantly, by being in the right place at the right time. Elvis didn't, however, become a world famous recording artist by himself. He used his vocal talents, good looks, and assertiveness to get his foot in the door of the music business. It was also the music business, or more precisely the people who make up the music business, that helped *Elvis* become the *King of Rock and Roll*.

If you do not have the talent or desire to be an artist or write a song there are still many entrepreneurial opportunities available. Artists need studio and tour musicians, record producers, audio engineers, managers, attorneys, booking agents, promotion agents, publicists, radio announcers, sales, and financial managers to help them build their careers. Entrepreneurs who are not label or mega entertainment corporation employees fill most supportive careers. *Elvis Presley's* talent combined with *Sam Phillip's* producing skills and *Colonel Parker's* managerial expertise helped create one of the most successful entertainment ventures in history. This is a stellar example of how entrepreneurship (Elvis, Sam Phillips and Colonel Parker) and the industry (RCA Records) embraced the numerous opportunities available for a successful profit that still exists today.

REVENUE STREAMS

Writing about the music and entertainment industry is akin to standing on quick sand as everything is changing so quickly. Educators need a technique to describe the complexity of the industry in a way that students and others can easily understand. Thus, the industry is often divided and analyzed into three functional revenue streams:

- ***SONGWRITING/ MUSIC PUBLISHING REVENUE STREAM***

    (Intellectual Properties, Copyrights & Music Publishing). Songs are the foundation of the music business. They bring the songwriters, producers, musicians, and the business world together. Once a song is written, it must be published, placed with an artist and recorded or performed publicly to make money. Businesses that use recordings or live performances of a song are usually required to pay for the use of the song through a performance license. Record labels pay mechanical license fees for the use of songs on their recordings. Visual production companies, including film and TV shows are required to pay for the use of a song in the production of the work through acquiring a sync license. In the end, consumers also pay for the use of the songs they hear in the purchase price of downloads, albums, and subscription rates for satellite radio and cable TV.

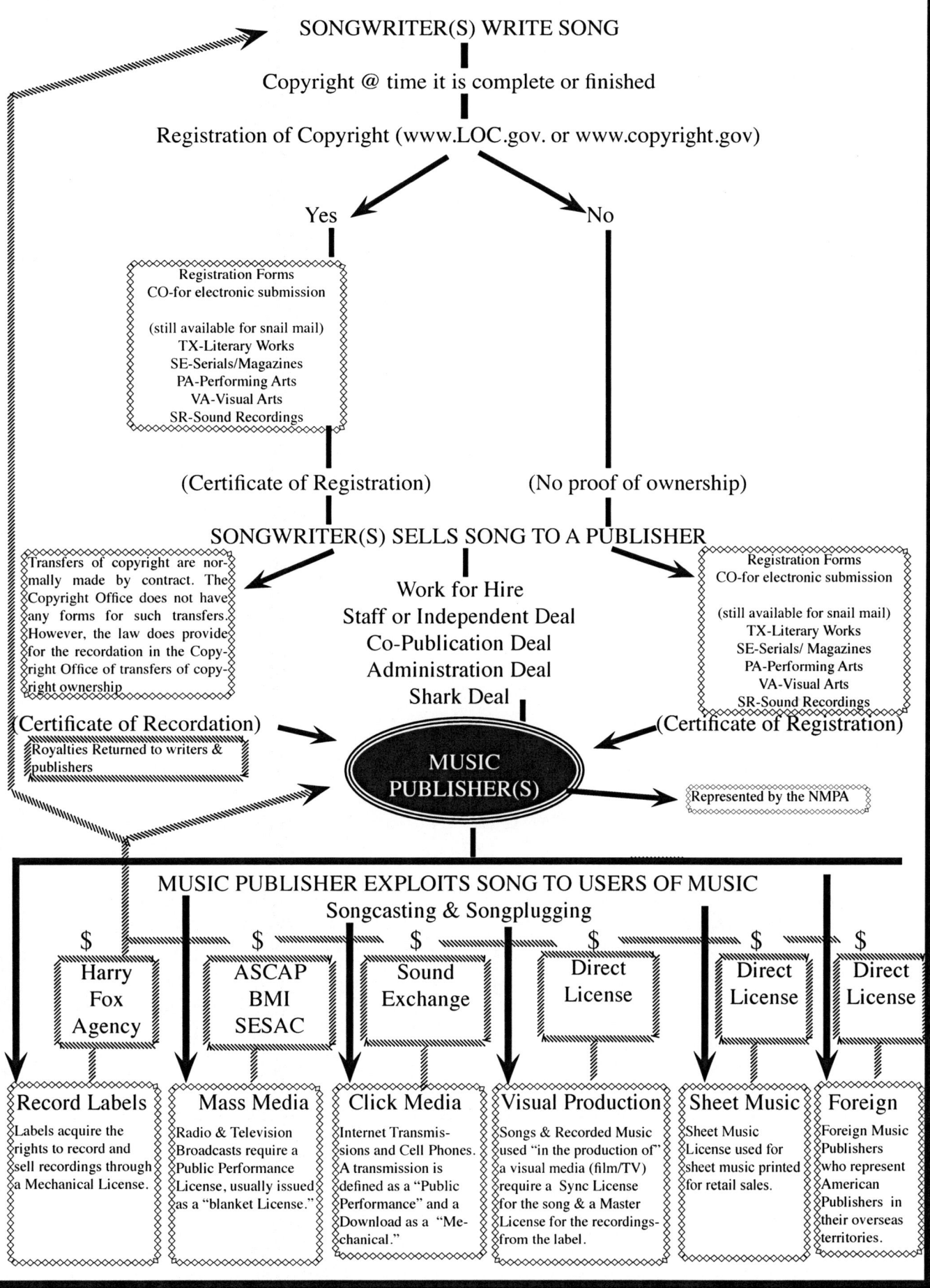

- ***RECORD LABEL REVENUE STREAM*** (Mega Entertainment Organizations & Labels). Record labels find and sign artists to their labels and songs to their publishing companies. They are the banks of the industry providing hundreds of thousands of dollars to recording artists to pay for advances, producers, musicians, audio engineers, BGV's (background singers), and studio rental time required to complete major album projects. Then they provide additional money to market the recordings to various types of consumers through promotion, publicity, and distribution to retail outlets. Labels range in size from worldwide distribution companies (mega entertainment organizations), such as *EMI, Sony, TimeWarner, Universal, and Bertelsmann,* to the one-person operation that offers digital downloads over the Internet. Favorite recording artists selected by different types of consumers usually reveal the personalities and lifestyles of the consumers through demographic and psychographic research. *Demographic research* is an analysis of comparison based on gender, age, and education. *Psychographic research* is a deeper analysis that groups individuals by their lifestyles tied to zip codes. The results are for marketing of tours, corporate sponsorships and merchandise. Thus the music business is really the emotion business based on enjoyment as perceived by various types of consumers, who attend the concerts, listen to and purchase the recordings. Clusters of consumer creative emotions often define various types of music genres and the image of the artists themselves. As an example, record labels may niche market some of their artist's recordings to hip-hop fans that may have a different lifestyle or musical preference than jazz, country, or classical fans. In addition, artists, publishers and songwriters also pay for non-label recordings and thus a sub-revenue stream may include musicians, singers, producers, audio engineers and the studio/digital recording business.

Creativity

How much is creativity worth?

To the person who creates the song, recording, film, etc., the reward is personal satisfaction. However, if you can turn your creativity into a business, what is it worth?

- *Global Creative Industries $2,200,000,000,000 ($2.2 Trillion).*

What percent of the population of the United States would have to buy your album to make it platinum (one million copies sold)?

- *Far less then one percent. (.0035 of one percent of the United States population estimated at 350 million).*

Your odds improve dramatically if you can sell one million copies to the six and one-half billion people on the earth. Then the odds are even better, only .00065 of one percent. Thus, if you can connect emotionally with your creative product to the point where either .0035% of one percent of the U.S. population or .00065% of one percent of the worlds population buy it, you can become rich and famous.... That is if...

If you understand how to turn your creative products into a... BUSINESS!

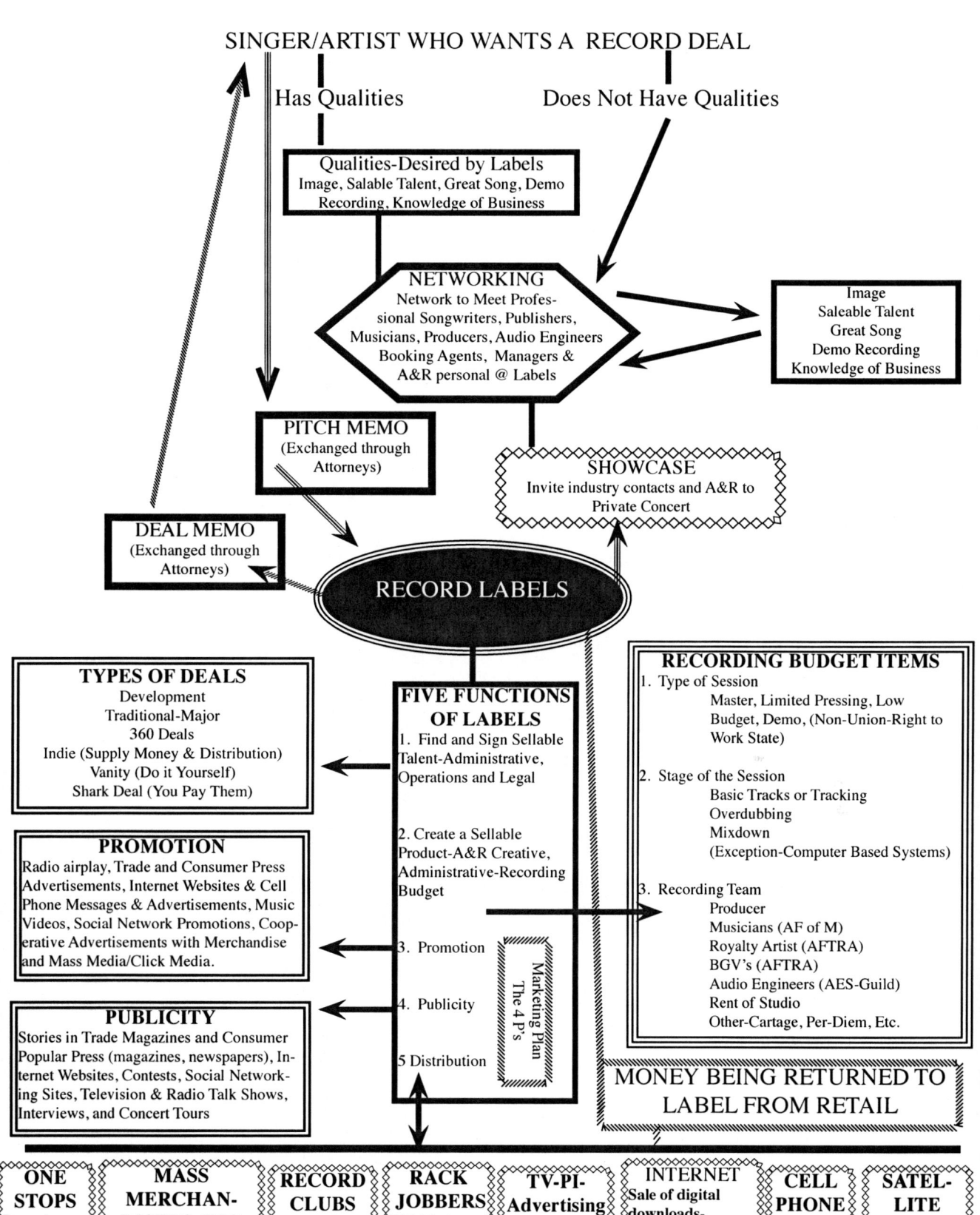

- **THE MANAGEMENT/TOURING REVENUE STREAM**

  The image exploitation, concert promotion tour, corporate sponsorships, endorsements, and merchandise business. Recording artists generally make the greatest share of their annual income from concert appearances, corporate endorsements sponsorships and merchandise. Even major artists may not sell enough albums to cover their recording and marketing expenses.

Learning the *three revenue streams* and all of the corresponding business and *creative opportunities* (careers) will leapfrog you ahead of the millions of others who want a job or career in this business. It is how it works, even as it goes through the *creative destruction* caused by technology (peer to peer file sharing and the internet), and the introduction of *360 deals* that combine the revenue streams together. Today's industry is actually growing with new and better jobs and creative opportunities than the traditional businesses that are in the mist of transformation. Indeed, consumers want more entertainment products not less. Getting them to pay for it, in some cases, may be a little tricky. Yet, even the consumers who illegally download music often find new acts to support through tours, merchandise, and actual album or single recording purchases.

FINANCIALS

Todays creative industries driven by music gross more money than ever! Annual industry related income from multiple sources report the following:

- Global Creative Industries $2,200,000,000,000 ($2.2 Trillion).
- National Creative Industries $850,000,000,000 ($850 Billion).
- Global Music Industries (all three revenue streams) $130,000,000,000 ($130 Billion).
- Internet Broadband $100,000,000,000 ($100 Billion)
- Radio Advertisement $34,000,000,000 ($34 Billion).
- Record Companies $21,000,000,000 ($21 Billion).
- Music Instruments Sales $19,000,000,000 ($19 Billion).
- Live Event/Concert Industries $17,000,000,000 ($17 Billion).
- Other Music Related Industries Sales $15,000,000,000 ($15 Billion).
- Music Retail Sales (non-label) $15,000,000,000 ($15 Billion).
- Portable Digital Players $10,000,000,000 ($10 Billion)
- Music Publishing $8,000,000,000 ($8 Billion).[9]

Music is what feelings sound like.

—Author Unknown[10]

---

9 IFPI. Radio advertising: PWC. Record company revenues: physical, digital, performance rights income and licensing income (IFPI). Musical instruments: Music Trades. Live: IFPI extrapolations of Pollstar data. Other music related sectors: music magazines (IFPI extrapolations of PWC data), music channels advertising revenues (Viacom), US satellite radio subscriptions (PWC), audio home system sales (CEA, EITO). Music retail: physical, digital and ringtone retail sales (IFPI, Informa). Portable digital players: IDC. Publishing: IFPI estimates based on CISAC data and performers' performance rights collections from IFPI data. National Creative Industries estimated from Census Data.
10 The Quote Garden/www.google.com, 2007.

THE MANAGEMENT/TOURING REVENUE STREAM

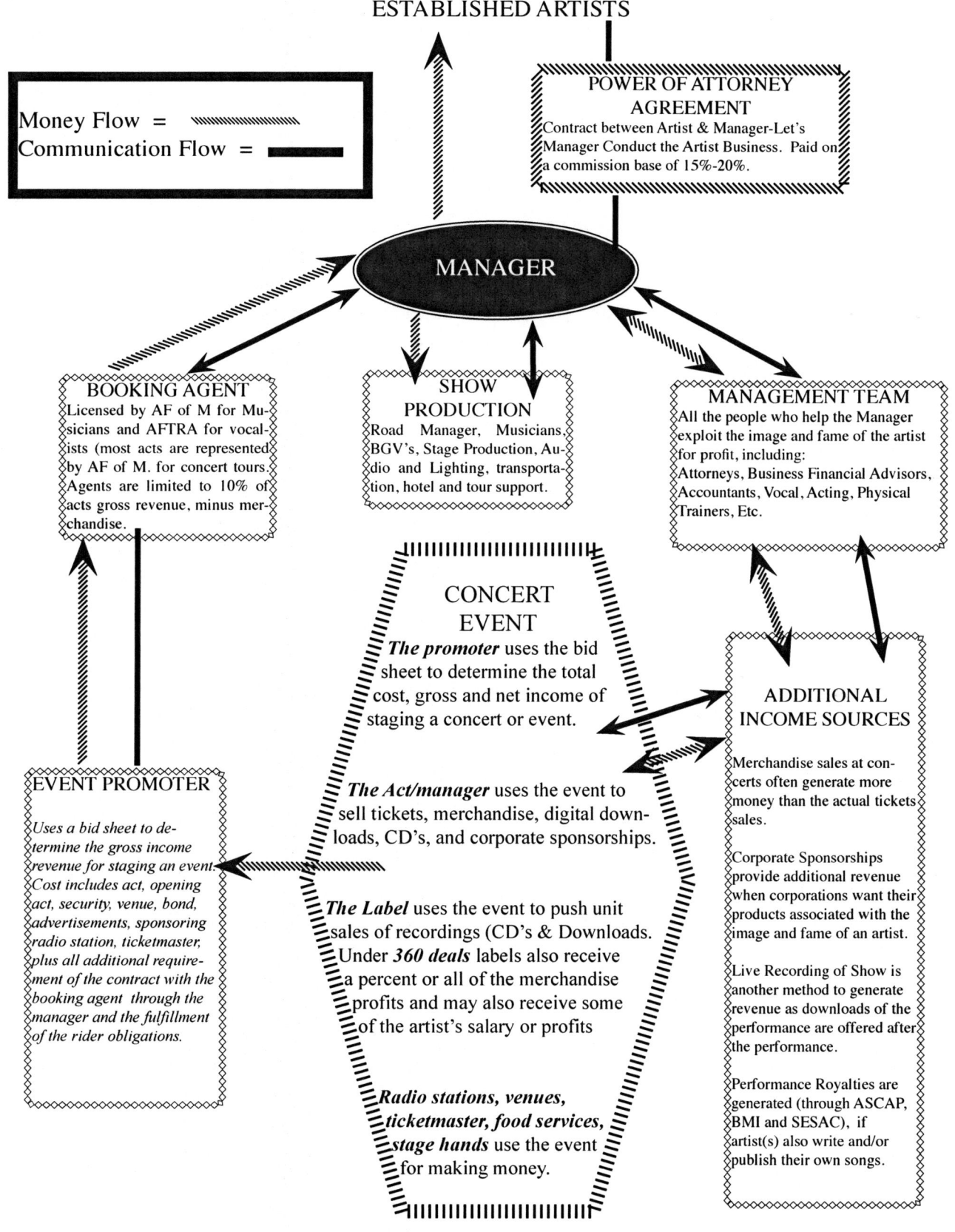

CAPTURING EMOTIONS AS SELLABLE PRODUCTS

If songs are the foundation of the business, then the recording process is the method used to build a sellable product. It is similar to building a house for sale. Think of the plans for the building as the song, the workers who put the nails in the studs, floors, and ceilings as the musicians, artists, audio engineers and producer. At the end of the process, in the home building business we have a house to sell. In the music industry, we have a recording to sell. Thus, studios and recording software are an integral part of the music business, the place where dreams are made and sometimes broken. Mixing a great song with the creativity of recording artists, background vocalists, musicians, producers, and audio engineers makes a successful recording. Equipment ranges from multi-million dollar consoles and soundproof rooms to digital tape recorders and Pro-Tools software linked to home computers. Budgets range from million dollar star-driven sessions to friends who agree to record some tracks for you. The pay-off is based on money, how many units are downloaded or sold and how many additional touring, corporate sponsorships, and merchandise purchases occur. And in the end, nobody really knows which recording will become the next number one _Billboard Magazine_ charted hit; the million dollar artists with the huge budget or the kid in the basement with access to the Internet.

"How can you sell ten million records and have to file for bankruptcy?"

—**TLC in an interview on VH-1**[11]

LAUNCHING THE PRODUCTS

Labels use the print media, mass media of radio, television, cell phones, iPods, the Internet and films to promote and circulate (publicize) their artists and available recordings. They use distribution outlets, Internet sites, PDA's, cell phones and various types of retail outlets to promote and sell the recordings. It costs money of course, which is then charged back to the artist's account at the label. The process of recoupment is the accounting method used by the labels to pay off the debt they have created in the artist's name through royalties that are supposed to be paid to the artist from record sales. The upside is that artists are given a shot at becoming a big star without having to use much of their own money. *The downside is that most recording artists never receive any royalties from units sold as the labels do not sell enough to break-even.* Artist royalties are only a small percent of the money consumer's pay for a product. Labels who are risking their investment receive a much larger share of income and thus, break-even faster and often make money before the artist.

EVENT MARKETING

Promoters rent venues for the dates of the concerts and then locally promote and advertise the event. Facility managers and their staff of event coordinators keep the arenas, theaters, and clubs in top shape for the concerts. *Stagehand union members* commonly provide the lighting and sound. *Publicists and marketing experts* provide artists' interviews to the mass and click media in an effort to promote concerts and the artists. Record labels provide free recordings to radio stations and in-store promotional items, called end caps and stand-ups, to retail outlets. And if you're not a signed recording artist yet, even non-label artists and musicians may attain a good living from personal performances as a member of an orchestra, nightclub band, or by playing in weddings, at parties and/or by providing the entertainment at a number of unique events. Others contributing to the management revenue stream include *business managers* who are hopefully financial experts and invest the artist's earnings into stock and bond markets, merchandise fulfillment providers who provide the merchandise, and corporate sponsors that provide financial support in exchange for icon and product identification.

---

11 Vh-1, Where are they now; Comcast (2000).

THE NEW MUSIC BUSINESS

The traditional music business model based on the three revenue streams are a very mature (dated) form of business compared to the new digital world of technology and the internet. Indeed, the entertainment industry and the music business specifically are reeling with revenue losses based on internet technology and consumers' peer to peer (p2p) file sharing. *It's hard to survive when more than 51 percent of the music acquired by consumers is not paid for or stolen through p2p.* In the last few years, the entertainment industry has slowly started to reinvent itself. Record labels are often seen as "stand alone" companies, when in reality they are generally just a small part of a global entertainment corporation. Corporate decisions made in Tokyo or Frankfurt may have serious repercussions for record labels, artists and their employees. In addition, new technology and e-commerce is causing perilous cracks in the industry's skeletal foundation. Companies are merging and closing doors on many existing artist deals and industry employees. Artists and others in the industry now have fewer major label options yet more entrepreneurial opportunities available. Examples are the tools we use every day; our iPods, cell phone, computers, and sites such as www.myspace.com, www.facebook.com, and www.youtube.com.

Therefore, music over the Internet is *fundamentally changing* the way artists, recording companies, retail channels, and end users, create, distribute, and buy music. Major artists are already netting huge profits by selling products over *iTunes, and www.musicnet.com* which supplies material to *Yahoo* and other websites. Unknown artists and even formerly established label artists now own their own website, bypassing the established distribution and retail chains to retain a larger share of the profits for themselves. Clearly, the days of being solely an artist are over. If you're in a rock band, start a business by creating your own label. Record and finance a demo, give it to the local station, put it on sale at the local record shop, and then invite local personalities to a showcase through Internet websites.

Artist/ Ranking	2008 Income in Millions	FORBES CELEBRITY 100 Accomplishments	Web Rank	Press Rank	TV Rank
Madonna (3)	$110	1. Hard Candy album 2. Top internatiional tour of 58 concerts in 17 countries grosses $280 million. 3. Personal life covered in many web, press, and TV suorces.	9	6	8
Beyonce (4)	$ 87	1. Released a double album, 2. Starred in two films 3. Performed at the Oscars 4. Performming at a 110-date international tour. 5. Has endorsement deals and sponsored by Nintendo, Crystal Geyser General Mills, L'Oréal, Giorgio Armani and Samantha Thavasa handbags.	2	20	16
Bruce Springsteen (6)	$ 70	1. 2008, bringing in $166 million on sales of 1.6 million tickets. 2. Headline Super Bowl halftime show. 3. Signed deal with Wal-Mart to sell greatest hits album	32	19	25
Britney Spears (13)	$ 35	1. Circus album sells 1.5 million copies in three months. 2. New tour grossing $24 million with the first 13 concerts.	10	16	11
Coldplay (15)	$ 70	1. Released studio album, Viva La Vida, streaming free on MySpace. 2. Album still sold 7 million units (best-selling album of 2008), 3. Earned a Grammy for Best Rock Album. 4. Viva la Vida tour grossed $72 million for 76 concerts in 16 countries.	64	17	35

Earnings estimates are for June 2008 to June 2009. Includes dollars earned solely from entertainment income. Management, agent and attorney fees have notbeen deducted. Figures rounded off where appropriate. Sources include Billboard, Pollstar, Adams Media Research, Nielsen SoundScan and Nielsen BookScan. Rankings are generated by combining earnings with other metrics: Web mentions on Google press clips compiled by LexisNexis; TV/radio mentions by Factiva; and number of times a celebrity's face appeared on the cover of 25 major consumer magazines. (www.Forbes.com (2009)

SUMMARY

The music business is based on the fans' ability to emotionally connect with the music and iconic artist's communicative messages on recordings, in concerts and played through the mass and click media. Consumers emotionally use the music and various related entertainment products for subconscious, self-definition and psychological elaboration. The artists creatively express their artistic talents while the business system exploits their products for profits. It's the people behind the stars and public personalities that often provide the majority of the "essence for success" in the creative and business systems. Record labels and other entertainment-based companies time and again finance the recordings and entertainment products. Managers, publicists and agents help develop images and career goals, and assist to promote, publicize, and market the images and corresponding products to consumers. The mass and click media provide distribution of images and products and in some cases retail products. The perception is that all the recording artists and stars have to do is sing, play their instrument, act and provide shameless self-promotion. Realistic industry success usually involves passion, a better world vision of humanity and society, street and learned knowledge, talent, an understanding of business principles, connections, money, and acceptance of an excellent team of experts who market products and images, searching for profits. All of this is, of course, based on a great song and the artist's ability to contribute artistically in some meaningful manner to a message of emotional importance to a various segment of consumers.

The reality is that it is highly unlikely that you are going to be discovered. You have to make things happen yourself. Professional musicians, artists, and industry insiders have assertively earned their own success by having a positive attitude, meeting the right people, perfecting their artistic and business intellectual talents, obtaining a quality education, and by being in the right place at the right time. Successful industry related entrepreneurs, who provide products, start businesses and materials that solve problems, create win-win situations, and provide better entertainment products to various segments of the world's population. In the music business, there is a balance between the creative and business-minded men and women who own, operate, or work at industry related companies that determines their own company's and industry's success.

Many of the successful people in the music and entertainment business have created their own shot at success. Luck is important, but successful people often create their own by setting personal goals, developing creative and analytical talents, having a positive attitude, attaining excellent communicative skills, and by gaining as much knowledge as possible about the society and profession they want to experience. Entrepreneurship is becoming one of the main keys to success in the music business. Creative artists are often sole proprietors who must fulfill the role of a business or hire others to control the business aspects of their artistic creations. In other words, successful musicians, vocalists, songwriters, producers, etc. are, in addition to being creative artist, businessmen and women make a living from their musical and artistic talents.

Industry professionals customarily associate with other colleagues for commonality, friendships, and to enhance their career opportunities. Nobody can make it in this business by him or herself. It's too big of an industry. Joining together with others who have similar interests and talents is a common practice among industry professionals. There are many opportunities you can find by working in teams with others who have similar interests, goals, and connections.

STUDY GUIDE-INDUSTRY OVERVIEW

1. Who is most responsible for a recording artist's success?

2. What is success actually based on?

3. Define Talent?

4. Describe the creative system careers:

    (a) Songwriting

    (b) Recording Artists and Vocalists

    (c) Musicians

    (d) Record Producers

    (e) Audio Engineers

5. Describe the business system careers/functions:

    (a) Music Publishers

    (b) Recording Studios

    (c) Record Labels

    (d) Promotion

    (e) Publicists/publicity

    (f) Artist Managers

(g) Booking Agents & Talent Agents

(h) Concert Promoters

(i) The Mass Media

(j) The Click Media

5. Where do the two industry systems (creative and business) meet?

6. List five other careers associated with the music and entertainment industry.

   (a)

   (b)

   (c)

   (d)

   (e)

7. List the three types of legal businesses.

   (a)

   (b)

   (c)

8. How important is entrepreneurship in the music and entertainment industry? List five positions that are mostly entrepreneurial.

   (a)

   (b)

   (c)

   (d)

   (e)

9. Name and explain the industries three revenue streams.

(a)

(b)

(c)

10. How much money do the music and entertainment industries gross annually?

   (a) Global Creative Industries

   (b) National (USA) Creative Industries

   (c) Record Labels

   (d) Music Industries Sales

   (e) Live Event/Concert Sales

   (f) Portable Digital Players

   (g) Music Publishing

11. What is the new Music Business based on?

Lecture Points

CAST OF CHARACTERS-Creative

SONGWRITERS

MUSIC PUBLISHERS

RECORDING ARTISTS

SINGERS/BACKGROUND SINGERS

MUSICIANS

RECORD PRODUCERS

AUDIO ENGINEERS & MERGE TECHNOLOGY ENGINEERS

Lecture Points

SUPPORTING BUSINESS SYSTEMS

RECORD LABELS

RECORDING STUDIOS

PROMOTION - PUBLICITY

ARTIST MANAGERS

BOOKING AGENTS

CONCERT PROMOTERS

BUSINESS MANAGERS

ATTORNEYS - CONSUMERS

MAJOR ENTERTAINMENT CORPORATIONS

SONY / BERTELSMANN'S AG (BMG)

EMI GROUP

VEVENDI UNIVERSAL (UMG)

TIME WARNER

Disney

PROTECTING CREATIVITY
® © ™
Intellectual Property Rights

Copyright is the means by which a person or a business makes a living from creativity.

—IFPI[12]

"Music is spiritual. The Music Business is not."

—Van Morrison[13]

"I don't think anybody steals anything; all of us borrow."

--BB King[14]

In a landmark U.S. Supreme Court decision, Justice Sandra Day O'Connor wrote that copyright protection --far from being inconsistent with the rights of free speech and freedom of information-- is the very engine of free expression. This principle is not new. Over two hundred years ago, Benjamin Franklin, Thomas Jefferson, James Madison, and the other champions of American democracy, considered copyright protection and the ownership of intellectual property so essential and complimentary to freedom of speech that they included a mandate for it in Article I, Section 8 of the U.S. Constitution.

—NMPA (National Music Publishers Association)[15]

COPYRIGHTS ©

We know what the word "copy" means and we know what the word "right" means, but "copyright" is a different matter. Why is it important to the music and entertainment industry? Better still, why is it important to the creative artist? Copyrights spring from a simple notion; the people who create, produce or invest in original creative works should be the ones who own the works (as examples, songs, recordings, films, and books) as their own property. To simplify it, the word "right" relates to the ownership rights called exclusive rights of the copyright. The word "copy" relates to the owner's right to receive payment for each copy made, distributed, performed, digitally transmitted or used by consumers. The trick is to create such a wonderful piece of art, song, or entertainment product that consumers will pay for the use of it. *United States* copyright industries contribute over *$255 billion* annually to the national gross domestic product and new jobs are created in copyright related industries at double the national economy rate.[16]

12 "What is a Copyright?" by the IFPI, ifpi.org (07/06/2000).
13 Forbes Book of Quotations: Thoughts on the Business of Life, (11/29/1999).
14 http://www.barryrudolph.com/utilities/quotes.html
15 The penalties for criminal infringement, set forth in Title 18 of the U.S. Code, are determined by its extent: if the infringer has made, in any 180-day period, ten or more copies of one or more copyrighted works with a total retail value of $2,500, the crime is a felony entailing up to five years imprisonment and/or a fine of up to $250,000 for individuals and $500,000 for organizations. 18 U.S.C. §§ 2319(a), 3571(b). For cases not meeting this threshold, the crime is a misdemeanor, with the maximum penalty of imprisonment for up to one year and/or a fine of up to $25,000 for individuals and $100,000 for organizations. Id. §§ 2319(c), 3571(b). There is also an increased penalty for repeat offenders, authorizing a sentence of up to 10 years. Id. § 2319.
16 Copyright and the U.S. Economy", Copyright Industries in the U.S. Economy: The Economists, Inc. as reported at:

At its simplest, most basic level, the music and entertainment industry is really about the business of selling the same performances and recordings over and over again. Labels sell recordings of a song created in a studio or by computers hopefully into the millions; radio plays the same copy of the recording trying to gain an audience in order to sell air time to advertisers; concerts are actually the basic same live performance of songs played in a different venue before different audiences; film production companies sell movies to mega entertainment companies (*EMI, Sony, Time Warner, Bertelsmann A.G., or Universal*) who sell viewing of the same film in theaters to millions and then later, copies on DVD's and digital downloads. The business model of the mass media is all about gathering an audience by using, playing, or airing someone else's copyrighted entertainment products. The truth is that almost everything from sports teams to talk shows (Rush Limbaugh) are considered an entertainment product copyrighted and thus owned by an individual or company who sells it and it's appearances to mass media outlets. With the success of the entertainment products come other cash generating copyrighted opportunities in endorsements, merchandise and corporate sponsorships. It's all based on copyrights and who owns them. The legal protection of creatively falls into four definitions under the umbrella of Intellectual Properties. They include:

- *Copyrights,*
- *Trademarks,*
- *Trade secrets,*
- *Patents.*

Patents provide protection for useful inventions and discoveries such as CD players, CDs, computer chips, film cameras, recording tape and film. Copyright laws are meant to encourage artistic and creative works (often using the inventions and discoveries covered under patent laws), to make among other things, musical recordings, paintings, photographs, literary works, choreographic works, computer-enhanced artwork, and films. Trademarks are tied to product and company identification. Company icons and logos identify a product as original and not as counterfeit merchandise. Trade secrets are tied to valuable information a company may possess that provides it with a competitive advantage over other businesses in an industry. Employees from one company are often required to sign a document that they cannot share trade secrets with a competitor after they leave their employer. Copyright is a form of protection provided by the laws of the United States (title *17 U. S. Code*) to the authors of original works of authorship, including literary, dramatic, musical, artistic, and certain other intellectual works.[23] It is illegal for anyone to violate any of the rights which are provided by the copyright law to the owner of the copyright.[17]

Consumers of entertainment products may understand the meaning of copyrights better by rearranging the words from copyright to right to copy. The person who created the work now owns it because it fits the definitions of property and copyright and thus, anyone who wants to use the work (by making or acquiring a copy of it), is required to pay for it (unless the creator wants to give it away free). The artist who created the work can now claim it as his/her own property and attempt to sell it. Copyright protects original works of authorship that are fixed in a tangible form of expression.

---

www.cic.org (09/23/98).

17 © 2007 Copyright claimed in Chapter 2 and 3 of this publication are exclusive of U.S. Copyright Office, Library of Congress, United States of America www.loc.gov.

Copyright works include the following categories:

- *Literary works*
- *Musical works, including any accompanying words*
- *Dramatic works, including any accompanying music*
- *Pantomimes and choreographic works*
- *Pictorial, graphic, and sculptural works*
- *Motion pictures and other audiovisual works*
- *Sound recordings*
- *Architectural works*[26]

HISTORICAL PERSPECTIVE

The origin of copyright law is related to the invention of the printing press in 15th century England. This new ability to inform the masses threatened the image of the English government. To control the distribution of Protestant religious heresy and political upheaval the government and church forced book publishers to obtain a license to publish.[18] This of course was a censorship law that allowed only the printing of books that were loyal or non-confrontational to the church and government.

STATUTE OF ANNE

The expiration of the license to publish law in 1695 initiated stiff competition between entrepreneurial book publishers who were seeking to profit from books expounding a different perspective and the established autocratic publishers.[19] In defiance of the lobbying efforts of political leaders and the established book publishers, the *English Parliament* passed the first known copyright law in 1710, called the Statute of Anne. It established the ultimate purpose of modern copyright laws, which is to enhance public welfare by encouraging the dissemination of knowledge.[20] The established book publishers lost their monopoly. The law encouraged the writing, printing and distribution of useful works (in this case books that were in some cases critical to the political establishment). It changed the world, as different levels of society were now able to communicate and express their views and make a profit at the same time.[21] Thus the Statute of Anne tied the new technology of the times (the printing press) to political action that shifted distribution rights and potential profits to the creators of the original works. The act defined ownership rights and provided a method of gaining financial rewards to the artists, scientists, and investment companies who created the works.

As a result of the invention of the personal computer, cell phones, PDA's and the Internet, think of all the political and social businesses that will grow and change in the next 20 years. Consider the impact on relationships, creativity and business

---

18 The Copyright Book: A Practical Guide, by William S. Strong (5th edition), The MIT Press, Cambridge (1999) p. 2.
19 Leaffer (1989).
20 Statute of Anne, 1710, as stated in Understanding Copyright Law (1989).
21 Ibid & The Constitutional Provision Respecting Copyright. The Copyright Law of the United States of America, (1993).

Back Then!

1790
Concerto for Pianoforte and Orchestra in D major (Coronation) by Wolfgang Amadeus Mozart 10/9 at Frankfurt-am-Main for the coronation of Leopold II.

President Washington appoints French-born engineer Pierre (Charles) L'Enfant, 35, to design the federal city with a Capitol to be built on an 85-foot hill at the intersection of what will be Pennsylvania Avenue and Constitution Avenue

Benjamin Franklin dies in Philadelphia April 17 at age 84.

Cincinnati gets its name as the 2-year-old town of Losantiville on the Ohio River is renamed by the Northwest Territory's first governor, General Arthur St. Clair.

Congress enacts the first U.S. copyright law.

Source Wikipedia.com

in the entertainment industries that all started with the invention of the printing press and some political courage. And at the same time, consider the problems technology once again brings to the copyright holders.

UNITED STATES CONSTITUTION

The authors of the United States Constitution did not miss the Statute of Anne's inference. *Article 1, Section 8* gives:

Congress the right to legislate copyright statute to promote the Progress of Science and Useful Arts, by securing for Limited Times to Authors and Inventors, the Exclusive Right to their respective Writings and Discoveries.[22]

Let's take a closer look at the statute.

- ***Promoting the progress of science and useful arts*** is accomplished by providing legal ownership and therefore, potential financial rewards to the individuals who invest their time and money into scientific discoveries (as an example inventions and medicines) and useful arts (such as the performing and creative arts) including songs, scripts, recordings, movies and other entertainment products.

- ***Copyright protection subsists from the time the work is created in fixed form.*** The copyright in the work of authorship immediately becomes the property of the author who created the work. Only the author or those deriving their rights through the author can rightfully claim copyright.[23]

- ***Accordingly, the copyright is instant and you do not need to apply for one.*** In reality, when you register your claim of a copyright with the Copyright Office, all you are doing is registering your claim of a copyright. *The government only registers the time and date of your claim. Therefore, the copyright office does not issue a copyright; it only registers your claim of one.*

- ***By securing for limited times means ownership rights are not forever but only for a stated period of time.*** After that period of time, (currently, life plus 70 years), the copyright falls into public domain, meaning it can be used freely by the general public.

- ***Exclusive Rights*** define the copyright owners six rights. *Section 106 of the 1976 Copyright Act* generally gives the owners of copyrights the exclusive rights to carry out for themselves or authorize others to accomplish them.

Back Then

Let's see what has changed in the world since 1909. The Titanic sank, the invention of radio, television, film, Al Gore's Internet, personal computers, the A-bomb, MP3's, iPods, iPhones, iTunes, and the list goes on. To say the least, we needed a new copyright law to deal with all of the changes between 1909 and 1976!

Bummer!

If a copyright originally secured before January 1, 1964 was not renewed by the end of its first 28-year coverage, then it fell into public domain and was not available for the 1909 renewal or the 1976 extension.

THE DART FUND

The recording industry portions of the DART royalties are determined by dividing the total number of records distributed by the various numbers of recording artists and record labels who have released a product. For example, if you are a recording artist and your label pressed and distributed 100,000 copies of your latest album on CD's, DCC's, you can divide the 100,000 by the total number of albums nationally distributed, over the same period of time, to determine the percent of DART recording artist royalties you will receive. Then simply multiply the total amount of DART recording artist's royalties collected by the government by your percent of total albums distributed.

---

22 www.loc.gov or www.copyrights
23 Ibid.

So, if the United States Constitution gives creative people exclusive or ownership rights, what are they?

EXCLUSIVE RIGHTS

To *reproduce the © work* in copies or phonorecords;

To prepare *derivative works* based upon the © work;

To *distribute* copies or phonorecords of the © work to the public by sale or other transfer of ownership, or by rental, lease, or lending;

To *perform the © work publicly*, in the case of literary, musical, dramatic, and choreographic works, pantomimes, motion pictures and other audiovisual works;

To *display the © work publicly*, in the case of literary, musical, dramatic, and choreographic works, pantomimes, and pictorial, graphic, or sculptural works, including the individual images of a motion picture or other audiovisual work; and

In the case of sound recordings to perform the © work publicly by means of a *digital audio transmission*.[24]

TYPES OF COPYRIGHT OWNERSHIP

There are several methods or ways to own a copyright:

- *Authorship Ownership*-This is the initial copyright vested in the original authors/creators of the work.

- *Works Made for Hire*-The employer or other person for whom the work was prepared is considered the copyright owner.

- *A Contribution to Collective Works*-The Copyright in each separate contribution to a collective work is distinct from copyright in the collective work as a whole and is vested initially in the author of the contribution.

- *Transfer of Ownership*-The ownership of a copyright may be transferred in whole or in part by any means of conveyance or by operation of law, and may be bequeathed by will or pass as personal property by the applicable laws of interstate succession. In addition, any of the rights specified by section 106 (exclusive rights) may be transferred... or owned separately.[25]

PHONORECORDS

Phonorecords are defined as objects in which sounds, other than those accompanying a motion picture or other audiovisual work, are fixed by any method now known or later developed and from which sounds can be perceived, reproduced or otherwise communicated, either directly or with the aid of a machine or device. Phonorecords also include the material objects in which the sounds are first fixed.[26]

---

24 Ibid.
25 Ibid.
26 Ibid.

SOUND RECORDINGS

Sound recordings are works that result from the fixations of a series of musical, spoken, or other sounds, but not including the sounds accompanying a motion picture or other audiovisual work, regardless of the nature of the material objects such as disks, tapes, or other phonorecords in which they are embodied.[27]

Following the instructions in the Constitution, Congress passed many copyright acts (legislation):

- *January 8, 1783*-The earliest copyright statute in the United States was passed by the General Court of Connecticut under the title of "An Act for the Encouragement of Literature and Genius." Dr. Noah Webster, famed lexicographer and one of Connecticut's most distinguished men, was directly instrumental in securing its enactment.

- *March 10, 1783*-The Continental Congress resolved that a committee be appointed to consider the most proper means of cherishing genius and useful arts through the United States by securing to authors or publishers their property in such new works. The committee chosen consisted of Hugh Williamson, Ralph Izard, and James Madison.[28]

Some of the most important acts affecting the length of the copyright and various registration and other processes are the laws of *1790, 1831, 1909, 1976, 1992, 1993, 1995, 1997, 1998, 2004 and 2006.*

ACT OF 1790

The Copyright Act of 1790 was the first copyright law of the United States. It was entitled *"An Act for the Encouragement of Learning, by Securing the Copies of Maps, Charts, and Books to the Authors and Proprietors of such Copies during the Times Therein Mentioned."*[29] It gave authors monopoly ownership rights (for a limited period of time) of approval for the copying and displaying of their creative works. It also specified by statute that writing was a particular form of expression. The monopoly ownership rights, later called *Exclusive Rights*, were granted for one 14-year term, plus an additional 14-year renewal term (if applied) for a total of 28 years.[30] The act also required the following formalities to be accomplished in order for the copyright registration to be secured; (a) The deposit of a printed title before publication in the clerk's office of the local U.S. district court; (b) The deposit of a copy of the work with the Secretary of State within six months after publication; and (c) The giving of a notice of the copyright by four advertisements in some newspaper.[31]

ACT OF 1831

Congress specified that music was a useful art that allowed for copyright protection and exclusive ownership rights.[32]

---

27 Ibid.
28 Notable Dates in American Copyrights 1783-1969, Compiled by James Rudd, Library of Congress, www.loc.gov, 2007.
29 1 stat, 24 Chapter, 15, Library of Congress by Internet www.loc.gov, 2007.

30 Ibid.
31 Ibid.
32 Legal Aspects of the Music Industry: An Insider's View of the Legal and Practical Aspects of the Music Business by Richard Schulenberg, Billboard Books (1999).

ACT OF 1909

The 1909 act was the third general revision of the copyright law. The President signed it into law in July of 1909. The act expanded the monopoly ownership to a total of 56 years (original and renewal period). It also allowed unpublished works protection; a *copyright notice* on the work (© date, owners name) was secured by publication, thus ending the need for newspaper copyright related advertisements. The works of foreign origin in foreign languages were exempted from the requirement of American manufacturing.[33] Additionally, the owners of musical compositions were granted mechanical recording rights under the *compulsory licensing* provisions.[34]

What was going through the lawmakers' minds about copyright laws and the development of the mass media back in 1909? They may have had a clue about the future of technology as *Thomas Edison* was in the process of inventing the phonograph, film camera, telephone and other related devices. Indeed, as the inventions of the entertainment industry (mass media) were being developed even into the 1970's, most of the relevant copyright laws were fixed under the 1909 act.

ACT OF 1976

The problem for the emerging music and entertainment industry was how to adapt the law of 1909 to the modern mass media and entertainment business. It was not until 67 years later that Congress addressed many of these issues in the 1976 copyright act. Some of our greatest songwriters, including the late *Irving Berlin*, were outliving their copyrights, so the 1976 act extended the term of a copyright to life plus 50 years. Joint authorship works were provided copyright protection for 50 years after the surviving author's death. *Pseudonymous, anonymous, and works for hire* (for example, songs written by a staff writer at a publishing company) were protected for 75 years from the date of first publication or 100 years from the date of creation, whichever expires first.[35]

The 1976 law retained the renewal system for works still under protection of the 1909 law. *Nineteen additional years* were added to the years of duration under the 1909 act. The original 28 years and 28 renewal years, plus 19 additional years provided for a total copyright term of 75 years for songs and copyrights that had not dropped into public domain.[36] Prior to the 1976 law, copyrights were granted federal protection for published works and state common law protection for unpublished or non-distributed materials. The word published in copyright law language is defined as distributed for sale to the public whereas in music industry terminology, it often means that a songwriter has a deal with a music publisher. In this case, we are discussing the legal definition tied to

---

> *Oldest Trademarks*
>
> Zildjian, the cymbal and gong company, owns the oldest continuously used U.S. trademark -- it should be noted, however, that the first two hundred years of the use of the Zildjian trademark were in Turkey as the family moved to the United States. Venetian glass blowers are thought of as using the longest continuously used trademarks. Wielicka, a salt mine in the Czech Republic, is reported to be the source of the oldest known trademark (circa 1241 A.D.) -- even though this trademark is really appellation of origin. Finally, in trademark treatises, it is usually reported that blacksmiths who made swords in the Roman empire are thought of as being the first users of trademarks.[4] Other notable trademarks that have been used for a long time include Löwenbräu, which claims use since 1383, and Stella Artois, which claims use since 1366.[1]
>
> 1 Wikipedia

---

33 35 stat, 1075, Public Law 3495 www.loc.gov, 2007.
34 Notable Dates in American Copyrights 1783-1969, Compiled by James Rudd, Library of Congress, www.loc.gov 2007.
35 The Copyright Law of the United States of America, pp. 67-68.
36 If a copyright originally secured before January 1, 1964 was not renewed by the end of its first 28-year coverage, then it fell into public domain and was not available for the 1909 renewal or the 1976 extension.

copyrights and not the music business lingo. The 1976 law terminated this dual copyright system. The 1976 law, which became effective January 1, 1978, provides federal copyright protection for all published and non-published works.[37]

Finally, the 1976 act required jukebox owners to obtain a *compulsory performance license* for each of their jukeboxes. Previously, jukeboxes were exempt from royalty payments. In addition, noncommercial broadcasters (NPR) were required to pay for music played over their airwaves.[38]

ACT OF 1992

The 1992 Audio Home Recording Act (commonly known as the Digital Audio Recording and Tape Act or *DART Act*) provides royalties to songwriters, publishers, producers, recording artists, and record companies to compensate for their loss of royalties due to consumer copying or dubbing of their CD's and other media. Back in the late 1980's the concern was that digital recorders would lower revenues because there was not any loss in sound quality when making copies. The federal government imposed a 3% royalty on recorders and a 2% royalty on tapes.[39] Computers, iPods, mp3 players, and CD-ROM drives are not covered in the DART act.

ACT OF 1993

The Copyright Royalty Tribunal Reform Act of 1993 eliminated the *Copyright Royalty Tribunal* (CRT) and replaced it with a system of ad hoc *Copyright Arbitration Royalty Panels* (CARPs) administered by the Library of Congress (Librarian) and the Copyright Office. CARP's job was to set statutory rates for the various licenses including the mechanical license record labels must acquire for the use of songs their recording artists record and the label sells to retail outlets.[40] [41] Carp was replaced in 2004 by a three-judge panel.

---

37 Ibid.
38 Legal Aspects of the Music Industry: An Insiders View of the Legal and Practical Aspects of the Music Business, by Richard Schulenberg, Billboard Books, Watsons-Guptill Publications/New York (1999), p 462.
39 The recording industry portions of the DART royalties are determined by dividing the total number of records distributed by the various numbers of recording artists and record labels who have released a product. For example, if you are a recording artist and your label pressed and distributed 100,000 copies of your latest album on CD's, DCC's, you can divide the 100,000 by the total number of albums nationally distributed, over the same period of time, to determine the percent of DART recording artist royalties you will receive. Then simply multiply the total amount of DART recording artist's royalties collected by the government by your percent of total albums distributed.
40 The Copyright Royalty Tribunal Reform Act of 1993, PL 103-198, eliminated the Copyright Royalty Tribunal (CRT) and replaced it with ad hoc Copyright Arbitration Royalty Panels (CARPs) administered by the Library of Congress and the Copyright Office. CARPs adjust copyright royalty rates and distribute royalties to eligible claimants.
41 www.loc.gov

Sonny Bono

Born in Detroit, Michigan to Italian immigrants, Santo Bono worked for the legendary record producer Phil Spector in the early 1960s. Later he achieved success, with his then-wife Cher, as part of the singing duo Sonny and Cher with songs "I Got You Babe" and "The Beat Goes On." They starred in a popular television variety show, The Sonny and Cher Show, and he acted in the TV shows Fantasy Island and The Love Boat. He tried to open a restaurant in Palm Springs, California and got so frustrated with the local government that he ran as mayor and won. Later he became a member of the US House of Representatives and sponsored copyright legislation. After his death, a similar bill was passed and named in his honor.

Uploading or downloading works protected by copyright without the authority of the copyright owner is an infringement of the copyright owner's exclusive rights of reproduction and/or distribution. Anyone found to have infringed a copyrighted work may be liable for statutory damages up to $30,000 for each work infringed and, if willful infringement is proven by the copyright owner, that amount may be increased up to $150,000 for each work infringed. In addition, an infringer of a work may also be liable for the attorney's fees incurred by the copyright owner to enforce his or her rights-source, www.loc.gov-copyrights.

ACT OF 1995

The Digital Performance Right in Sound Recordings Act of 1995 authorizes copyright owners to be paid for digital transmissions of their recordings, including interactive digital audio transmissions.[42] Thus, the 1995 digital transmission act expands the previous compulsory licenses by including audio digital transmissions. It also creates a new compulsory license for digital subscription transmission services and yet exempts non-interactive service.

ACT OF 1997

The No Electronic Theft Act (NET ACT) is significant because companies that do not make a monetary profit or commercial gain (such as Napster), yet who infringe on sound recording copyrights can be criminally prosecuted. Punishment includes up to three years in prison and/or $250,000 fines.[43]

The NET Act amended the definition of commercial advantage or private financial gain to include the receipt (or expectation of receipt) of anything of value, including receipt of other copyrighted works.[44 & 45]

THE DMC

The Digital Millennium Copyright Act in 1998 includes cable and satellite digital audio services, webcasters, and all future forms of digital transmission. Non-interactive transmissions are still subject to statutory licensing.[46] The DMC implements the 1996 *World Intellectual Property Organization* (WIPO) treaties for the protection of copyrights, performances and phonorecords. The treaty significantly helps to protect the United States and WIPO members' creative works by addressing copyright issues concerning the Internet, online service providers, computer programs, web casting, digital movies, digital music transmission and downloads.[47]

ACTS OF 1998

Three important acts were passed in 1998. ***The Fairness in Music Licensing Act*** is considered as one of the most damaging laws ever passed by Congress concerning music performance copyrights. Indeed, most music copyright holders consider it to be the *Non-Fairness in Music Licensing Act of 1998* because it exempts many "establishments," defined as food service and drinking establishments, with less than 3,750 square feet of gross space and other types of small businesses of less than 2,000 gross square feet.[48]

---

42 Chairman Moorhead joined by Chairman Hyde and Representatives Conyers and Gekas introduced H.R. 1506 on April 7, 1995; legislation to provide a sound recording public performance right had also been introduced in the Senate. The Copyright Office has supported the principle behind H.R. 1506 for many years.

43 The penalties for criminal infringement, set forth in Title 18 of the U.S. Code, are determined by its extent: if the infringer has made, in any 180-day period, ten or more copies of one or more copyrighted works with a total retail value of $2,500, the crime is a felony entailing up to five years imprisonment and/or a fine of up to $250,000 for individuals and $500,000 for organizations. 18 U.S.C. §§ 2319(a), 3571(b). For cases not meeting this threshold, the crime is a misdemeanor, with the maximum penalty of imprisonment for up to one year and/or a fine of up to $25,000 for individuals and $100,000 for organizations. Id. §§ 2319(c), 3571(b). There is also an increased penalty for repeat offenders, authorizing a sentence of up to 10 years. Id. § 2319.

44 The Digital Millennium Copyright Act of 1998, U.S. Copyright Office Summary, 1998.

45 Statement of Marybeth Peters The Register of Copyrights before the Subcommittee on Courts and Intellectual Property Committee on the Judiciary. United States House of Representatives 105th Congress, 1st Session-September 11, 1997. No Electronic Theft (NET) Act of 1997 (H.R. 2265)

46 www.loc.gov 2007.

47 Legal Aspects of the Music Industry: An Insiders View of the Legal and Practical Aspects of the Music Business, by Richard Schulenberg, Billboard Books, Watson-Guptill Publications/New York (1999), p 462).

48 (i) in the case of an establishment *other than a food service or drinking establishment*, either the establishment in which the communication occurs has less than 2,000 gross square feet of space ... (I) if the performance is by audio means only, the

In other words, the businesses may use radio broadcasts and other musical performances in their businesses, and make money without paying the music publishers, songwriters and labels for the music they are using to make a profit. Many in the music and entertainment industry, who will lose hundreds of millions of dollars, consider this a political move against the creative songwriters and music publishers who should be paid for their songs/copyrights.[49][50]

SONNY BONO

The ***Sonny Bono Copyright Term Extension Act of 1998*** adds an additional 20 years to the term of a copyright. Thus the life plus 50 years that was granted in the 1976 Act is now life plus 70 years. The 1976 Act gave copyrights still under duration and created prior to the 1976 act an additional 19 years to extend the 56 years granted under the 1909 act to 75 years. The *Sonny Bono Act* extended those copyrights an additional 20 years for a total of 95 years.[51]

P2P EFFECTS ON COPYRIGHT OWNERS

...Mr. Chairman, make no mistake. The law is unambiguous. Using peer-to-peer networks to copy or distribute copyrighted works without permission is infringement and copyright owners have every right to invoke the power of the courts to combat such activity. Every court that has addressed the issue has agreed that this activity is infringement.[52] It can also be a crime and the perpetrators of such a crime are subject to fines and jail time.[56]

—**Statement of Marybeth Peters, <u>The Register of Copyrights</u>, as stated before The Committee on the Judiciary, United States Senate, 108th Congress, 1st Session, September 9, 2003.**[53]

Peer-to-peer file sharing has provided both a marketing boom and copyright protection nightmare to the music and entertainment businesses. In general, these industries have been very slow to embrace the opportunities of digital technology. However, this business is also a talent-driven, creative industry, and as such, it is totally dependent on copyright protection.[57] Lawsuits by *Metallica* and the *RIAA (Recording Industry Association of America)* against *Napster* and other file sharing companies and consumers have <u>curbed the illegal use and sharing of copyrighted non-free music.</u>[54]

performance is communicated by means of a total of not more than 6 loudspeakers, of which not more than 4 loudspeakers are located in any one room or adjoining outdoor space; or (II) if the performance or display is by audiovisual means, any visual portion of the performance or display is communicated by means of a total of not more than 4 audiovisual devices, of which not more than 1 audiovisual device is located in any 1 room, and no such audiovisual device has a diagonal screen size greater than 55 inches, and any audio portion of the performance or display is communicated by means of a total of not more than 6 loudspeakers, of which not more than 4 loudspeakers are located in any 1 room or adjoining outdoor space...
Source § 110. Limitations on exclusive rights: Exemption of certain performances and displays-www, loc.gov 2007.
49 Also included in this bill, Section 2(d) entitled "Performances at Children's Camps," created a new exemption for performances of nondramatic musical works at organized children's camps if the children sing the work, play games or dance to it, or if the performance is instructional. ASCAP had poor media coverage when they tried collecting royalties from Girl Scout camps regarding their performance of musical works around the campfires.
50 Statement of Marybeth Peters The Register of Copyrights before the Subcommittee on Courts and Intellectual Property Committee on the Judiciary. United States House of Representatives 105th Congress, 1st Session-September 11, 1997. Fairness in Musical Licensing Act of 1997 (H.R. 789), www.loc.gov, 2007.
51 The Sonny Bono Copyright Term Extension Act, signed into law on October 27, 1998, amends the provisions concerning duration of copyright protection. Effective immediately, the terms of copyright are generally extended for an additional 20 years. www.loc.gov, 2007.
52 See Napster at 1014; In re: Aimster Copyright Litigation, 334 F.3d 643, 645 (7th Cir. 2003)(hereinafter "Aimster"); Metro-Goldwyn-Mayer Studios, Inc. v. Grokster, Ltd., 259 F.Supp. 2d 1029, 1034-35 (C.D. Cal. 2003) (hereinafter "Kazaa").
53 www.loc.gov, 2007- Statement of Marybeth Peters The Register of Copyrights before the Committee on the Judiciary, United States Senate 108th Congress, 1st Session, September 9, 2003.
54 Uploading or downloading works protected by copyright without the authority of the copyright owner is an infringement of the copyright owner's exclusive rights of reproduction and/or distribution. Anyone found to have infringed a copyrighted

The Penalty

The penalties for criminal infringement, set forth in Title 18 of the U.S. Code, are determined by its extent: if the infringer has made, in any 180-day period, ten or more copies of one or more copyrighted works with a total retail value of $2,500, the crime is a felony entailing up to five years imprisonment and/or a fine of up to $250,000 for individuals and $500,000 for organizations. 18 U.S.C. §§ 2319(a), 3571(b). For cases not meeting this threshold, the crime is a misdemeanor, with the maximum penalty of imprisonment for up to one year and/or a fine of up to $25,000 for individuals and $100,000 for organizations. Id. §§ 2319(c), 3571(b). There is also an increased penalty for repeat offenders, authorizing a sentence of up to 10 years. Id. § 2319.

The Bern Convention

The Bern Convention was developed at the instigation of Victor Hugo as the Association Littéraire et Artistique Internationale. Thus it was influenced by the French "right of the author" (droit d'auteur), which contrasts with the Anglo-Saxon concept of "copyright" which only dealt with economic concerns. Under the Convention, copyrights for creative works are automatically in force upon their creation without being asserted or declared. An author need not "register" or "apply for" a copyright in countries adhering to the Convention. As soon as a work is "fixed", that is, written or recorded on some physical medium, its author is automatically entitled to all copyrights in the work and to any derivative works, unless and until the author explicitly disclaims them or until the copyright expires. Foreign authors are given the same rights and privileges to copyrighted material as domestic authors in any country that signed the Convention.[1]

1-a-Wikipedia.com

The bottom line is profits from artistry and creativity encouraged by the promotion, publicity and distribution of sellable entertainment products that satisfy consumers' emotional wants and needs.[55] Digital music sold on-line to consumers is very profitable. It is a new and exciting method for consumers to acquire music quickly. Record labels actually make more money from each song/album sold because they are cutting out the middlemen distribution and retail record stores, TV outlets, and record clubs. As a result the industry has benefited from selling recordings through traditional retail outlets, plus Internet music web sites such as iTunes and musicnet.com. The only calamity is how to protect copyrights and assure royalty payments to the copyright holders.

SUPREME COURT DECISION ON PEER-TO-PEER FILE SHARING

In 2004, the *United States Supreme Court* issued its decision in the *Metro-Goldwyn-Mayer Studios vs. Grokster Ltd. Lawsuit* clearly stating that failure to pay for copyrighted products obtained free over the Internet is illegal. The decision was not against the use of downloading of entertainment digital products over the Internet, just the failure to pay the copyright holders' royalties and license fees.

...Discovery revealed that billions of files are shared across peer-to-peer networks each month. Respondents are aware that users employ their software primarily to download copyrighted files, although the decentralized networks do not reveal which files are copied and when. Respondents have sometimes learned about the infringement directly when users have e-mailed questions regarding copyrighted works, and respondents have replied with guidance. Respondents are not merely passive recipients of information about infringement. The record is replete with evidence that when they began to distribute their free software, each of them clearly voiced the objective that recipients use the software to download copyrighted works and took active steps to encourage infringement. After the notorious filesharing service, Napster, was sued by copyright holders for facilitating copyright infringement, both respondents promoted and marketed themselves as Napster alternatives. They receive no revenue from users, but, instead, generate income by selling advertising space, then streaming the advertising to their users. As the number of users increases, advertising opportunities are worth more. There is no evidence that either respondent made an effort to filter copyrighted material from users downloads or otherwise to impede the sharing of copyrighted files...[56]

work may be liable for statutory damages up to $30,000 for each work infringed and, if willful infringement is proven by the copyright owner, that amount may be increased up to $150,000 for each work infringed. In addition, an infringer of a work may also be liable for the attorney's fees incurred by the copyright owner to enforce his or her rights-source, www.loc.gov-copyrights, 2007.
55 Copyrights and Digital Files, www.loc-copyrights, 2007.
56 METRO-GOLDWYN-MAYER STUDIOS INC. ET AL. v. GROKSTER,

JUSTICE SOUTER delivered the opinion of the Court:

The question is under what circumstances the distributor of a product capable of both lawful and unlawful use is liable for acts of copyright infringement by third parties using the product. We hold that one who distributes a device with the object of promoting its use to infringe copyright, as shown by clear expression or other affirmative steps taken to foster infringement, is liable for the resulting acts of infringement by third parties.[57]

ACT OF 2004

Copyright Royalty and Distribution Reform Act of 2004 replaced the Copyright Arbitration Royalty Panels (CARP) with three federal judges. The judges serve scattered six-year terms and send all compulsory license fee recommendations to Congress.[58]

NOTICE OF INTENTION

In 2004, the Copyright Office established a new method to keep track of all digital recordings. The *Notice of Intention* requires individuals and labels that are obtaining a compulsory license to make and distribute a new recording within 30 days after making the recording and before distribution must notify the copyright holder of their activities.[59]

NEIGHBORING RIGHTS

The United States accounts for about 30% of the global recorded music market, which of course, means that about 70% of recorded music sales are in foreign territories. Thus, it is important for the United States to help and protect American creative artists' products, films, recordings and songs that are used and sold in the World, and at the same time, to protect foreign artists' products used and offered for sale in the United States. Neighboring Rights are similar to but not often the same as *United States Copyright Law*. Indeed, sometimes the persons, companies or governments receiving fees or royalties are not the copyright owners.

LTD., ET AL., October 2004 Supreme Court of The United States decision June 27, 2005 http://www.supremecourtus.gov/
57 Ibid.
58 Copyright Royalty and Distribution Reform Act of 2004 (P.L. 108-419) on Nov. 30, 2004, www.loc.gov copyright law 2007.
59 A "Notice of Intention" is a Notice identified in section 115(b) of title 17 of the United States Code, and required by that section to be served on a copyright owner or, in certain cases, to be filed in the Copyright Office, before or within thirty days after making, and before distributing any phonorecords of the work, in order to obtain a compulsory license to make and distribute phonorecords of nondramatic musical works.

The Bern Convention Again

A song is considered a Bern Convention work if: (a) in the case of an unpublished work, one or more of the authors is a native of a nation adhering to the Bern Convention; or, if the work is published, one or more of the authors is a national of a nation adhering to the Bern Convention on the date of the first publication, or (b) if the work is first published in a nation adhering to the Bern convention.

A "Notice of Intention" is a Notice identified in section 115(b) of title 17 of the United States Code, and required by that section to be served on a copyright owner or, in certain cases, to be filed in the Copyright Office, before or within thirty days after making, and before distributing any phonorecords of the work, in order to obtain a compulsory license to make and distribute phonorecords of nondramatic musical works.

The Copyright Notice
The copyright law suggests that a notice be affixed to all non-sound recording copies (lyric sheets as an example), "in a manner and location" that will provide "a reasonable notice of the claim of copyright." The copyright notice consists of three elements:

1. The symbol ©, or the word "Copyright", or the abbreviated "Copr.";
2. The year of creation (unpublished) or the year of first publication (if distributed);
3. The name(s) of the owner of the copyright in the work, an abbreviation by which the name(s) can be recognized, or a generally known alternative designation of the owner.

Copyright does not protect names, titles, slogans, or short phrases. In some cases, these things may be protected as trademarks. Contact the U.S. Patent & Trademark Office, 800-786-9199, for further information. However, copyright protection may be available for logo artwork that contains sufficient authorship. In some circumstances, an artistic logo may also be protected as a trademark.

Public performance (mass media) reproduction rights (copies), broadcast rights (radio/TV broadcast) and even moral rights and their respective royalties and payments are often different in various countries and territories.[60] Regretfully, there is not an automatic worldwide copyright protection registering system available for creative works. Hence, international copyright treaties have been negotiated to provide copyright protection in as many countries as possible.[61] The treaties are often named after the city in which they were held.

GENEVA

In Geneva in 1952, the United States became a part of the *Universal Copyright Convention* to protect American copyrights in foreign countries that ratified the treaty. The treaty became effective in the United States, September 16, 1955.[62]

GENEVA PHONOGRAMS CONVENTION

The Geneva Phonograms Convention is the Convention for the Protection of Producers of Phonograms Against Unauthorized Duplication of Their Phonograms, concluded in Geneva, Switzerland, on October 29, 1971. The effective United States date is March 10, 1974.[63]

PARIS

The *Universal Copyright Convention* was updated in Paris in 1971. The Effective United States date is July 10, 1974.[64]

BRUSSELS

The 1974 Brussels convention related to the distribution of programs transmitted by satellites became effective in the United States March 7, 1985.[65]

THE BERN CONVENTION

The *Bern Convention for the Protection of Literary and Creative Works* is recognized as a primary international copyright agreement. It ensures international copyright protection for American citizens' creative works in the 80-plus Bern member countries. In return, international members' creative works are protected in America.[66] Effective date in the United States was March 1, 1989. The *Copyright Law of 1976* was modified in order for the United States to become a member of the *Bern Convention*. Previously, a copyright notice had to be placed on all published "works." Now in the United States the copyright notice is no longer required. However, it is a good idea to place it on songs, recordings, music videos, printed sheet music, and other creative works.[67]

---

60 This Business of Music, by M. William Krasilovsky and Sydney Shemel with contribution by John M. Gross and Jonathan Feinstein, 10th edition, Chapter 7, page 68, Billboard Books, Watson-Guptill Publications, New York 2007.
61 As an example, Krasilovsky claims an American copyrighted sound recording only receives 50 years of protection in England, yet songs and books receive life plus 70 years, the same as in the United States.
62 International Copyrights Relations of the United States, Cirular 38A, The Copyright Law, LIBRARY OF CONGRESS (07/26/2000).
63 Ibid.
64 Ibid.
65 Ibid.
66 A song is considered a Bern Convention work if: (a) in the case of an unpublished work, one or more of the authors is a native of a nation adhering to the Bern Convention; or, if the work is published, one or more of the authors is a national of a nation adhering to the Bern Convention on the date of the first publication, or (b) if the work is first published in a nation adhering to the Bern convention.
67 The copyright law suggests that a notice be affixed to all non-sound recording copies (lyric sheets as an example), "in a manner and location" that will provide "a reasonable notice of the claim of copyright." The copyright notice consists of three

THE WTO AND WIPO

The World Trade Organization and The World Intellectual Property Organization have passed legislation in support of worldwide copyrights protection. WTO ratified the Marrakech Agreement of April 15, 1994 that supports intangible property and copyrights of the Uruguay Round Agreements. The effective United States date is January 1, 1995. The "WIPO Performances and Phonograms Treaty" was concluded in Geneva, Switzerland, on December 20, 1996. *It protects rights management information (RMI) or electronic watermarks that are placed in copyrighted products.* The RMI is then used to electronically label and thereby protect music and entertainment products from consumers who want to use or copy the music for free. RMI also allows copyright holders to offer licenses to consumers, distributors (repackagers) and businesses that want to use their products.[68]

NOT PROTECTED

Copyright works must be an expression, not an idea. It is an old truism in copyright law that you cannot copyright an idea but only your expression of it; ideas are in fact considered in the public domain. Thousands of songs use the same title and slogans that have been used in many books, films, and commercials, without the need to gain permission from anyone. In some cases, titles and slogans can be protected by federal trademark law and by state laws against unfair competition and misappropriation. However this is rare and, in general, copyright law does not protect unique ideas, titles, and slogans. Several categories of material are generally not eligible for federal copyright protection. These include among others:

- *Works that have not been fixed in a tangible form of expression, for example, choreographic works that have not been notated or recorded, or improvisational speeches or performances that have not been written or recorded.*

- *Titles, names, short phrases, and slogans; familiar symbols or designs; mere variations of typographic ornamentation, lettering, or coloring; mere listings of ingredients or contents.*

- *Ideas, procedures, methods, systems, processes, concepts, principles, discoveries, or devices, as distinguished from a description, explanation, or illustration.*

- *Works consisting entirely of information that is common property and containing no original authorship (for example: standard calendars, height and weight charts, tape measures and rulers, and lists or tables taken from public documents or other common sources).*[69][70]

---

elements:
The symbol ©, or the word "Copyright", or the abbreviated "Copr."; The year of creation (unpublished) or the year of first publication (if distributed); The name(s) of the owner of the copyright in the work, an abbreviation by which the name(s) can be recognized, or a generally known alternative designation of the owner.

68 International Copyrights Relations of the United States, Cirular 38A, The Copyright Law, LIBRARY OF CONGRESS (07/26/2000).

69 Copyright does not protect names, titles, slogans, or short phrases. In some cases, these things may be protected as trademarks. Contact the U.S. Patent & Trademark Office, 800-786-9199, for further information. However, copyright protection may be available for logo artwork that contains sufficient authorship. In some circumstances, an artistic logo may also be protected as a trademark-Source www.loc.gov-copyright Frequently Asked Questions, 2007.

70 www.loc.gov-copyright Frequently Asked Questions, 2007

SUMMARY

The copyright law is continually being defined by the legal actions of copyright owners against individuals or companies who have failed to gain permission to make payments for their use of copyrighted works such as songs, recordings, TV productions, musical arrangements, films and other creative works. Copyright protection subsists in original works of authorship fixed in any tangible medium of expression, now known or later developed, from which the work can be perceived, reproduced, or otherwise communicated, either directly or with the aid of a machine or device.

In the music and entertainment business, works of authorship include: (a) literary works, (b) musical works, including any accompanying words, (c) dramatic works, including any accompanying music, (d) pantomimes and choreographic works, (e) pictorial, graphic, and sculptural works, (f) motion pictures and other audiovisual works, and (g) sound recordings. If you want to be a part of the music business, be grateful that the United States Congress and countries around the world provide protection to the creators of songs, music, books, music videos, and entertainment products.

The copyright law provides the legal foundation for ownership and justifies the corresponding financial rewards. Songwriters initially own the songs they write, record companies own the albums they financially produce, and movie and music video scriptwriters own their scripts, films and television shows. Without strong American and international copyright law, conventions and treaties, the ownership of creative products would be meaningless. The music business, indeed the entire entertainment industry as we currently know it, would cease to exist without the copyright law. The men and women who invest so much of their time and effort into creating the songs, recordings and all the other entertainment products we enjoy and purchase would not be paid for their worthy endeavors. Music makes life so much more enjoyable. It is important that the individuals who create the music and entertainment products that enrich our lives be financially rewarded for their efforts.

STUDY GUIDE-COPYRIGHTS

1. What is a copyright?

2. Define the four types of Intellectual Properties and what they protect.

    (a)

    (b)

    (c)

    (d)

3. List the 8 types of copyrightable works.

    (a)

    (b)

    (c)

    (d)

    (e)

    (f)

    (g)

    (h)

4. Why is the Statute of Anne considered so important?

5. Write (in the space below) Article 1, Section 8 of the United States Constitution.

6. Explain the five points listed in the textbooks about the rights authors and inventors have as described in Article 1, Section 8 of the United States Constitution.

    (a)

    (b)

    (c)

    (d)

    (e)

7. List and explain the 6 Exclusive Rights.

    (a)

    (b)

    (c)

    (d)

    (e)

    (f)

8. Explain the four types of copyright ownership.

   (a)

   (b)

   (c)

   (d)

9. What is a Phonorecord?

10. List the key points of the following copyright acts.

    (a) 1790

    (b) 1831

    (c) 1909

    (d) 1976

    (e) 1992

    (f) 1993

    (g) 1995

    (h) 1997

    (i) The DMC

    (j) 1998

(k) The Sonny Bono Act

(l) 2004

11. Is peer to peer file sharing legal? Why?

12. Explain the Supreme Court Decision on p2p.

13. What is the "Notice of Intent" used for? Who is notified?

14. Foreign countries account for what percent of global recorded music sales?

15. Why is the Bern Convention important and what did the United States have to change in the copyright law in order to become a member?

16. List four categories of material that are not generally protected by copyright law.

(a)

(b)

(c)

(d)

Chapter Two
Lecture Points

COPYRIGHTS

HISTORY

BASICS

OWNERSHIP

BASIC RIGHTS

HOW DO I GET ONE?

TRANSFERRING

Chapter Two
Lecture Points

INFRINGEMENT

PUBLIC DOMAIN

CO-OWNERS

WHO WROTE IT?

SAMPLING

PLAGIARISM

Chapter Two Notes

Chapter Two Notes

COPYRIGHT REGISTRATION

ELECTRONIC REGISTRATION
TRADITIONAL FORMS

POOR MAN'S COPYRIGHT

No provision in the copyright law states that sending yourself a copy of your creative work through the United States mail is going to protect your claim of a copyright.[71] In fact, it is not.[72]

A WORK-FOR-HIRE

A *work-for-hire* is a work prepared by an employee within the scope of his or her employment or work specially ordered or commissioned for use as a contribution to a collective work. The copyright holder of the work-for-hire song is the employer of the songwriter (unless agreed upon in writing for shared ownership), not the person who created the work or song. *Section 101* of the Copyright Law defines a work-for-hire as:

- A work prepared by an employee within the scope of his or her employment; Or
- A work specially ordered or commissioned for use as:
- A contribution to a collective work
- A part of a motion picture or other audiovisual work
- A translation
- A supplementary work
- A compilation
- An instructional text
- A test
- Answer material for a test
- An atlas

AUTHORSHIP

Songwriters are the authors of the songs they create unless the work is a work-for-hire. Thus, it is often wise to negotiate authorship (author/songwriter status) on the copyright registration form with the employer to insure that your work will be acknowledged.

FIXATION PROCESS

The copyright law provides copyright protection at the moment an original work is "fixed" into a tangible medium. The work must be original (not a copy or derived from another source), and it must be placed into a tangible (physical) form such as written onto a piece of paper or recorded onto a data CD, DVD, computer hard drive, film or video tape. Performing a song live does not protect the song as it has not been placed into a tangible form, it has just been played, heard, and then it is gone. Thus, works are not regarded as copyrighted until they are recorded into a tangible form.

---

[71] The practice of sending a copy of your own work to yourself is sometimes called a "poor man's copyright." There is no provision in the copyright law regarding any such type of protection, and it is not a substitute for registration.
[72] www.loc.gov-copyright Frequently Asked Questions, 2007

PUBLICATION

The term "publish" in the music business often means acquiring a music publishing deal to distribute your songs for production. However, in copyright language, publish means *distribution* of the product for sale to the public. A public performance or display of a work does not in itself constitute publication.[73] Here is how the Copyright Office defines "Published" and "Unpublished" works.

- A Published Work-works published in a single unit of publication and owned by the same copyright claimant.

- An Unpublished Work-works by the same author(s) and owned by the same copyright claimant(s), organized in a collection under a collection title.

WHY REGISTER YOUR CLAIM OF COPYRIGHT

If you plan to commercially exploit your songs, recordings, books, music videos, movie scripts, etc., you should register your copyright (claim of ownership). The United States Government recognizes the person or company who registers a claim of copyright as the copyright owner. It does not analyze the authenticity of the claim. Registration of a copyright customarily protects the copyright holder from unauthorized use or infringement of their creative work. The copyright office only records the date and time of your claim. If a registered song is actually an infringement of another song, then the original copyright holder may have to take legal action to prove creative authorship.

THE UNITED STATES COPYRIGHT OFFICE

www.loc.gov or www.copyright.gov

The U.S. Copyright Office was established in the *Library of Congress* in 1870. The office registers more than 500,000 claims to copyright annually.

CERTIFICATE OF REGISTRATION

Copyright registration is effective on the date the *Copyright Office* receives your properly completed forms, deposit of a copy of the work, and application fee. Once it has processed the forms, copy(s), and application fee, the *Copyright Office* will determine whether the materials deposited constitute copyrightable subject matter. If so, the Registrar will issue to you a certificate of registration.[74]

REGISTRATION PROCESS

It is very easy to register your claim of a copyright. *The Copyright Office, Library of Congress* encourages the use of the Internet to download the proper forms. Just visit www.loc.gov or www.copyright.gov and select Copyrights from the left hand menu. Select the proper form and instructions and print them out. Fill out the forms, send one of two copies of the creative work you are claiming a copyright for and do not forget the fee (currently $45).[75]

---

73 The Copyright Law of the United States of America, pp. 35-58, (1993).
74 If you have a question about the status of your application, the Copyright Office will furnish free information after sixteen weeks, although return of your certificate may take eight months. You will receive a certificate of registration to indicate your song or creative work copyright has been registered or an email, letter or telephone call seeking additional information. If the application cannot be accepted, a letter explaining why it was rejected will be sent.
75 Enclose one copy for unpublished works (not distributed) and two for published works. The U.S. Copyright Office receives over 600,000 applications for copyright annually.

ELECTRONIC REGISTRATION

In July of 2007, the *Copyright Office* set in motion the ***Internet Digital Registration Beta Test***. Shortly after the success of the test, the Copyright Office began the new electronic registration by using eCO forms. Thus, we are encouraged to use the new digital forms and submit our copies digitally. *The office uses the The Adobe® LiveCycle® Barcoded Forms bar-codes to automate the extraction of data from paper forms and deliver it to core systems for processing. This dramatically reduces costs, errors, and time compared to manual data entry and solutions based on optical character recognition (OCR).[76] The following are examples of the 6 page digital registration forms. Notice that on CO 1, you select the type of registration instead of using the old snail mail PA, SR or other type of form.*

QUESTION?

CAN I REGISTER MORE THAN ONE OF MY SONGS AT A TIME?

Unpublished collections of two or more musical works can be submitted for registration on a single form with a single fee and deposit of one complete copy or phonorecord; if on unpublished works the author(s) are claiming full authorship (both wrote the music and lyrics or one wrote the lyrics and the other(s) the music on all the songs submitted. On published songs both the author(s) are claiming ownership of the copyright. However, you cannot submit a collection of songs on one form for one fee, if some of the songs submitted were by one author and some by another. That requires separate registration, with each author claiming the copyright for his or her own respective work. Thus, a separate registration is required as it may simplify identification of the work for purposes of licensing, transfer, permission, and distribution of royalties later if the song becomes a hit.

Parody
Make it funny and it May Be Legal

A parody is a work that ridicules another, usually well-known work, by imitating it in a comic way. Judges understand that by its nature, parody demands some taking from the original work being parodied. Unlike other forms of fair use, a fairly extensive use of the original work is permitted in a parody in order to "conjure up" the original.[1]

---

1 http://fairuse.stanford.edu/Copyright_and_Fair_Use_Overview/chapter9/9-a.html#2

Save the Stamp

The practice of sending a copy of your own work to yourself is sometimes called a "poor man's copyright." There is no provision in the copyright law regarding any such type of protection, and it is not a substitute for registration. Thus, sending a letter to yourself with a copy of your song in it does not protect your claim of copyright.

Save another Stamp!

Now you can register your claim of copyright on line. It is much quicker and will cost you less. The on line registration was beta tested in 2007 and accepted for operation in 2008. Contact www.copyright.gov for additional information.

---

76 Form co2d.pdf from the copyright office-www.copyright.gov 2009.

APPLICATION FOR COPYRIGHT REGISTRATION

* Designates Required Fields

1 WORK BEING REGISTERED

1a. * Type of work being registered (Fill in one only)
- ○ Literary work
- ○ Performing arts work
- ○ Visual arts work
- ○ Motion picture/audiovisual work
- ○ Sound recording
- ○ Single serial issue

1b. * Title of this work (one title per space)

[Remove]

[Click here to create space to add an additional title]

1c. For a serial issue: Volume [ ] Number [ ] Issue [ ] ISSN [ ]
Frequency of publication: [ ] ○ Other [ ]

1d. Previous or alternative title

1e. * Year of completion

Publication (If this work has not been published, skip to section 2)

1f. Date of publication [ ] (mm/dd/yyyy) **1g.** ISBN [ ]

1h. Nation of publication ○ United States ○ Other [Clear Response] Other [ ]

1i. Published as a contribution in a larger work entitled

1j. If line 1i above names a serial issue Volume [ ] Number [ ] Issue [ ]

1k. If work was preregistered Number PRE-

For Office Use Only

Form CO · Application for Copyright Registration

2 AUTHOR INFORMATION - Entry Number

2a. Personal name *complete either 2a or 2b*

First Name | Middle | Last

2b. Organization name

2c. Doing business as

2d. Year of birth   **2e.** Year of death

2f. ☐ Citizenship ○ United States ○ Other   Other _____
       ☐ Domicile   ○ United States ○ Other   Other _____

2g. Author's contribution: ☐ Made for hire   ☐ Anonymous
        ☐ Pseudonymous (Pseudonym is: _____)

Continuation of Author Information

2h. * This author created *(Fill in only the authorship that applies to this author)*

☐ Text   ☐ Compilation   ☐ Map/technical drawing   ☐ Music
☐ Poetry   ☐ Sculpture   ☐ Architectural work   ☐ Lyrics
☐ Computer program ☐ Jewelry design   ☐ Photography   ☐ Motion picture/audiovisual
☐ Editing   ☐ 2-dimensional artwork ☐ Script/play/screenplay ☐ Sound recording/performance

Other: _____

Form CO · Application for Copyright Registration
UNITED STATES COPYRIGHT OFFICE

3 COPYRIGHT CLAIMANT INFORMATION   - Entry Number

Claimant *complete either 3a or 3b - If you do not know the address for a claimant, enter "not known" in the Street address and City fields. You must give the address for at least one claimant.*

3a. Personal name
First Name | Middle | Last

3b. Organization name

3c. Doing business as

3d. Street address *

Street address (line 2)

City * | State | ZIP / Postal code | Country

Email | Phone number

3e. If claimant is **not** an author, copyright ownership acquired by: ○ Written agreement ○ Will or inheritance ○ Other

Other: _____

66

UNITED STATES COPYRIGHT OFFICE
Form CO · Application for Copyright Registration

[Print Form] [Clear Form]

4 LIMITATION OF COPYRIGHT CLAIM

Skip section 4 if this work is all new.

4a. Material excluded from this claim *(Material previously registered, previously published, or not owned by this claimant)*

☐ Text ☐ Artwork ☐ Music ☐ Sound recording/performance ☐ Motion picture/audiovisual

Other: [ ]

4b. Previous registration(s)   Number [   ]   Year
                                  Number [   ]   Year

4c. New material included in this claim *(This work contains new, additional, or revised material)*

☐ Text   ☐ Compilation   ☐ Map/technical drawing   ☐ Music
☐ Poetry   ☐ Sculpture   ☐ Architectural work   ☐ Lyrics
☐ Computer program ☐ Jewelry design   ☐ Photography   ☐ Motion picture/audiovisual
☐ Editing   ☐ 2-dimensional artwork ☐ Script/play/screenplay   ☐ Sound recording/performance

Other: [ ]

UNITED STATES COPYRIGHT OFFICE
Form CO · Application for Copyright Registration

[Print Form] [Clear Form]

5 RIGHTS AND PERMISSIONS CONTACT

[Clear Section]

☐ Check if information below should be copied from the **first** copyright claimant

First Name [   ]   Middle [   ]   Last [   ]

Name of organization [   ]

Street address [   ]

Street address (line 2) [   ]

City [   ]   State [   ]   ZIP / Postal code [   ]   Country [   ]

Email [   ]   Phone number [   ]

UNITED STATES COPYRIGHT OFFICE
Form CO · Application for Copyright Registration

6 CORRESPONDENCE CONTACT

☐ Copy from first copyright claimant   ☐ Copy from rights and permissions contact

First name *   Middle   Last *

Name of organization

Street address *

Street address (line 2)

City *   State   ZIP / Postal code   Country

Email *   Daytime phone number

SNAIL MAIL COPYRIGHT REGISTRATION FORMS

The *Copyright Office* encourages the use of the electronic registration process and CO forms. The older snail mail forms which are being phased out include:

- *TX:* For published and unpublished non-dramatic literary works.
- *SE:* For serials and works to be issued in successive parts including periodicals, newspapers, magazines, newsletters, annuals, journals, etc.
- *PA:* For published and unpublished works of performing artists (musical and dramatic works, pantomimes and choreographic works, motion pictures and other audiovisual works).
- *VA:* For published and unpublished works of visual arts including pictorial, graphic, and sculptural works.
- *SR:* For published and unpublished sound recordings.

COLLABORATION TEAM

Collaborative works are songs that are created by lyricists and music composers. The lyricists provide the words, the composers the musical notations. Collaborations allow lyricists to work with composers who are better at creating the music than the lyrics and vice versa. Successful collaboration teams include *Rodgers and Hammerstein, the Gershwins, Jay Livingston and Ray Evans*, and many of today's famous songwriters. Copyright ownership is usually divided into 50/50 shares that are negotiated in legal written agreements before the collaboration work begins. It is important to agree before you start a project on the amount of the share you will receive.[77]

CO-SONGWRITING

Co-writing means writing with one or more other writers and joint ownership of the copyright. Registration is attained with the names of all the contributing authors of the work. Royalties are usually divided equally or paid according to any previous agreements by corresponding music publishers and performance rights organizations.[78] The duration of the copyright is life plus 70 years of the surviving author.

---

[77] Songwriters should not pay a lyricist or composer to be a collaborator. Money paid up-front is considered unethical, as payment is usually collected through the publishing of the song and the amount of copyright ownership (shares) each participant retains.

[78] Such as ASCAP, BMI or SESAC in the United States and SOCAN in Canada.

MUSICAL ARRANGEMENTS

The copyright law usually addresses *musical arrangements, orchestrations, etc. as a work-for-hire* when a business or musical enterprise commissions the work. The arrangement of a previously public domain musical work is considered a derivative of an original work and the arrangement is therefore copyrightable.

SAMPLING

Sampling is the process of using a portion of an already existing recording in a new recording or performance. The recording artist, act, or author integrates previously recorded material with original material. The use of a previously recorded and therefore copyrighted material (records, etc.) in a new production is considered a copyright infringement. Permission is required from both the sampled song's music publisher and record label.[79] Recent court action has indicated that the use of even one note or part of one recorded note is a copyright violation.

FAIR USE RIGHTS

Individuals and companies (labels) pay for the use of songs, recorded music, etc., created by or leased to them by the copyright holder. *Fair Use Rights are the exception to the exclusive rights of the copyright law.* It allows for free use of copyrighted works in criticism or commentary, news reporting, teaching, academic scholarship, and research. No payment for the use of the materials in these situations is required. However, there are some determining factors, including nonprofit purpose, the type of copyrighted material used, the amount used, and the affect of the used portion on the commercial market or value of the original source.[80]

COMPULSORY (MECHANICAL) LICENSE

The *copyright owner* (through the exclusive rights) in general may determine who may use their creative works. However, the government has determined that the copyright owner must grant permission for others to use their creative work in the following six areas, when requested:

- Cable television stations
- Jukebox owners
- Public broadcasting, including PBS-TV and PBS-Radio
- Satellite re-transmission operators
- Music producers
- Digital Transmissions[81]

---

79 Sampling is also the term used to describe the second stage of the analog to digital recording process. In digital recording music is converted to electronic signals by microphones or other recording devices. Then, the electronic signals are sampled and converted into binary codes. Sampling is also the turn used to rip as little as one recorded note from a previous recording and then use it in a new recording. Recent legal ruling indicate that even the use of one note is a copyright infringement of the songwriters/publisher and record label.
80 Sections 107 through 121 of the 1976 Copyright Act establish limitations on these rights. In some cases, these limitations are specified exemptions from copyright liability. One major limitation is the doctrine of "fair use," which is given a statutory basis in section 107 of the 1976 Copyright Act. In other instances, the limitation takes the form of a "compulsory license" under which certain limited uses of copyrighted works are permitted upon payment of specified royalties and compliance with statutory conditions.
81 Sections 107 through 118 of the Copyright Law, www.loc.gov, 2007.

Compulsory Licenses are only available after the initial release (publication) of a composition or creative work. Music users are stilled required to pay for their use of the music, songs, and compositions they re-record, download, play or retransmit.[82]

RECAPTURING ASSIGNED COPYRIGHTS

The author(s), surviving spouse, surviving children or grandchildren, may accomplish recapturing of an assigned copyright usually (from a publishing company back to the original copyright owner):

- At any time during a five-year period beginning at the end of the 35th year from the date of assignment to the music publisher etc., or (if published) at the end of the 35th year from the date of publication.

- The notice must state the effective date of termination (which must fall within the five-year period), and it must be served to the music publisher etc., not less than two or more than ten years before that date.

- A copy of the notice must be filed and recorded with the Copyright Office before the date of termination.[83]

KEY INDUSTRY RELATED TERMS

Audiovisual works consist of a series of related images (pictures, etc.), which are intrinsically intended to be shown by the use of machines or devices, such as projectors, viewers, or electronics equipment, together with accompanying sounds, such as films or tapes, in which the works are embodied.

A collective work is a work, such as a periodical issue, anthology, or encyclopedia, in which a number of contributions (which are separate and independent by themselves) have been assembled into a new collective work.

A compilation is a work formed by the collection and assembling of pre-existing materials or of data that are selected, coordinated, or arranged in such a way that the resulting work as a whole constitutes an original work of authorship. Compilations include collective works.

The Best Edition of a work is the edition published (distributed) in the United States at any time before the date of deposit, which the Library of Congress determines to be most suitable for its purposes.

Copies are material objects other than phonorecords, in which a work is fixed by any method now known or later developed, and from which the work can be perceived, reproduced, or otherwise communicated, either directly or with the aid of a machine or device.

The copyright owner is the person or company who created the original work or who purchased the work from the person who created the work as a work-for-hire.

A derivative work is a work based upon one or more pre-existing works, such as a translation, musical arrangement, dramatization, fictionalization, motion picture version, sound recording, art reproduction, abridgment, condensation, or any other form in which a work may be recast, transformed, or adapted. A work consisting of editorial revision, annotations, elaboration, or other modifications, which, as a whole, represent an original work of authorship, is a derivative work.

A digital transmission is a transmission in whole or in part in a digital or other non-analog format.

To display a work means to show a copy of it either directly or by means of a film, slide, television image, or any other device or process or, in the case of motion picture or other audiovisual work, to show individual images non-sequentially.

---

82 Most compulsory licenses for music recordings are issued by the Harry Fox Agency found at www.nmpa.org.
83 www.loc.gov

The term financial gain includes receipt, or expectation of receipt, of anything of value, including the receipt of other copyrighted works.

A food service or drinking establishment is a restaurant, inn, bar, tavern, or any other similar place of business, in which the public or patrons assemble for the primary purpose of being served food or drink, in which the majority of the gross square feet of space, that is nonresidential is used for that purpose, and in which non-dramatic musical works are performed publicly.

A joint work (or collaboration) is a work prepared by two or more authors with the intention that their contributions be merged into inseparable or interdependent parts of a unitary whole. Duration of the copyright is 70 years after the death of the surviving author.

Literary works are works, other than audiovisual works, expressed in words, numbers, or other verbal or numerical symbols or indicia, regardless of the nature of the material objects, such as books, periodicals, manuscripts, phonorecords, film, tapes, disks, or cards, in which they are embodied.

Ownership of a copyright may be transferred in whole or in part, including any or all of the exclusive rights.

To perform a work means to recite, render, play, dance, or act it, either directly or by means of any device, process or, in the case of a motion picture or other audiovisual work, to show its images in any sequence or to make the words accompanying it audible.

A performing rights society is an association, corporation, or other entity that licenses the public performance of non-dramatic musical works on behalf of copyright owners of such works, such as the American Society of Composers, Authors and Publishers (ASCAP), Broadcast Music, Inc. (BMI), and SESAC, Inc.

Sound recordings are works that result from the fixation of a series of musical, spoken, or other sounds, but not including the sounds accompanying a motion picture or other audiovisual work, regardless of the nature of the material objects, such as disks, tapes, or other phonorecords, in which they are embodied.

A transfer of copyright ownership is an assignment, mortgage, exclusive license, or any other legal conveyance, of a copyright or any of the exclusive rights comprised in a copyright, whether or not it is limited in time or place of effect, not including a non-exclusive license.

STUDY GUIDE-COPYRIGHT REGISTRATION

1. Does sending a copy of your musical work to yourself in a sealed envelope protect your song? Why not?

2. Define a work for hire? What does it mean? Who owns your creative rights?

3. Define fixed into a tangible medium. Why is it important?

4. Define the word "published" in copyright language.

5. What is a certificate of registration? Where do you get one and how much does it cost?

6. Which copyright form would you use if you want to claim copyright protection on the lyrics, music, and sound recording of one of your songs?

7. Is sampling legal?

8. What is a fair use right/defense?

9. If you want to record a popular song you have heard on the radio, press CD's and then sell it, what kind of license is required?

10. How can a person recapture their copyright after it has been sold to a publisher?

11. Describe the steps (on each form) to register a claim of copyright digitally?

    1.

    2.

    3.

    4.

    5.

12. Describe the steps to register a claim by snail mail.

    1.

    2.

    3.

Lecture Points
Chapter Three

THE COPYRIGHT FORM

TITLE AND NATURE OF THE WORK

PREVIOUS OR ALTERNATE TITLE

NATURE OF WORK

THE AUTHOR

WORKS MADE FOR HIRE

NATURE OF AUTHORSHIP

DATES OF BIRTH AND DEATH

Lecture Points
Chapter Three

NATIONALITY

CREATION AND PUBLICATION

DATE AND NATION OF FIRST PUBLICATION

THE COPYRIGHT CLAIMANT

TRANSFER

PREVIOUS REGISTRATION

DERIVATIVE WORK OR COMPILATION

DEPOSIT ACCOUNTS AND CORRESPONDENCE

CERTIFICATION

MAILING INFORMATION

THE SONG BUSINESS

COMMUNICATION THEORIES
BECOMING A PROFESSIONAL SONGWRITER

"I think that people need to get the stars out of their eyes and realize that they're going into it as a business."

—**Desmond Child, Songwriter**[84]

"I learned very early in life that 'Without a song, the day would never end; without a song, a man ain't got a friend; without a song, the road would never bend.. without a song.' So I keep singing a song."
—**Elvis Presley**[85]

THE SONG BUSINESS

The industry is desperate for great songs not good songs to invest their money and creative talents into. They are the foundation for almost everything else that follows including recordings, film sound tracks, commercials, radio and the mass media, and tours. It is their communicative success that generates the industry's bottom line. Thus the difference between a good song and a great song is millions of dollars for the songwriter, publisher, artist and the label.

Many successful songwriters are first known as 20-year over-night wonders. It's a saying used in the industry to describe someone who has seemingly achieved success quickly but has actually been working at it for many years. Thousands of potential songwriters each year send CDs and attachments in emails to music publishers. Most are rejected or returned with a "not soliciting new material" or "not what we are looking for" rejection letter. However, every so often, an unknown writes a great song, gets it picked up by a publisher who places it with a major artist who records it and, before you know it, bam-smash hit.

ENTERTAINMENT AS EMOTIONAL COMMUNICATION

Why are songs and other entertainment products important to consumers? The theory is that consumers use them to satisfy their own wants and needs to live a more satisfying life by using the emotional, communicative message encapsulated in the complexity of the recording of a song, the artist image and performance. It allows consumers to celebrate their emotions and understand themselves better. Thus, music and other entertainment events and products are complex forms of communication sold to consumers to help them subconsciously define and celebrate their constructed ethos and pathos.

---

84 The Music Business Handbook & Career Guide, Baskerville (1990).
85 http://www.artquotes.net/entertainment-quotes/famous-singers/elvis-presley/index.htm

Imagination is the capacity to consider objects or events in their absence or as they might be. Imagination may refer to many things, such as fantasy, ingenuity, daydreaming, and make-believe. But it often involves the use of mental imagery, which is the ability to call to mind the sensations of sights, sounds, tastes, smells, and touches that have been experienced. Through mental imagery, people can also create mental sensations of situations or conditions they have not actually experienced. Imagination plays an important role in creativity, including the formation of abstract ideas. Mental images can substitute for the real thing allowing a person to plan how to paint a picture, compose a song, and so on.

— S. M. Kosslyn, Ph.D., John Lindsay Professor of Psychology, Harvard University[86]

COMMUNICATION THEORIES

Theories about wants and needs and how we learn appear to fall into three categories:

- ***Stimulus-response relationships*** claim that learning is the forming of habits by connecting a stimulus and a response that did not exist (to us) before. Thus, psychologists believe that we use past experiences to solve new problems and thus we change our behavior (behavior modification).

- A second group of psychologists believes that ***cognition or the act of knowing*** is more important than the stimulus-response relationships quoted previously. They believe and emphasize the importance of the learners' need to discover and perceive new relationships to achieve insights and understanding.

- A third group of psychologists believe that human learning is based on our needs to ***express creativity***. Thus, they claim that almost any activity including athletics, business dealings, and homemaking can serve as a creative outlet. The psychologists also believe that a person must become involved in challenging activities and must do reasonably well to have a satisfying life.

—Leonard M. Horowitz, Ph.D., Professor of Psychology, Stanford University[87]

There is little doubt that the quality of a song's message, the performance of the vocalists and the musicians must all come together to touch the emotions of various types of listeners. Music affects the pulse rate, respiration, and concentration. However, the emotions being created by listeners seem to last only as long as the music is being heard or replayed in our minds.[88]

The brain seems to be a sponge for music and, like a sponge in water, is changed by it.

—From a recent article in Newsweek Magazine by Sharon Begley[89]

The psychologists supporting the humanistic theory (third listed above) state that:

...Each person must become involved in challenging activities-and must do reasonably well at them-to have a satisfying life. The individual gains a sense of control, growth, and knowledge from such activities. For learning to occur, people must feel free to make their own decisions. They also must feel worthy, relatively free from anxiety, self-respecting, and respected by others. Under these conditions,

---

86 World Book "Imagination" S. M. Kosslyn, Ph.D., John Lindsay Professor of Psychology, Harvard University (2006).
87 Leonard M. Horowitz, Ph.D., Professor of Psychology, Stanford University, plus Banner, James M., Jr., and Cannon, H. C. The Elements of Learning, Yale, 1999. Bransford, John D., and others, eds. How People Learn, 1999. Reprint. National Academy Pr., 2000. and Levine, Melvin D.A Mind at a Time, Simon & Schuster, 2002. Discusses several ways people learn.
88 Philosophy In A New Key, Susanne Langer (1951). Langer suggests that Music is known to affect pulse rate and respiration, to facilitate or disturb concentration, to excite or relax the organism, while the stimulus lasts. But beyond evoking impulses to sing, tap, adjust one's step to musical rhythm, perhaps to stare, hold one's breath or take a tense attitude, Langer feels that music does not ordinarily influence behavior.
89 Music on the Mind by Sharon Begley, Newsweek, (07/24/2000).

their own inner drives will lead them to learn... to increase people's awareness of their own thoughts and of the world around them.

—**Leonard M. Horowitz, Ph.D., Professor of Psychology, Stanford University**[90]

Research also appears to indicate some forms of human intelligence are actually enhanced by music.

There is an indication that our brains may even be pre-wired for it! Scientists have interspersed PET scans and MRIs with snatches of Celine Dion and Stravinsky to show a correlation for the biological foundations of music... Music affects the mind in powerful ways: it not only incites passion, belligerence, serenity or fear but does so even in people who do not know from experience, for instance, that a particular crescendo means the killer is about to pop out on the movie screen... Research at the University of California and the University of Wisconsin recently found a connection between the use of music and young people's improved math skills. They found that the neurons connecting the two sides of the brain in young musicians are larger which appears to help planning and foresight skills.

—**From a recent article in Newsweek Magazine by Sharon Begley**[91]

"Music hath charms to soothe the savage beast."

—**James Bramston**[92]

CONSTRUCT THEORY

This brings us to a very important question. George Kelly's ***Theory of Personality*** may provide us some clues about consumer selections of music. Remember, labels define talent by how much money an act can generate. So, consumers have to connect with an act and their songs at such a high level of personal satisfaction that they will actually pay to listen, see the act, download or buy a CD.

A person chooses for him/herself that alternative in a dichotomized construct through which he/she anticipate the greater possibility for extension and definition of his/her system.

—**George Kelly**[93]

Consumers tend to select the type of music and acts that help them understand/define or celebrate their subconscious self. After many replications, called impressions, the selections may tend to help the mind shape the personality and ways of thinking. Therefore, music is one of the many energy events we use to help us understand and celebrate our personality and position in life. In general, research appears to suggest consumers create for themselves the following emotions when they hear various forms of music. How the emotions are turned into meanings specific to an individual is not understood.[94]

---

90 Leonard M. Horowitz, Ph.D., Professor of Psychology, Stanford University, plus Banner, James M., Jr., and Cannon, H. C.The Elements of Learning. Yale, 1999 Bransford, John D., and others, eds. How People Learn. 1999. Reprint. National Academy Pr., 2000. and Levine, Melvin D.A Mind at a Time. Simon & Schuster, 2002 Discusses several ways people learn.
91 Music on the Mind by Sharon Begley, Newsweek, (07/24/2000).
92 James Bramstom, Man of Taste, The Quote Garden, www.google.com, 2007.
93 A theory of personality, The psychology of personal constructs by George A. Kelly, Norton Publications (1963).
94 Philosophy in A New Key by Susanne Langer (1951), and Charles Disserens Influences of Music on Behavior (1926). Both Langer and Disserens are dated references, however, they are still considered benchmark research efforts that are often listed as suggested reading for music students.

Sadness	Seriousness	Excitement	Happiness
Relaxation	Amusement	Sentiment	Longing
Patriotism	Devotion	Irritation	Wanting to Dance

"I think the worst mistake an aspiring musician can make is not taking the business seriously... Do your homework. Learn the business. Because there's a lot more to it than just picking up your ax and playing."

— **George Porter, Recording Artist/Musician**[95]

It is up to the business side of the industry to find and exploit in a positive, profitable way the talented individuals who have used their creativity to hopefully create saleable products. Welcome to the business of music where talent and creativity tied to business principles are once again required for success. The bottom line is that financial success will depend on how well consumers connect emotionally to the music products and the iconic acts. It will also depend on how well the business system delivers their entertainment products to consumer eyes and ears so that they can get excited about it and buy it. The greatest entertainment products never make any money until consumers know they exist.

"We didn't know this was a business, we just thought it was a rock & roll party."

— **Vince Neil of Motley Crue'**[96]

HISTORICAL PERSPECTIVE

Early in the history of our nation, songwriters made deals with book publishers to print and sell their latest songs. Printed copies of the lyrics or sheet music were the only methods of mass distribution available to songwriters. Book publishers hired salesmen to sell the sheet music wholesale to local five-and-dime stores, who, in turn, sold them to the public at retail. It didn't take long for the book publishers to see the potential profits in music publishing. In 1892, the song *After the Ball* sold over one million copies of sheet music.[97] Seeing the potential profits in music publishing, many of the book publishers became entrepreneurial music publishers and moved to *Tin Pan Alley* in New York City. There they created and placed their new songs with the most popular *Broadway and Vaudeville* shows.

World War II spread American music around the world. World markets were created as recorded music was broadcast on American armed forces radio stations to the troops and the local populace. Even in the 1930's and 40's music publishers viewed radio and nightclub performances as promotion for record sales. Back then a typical promotion cycle involved

> ### *Susanne K. Langer 1895-1985*
>
> Susan K. Langer was an aesthetician or a specialist in the branch of philosophy dealing with beauty, art, and the human perception of these subjects. After studying at Radcliffe College and in Vienna, she taught at Connecticut College. Her publications focused on a philosophy of art derived from a theory of musical meaning, involving the use of music as paradigm of a symbol system; she regards the principles of musical form as structurally the same as those of the patterns of human feeling.
>
> She was often considered a maverick, for these considerations had played only a minor role in philosophy for many decades before she began to write. Even within the field of aesthetics, Langer was unusual; she had little interest in the concept of beauty. Instead, she believed that art and music were fundamental forms of human activity, related to and equal in significance to spoken language although different in their basic structures. Langer's book Philosophy in a New Key (1942) was for many years one of the most frequently assigned philosophy books in liberal arts college courses.

---

95 The Recording Industry Career Handbook by The NARAS Foundation, (1995)..
96 Behind the Music, VH-1, Intermedia Cable, Nashville, TN (12/14/1998).
97 The Recording Industry Career Handbook by NARAS Foundation (1995).

consumers hearing the songs on radio and then seeing and hearing the artists' songs in films. The purpose was to create potential consumer excitement (momentum) from the radio airplay that in turn encouraged people to see the films that promoted record sales. Many veteran Vaudeville performers became radio stars and later moved to television. Television was invented in the late 1930's, but it's development was delayed until the late 1940's by *World War II* and economics during the war. In the late 1940's and mid-1950's, *Rock & Roll* evolved from the *Beale Street Blues, minstrels, country folk music, and Chicago's Electric Blues* to become the language of independence for teenagers. Teenagers with time and money together created a huge new music industry.[98]

SONGWRITING AS A PROFESSION

It customarily takes many years to achieve the competencies and industry contacts required to be successful. So, how can you become a professional songwriter, composer or arranger? And if you are not a writer, what are some of the things you should understand about the mindset of creative writers?

- *Have talent.* Some type of natural talent is cardinal to being a successful songwriter. The ability to observe social and personal situations and the ability to interpret the social consciousness artistically is important. An ability to convey thoughts and observations emotionally through musical notations and lyrics is paramount. Being able to play an instrument in tune is one thing; being able to create and convey emotional messages is clearly another.

- *Become an educated person.* Formal education in music, literature, business, psychology, sociology, world history, etc., are enriching. Great songwriters often write their best songs about their own life experiences or passions. Research the great philosophers, writers, poets, and leaders whose works you admire and find out what inspired their passions.

- *Become a professional songwriter.* Join professional songwriters organizations. There are many such organizations across the country where songwriters encourage each other, co-write, and get advice from the experts. Network, network, network! Build friendships and acquaintances through the local and national songwriter organizations and attend national seminars in New York, Los Angeles, and Nashville. Co-write with someone who is better than you. Writing with others helps you see a lyric and hear music from a different perspective and often improves songwriting.

- *Have a professional in the business listen to your songs.* Performance Rights Organizations such as *ASCAP, BMI, and SESAC* will usually take a few minutes to listen to new writers. They have a staff whose job is to help and find new writers. Let them listen to your work and if they like what they hear they will often refer you to established music publishers. The door is now open for you to pitch your songs and seek a deal. Once a writer is signed with a music publisher then one of the PRO's will become their exclusive performance license representative.[99] Referrals by an established writer who is a member of ASCAP, BMI, or SESAC will also increase your promise of a quick appointment and your possibility of being offered a contract.

---

98 The History of Rock & Roll (Part One) Cinemax Productions (videotape).
99 ASCAP, BMI, and SESAC represent writers and publishers by licensing the use of songs in a public performance such as radio stations airplay.

- *Select the right publisher.* Select the type of publisher who has a successful track record in your musical genre, such as hip-hop, country or rap. As an example, if you're writing rock music, find a publisher who has been successful in rock music. Successful publishers know the right people, have the contacts and can successfully place your songs with them.

CAREER SONG

Record producers and smart recording artists search for great songs that will establish their career. It's a song that becomes so popular that the artist is always associated with it, for example, *Bing Crosby and White Christmas, Carl Perkins and Blue Suede Shoes, and Led Zeppelin and Stairway to Heaven.*

WHAT TO "LOOK FOR" IN A MUSIC PUBLISHER

Find a music publisher who is well connected to the most successful people in the industry and who can place your songs with those individuals. They should be a progressive middleman between you (as a songwriter) and the record labels, producers, artist managers, and recording artists who are looking for your genre of songs. Find a publisher who will help you become a better songwriter by offering you constructive criticism and positive creative and financial support. Make sure they are honest business people who have a good reputation and passion for your song and your success, as well as their own.[100]

PROFESSIONAL SONGWRITING ORGANIZATIONS

www.nashvillesongwriters.com

The *SGA* (The Songwriters Guild of America) was formed in 1931 by songwriters *Billy Rose, George M. Meyer, and Edgar Leslie*. As a voluntary songwriter association run by and for its members, it is devoted to providing songwriters the services and activities they need to be successful in the music business. For beginning songwriters the SGA offers workshops, critique sessions, pitch opportunities, access to catalogs, award events and news. For established writers the SGA also offers publishing company audits, catalog administration and financial evaluations, medical and life insurance, and legislative and legal support. The guild's support of songwriting as a profession before congress provided several important legal provisions in the 1976 copyright act. The guild continues to lobby before Congress for the professional aspects of songwriters including the royalty effects of digital downloading.[101]

The *NSAI* (Nashville Songwriters Association International) sponsors regional workshops in various locations in the U.S. and Europe. The purpose of the workshops is to further the knowledge and craft of songwriting among participants through a series of specific songwriting lessons. The NSAI also offers a Song Evaluation Service to its members. Songs submitted are evaluated for their commercial appeal based on the theme, lyrics, melody and overall impact. Once a year, the NSAI also sponsors Tin Pan Ally South, which is a series of shows, workshops, and opportunities for songwriting members to network and write with professional writers.

WHAT PUBLISHERS "LOOK FOR" IN SONGWRITERS

Music publishers search for songwriters who see songwriting as a passion and as a craft they work at daily. Yet, what music publishers really want are the types of songwriters who consistently deliver potential hit songs that turn into profitable hits. Additional characteristics include:

---

100 Follow the golden rule in the music business. Never say anything bad about anyone. It is always better to be seen as an honest and positive person, the type of person insiders like to have as a friend, respect and want to work with in the future.
101 The History of the Songwriters Guild and Services, 2007.

- ***Songwriters who view the songwriter and music publisher relationship as a career partnership.*** Although in many cases, it is often adversarial, music publishers appreciate songwriters who understand the business aspects of publishing. However, determining the "value" of a song is very difficult. If a song does not perform as well as expected, the writer may blame the publisher and the publisher may blame the writer. The equity of a song and its cumulative value are better judged over a period of a year as it takes time to determine the real value of a copyright.

- Many of today's great writers had to learn how to write songs from the master writers who came before them. ***Numerous music publishers still provide this mentoring process to young talented writers they feel have the potential to write the next great hit song.*** Of course you'll always want to give them co-writing credits.

- ***Publishers appreciate writers who help place their own songs with industry insiders and major acts.*** Writers know many insiders and thus, they can help the publishers and themselves by networking and letting artists, managers, and A&R at the labels know about their newest material.

- ***Writers often offer their musical talents and vocal abilities to demo record their songs.*** Publishers use songwriters with good voices to record their own demos to pitch. [102]

- ***Writers with great voices are seen as a bonus, as they have the potential to develop into recording artists.*** Songwriters that are later signed to labels as recording artists may owe the music publishing company who helped develop their vocal talents and label connections recording points (royalties).

What is a Public Performance?

In the case of an establishment other than a food service or drinking establishment, either the establishment in which the communication occurs has less than 2,000 gross square feet of space ... (I) if the performance is by audio means only, the performance is communicated by means of a total of not more than 6 loudspeakers, of which not more than 4 loudspeakers are located in any one room or adjoining outdoor space; or (II) if the performance or display is by audiovisual means, any visual portion of the performance or display is communicated by means of a total of not more than 4 audiovisual devices, of which not more than 1 audiovisual device is located in any 1 room, and no such audiovisual device has a diagonal screen size greater than 55 inches, and any audio portion of the performance or display is communicated by means of a total of not more than 6 loudspeakers, of which not more than 4 loudspeakers are located in any 1 room or adjoining outdoor space...

---

[102] "Pitch" is the term used by industry insiders to describe personal meetings set up by music publishers and record labels to audition new songs for recording artists.

Lecture Points
Chapter Four

Songwriting

Inspiration for lyrics, poetic devices, writing principles, themes of love

POETIC DEVICES

ALLITERATION

ASSONANCE

SIMILES

METAPHORS

ALLEGORY

PERSONIFICATION

HYPERBOLE

IRONY

ANTITHESIS

CHARACTERIZATION

Lecture Points
Chapter Four

TOP TEN WRITING PRINCIPLES

SIMPLICITY

CLARITY

COMPRESSION

EMPHASIS

CONSISTENCY

COHERENCE

SPECIFICITY

REPUTATION

UNITY

GENUINE FEELING

Lecture Points
Chapter Four

THE KEY DECISIONS

CHOOSE THE GENDERS

SELECT THE VIEWPOINT

DECIDE VOICE

DEFINE THE TIME FRAME

SET THE SCENE

IDENTIFY THE TONE

PICK THE DICTION

DETERMINE THE SONG FORM

BECOME THE CHARACTER

KNOW THE AUDIENCE

Lecture Points
Chapter Four

THE THEMES OF LOVE

FEELING THE NEED

I THINK I'VE JUST FOUND HER/HIM

THE BIG COME ON

THIS IS IT, I'M IN LOVE

THE HONEYMOON IS OVER

CHEATING

LEAVING

REMEMBERING HOW IT USED TO BE - PHILOSOPHY

THE SHAPE AND FORM HIT SONGWRITING

VERSE

PRE CHORUS

CHORUS (the hook)

BRIDGE

Chapter Four Notes

Chapter Four Notes

SINGLE SONG AGREEMENT

This Agreement is made as of this ____ day of _____, 2008, by and between _____, whose address is _____, ("Writer") and _____ _____ ("Publisher") whose address is _____.

1. Grant of Exclusive Rights;

Sample

1.1 With respect to the following musical composition(s) ("Original Works")

TITLE	WRITER(S)	PERCENTAGES

WRITER does hereby agree to and does assign and transfer to PUBLISHER all rights of whatsoever nature known, or which may hereafter come into existence, including, but not limited to the exclusive rights set forth in Title 17 U.S.C. section 106 (1977) in and to said Original Works invented, written, and conceived, arranged, composed, created or originated by WRITER and the right to secure copyrights thereon throughout the entire world in the name of PUBLISHER and all renewal and extension copyrights thereof and all right, title, and interest both legal and equitable in and to the same, it being understood and agreed that said Original Works and copyrights thereof and each and every right in said Original Works, whether now known or hereafter to become known covering the use or any manner or type of use of said Original Works, are and shall be the sole and exclusive property of PUBLISHER.

1.2 PUBLISHER shall have the right to grant licenses for the reproduction, printing, recording, arrangement, or performance of any Original Works without restriction.

1.3 PUBLISHER shall have the right, in its sole discretion, to re-title, translate, arrange and otherwise edit, review and adapt said Original Works created hereunder. In the event said Original Work is an instrumental composition, PUBLISHER shall have the right to have lyrics written for said Original Work by a writer or writers designated by PUBLISHER, said lyrics shall require only the approval of PUBLISHER.

1.4 WRITER agrees that WRITER shall deliver to PUBLISHER Original Works created hereunder in such a form as is deemed suitable by PUBLISHER. Unless otherwise specified by PUBLISHER, any form, as established by prior course of dealings between PUBLISHER and WRITER, or usual and customary industry practices shall be deemed suitable.

2. Separate Agreements. At PUBLISHER's request, WRITER agrees to execute an Assignment of Copyright between WRITER and PUBLISHER for every Original Work created hereunder. WRITER agrees to execute any other documents as requested by PUBLISHER to effectuate such transfer of ownership. Upon WRITER's failure to do so, PUBLISHER shall have the right pursuant to the terms and conditions hereof, to execute such separate agreements on behalf of WRITER. Such separate agreements shall supplement and not supersede this Agreement. In the event of any conflict between the provisions of such separate agreement and this Agreement, the provisions of this Agreement shall govern. The failure of either party to execute such separate agreement shall not affect the rights of either party.

3. Power of Attorney. WRITER hereby irrevocably constitutes, authorizes, empowers and appoints PUBLISHER, and PUBLISHER's successors and assigns, WRITER's true and lawful attorney in WRITER's name, place and stead to execute and deliver any and all documents, which PUBLISHER may from time to time deem necessary to effectuate the intent and purpose of this Agreement, this power being coupled with an interest and irrevocable for any cause or in any event. Such power of attorney shall include, without limitation, such documents as PUBLISHER deems necessary to secure to PUBLISHER and PUBLISHER's successors and assigns the worldwide copyrights for the entire term of copyright and for any and all renewals and extensions under any present or future laws throughout the world.

4. Royalties.

4.1 PUBLISHER, shall pay WRITER a royalty of fifty percent (50%) of any and all sums actually received by PUBLISHER, or its authorized agent, less the following:

(a) all outstanding recoupable advances between PUBLISHER and WRITER hereunder;

(b) any administration or collection fees, foreign taxes, etc. actually charged by PUBLISHER, its authorized agents, or foreign subpublishers;

(c) royalties payable to co-writers; and

(d) any other sums or monies due PUBLISHER by WRITER of any nature.

4.2 Royalties on foreign sales shall be payable by PUBLISHER only after PUBLISHER, or an authorized agent of PUBLISHER, has received payment in the United States in United States currency, and shall be payable at the same rate of exchange as received by PUBLISHER.

4.3 Notwithstanding anything herein to the contrary, WRITER shall not be entitled to any portion of any sums received by PUBLISHER with respect to public performance of any Original Works from any performing rights society which pays a portion of performance fees directly to writers or composers and WRITER shall receive the writer's share of public performance royalties directly from the performing rights society.

4.4 Such royalties shall be paid in instances where WRITER is or was the sole author, composer, and arranger of the Original Works. With regard to Original Works where WRITER is or was only one of two or more authors, writers, or collaborators, WRITER shall be paid only the portion of such royalties equal to WRITER's percentage of authorship of said Original Work.

4.5 PUBLISHER or any of its affiliates, subsidiaries, or parent companies shall have the right to cross-collateralize this Agreement and any previous exclusive songwriter agreement, single song agreement, arranger's agreement or similar type of agreement between WRITER and PUBLISHER or any of its affiliates, subsidiaries, or parent companies. PUBLISHER or any of its affiliates, subsidiaries, or parent companies shall also have the right to cross-collateralize Original Works created hereunder.

4.6 In the event PUBLISHER creates or causes to be created a separately copyrighted arrangement or translation of any Original Work, or in the event PUBLISHER causes to be created lyrics for an instrumental composition, WRITER agrees that PUBLISHER may pay to the author or composer of such arrangement or translation, a portion, but not exceeding one-half (1/2), of the royalties due WRITER for said Original Work. In such event WRITER shall receive such royalties due WRITER for said Original Work less such portion.

4.7 No royalties will be earned or payable on Original Works contained in any uses pursuant to paragraphs 4.6 herein;

> a) given away or furnished on a "no charge" or "service charge" basis for promotional purposes or furnished as a sales inducement or otherwise to distributors, subdistributors, dealers and others   otherwise distributed as part of promotional activities; or
>
> b) sold as cutouts, scrap, salvage, overstock or closeout units.

5. Writer's Name And Likeness. PUBLISHER shall have the perpetual, non-exclusive worldwide right to use and to permit others to use: WRITER's name, both legal and professional and whether presently or hereafter used by WRITER; WRITER's approved likeness; WRITER's facsimile signature; and other identification and biographical material concerning WRITER. Such use shall be for purposes of trade and otherwise, without restriction, in connection with Original Works produced hereunder.

6. Writer's Warranties.

6.1 WRITER represents and warrants that WRITER has the authority to enter into and perform all the terms of this Agreement and that WRITER is under no disability, restriction or prohibition, whether contractual or otherwise, with respect to WRITER's right to execute this Agreement, to grant the rights granted by WRITER to PUBLISHER hereunder and to perform each and every term and provision hereof.

6.2 WRITER warrants that all of the lyrics and music or Original Works delivered by WRITER to PUBLISHER hereunder shall be WRITER's own original compositions or arrangements and that no part thereof shall be an imitation or copy of any other copyrighted work.

6.3 WRITER further covenants and agrees to protect and defend the right, title, and interest of PUBLISHER in said Original Works hereby sold and assigned to PUBLISHER, to the fullest extent and to hold PUBLISHER free and harmless of and from all loss, liability, and damage in any action brought against PUBLISHER by reason of the inclusion in said works of material owned or copyrighted by others or on account of WRITER's violation of any warranties contained herein. All costs, fees, and expenses paid or incurred by PUBLISHER in defending, protecting, or perfecting its title to the Original Works, and the copyright thereon, shall be charged against WRITER and deducted from all sums due or becoming due from PUBLISHER to WRITER.

7. Royalty Payments.

7.1 PUBLISHER, or an authorized agent, will compute royalties and payments due on or about forty-five (45) days after the end of a calendar quarter, for that quarter, and if royalties or other payments are due WRITER, PUBLISHER will make such payments less any then unrecouped advances paid to WRITER or on WRITER's behalf pursuant to this Agreement. If WRITER has accounts of any nature with PUBLISHER or PUBLISHER's affiliates and if WRITER owes PUBLISHER or PUBLISHER's affiliates money in such accounts(s), PUBLISHER may apply all royalties or payments which might be due and payable to WRITER to reduce the balance in WRITER's account(s).

7.2 WRITER, or a Certified Public Accountant representing WRITER, shall have the right, during PUBLISHER's normal business hours, and at WRITER's expense, after giving PUBLISHER, or an authorized agent of PUBLISHER, at least thirty (30) days advance notice in writing, to examine PUBLISHER's, or an authorized agent of PUBLISHER, books and records insofar as they pertain to the royalties or payments payable to WRITER.

7.3 Any payments to be made to WRITER hereunder shall be made to WRITER at the address set forth at the beginning of this Agreement. PUBLISHER shall make payment by a single check made payable to WRITER, or such agent as WRITER may designate in writing in accordance with the provisions of this Agreement governing notices.

7.4 All statements and all accounts rendered to WRITER hereunder shall be binding upon WRITER and not subject to any objection for any reason whatsoever unless specified objections in writing, setting forth the basis thereof, is given to PUBLISHER, or PUBLISHER's authorized agent, within two (2) years from the date the statement is rendered. No action, audit, or proceeding of any kind or nature may be instituted or maintained by WRITER with respect to any statements recorded hereunder unless such action or proceeding is commenced within one (1) year after delivery of such written objection by WRITER to PUBLISHER.

8. Suits and Actions Involving Original Works. PUBLISHER shall have the sole right to prosecute, defend, settle and compromise all suits and actions respecting the Original Works, and generally to do and perform all things necessary to prevent and restrain the infringement of copyrights therein or other rights with respect to the Original Works. If PUBLISHER recovers any moneys as a result of a judgement or settlement, the moneys shall be apportioned between PUBLISHER and WRITER fifty percent (50%) for PUBLISHER and fifty percent (50%) for WRITER pro-rated by WRITER's portion of ownership, if any, in the Original Works, after first deducting the expense of obtaining the moneys, including attorney's fees. WRITER shall have the right to obtain counsel for WRITER, but at WRITER's own expense, to assist in any such matter. Any judgements against PUBLISHER and any settlements by PUBLISHER of claims against it, respecting the Original Works, together with costs and expenses including attorney's fees, shall be covered by the indemnity provisions.

9. Indemnification. WRITER hereby agrees to and does hereby indemnify, save, and hold PUBLISHER harmless from any damages, liabilities, costs, losses and expenses including legal costs and attorney's fees arising out of or connected with any claim, demand, or action by a third party which is inconsistent with any of the warranties, representations, or covenants made by WRITER in this Agreement. WRITER agrees to reimburse PUBLISHER, on demand, for any payment made by PUBLISHER at any time with respect to any such damage, liability, cost, loss or expense to which WRITER's indemnity applies. PUBLISHER shall notify WRITER of any such claim, demand, or action promptly after PUBLISHER has been formally advised thereof. Pending the determination of any such claim, demand, or action, PUBLISHER shall have the right, at PUBLISHER's election, to withhold payment of any moneys otherwise payable to WRITER under this or any other Agreement between WRITER and any of PUBLISHER's affiliates.

10. Notices. All notices to be given to WRITER or PUBLISHER hereunder shall be addressed WRITER or PUBLISHER at the addresses set forth on page 1 or at such other address as WRITER or PUBLISHER shall designate in writing from time to time. All notices shall be in writing and shall either be served by personal delivery, mail, or telegraph, all charges prepaid. Except as otherwise provided herein, such notices shall be deemed given when personally delivered, mailed or delivered to a telegraph office, all charges prepaid, except that notices of change of address shall be effective only after actual receipt thereof.

11. Entire Agreement. This Agreement sets forth the entire understanding between WRITER and PUBLISHER concerning the subject matter hereof. No modification, amendment, waiver, termination or discharge of this Agreement or of any of the terms or provisions hereof shall be binding upon either party unless confirmed by a written instrument signed by WRITER and by a duly authorized officer of PUBLISHER. No waiver by WRITER or PUBLISHER of any term or provision of this Agreement or of any default shall affect WRITER's or PUBLISHER's respective rights thereafter to enforce such term or provision or to exercise any right to remedy in the event of any other default, whether or not similar.

12. Separability. If any portion of this Agreement shall be held void, voidable, invalid, or inoperative, no other provision of this Agreement shall be affected as a result thereof, and, accordingly, the remaining provisions of this Agreement shall remain in full force and effect as through such void, voidable, invalid, or inoperative provision had not been contained herein.

13. Notice of Breach. Before PUBLISHER or WRITER may assert that the other is in default in performing any obligation contained herein, the party alleging the default must advise the other in writing of the specific facts constituting default and the specific obligation breached. The other party shall be allowed a period of thirty (30) days after receipt of such written notice to cure the default. No breach of any obligation shall be deemed to be incurable during such thirty (30) day period.

14. Relationship of Parties. Nothing herein contained shall constitute a partnership or a joint venture between WRITER and PUBLISHER. Neither party hereto shall hold itself out contrary to the terms of this paragraph, and neither WRITER or PUBLISHER shall become liable for any representation, act, or omission of the other contrary to these provisions. This Agreement shall not be deemed to give any right or remedy to any third party whatsoever unless said right or remedy is specifically granted by PUBLISHER in writing to such third party.

15. Binding Effect and Benefit of Agreement. This Agreement shall be binding upon and shall inure to the benefit of PUBLISHER and its designees, successors, and assigns, as well as to WRITER or his heirs, executors, administrators, personal representatives and/or assigns.

16. Assignment. PUBLISHER may assign, license or otherwise transfer to any other entity any or all of PUBLISHER's rights, privileges and property under this Agreement including, without limitation, the right to WRITER's services. In the event of any assignment, the obligations of PUBLISHER shall be binding upon any such assignee or assignees for the express benefit of PUBLISHER and WRITER.

17. Controlling Law. This contract shall be deemed to have been made in the State of Tennessee, and its validity, construction and effect shall be governed by the laws of said state. Any disputes arising between the parties shall be brought in the state and/or federal courts located in Nashville, Davidson County, Tennessee.

IN WITNESS WHEREOF, the parties hereto have executed this Agreement and the accompanying Schedules and Appendices as of the date first written above.

PUBLISHER:

By:_____

WRITER:

_____

Name:

Social Security No:

Date of Birth:

COPYRIGHT ASSIGNMENT

For and in consideration of the mutual covenants, promises and undertakings set forth in separate publishing agreements between _____ (WRITER) and _____, with respect to the composition(s) described below, WRITER assigns, transfers, sets over and conveys to _____, all WRITER's right, title, and interest in and to the following musical composition(s):

    TITLE   WRITER(S)   PERCENTAGES

The within assignment, transfer and conveyance includes, without limitation, the lyrics, music and title of said composition(s) any and all works derived therefrom, the United States and worldwide copyright therein, and any renewals or extensions thereof, and any and all other rights that WRITER now has or to which WRITER may become entitled under existing or subsequently enacted federal, state or foreign laws, including, without limitation, the following rights: To reproduce the composition(s) in copies or phonorecords, to prepare derivative works based upon the composition(s), to distribute copies or phonorecords of the compositions, and to perform and display the compositions publicly. The within grant further includes any and all causes of action for infringement of the compositions, past, present, and future, and all proceeds from the foregoing accrued and unpaid and hereafter accruing.

THIS ASSIGNMENT IS EFFECTIVE THE   DAY OF   ,
.

                                    WRITER:

STATE OF TENNESSEE

COUNTY OF DAVIDSON

    Personally appeared before me, a Notary Public in and for said county and state, WRITER, the within named publisher, with whom I am personally acquainted, and who acknowledge execution of the foregoing Assignment of Copyright for the purposes therein contained.

    Witness my hand and official seal at office on this   day of
,   .

My commission expires:

                                    NOTARY PUBLIC

SINGLE SONG CONTRACT NEGOTIATION POINTS

The following points are examples of the language and issues you will often find in single song contracts. Additional items to consider that you will usually find somewhere in the contract include the following;

Accounting Statement-Music publishers will provide a semi-annual accounting statement that lists the money the publisher paid the songwriter in advance, plus chargeable expenses against the money credited or due to the songwriter from the royalties.

Advances-Money paid to the writer from the music publisher for the right to exploit their song(s). Advances are not considered a salary. They include a one-time payment for a song, the cost of the demo recording, hiring of an independent promoter, legal cost, and even travel expenses including per diem. Advances are repaid to the publisher by the publisher themselves from collected song royalties.

Administrative Rights-Whoever controls the administrative right of a copyright controls the potential revenue-generating assets of a song. Administrative rights include the right to assign or transfer the copyright at any time, the right to control licensing and the right to collect royalties for the use of the song.

Authorship-The legal relationship between the songwriter and a publisher will determine "who" is the author of a "work." If the songwriter is a work-for-hire employee, then the publisher is usually considered the "author" of a song. If the songwriter is an independent contractor, or staff writer or owns their publishing company (as in co- or sub–publishing), then, the songwriter is usually considered the author of a song.

Bonuses-Negotiated non-recoupable monies paid to songwriters (and often recording artists and producers) for albums that reach various sales levels, usually gold (500,000), platinum (1,000,000), or multi-platinum.

Cross Collateralization-In songwriter deals, if a claim is made against a writer's song, then the publisher may hold payment of all royalties from all the songwriter's "works" held by that publisher. In a recording contract, the cross collateralization clause usually refers to the withholding of royalties from the sale of one or more different albums to cover the labels' financial losses from the artists' other albums.

Demo Recordings-It is often the music publisher's obligation to record a song for presentation to a major recording artist, the A & R Department at record labels, record producers, and artist managers. Expenses for the quick recording are recoupable out of the songwriter's future royalties. The quality of the recording (number of musicians, tracks, etc.), ownership of the master tape, and a share of the expenses are rarely negotiable, depending on the level and status of the songwriter based on the number of hits and money generated by the songs written.

Exclusivity-A songwriter will only write for the music publisher they are signed with and all material created during the contractual agreement will be represented and owned by that specific music publisher. There are exceptions that may be negotiated as a separate agreement, including specific genres of music that the publisher or co-publisher does not represent on specific songs.

Float-If a writer assigns performance royalties to be paid through a music publisher (performance royalties are usually paid directly to the songwriter by the Performance Rights Organization), the publisher will often "float" the payment in order to earn interest off of the monies. This is a practice that is not supported by songwriter organizations.

Free Goods-For songwriters and music publishers, free goods are the songs on the CDs, and digital downloads that labels and Internet sites provide to retail outlets and consumers. Free goods given to retail and Internet sites encourage the outlets to stock and move the items. Consumers are provided a free 30 second download to encourage them to purchase the product.

Catalog-A listing of all the songs (copyrights) a music publisher owns and controls.

Collaboration-When two or more people work together to create a song, recording, etc. It is suggested that all the specific items of the agreement be in writing, including exceptions of the traditional royalty splits, permission to change each other's lyrics, and a listing of who will pay demo recording, legal, and promotion expenses. However, once the working arrangement is decided, a written agreement concerning the actual copyright is not required. The Copyright Law calls the songs written by more than one individual a "joint work." Ownership is shared salary or employment benefits, then they are considered an independent contractor.

Moral Rights-The changes in a song that someone may want to make when recording a cover version are called moral rights. You can somewhat control others' negative creativity legally by contractually obligating the publisher to seek the writers approval for any major changes in the music, lyrics, title, or when a song is to be used in movies (synchronization license or transcription licenses). If the movies or commercials are about something the writers do not support (example, smoking ads), then the writers will have the right to reject or control the song's use only if stated in the single song contract.

Originality-In a song contract the writer has to state that a "creative work" is original and not plagiarized from another person's creative efforts. This statement provides legal "proof" the publisher can use to protect itself (sometimes against the writer) if sued by other writers who claim authorship.

Reversion Clause-A provision in the songwriters/music publishers contract that states if the publisher does not obtain a commercial sound recording (or some other form of written performance) then they return your song's copyright within a specified time.

Independent Contractor-If writers uses their own musical instruments, don't have to meet a publisher song quota, have their own demo-recording studio or pay for their own recordings.

Transfer of Copyright and all Exclusives Rights-The Writer hereby assigns, transfers and delivers to the Publisher an original musical composition written and/or composed by the named songwriter(s). The Writer also assigns to the Publisher the title, words and music thereof, and the right to secure the copyright ownership registration throughout the world.

Representation-Both the Publisher and Writer agree this contract shall be subject to any existing agreements between the parties hereto and their following performance rights organizations, ASCAP, BMI, SESAC, mechanical rights organization, The Harry Fox Agency, and digital rights management agency, SoundExchange.

Warrants and Rights-The Writer hereby warrants the composition is his(s)/her(s) sole, exclusive, and original work; that he/she has the legal right to complete this contract, (they are not signed with anyone else), and that there is no known adverse claim to the above stated/listed composition.

Best Efforts-The Publisher hereby agrees to use their best efforts to exploit the copyright to all forms of music users in the music and entertainment industry including artists, labels, film and Television production companies, advertisement agencies, digital media, mass media and other companies that use music in their forms of business.

Type of Deal-The Publisher(s) and Writer(s) additionally agree that this contract represents the following type of deal with the following restrictions and definitions of revenues and copyright ownership.

Staff Writer Advances/Royalties and Additional Payments-In consideration of this contract, the Publisher agrees to pay the Writer as follows; $_____ advance against royalties, receipt of which is hereby acknowledged, which sum shall remain the property of the Writer and shall be deductible only from (2,000,000 plus).

ADDITIONAL TERMS

Term-The length of a songwriter/music publisher "deal" may be for a single song, a group of songs, or a period of time, from 1 year, plus another 1-year option, to a multi-year contract.

Value-The "worth or value" of a music publishing company.

Ensemble-A group of musicians or singers who perform together.

Falsetto-Tones in an upper register beyond the full-voice range of a vocalist.

Genre`-A distinctive artistic style, form, or content of music.

Harmonic-A tone produced by a fundamental tone which can be natural or artificial.

Initiation Fees-None of the PRO's requires an initiation fee for writers at the time they join the organization. BMI requires a onetime $100 administration fee to publishers when they join.

ISCI Number-A standard coding number used in the industry (consisting of four letters and four numbers) to track the song's use by mass media performances and record sales.

Local-A song performance payment based on a local, instead of national, usage.

Lyric-Words of a song.

Passage-Section of a composition of pitches.

Superthemes-A term used by BMI to describe music used as theme music on 30-minute or longer network TV shows for more than 13 weeks, if the theme is the only theme music used, is played 40 seconds or more and is used as the opening and/or closing theme.[97]

Symphony-One of the extended compositional forms for full orchestra (in most cases, a sonata for orchestra).

Symphony Orchestra-A large orchestra composed of brass, string, wind, and percussion sections.

Timbre-The quality of a sound that distinguishes it from other sounds

STUDY GUIDE-THE SONG BUSINESS

1. Define how music and entertainment is used by consumers.

2. Explain three communication theories.

    (a)

    (b)

    (c)

3. According to *Construct Theory* why do consumers subconsciously choose to listen to certain recordings/acts, performances?

    (a)

    (b)

4. List five things you can do to improve your chances of becoming a professional songwriter.

    (a)

    (b)

    (c)

    (d)

    (e)

5. What are four things you should do when preparing to pitch your songs to a music publisher?

    (a)

    (b)

    (c)

    (d)

6. Why is a career song so important to artists? To the writer? To the publisher?

7. What should a songwriter look for in a music publisher?

8. List two professional songwriter organizations and look up their websites.

    (a)

    (b)

9. Besides being able to write great songs, list two things music publishers also look for in songwriters.

    (a)

    (b)

Lecture Points
Chapter Five

WRITER

PUBLISHER

ORIGINAL WORKS

ASSIGNMENT OF COPYRIGHT

POWER OF ATTORNEY

GRANT OF EXCLUSIVE RIGHTS

MUSICAL COMPOSITION

CONTROLLING LAW

COVENANTS AND AGREES

RIGHT TO PROSECUTE, DEFEND, SETTLE AND COMPROMISE

Chapter Five Notes

Chapter Five Notes

Chapter Five Notes

6 MUSIC PUBLISHING
TYPES OF PUBLISHERS
TYPES OF DEALS
SPLITS & SHARES

PITCHING SONGS TO MUSIC PUBLISHERS

Music publisher's profits correspond directly with their ability to find and sign potential hit songwriters and their songs. But, they rarely have the extra time to listen to all of the unsolicited tapes sent from amateurs to their offices. Publishers know that the most profitable songs originate from established, professional staff and known independent songwriters. However, professional songwriters were also once amateurs themselves. They had to learn to *thrive on rejection* and to perfect their ability to write great commercial songs. Assuming you've developed your songwriting as a craft, joined the professional songwriting organizations, learned the business, written some great songs, registered your copyrights, and networked in the business to the point where you know the right people then it is time to pitch your songs to the right publisher.

- *Demo record* three to four of your songs in an inexpensive yet "quality" recording studio or on your home computer. Don't waste money on a major recording studio production by overproducing the demo recording. In most cases, all you need is a couple of instruments (guitar, bass, etc.) and your vocal mixed louder than the instruments.[103] Try to capture the "feel" or "emotion" in the demo that best displays the essence of your songs.

- *Provide lyric sheets* (typed lyrics of the songs) or printed lead sheets (lyrics and the musical notations of melody, chords, and rhythm). Publishers usually read the lyrics as they are listening to the demo. Sometimes the voice is mixed too low or there is a word or two they can't understand without lyric sheets. Make their job easy by providing cued up CD's (when possible) and lyric sheets.

- *Set up an appointment.* Make sure the publishers are accepting demos. Publishers are much more likely to listen to your demos if they know who you are and are expecting the discs. Let them know that you are submitting material. Many publishers have Internet web pages and use email more than snail mail. The copyright notation is not required, yet it is a good idea to place it on the disc along with your name and address. Write a brief cover letter detailing your association with the publisher, how you know of them or who referred them to you. Many publishers will not see you unless you are referred to them by someone in the business or by someone at *ASCAP, BMI or SESAC*.

- *Keep a journal* of where you have sent the email and demos. Send publishers a thank you note for reviewing the material. After a few days email, call or write to ask about the status of the review process. Most likely, if the music publisher knows you (established through your networking), they will often listen to your material. If they hear positive talent in your songs, they may help you improve your skills or better still, offer you a contract. They know that once you get good enough, you will come to them first with your potential hits. That's why they are in business, to make a profit by exploiting your great song's copyright.

---

[103] Recording "strings," additional instruments, and vocal overdubs is a waste of your money as most demo's will be re-cut in a professional studio with AF of M musicians if the song is placed with a publisher or label.

THE BUSINESS OF MUSIC PUBLISHERS

- *Major publishers* are part of a label that is a component of a mega entertainment corporation such as Sony, EMI, Universal, Time Warner, and Bertelsmann. Major music publishers are considered full-line, stand alone operations, as they have many departments within the typical major or affiliate record label structure and yet they act and operate as a separate company.

- *Independent publishers* are not affiliated with any one label or mega entertainment corporation. On the other hand, they frequently sign co- and sub-publishing deals with major entertainment corporations and other publishing companies for distribution and administrative assistance. Some independent publishers are full-line, others are one-person operations owned usually by a major writer or recording artist. Owning a music publishing company increases revenues to the songwriters and recording artists as they retain control of their copyrights, or a share of their copyrights and a share of the publishing revenues generated.

- *Specialty publishers* usually limit their catalogs to one or two genres of music. Examples include concert or classical music arrangements for ballet, opera, and symphony performances, gospel or Christian music for religious record labels and church performances, childrens music, jazz, big band, and other types of specialty niches.

- *Foreign publishers* may or may not be affiliated with a mega organization. Most are full-line companies doing business in their perspective countries or world territories. Most have cooperative agreements with mega entertainment corporations and American music publishers. Foreign royalties collected by foreign music publishing companies acting as agents for the American publishing companies often retain between 20%-50% of the royalties collected.

- *Vanity publishers* are owned by the songwriter(s) who place their songs into their own companies. They are often not connected to the powerful personalities in the industry. Thus, they rarely attain any significant music publishing royalties. Besides, once they start receiving royalties they are really considered small indie publishers by the industry.

QUESTION?			
Why do record labels alway want to use the Controlled Composition Clause for their Mechanical License?			
Statutory Rate	*(9.1 cents)*		*CCC Rate (75%) of SR*
One Song	9.1 cents		6.825 cents
1-Ten Song Album-	91 cents		68.25 cents
1 Million albums	$910,000.00		$682,500.00
*Saving the labels on just one million selling album $227,500.00			

DEPARTMENTS

Music publishers range in size from sole proprietorships (one-person) to partnerships (two or more owners) to fully staffed, multi-departmental, international corporations. Full-Line music publishers have many departments and industry connections. Whatever their size, successful publishers use sub- or co-publisher deals with other publishers who take care of the following tasks:

- *Acquisitions*-analyze songs that have been submitted. The creative department in smaller publishing companies may also screen songs. They are looking for needles in a haystack as hundreds of songs are submitted to major music publishers and yet only a few are great enough to use. Submissions are also accepted as enclosures in email over the Internet as long as the publisher has agreed to accept the song for review. For legal purposes, most unsolicited songs are never listened to unless the publisher knows you or has agreed to listen to your material.

- *Legal*-(business affairs) may be part of acquisitions in smaller music publishing companies. The legal department secures the song's copyright from the writer, registers the transaction with the Copyright Office in Washington D.C., and files the returned Certificate of Registration.

- *Administration*-takes care of the business, by offering licenses to the users of the company's songs. They also register newly acquired songs with a corresponding performance rights organization such as ASCAP, BMI, and SESAC, and notify their foreign administrative publishers of the new acquisitions.

- *Payroll or the royalty department*-use computer programs to correlate the use and projected royalties due from various sources and payments to writers and copyright owners (co-publishers) on a quarterly basis.

- *Creative*-consists of staff writers who are paid an advance to write their quota of acceptable songs; audio engineers; musicians and singers, and songpluggers, who pitch the demos to recording artists, labels, artist managers, and producers. Staff writers co-write with new and other professional industry writers.

THE NATIONAL MUSIC PUBLISHERS ASSOCIATION
www.nmpa.org

The National Music Publishers' Association is the largest U.S. music publishing trade association with over 600 members. Its mission is to protect, promote, and advance the interests of music's creators. The NMPA is the voice of both small and large music publishers, the leading advocate for publishers and their songwriter partners in the nation's capital and in every area where publishers do business. The goal of NMPA is to protect its members' property rights on the legislative, litigation, and regulatory fronts. In this vein, the NMPA continues to represent its members in negotiations to shape the future of the music industry by fostering a business environment that grows both creative and financial success.[104]

SONGCASTING

Songcasting or the songpluggers act of placing the right song with the right recording artist provides music publishers with their long-term financial successes. Songcasting the appropriate song to the greatest possible selling artist gives the music publisher, and the artist fame and fortune. Recordings are communicative messages that have to emotionally connect with the public to sell. If the recording fails to excite the consumer, then the songwriter(s), music publisher, record company, recording artist, and record producer have failed. Hundreds of thousands of dollars and professional credentials are sometimes forfeited in this process of an ineffective recording.

---

[104] Mission Statement of the NMPA, www.nmpa.org, 2007.

SPLITS AND SHARES

What is available for negotiation in a typical contract? Two issues;

- The *ownership of the copyright* which is valuable due to the money it makes from licensing the song to labels, radio air play, live performances, it's use in media and films, etc., and the potential future royalties it may make in the future.

- A 50%/50% *split of the total revenues generated into music publishing and songwriter shares* allows the songwriter(s) and publisher(s) an equal split of the money the song's use (through licenses) has generated. The amount of the splits into shares of money generated are not always 50/50. When a songwriter also owns their own publishing company as in a co-pub or administrative deal, then the songwriter/publisher can retain all of the songwriters share (50% of the total money generated), and half of the other music publishers share (25% of the total income). Therefore, in co-pub and administrative deals the original songwriter(s) who is also a music publisher(s) retail 75% of the total money generated and the co-pub or administrative music publisher receives the final 50% of the music publishers share or (25% of the total money generated).

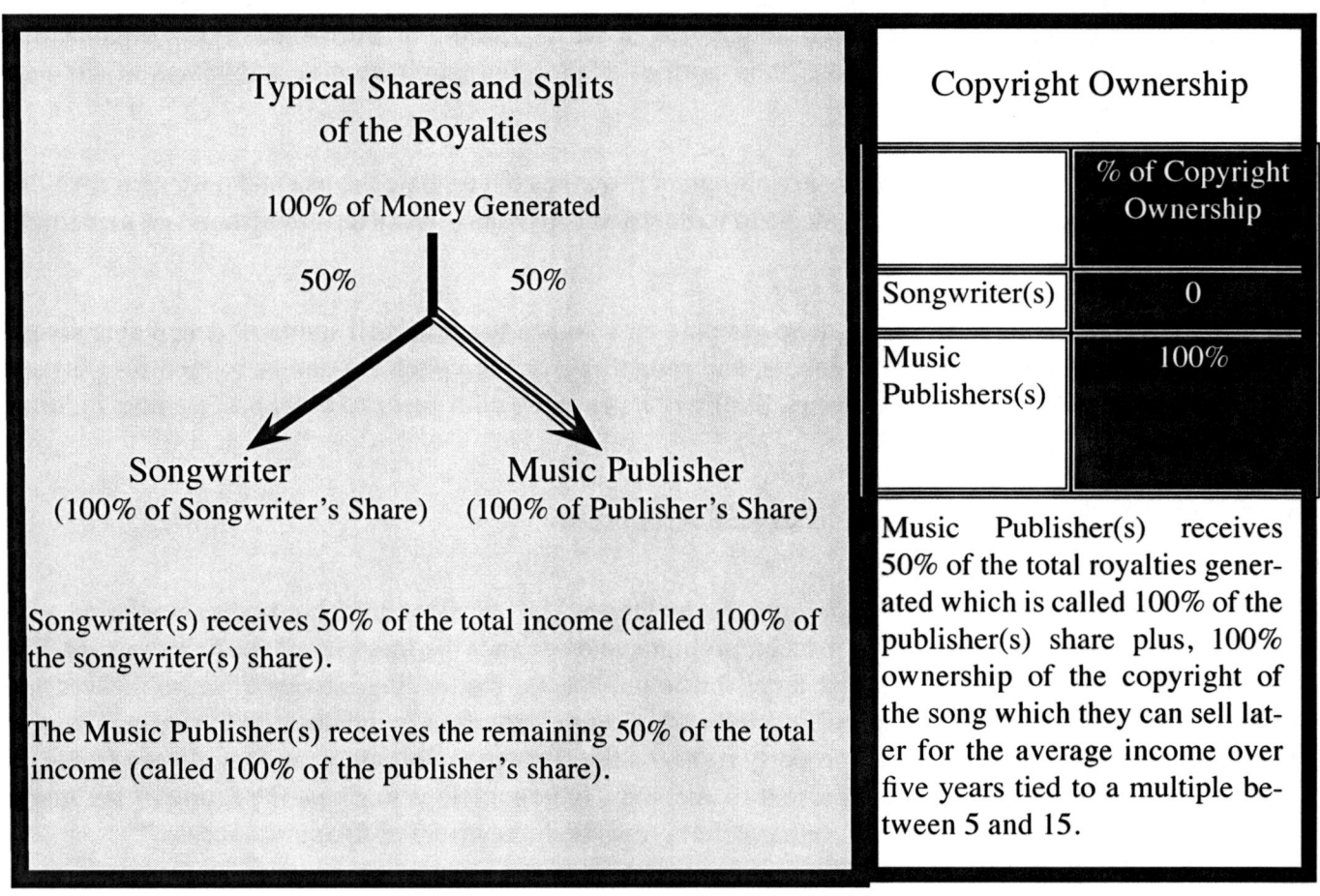

Typical Shares and Splits of the Royalties

100% of Money Generated

50% → Songwriter (100% of Songwriter's Share)

50% → Music Publisher (100% of Publisher's Share)

Songwriter(s) receives 50% of the total income (called 100% of the songwriter(s) share).

The Music Publisher(s) receives the remaining 50% of the total income (called 100% of the publisher's share).

Copyright Ownership

	% of Copyright Ownership
Songwriter(s)	0
Music Publishers(s)	100%

Music Publisher(s) receives 50% of the total royalties generated which is called 100% of the publisher(s) share plus, 100% ownership of the copyright of the song which they can sell later for the average income over five years tied to a multiple between 5 and 15.

VALUE OF COPYRIGHT OWNERSHIP

Thanks to consumers, fans, and businesses who continue to purchase and use music, publishers with great copyrights (songs) own a very valuable asset. Music publishers build their company's *value or equity* through the revenues generated from the songs they own. The wonderful thing about the music business is that great songs and standard recordings continue to make money long after the original recordings are released. Great hits are purchased by new generations, used in commercials, re-recorded as cover-tunes in different languages, in different nations. As an example, *The Beatles* songs have made more money since they disbanded then when they were an actual group recording and performing. Much of the money still comes from artists royalties tied to the record deals and recordings that still sell very well. However, even more money comes from the songwriting and music publishing that are still valid some 40 plus years after the songs were written published and recorded. So, if you can write, publish and record a great song that becomes part of the popular culture, you will probably be very rich and so will your children and grandchildren. Most of us have to work next week to pay the bills from last week. In the music business, great songs continue to generate money for the duration of the copyright and as long as it continues to be used. Remember, duration of a copyright, thanks to *The Sonny Bono Act of 1998*, is now life of the author, plus 70 years.

BUSINESS EQUITY OF THE COPYRIGHT

Music publishers sell their business using a factor of between 5-15 times the average gross revenues generated over several years to determine the value of their businesses. Thus, a music publishing company that averages a gross income of $10 million could be sold (if they can find the right buyer) for as much as $150 million ($10 million average gross income times a factor of 15). The concept is that even if the new publisher who bought the company leaves it alone, it will continue to generate enough income to pay for itself in 15 years. In addition, during those 15 years, the value of the songs may increase and the new company may be able to exploit the copyrights in a new innovative way that will once again increase the value or equity of the purchased company. Even small publishing companies with a small average income are valuable assets. As an example, a company that has a few songs that average only $100,000 a year (a number one song on top forty radio will generate about half a million), and a factor of 15 would bring the owner $1.5 million, plus continued songwriter's share royalties. Some songwriters may also leverage their potential future royalty revenues for bank loans and stock market mutual funds. This is not advised as the bank may end up with your copyrights or songwriter's share of royalties if you cannot repay the loan.[105]

SINGLE SONG CONTRACTS

Single song contracts are provided on all deals. Publishers require writers to complete and sign a single song contract for each song submitted and accepted. A power of attorney clause authorizes the music publisher to complete agreements with music users without the songwriter's signature. Independent songwriters may use a one-time single song agreement to develop a working relationship with a publisher. Publishers may also add a right of first refusal clause with staff writers that stipulate they will have the right to offer the writer a single song contract before any other publisher is allowed to hear the song. The bottom line is simple; no matter what type of deal writers negotiate, a single song contract will be used for each song being sold to the publisher.[106] In general, it will give the publisher 100% ownership of the copyright and 100% of the publisher's share of the revenue stream, which is 50% of the total revenues generated from licenses.

TYPES OF DEALS

There are several types of publishing deals and hundreds of variations that can be negotiated. Deals include: a work-for-hire, staff writer deal, co-publishing and sub-publishing agreements and the shark deal.

- *A work-for-hire deal* returns us to the days of Tin Pan Alley when songwriters were paid a salary up front for their songs. Examples of a work-for-hire include specific "one-time jobs," such as writing jingles or commercials for radio or TV. The employer of the work-for-hire is considered the author and copyright holder of the music.

---

105 Equity is usually defined as the amount of a company you own. So, if you own 75% of the company (music publishing) then you would receive 75% of the purchase price, in addition to all the money you made each year from songwriter royalties. Lastly, you are only selling your copyright ownership not your part of the songwriting revenue stream.

106 The word "sold" does not mean that money is being transferred in the single song agreement. Usually the contract is about the rights of the publisher and writer to offer the song for usage to the industry and payment methods.

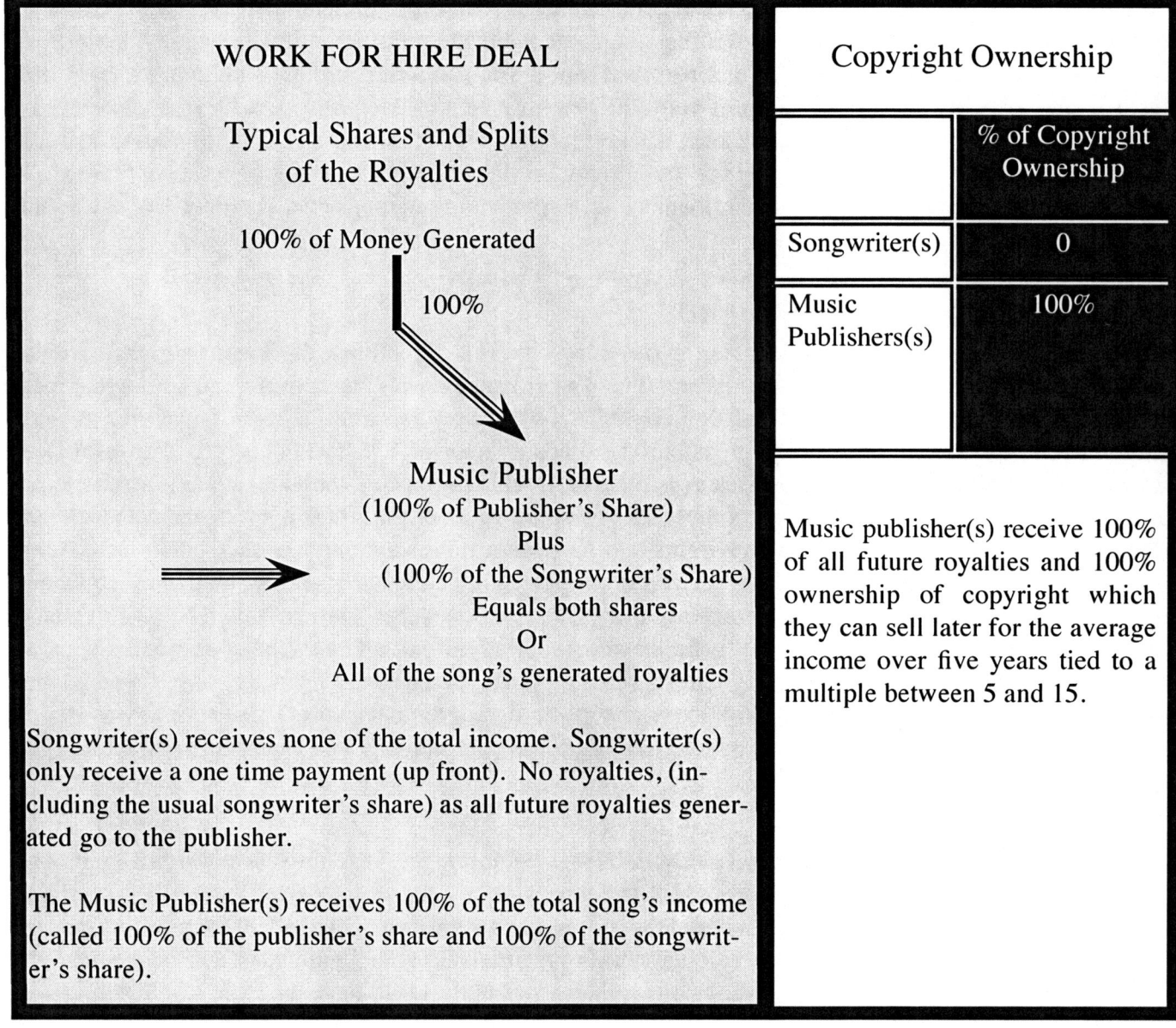

However, songwriters gain valuable industry experience and contacts. The disadvantage is that your employer owns everything you write and all future royalties are paid to the copyright holder which, of course, is not you. As a work-for-hire the songwriter is given a one-time payment and the employer receives the copyright (ownership of the song) and all revenues (both songwriter and music publisher's shares).

- *Staff writer* positions at a music publishing company are desirable because they provide songwriters with an opportunity to improve their songwriting skills, make industry contacts, network with other writers, co-write, and make a reasonable living at the same time. Novice staff writers are often surprised to learn that the songs they write are owned by the music publisher who is paying them, instead of themselves. On the other hand, the music publisher is in effect betting the advances that the writers will be able to create songs that will recoup the writer's advances, plus a profit. Staff writers are paid in exchange for a quota of acceptable songs and the songwriter's share after recoupment.[107]

---

[107] The quota is often 8-12 acceptable songs.

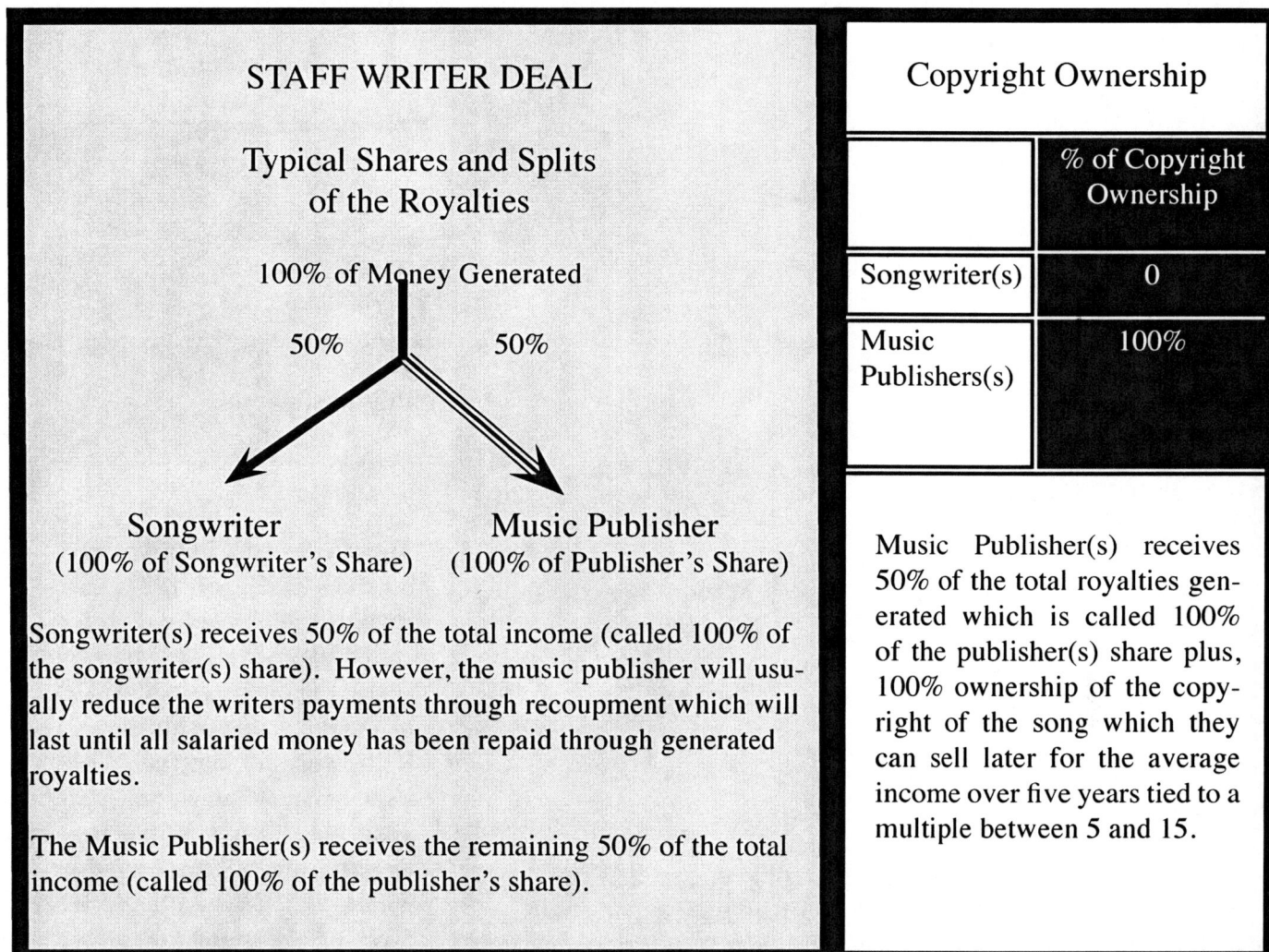

They are considered exclusive writers for the music publisher who is paying their advances. They are usually paid advances quarterly over a year, which the music publisher will recoup from royalties, if indeed there are any. Once the song's "royalties" repay the writer's advances, the remaining royalties are split into a songwriter's share and a publisher's share. The more successful the writer, the more the payment schedule favors the writer. A powerful publisher may have a contract that is skewed favorably toward the company. Beginning salaries often range from $18,000 to $30,000 while very successful writers can earn hundreds of thousands of dollars per year in salaries and royalties.[108&109]

- *Co-publishing agreements* help songwriters capture more of their song's equity by establishing co-ownership of their songs at the time of publishing. In addition, producers, recording artists (with their own publishing companies) and smaller independent music publishers generally make co-publishing deals with larger, better connected publishers. In a co-pub deal the songwriter, producer, label, or recording artist (whoever owns the song) gives up only half of their copyright of the song (ownership), in exchange for the other publisher's (the co-publisher) legal work and collecting of the royalties worldwide. In addition, the total royalties are split 75/25 with 75% of the total generated revenues going to the original publisher (100% of the songwriter's share and 50% of the publisher's share) and the remaining half of the music publisher's share of the revenue stream (25% of the total) going to the co-publisher.

---

108 Some writers put a "right of first refusal" option in their contracts which allows them to "pitch" their songs to other publishers if the song is rejected by their contracted publisher.

109 In a staff writer deal the songwriter gives up his or her copyright of the song (ownership) in exchange for a small salary (that will be recouped) out of royalties. In addition, the total royalties the song generates is split 50/50 with half of the generated revenues becoming the songwriter's (songwriters share) and the other 50% being the music publisher's (publisher's share).

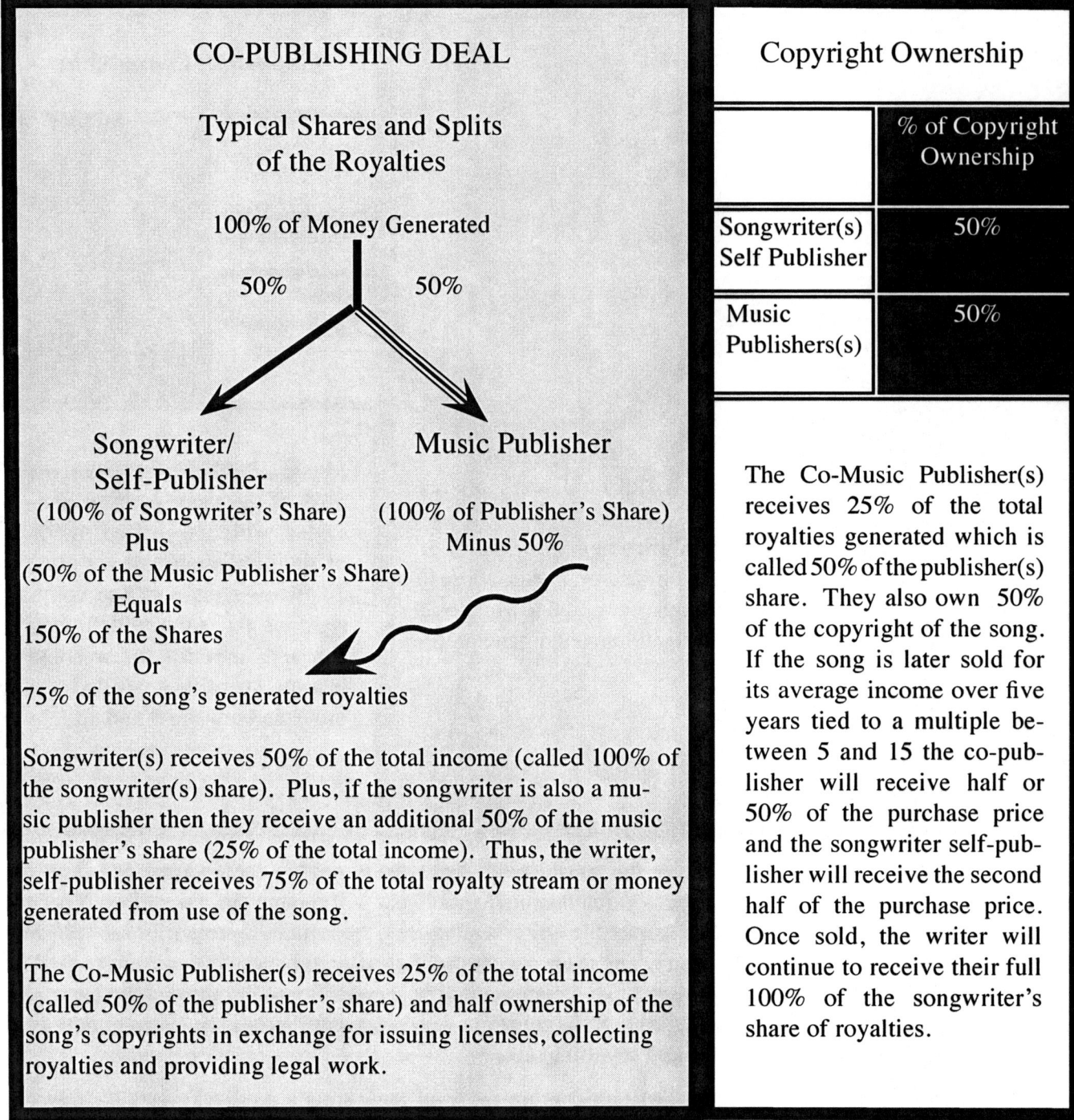

This of course, means that anyone can be a one-person music publishing company which is a great opportunity for students and entrepreneurs. All you need to be successful in the business is a great song and a co-publishing deal with a world-wide publishing company that can take care of all of the paperwork in exchange for 50% ownership of the song and 50% of the publishing share of the revenue stream. Industry terminology and the practice of converting percentages to shares tend to make co-publishing agreements complex. Here is an example of what is really happening. The typical single-song contract has a 50/50 split of all royalties except printed sheet music and folios where the writer(s) may be paid as much as 10% of the suggested retail price. The maximum percent of any whole is 100%. Yet, the music business splits the 100% of a song's potential collected revenue into 50% songwriter and 50% publisher shares and then reconverts each 50% share into a 100% share for the writers and publishers. Co-publishing often works to the advantage of both the songwriter/publisher and established industry music publishers. The music publisher receives a share of the equity (copyright ownership) that can quickly increase the value of their catalog and the songwriter/publisher receives the major connections, distribution, and industry power of the major music publisher. Co-publishing ordinarily occurs during the acquisition of a song when more than one publisher is involved. Songwriter, music producer, and recording artist-owned publishing companies need co-publishing deals with the major publishers for distribution around the world and in the entertainment centers of the United States, Asia, South America, and Europe.

- *Administration-Publishing Deals* allow songwriters who own their own publishing companies to keep absolute ownership of their song's copyright. An administrative-publisher or exclusive agent simply issues mechanical licenses, registers songs with the corresponding performance rights organizations and commonly collects royalties in exchange for 50% percentage of the publisher's share of the revenues collected. Administrative agreements are advantageous to songwriters who demo record their own songs and have the networking contacts to place them with major recording artists. These types of deals frequently occur between two or more publishers after the acquisition of a song by one publisher who then licenses second or third publisher to administer and exploit the song's potential equity. Publishers seek administrative-publisher deals to handle various aspects of the business including the paper business (printing of sheet music and sales), legal, documentation, and demo recording.

ADMINISTRATIVE-PUBLISHING DEAL

Typical Shares and Splits of the Royalties

100% of Money Generated

50% → Songwriter/Self-Publisher
(100% of Songwriter's Share)
Plus
(50% of the Music Publisher's Share)
Equals
150% of the Shares
Or
75% of the song's generated royalties

50% → Music Publisher
(100% of Publisher's Share)
Minus 50%

Songwriter(s) receives 50% of the total income (called 100% of the songwriter(s) share). Plus, if the songwriter is also a music publisher then they receive an additional 50% of the music publisher's royalty share (25% of the total income). Thus, the writer, self-publisher receives 75% of the total royalty stream or money generated from use of the song.

The Co-Music Publisher(s) receives 25% of the total income (called 50% of the publisher's share) and half ownership of the song's copyrights in exchange for issuing licenses, collecting royalties and providing legal work.

Copyright Ownership

	% of Copyright Ownership
Songwriter(s) Self-Publisher	100%
Music Publishers(s)	0%

The only difference between a Co-Pub Deal and an Administrative Publishing Deal is in the ownership of the copyright. The royalty streams remain the same as in the Co-Pub Deal. In the Administrative Deal the Songwriter Self-Publisher retains 100 % ownership of the Copyright. If the song is later sold for its average income over five years tied to a multiple between 5 and 15 the songwriter self-publisher will receive 100% of the purchase price. Once sold, the writer will continue to receive their full 100% of the songwriter's royalties. Thus, Administrative deals are great for writers who are also publishers. However, to get an Administrative or Co-Deal you will need to have a great song that the other publisher wants.

- *Avoid the Song Shark Deal.* Whenever a publisher compliments your song and then asks you to put up some money to share the expenses, you are probably being cheated. You don't pay them, they pay you! It is your song, your property, not theirs. Be careful! There have been many examples of songs sold to music publishers (mostly in the 1950's and early 1960's) for a set fee of a few hundred dollars or less. Many of the songs became hits, yet the writers did not receive any additional revenues as they had already sold all of their ownership (copyright of the song). Notice of the transfer of the rights must be in writing and signed by you (the original author of the song) and by a representative of the music publisher.[110] Unethical music publishers, who offer shark deals, are considered rip-off artists as they are in the business of making money off of you, the songwriter. The only money shark publishers usually make is what you paid them to publish your song. In most cases, they do not have the industry contacts to place your song with a major artist, producer, or label and correspondingly, you will almost certainly never receive any royalties.

CERTIFICATE OF REGISTRATION

If the copyright is not registered by the original songwriter(s) then the publishing company will register the song under their name as owners of the copyright and the songwriter as the author of the song once the single song contract is signed. They will receive back in the mail a copy of the registration form with the registration number added and the date and time it arrived at the Library of Congress, Copyright Office.

CERTIFICATE OF RECORDATION

If the song has been registered by the original songwriter(s) then the publishing company is required to notify the copyright office that they are the new owners of the copyright. Once the Copyright Office has received the fees, transfer of ownership and other documents, the Register of Copyrights will review the paper work and return the original documents as a Certificate of Recordation under the same registration number as the original registration.[111]

ARTIST LINE

It is very difficult to accurately estimate a song's potential earnings. However, music publishers have computerized the average previous earnings of their songs recorded by major artists. When a song is placed with a specific artist, the music publisher may glance at the average previous earnings to determine the song's potential income from performance and mechanical licenses. Artists are ranked as follows:

- *A-line artists* are considered superstars with platinum recordings of one million units or more.

- *B-line artists* have gold record sales of 500,000 units or more.

- *C-line artists* are signed to a major label and have not sold gold or platinum.

New artists are considered a "risk" as their recordings have not yet been released to the public for sale, the results of which determine if they are an "A", "B", or "C-line" artist.

---

110 The Essential Songwriter's Contract Handbook, NSAI (The Nashville Songwriters Association International), (1994), p. 28.
111 Summary of the Copyright Office, Library of Congress form Recordation of Transfers and other documents. U.S. Government Printing Office, April, 1988, 202135/60.045.

Type of Deal	Revenues Stream Writer's Share	Revenues Stream Publisher's Share	Copyright Ownership Writer(s) Share	Copyright Ownership Publisher(s) Share	Summary
Work for Hire	*None*	100% of Publisher's share (50% of total song income) plus 100% of Songwriter's share (50% of song income) for a total of 100% of the combined revenue stream.	*None*	100%	**Writer** receive a one time fee **Publisher** receives all songwriting and publishing royalties plus copyright ownership
Staff writer	*100% of Songwriter's Share of Royalties (50% of total Income)*	*100% of Publisher's Share of Royalties (50% of total Income)*	*None*	100%	**Royalties** split 50/50. **Publisher** receives 100% of copyright ownership
Co-Publishing *Songwriter owns a working publishing company	*100% of Songwriter's Share of Royalties (50% of total Income)*	*50% of Publisher's Royalties (25% of total Income)*	*50% of Publishing Copyright Ownership*	*50% of Publishing Copyright Ownership*	**Songwriter/ Publisher** receives 75% of royalties **Co-publisher** receives 25% of Royalties **Ownership** split 50/50
Administrative- Publishing *Songwriter owns a working publishing company	*100% of Songwriter's Royalties (50% of total Income)*	*50% of Publisher's Royalties (25% of total Income)*	*100% of Publishing Copyright Ownership*	None	**Songwriter/ Publisher** receives 75% of royalties and 100% of copyright ownership **Co-publisher** receives 25% of Royalties

LICENSES

Permission to use a copyright is usually granted through the issuing of a license. Compensation for the use of the song is paid as a licensing fee either directly to the publisher or through their agents such as the Harry Fox Agency, ASCAP, BMI, and SESAC. Remember music publishers and songwriters (and other creative artists) gain their ownership rights from the Copyright Law and control six Exclusive Rights, (reproduction, distribution, derivative, public performance, public display and digital transmission). Licenses used in the music industry are:

- *Mechanical*-songs used in an audio reproduction and distribution for sale by labels.

- *Sync (synchronization)*-songs used in a visual production and distribution (as examples movies, TV shows, web sights, computer animation games).

- *Blanket (Public performance)*-songs used in the operation of a business (for example, radio station airplay, or a broadcast in a movie on network and local TV stations).

- *Print*-used for music sheets, books, arrangements, and folios.

- *Transcription*-A combination of a mechanical and performance license used by companies to re-record hits and then sell or transmit copies for in-store broadcast at hotel chains, malls, and retail chain stores.

THE HARRY FOX AGENCY

www.harryfox.com

In 1927, the *National Music Publisher's Association* established HFA to act as an information source, clearinghouse and monitoring service for licensing musical copyrights. HFA provides services for publishers, licensees, and a broad spectrum of music users. Thus, HFA is the foremost mechanical licensing, collections, and distribution agency for U.S. music publishers.[112]

MECHANICAL LICENSES

Record labels must acquire the right to record and sell a song (the music publisher's copyright and therefore property) before they offer the recordings for sale and give them to radio stations for airplay. *About 85% of all mechanical licenses are provided to labels through the Harry Fox Agency in New York City.* It acts as a licensing agent for most of the music publishers in America, is a part of the National Music Publishers Association of America, and also collects foreign mechanical royalties.[113]

HOLDS AND FIRST USE RIGHTS

Only the copyright holder (the music publisher) may determine which artist or label may first record a new song their staff writers have created or they have acquired through a single song contract. Thus, music publishers exploit their new songs to the most established artists through networking, songpluggers, emails and Internet sites to the labels, producers, managers, and the artists themselves. If an artist decides to record the song in the future, they (usually through their producer) place the song on hold. This simply means the artist is interested in recording the song on their next album. It is not unusual to have a first, second, and even third hold as different artists express their desire to record the song, and if the first hold artist passes, then the right falls to the second hold.

---

[112] www.nmpa.com
[113] The NMPA was formed in 1917 to maintain high standards of commercial honor and integrity among its members, to promote equitable principles of trade and business, and to foster and encourage the art of music and songwriting. The NMPA formed The Harry Fox Agency in 1927 to provide a clearinghouse and monitoring service for licensing musical copyrights.

THE STATUTORY RATE LICENSES

Once an artist (in cooperation with their producer) decides to record a song the label must acquire the legal right to record and distribute the song. A Mechanical License fee called the Statutory Rate is used to determine the total cost of the license. The fee is currently 9.1¢ per song for a song under 5 minutes in length, times the number of units pressed and sold. Therefore, if a label presses or digitally downloads a combination of 1,000,000 units the cost for the license is 9.1¢ x 1,000,000 or $91,000. A ten-song album will cost the label ten times that amount, as they owe the publishers 9.1¢ per song times 10 songs on the album which equals 91¢ per album, times the 1,000,000 units delivered or sold for a total mechanical fee of $910,000.[114]

NEW STATUTORY RATES

The new schedule of mechanical rates, which will be in effect after final publication in the Federal Register until December 31, 2012, is:

- *Physical recordings: 9.1 ¢ for recordings five minutes or less; for recordings over 5 minutes, 1.75 ¢ for each minute, rounded up.*

- *Permanent Digital Downloads: 9.1 ¢ for recordings five minutes or less; for recordings over 5 minutes, 1.75 ¢ for each minute, rounded up.*

Mastertone Ringtones:
- *24¢ (mono-and polyphonic ringtones are not included).*

Webcaster streaming (such as Pandora),
- *For larger services earning more than $1.25 million, must pay the greater of 25% of gross income or 0.093 cents per listener, per song. The rates will increase each year until they hit 14 cents per listener, per play in 2015.*[1]

1. Pandora Sings New Tune with Royalty Agreement, Funding, www.ft.com 2009

CONTROLLED COMPOSITION CLAUSE

Labels want to save money on album projects and one of the ways to do this is to pay only 75% of the statutory rate for mechanical licenses. As stated earlier, if the main artist owns, controls or has written all or part of the composition, then the label can declare the song a controlled composition.

COVER TUNE MECHANICALS - COMPULSORY LICENSE

The Compulsory License, as discussed in our chapter on *Protecting Creativity*, states that in the music industry once the first use rights have been used, then anyone may record the song without getting special permission from the copyright holder (publisher). To obtain a Compulsory License for an already released song the Harry Fox Agency suggests sending a check for the mechanical royalties owed, which is the statutory rate times the number of songs x the number of units you plan to sell.[115]

---

[114] The next increase in the Statutory Rate is scheduled for January 1, 2008. Hearings have been held, yet a decision has not been made.

[115] www.harryfox.com

FOREIGN MECHANICAL ROYALTIES

Unlike the American practice of individual song mechanical licenses, most foreign countries require one mechanical license for all the songs on an album. Registration is mandatory. Mechanicals are collected by government-owned agencies and turned over to the foreign music publishers. A percentage of the retail price is collected for the mechanicals that are split among all the songs on the album and between the foreign and American publishers. Therefore, there is not a set foreign mechanical rate, and the amount of money collected varies from country to country and album to album. Totals collected also depend on the number of songs on the album and how many albums were sold. Foreign administrative publishers often collect the mechanicals from the government agencies and split the royalties with American publishers by making payments directly or through The Harry Fox Agency.[116][117]

[116] Foreign Administrative publisher splits range from 10% to 25% for collecting American product and up to a 50/50 split for foreign-recorded "cover tunes."

[117] Foreign Administrative publisher splits range from 10% to 25% for collecting American product and up to a 50/50 split for foreign-recorded "cover tunes." Passman, All You Need To Know About the Music Business (1993), pp. 242-243, & The Essential Songwriter's Contract Handbook by NSAI (The Nashville Songwriters Association International) (1994), p. 50.

INDIRECT ROYALTY "SPLITS"

Publishers typically split mechanical royalties from The Harry Fox Agency 50/50 with their signed songwriters. However, most music publishers also have the policy of first recouping (deducting) any advances paid to the staff writer out of the writer's share of the royalties. As a result, the negotiated percentages of revenues paid to the songwriters are usually 50% of the total revenues collected from mechanicals minus the recouped advances paid originally by the publisher.

RECOUPMENT

The royalties collected from a song's use in recordings from mechanical, print, and sync licenses are used to repay the music publishers advances. Thus, after the splits are determined, the publisher often repays itself from the songwriters share to *recoup* its advances.

MEMORANDUM OPINION ON RINGTONES

The Copyright Royalty Board responding to a request by the RIAA (Recording Industry Association of America, Inc.), was asked two questions (a) Does a ringtone, made available for use on a cell phone or similar device, constitute a delivery of a digital phonorecord (recording) that requires a statutory licensing (royalty payment), and (b) If so, what are the legal conditions and limitations on such licensing?[118] In general, the Board found in favor of the *RIAA* and declared that ringtones and mastertones are excerpts of a pre-existing sound and thus, fall within the scope of the statutory license as derivative work.[119] Music publishers and songwriters will now receive a mechanical license statutory rate of 9.1¢ for *mono-and polyphonic ringtones and 24¢* for master ringtones until the year 2012.[120]

SOUNDSCAN

Nielsen's SoundScan is an information system that tracks sales of music and music video products throughout the United States and Canada. Sales data from point-of-sale cash registers is collected weekly from over 14,000 retail mass merchant and non-traditional stores. Weekly data is compiled and made available every Wednesday. Nielsen SoundScan is the research sales source for the *Billboard* music charts.[121]

SYNC (SYNCHRONIZATION) LICENSE

Sync Licenses are required for the use of music in the production of a visual presentation. Film, TV and digital media production companies are required to obtain a sync license for the music and songs they plan to use in their productions. The Harry Fox Agency represents small independent music publishers and SESAC publishers for sync licenses. On the other hand, most music publishers license their songs and music directly to the production companies. Live TV shows (taped for delayed broadcasts, such as Letterman or Leno) must have all sync licenses in place before the productions are created and aired. Music videos are filmed only after the licenses are secure, however, movies are often being produced as the licenses are negotiated. Statutory rates are not required on sync licenses and thus, fees are negotiated. If the price for one song is too high another is selected from a different publisher.

---

118 Mechanical and digital Phonorecord Delivery Rate Adjustment Proceeding-docket no RF 2006-1, source www.loc.gov-copyright, 2007.
119 Ibid.
120 The statutory rate fee is set by the three-judge panel and will usually increase every two years.
121 www.soundscan.com

PERFORMANCE RIGHTS ORGANIZATIONS

Performance rights organizations collect performance royalties from the users of music in a public performance for their affiliated writers and publishers. There are three such Performance Rights Organizations in the United States and many others around the world. *The American Society of Composers, Authors, and Publishers (ASCAP), Broadcast Music Incorporated (BMI), and SESAC* are the three American performance rights organizations. SESAC is now the registered name for The Society of European Stage Authors and Composers, which is no longer used. After business fees are deducted, the remaining royalties are split 50/50 and sent to the songwriters and music publishers. Performance royalties are collected for the performance of a song, not for the recording artists who sing it.[122] The 50% sent to the writer is considered a 100% writer's performance share (royalty), and the 50% sent to the music publisher is considered 100% of the publisher's performance share (royalty).[123]

ASCAP

www.ascap.com

The American Society of Composers, Authors and Publishers was formed in 1914 to help music publishers and songwriters collect their public performance royalties. It is a non-profit organization owned and operated by its songwriter and music publisher members. The *Board of Advisors* consists of twelve publishers and twelve songwriters.[124]

BMI

www.bmi.com

In the late 1930's, ASCAP raised its fees for performance royalties. In retaliation, many broadcasters formed their own performance rights organization, *BMI*, in 1940. These stations refused to play any ASCAP songs. After lawsuits, the justice department filed a civil lawsuit alleging antitrust violations on the parts of ASCAP, BMI, NBC and CBS. The performance rights organizations settled and radio stations returned to broadcasting music licensed by all the performance rights organizations. BMI is a non-profit company still owned and operated by the 675 original radio stations that formed the organization.[125]

SESAC

www.sesac.com

SESAC is a different story. Much smaller than ASCAP and BMI, it is a privately owned for-profit business. Paul Heinecke formed SESAC in 1930 to represent European publishers and religious works. In 1992, three venture capitalists and the merchant-banking house of Allen & Company purchased the company. During the last several years, SESAC has been the leading technology innovator of the performance rights organization by using BDS (Broadcast Data Systems) and watermark technology for performance tracking and royalty distribution.[126]

---

122 In some European countries, a fee is collected and paid to the recording artist for the number of times their recordings are played on radio stations. The DMC copyright act now requires the collection agency SoundExchange to collect royalty fees for vocal performances of digital transmissions.
123 The Music Business Handbook & Career Guide, Baskerville (1990).
124 www.aacap.com
125 www.bmi.com
126 www.sesac.com

AFFILIATION/MEMBERSHIP

Songwriters and publishing companies may only affiliate with one performance rights organization at a time. Thus writers are often called ASCAP, BMI or SESAC writers, while music publishers are ASCAP, BMI, or SESAC publishers. In reality, to get around the single affiliation situation most publishers form three separate publishing companies with different names and affiliate each company with a different performance rights organization. BMI and SESAC writers and publishers are designated as affiliates, ASCAP writers and publishers are considered members. ASCAP, BMI and SESAC participation requires slightly different professional writing standards of at least one song commercially published, recorded, or likely to be performed. Music publishers must also have the ability and finances to exploit a song's potential equity.

ASCAP sued Woody's River Room Bar near Sarasota for $150,000 for failing to pay royalties for copyrighted songs played by a DJ. The general manager Pat O'Leary, of the 250-seat restaurant/bar, claimed it was a surprise and that the failure was a clerical error and that the licensing fee would be paid and would cost less than the fine. According to a report in the Sarasota Herald-Tribune, ASCAP sent a private investigator to the bar to document any unlicensed music being played.
—**Fox News**[127]

BLANKET LICENSE

ASCAP, BMI and SESAC license radio, television, cable TV stations and networks to pay for the music they use in their businesses. They license hotels, motels, restaurants, nightclubs, concert halls, specific concert performances, airlines, trade shows, amusement parks, malls, and almost any other source of music performance venues they can find.[128] Their job is to find the businesses and collect licensing fees for their use of the songs. They offer the license in the form of a blanket license to cover all the songs' licenses of their organization.[129]

BLANKET LICENSE FEES

Fees for *blanket licenses* are determined by weighing various factors, including the type of media (radio, TV, etc.), the size of the prospective broadcast audience (national, local, etc.), and the type of performance (music in movies, TV show, theme music, etc.). None of the performance rights organizations sample hotels and concerts for violations. However, many business owners are not aware of the copyright law and their obligation to pay for the music they use in the daily operation of their businesses. Many become frustrated when confronted with a bill for the music they thought was free. However, once the law is explained, most understand why the copyright owner should be paid. License fees are estimated and issued on the size of the facility's potential occupancy rate and the use of the music (CD's being played, live band, etc.).

DIRECT PAYMENTS

Performance rights royalties are split by ASCAP, BMI, and SESAC and sent separately to the writers and publishers. Fifty percent is equal to 100% of the writer's share and the remaining 50% is equal to 100% of the publisher's share. As stated earlier, mechanical fees are paid differently as The Harry Fox Agency and other mechanical collection agents pay all the royalties to the publisher who splits the royalties (minus recoupment) with the writer.

---

127 Fox News by Maurice Boyer, Friday February 23, 2007.
128 The Music Business Handbook & Career Guide, Baskerville (1978).
129 Ascap, Bmi, and Sesac.com

COLLECTIONS

Until recently, both ASCAP and BMI used random sampling and statistical analysis to determine the number of performances and, therefore, payments to their writers and publishers. ASCAP recorded a random sample of local radio and television broadcasts and generalized the results to national performance figures. They sampled TV networks, PBS, and cable channels. BMI required a random sampling of radio stations to log (keep a list of each song's performance). BMI used producers' cue sheets to determine music performances for national and cable TV performances. All three used *TV Guide* to calculate TV local performances. SESAC used field monitors to check for music usage and *Broadcast Data Systems (BDS)* to calculate performances. The BDS system monitors and digitizes an airplay performance by comparing the radio stations' broadcast to a digital fingerprint of the recording stored in its data bank. If there is a correlation, the monitor tallies an airplay performance. BDS is now used to monitor actual airplay performances by the three performance rights organizations. Not everyone has been happy with the Performance Rights Organizations. However, in 1967, the *United States Supreme Court* approved a lower court ruling that upheld the rights of songwriters and music publishers to authorize an agency to represent them in the collection of performance royalties. The ruling states:

... a central licensing agency such as ASCAP, is the only practical way that copyright proprietors may enjoy their rights under federal copyright laws and that broadcasters and others may conveniently obtain licenses for the performance of copyrighted music.

THE FAIRNESS IN MUSIC LICENSING ACT

The poorly named *Fairness in Music Licensing Act* exempts many establishments, defined as food service and drinking establishments, with less than 3,750 gross square feet and other types of small businesses of less than 2,000 gross square feet, from paying performance licenses fees. These establishments can use radio broadcasts and other musical performances in their businesses, (and make money) without acquiring a blanket license. Each business is limited to six or less loudspeakers (not more than four in any one room) to qualify for the exemption.[130]

IN THE PIPELINE

For publishers who do not have sub-publishing agreements in foreign territories, ASCAP, BMI, and SESAC collect performance rights monies from other nations' PRO's and pay their respective songwriter and publisher members. However, foreign royalty payments may take up to 2-5 years for collection and payments. This time period or delay in foreign payments compared to domestic payments is called "in the pipeline", as royalties have been earned and will be paid eventually.

PAYMENT RATES AND SCHEDULES

ASCAP and BMI pay competitively but not equally for the same chart placement. Different levels of payment are offered for different genres of music. To make it even more confusing, ASCAP and BMI do not pay the same amount of money for songs within the same genre. In other words, due to the way the charts are compiled by the PRO's payment scheme methodology and competition from the other PRO's, some number one records receive more airplay (performances and, therefore, money) than other number one records.

PRINT LICENSE

A print license is used to secure payments to the music publishers and songwriters of sheet music, music books, arrangements, and folios. The songwriter usually receives about 8-10% of the money collected from the suggested retail list price of the material sold. Print or sheet music is often handled by

---
130 See Chapter 2 Protecting Creativity.

a specialized administrative publisher who prints the sheet music, catalogs, and folios and distributes them to retail outlets.

TRANSCRIPTION LICENSE

Trade organizations (hotels, restaurants, etc.), license the music to the users they represent such as individual hotels, restaurants, malls, and retail stores. The trade organizations often contact companies to re-record popular music in very mellow arrangements in order to sway consumer moods and encourage purchasing. *Elevator music* helps the riders maintain a pleasant mood even when they are packed tightly together in a very small space moving quickly up and down inside a building. The license is the combination of a mechanical (reproduction and distribution) and blanket license (public performance) limited to the songs re-recorded and played in the subscriber's establishment. The number of retail outlets, size, and consumer traffic in the stores determine transmission license fees.

BEST EFFORTS

Publishers can only be pro-active concerning a song's potential selection by an artist to record. Contracts customarily state that music publishers have satisfied their contractual obligations when they have, to the best of their ability, attempted to place a song with music users. It is very difficult for a songwriter (or their attorney) to define and prove that a music publisher did not attempt to place the song with various music users. In addition, publishers can usually provide a stack of invoices and paid statements as proof of their attempt to place the song with record labels, recording artists and other types of music users.

TERMINATION OF CONTRACT

Sometimes the marriage between the songwriter and music publisher fails. The quality of their agreement means very little unless both profit. Written contractual goals that are not fulfilled often lead to either side terminating the contract. However, legal action is customarily required to prove non-performance of a contractual agreement. Publishers may default in their contractual obligation if they fail to provide licenses to music users, pay royalties in a timely manner, place the song with a major recording artist or an artist signed with a record label, provide sheet music (of the song) to music stores and other retail outlets, place the song in radio and TV commercials, advertisements, and movie soundtracks, or protect the copyright against infringement.[131]

REASSIGNMENT PROCESS

Writing a *letter of termination* to a publishing company requesting release from a single-song contract is the first step in recapturing your song's copyright due to a non-performance default or reversion clause not being met by the music publisher. You are not blaming the publisher of failing to meet their obligation; you're simply requesting the return of your copyright. If the publisher has failed to successfully license your song with music users, they may agree to terminate the contract. It must be a mutual agreement or you'll end up in court. Writing a Notice of Breach to the publisher that states and defines a specific area of the contract that has not been satisfied is a more serious approach. Publishers are usually given a 60-day notice to alleviate the situation. If the notice is ignored, legal action may be required to terminate the contract.[132] Publishers may negotiate some payment to help cover expenses. In either case, termination of the contract should state that all future rights are being assigned to another publisher or returned to you, the original copyright holder.

---

[131] Placement is defined as the use of the song in an actual master recording being distributed for sale to the public. An artist (or producer) placing a hold on a song (for a recording to be made in the future) is not considered compliance of the publisher's obligation to get a song recorded.

[132] The Musicians Business & Legal Guide, Holloran, (ed.) Prentice Hall (1991), p. 335.

SUMMARY

There are several "sources" of revenue for songwriters and music publishers in the music business. They include Mechanical Licenses, which are offered directly by music publishers or through a mechanical rights collection agency (such as The Harry Fox Agency) who represents the publishers. They collect royalties from record labels for the use of songs on albums, CDs, digital downloads, cell phone ringtones and mastertones. Royalties are paid to the publishers who recoup any advances out of the songwriter's share. Performance Licenses are issued by performance rights organizations (ASCAP, BMI, and SESAC) that represent the song publishers and songwriters individually. They collect royalties from businesses that use public performances in their daily operation. Sound Exchange collects royalties for labels and others for internet streaming. The Fairness in Music Licensing Act, however, exempts drinking establishments and restaurants of 3,750 square feet or less and small businesses of 2,000 square feet or less from the blanket license's requirement. Royalties are split and paid (after commissions) separately to the songwriter's (share) and a music publisher's (share). Other revenue sources include Print Licenses used for printing and selling sheet music in retail outlets, Sync Licenses for music used in the production of mass media TV, motion pictures, and Internet videos and Transcription Licenses for music used in hotels, restaurants and other business chains that use in-house music systems.

Music publishing is a gamble. Nobody knows which songs will become hit recordings. A successful song has equity that is divided into writer and publisher "shares" from the royalties collected. There are several types of contracts including "work-for-hires", staff writer deals, co-publishing and sub-publishing agreements and the one you should avoid, the shark deal. All of the deals will be supplied and signed with the use of a power of attorney agreement in the single-song contract that gives signature rights to the publishing company.

Major Music publishers have their own departments to handle specific tasks or sub-out duties to administrative publishers and co-publishers in exchange for a percentage of the royalties collected. Acquisitions are always searching for new songs and writers to sign. Attorneys or legal assistants work in Business Affairs negotiating with writers the agreements in the single song contracts. Publishers file a Certificate of Registration or Recordation with the Copyright Office in the Library of Congress depending on previous registrations. The Creative Department consists of staff writers who are paid a salary to write a quota of acceptable songs.

STUDY GUIDE-PUBLISHING

1. List and explain the five types of music publishers.

    (a)

    (b)

    (c)

    (d)

    (e)

2. List and explain the five departments often found at a music publisher.

    (a)

    (b)

    (c)

    (d)

    (e)

3. What is the NMPA and who do they represent?

4. Name the agency that is part of the NMPA and issues and collects mechanical licenses' fees.

5. What is songcasting? Why is it important?

6. What is available for negotiation in a typical single song contract?

    (a)

    (b)

7. Why can ownership of a copyright be profitable?

8. Explain a single song contract. On what types of deals is it used?

9. List and explain five types of songwriter deals.
    (a)

    (b)

    (c)

    (d)

    (e)

10. Explain the difference between a Certificate of Registration and a Certificate of Recordation.

11. List five types of licenses music users must obtain to legally use a copyrighted song (property). Explain the function of the license and the type of business required to obtain the licenses.
    (a)

    (b)

    (c)

    (d)

    (e)

12. What type of license does the Harry Fox Organization issue and collect fees for?

13. What is the current statutory rate?

14. If a record label records a ten song album (all songs under five minutes) then:

    (a). What type of license must they obtain for each song?

    (b) How much money will the license fee cost per album?

    (c) If the label sells one million units of the album, how much will the license(s) cost the label?

    (d) What would the license(s) be under the controlled composition clause?

15. Explain holds and first use rights.

16. Do you (or anyone else) have the right to record a cover tune that is popular on radio? Why?

17. If you record a cover tune, press 1,000 units (CD's) or sell 1,000 downloads, how much money would the license cost you?

18. What is the cost of retaining a song from a music publisher that will be recorded and sold as a ringtone? What type of license is required?

19. List and describe the three performance rights organizations.
    (a)

    (b)

    (c)

20. Which one is the largest in terms of membership?

21. Which one is by far the smallest in membership?

22. Which one is owned by its members (who are writers and music publishers)?

23. How many PRO's can a writer belong to at any time?

24. Which PRO is the hardest to become a member of?

25. What are blanket licenses and how do they work?

26. How are the songwriters and music publishers paid by fees collected by Harry Fox on mechanical licenses?

27. How are the songwriters and music publishers paid by fees collected by the PRO's on blanket licenses?

28. Explain the Fairness in Music Licensing Act. Whom does it effect?

29. Explain recoupment. What does it mean and how does it work?

30. You and a co-writer have written a platinum selling song on Elton John's last album. The song was recorded under the controlled composition clause with Elton John owning 25% of the publishing share, you owning 25% of the publishing share and John's label owning 25% of the publishing share. The song becomes a number 1 top 40 radio hit in the United States and BMI collects about $500,000. A movie company pays $300,000 for the use of the song for the opening and closing credits of a new Tom Hanks movie. Ford Motor Company has also paid $250,000 for the use of the song for a national TV commercial to run between January 1 to June 30 of this year.

    (a) What is your percent of the songwriter's share of the royalty stream?

    (b) What is your percent of the music publishers share of the royalty stream?

    (c) What is your percent of the total song royalty stream?

    (d) How much money did each license generate?
        (a) Mechanical

        (b) Blanket

        (c) Sync

    (e) How much money (gross) did the license(s) generate?

    (f) How much money did you make?

Lecture Points
Chapter Six

CREATIVE

MEET WITH NEW WRITERS

WORK WITH THEM

LISTEN TO TAPES

VISIT CLUBS AND RECORDING STUDIOS

PRODUCE DEMO TAPES

INITIATE COLLABORATIONS

CASTING SONGS

Lecture Points
Chapter Six

ACTIVITIES OF THE MUSIC PUBLISHER

PROMOTION

RESEARCHING PROJECTS

TRADE MAGAZINES

TIP SHEETS

MAKE AND MAIL COPIES

LYRIC SHEETS

MAINTAIN FILES ON PRODUCERS, A&R MEN, STUDIOS, ETC.

BUSINESS

HIRE PERSONNAL

ESTABLISH COMPANY POLICY

NEGOTIATE CONTRACT

Lecture Points
Chapter Six

LICENSES

ADMINISTRATION

FILE COPYRIGHT FORMS

FILE WITH THE PREFORMING RIGHTS ORGANIZATIONS

FILE WITH MECHANICAL RIGHTS ORGANIZATIONS

COLLECT ROYALTIES

ROYALTY ACCOUNTING

TAX ACCOUNTING

FINANCIAL PLANNING

PAY WRITER ROYALTIES

TYPES OF WRITER/PUBLISHER CONTRACTS

Chapter Six Notes

Chapter Six Notes

7 LABELS

Signing Acts,

Creating Products,

Distribution,

Promotion

Publicity

This story is about a bidding-war band that gets a huge deal with a 20 percent royalty rate and a million-dollar advance. (No bidding-war band ever got a 20 percent royalty, but whatever.) This is my "funny" math based on some reality ... What happens to that million dollars? They spend half a million to record their album. That leaves the band with $500,000. They pay $100,000 to their manager for 20 percent commission. They pay $25,000 each to their lawyer and business manager. That leaves $350,000 for the four band members to split. After $170,000 in taxes, there's $180,000 left. That comes out to $45,000 per person. That's $45,000 to live on for a year until the record gets released. The record is a big hit and sells a million copies... So, this band releases two singles and makes two videos. The two videos cost a million dollars to make and 50 percent of the video production costs are recouped out of the band's royalties. The band gets $200,000 in tour support, which is 100 percent recoupable. The record company spends $300,000 on independent radio promotion. All of those independent promotion costs are charged to the band. Since the original million-dollar advance is also recoupable, the band owes $2 million to the record company. If all of the million records are sold at full price with no discounts or record clubs, the band earns $2 million in royalties, since their 20 percent royalty works out to $2 a record. Two million dollars in royalties minus $2 million in recoupable expenses equals ... zero!

— **Courtney Love, Recording Artist**[133]

Record companies, believe me, no matter what record company you're with, they're going to try to hype you, because, really, all record companies are interested in is making money.

—**Elton John**[134]

MEGA ENTERTAINMENT INDUSTRY COMPANIES

Mega Entertainment Corporations control most of the world's entertainment consumer markets. They are *Bertelsmann AG of Germany, The Walt Disney Company, (which just made the list this year), EMI of England, Sony of Japan, TimeWarner of the United States and Vivendi Universal of France.* Historically these world-wide, dominant, billion-dollar entertainment businesses were built on the consumer acceptance of various types of entertainment products created from the inventions and developments in audio recording, film production, the popular print press, television, radio, photography, computers, and other forms of innovation and technology. For the last 125 years, these companies and their earlier

---

[133] Courtney Love Does the Math. Courtney Love's speech to the Digital Hollywood Online Entertainment Conference, given in New York on May 16, www.salon.com, (07/03/2000).
[134] http://www.artquotes.net/entertainment-quotes/famous-singers/elton-john/index.htm

enterprising business versions that have either merged or been bought out by them, have controlled between 80% to 90% of the audio recordings, films and mass media entertainment products in the various world market. Independent productions have made up the remaining market shares.

The formula for success is straightforward enough: Produce something for a fixed cost and exploit the —— out of it, selling it over and over in different markets, venues, and formats. And if enough people see it (or hear it) the property becomes a cultural touchstone that can continue to draw in revenue for decades.

— Author Unknown quote from Business Week Magazine[135]

HISTORICAL PERSPECTIVES

Over the years, many of the small entrepreneurial recording and film ventures have merged into five diversified world entertainment corporations. These companies with the money, business structure, and distribution systems can create, produce, market, promote, publicize, distribute, and deliver music, movies, computer games, and other entertainment products consistently to the global markets.

TRADITIONAL MEGA ENTERTAINMENT CORPORATIONS

Carl Bertelsmann started **Bertelsmann AG** in 1835 as a lithographic printing company. Today, it is Europe's leading media company and is number two in the world after TimeWarner. One of Bertelsmann's first books, a hymnal, helped the company to grow, despite the poverty and low literacy rate in the 1830's. The Nazis shut down the company during WWII. Its major growth was in the 1950's when it developed the "book club" marketing concept that created huge profits from the sale of print media distributed directly to consumer homes. At one point in time, Bertelsmann's book clubs had over 25 million members in 15 countries, and BMG Direct (the direct music/record club) had over four million American record club members.[136] *Bertelsmann* is an international media company encompassing television (RTL Group), book publishing (Random House), magazine publishing (Gruner + Jahr), music (BMG), media services (Arvato), and media clubs (Direct Group) in more than 50 countries. Bertelsmann's claim is to inspire people around the world with first-class media and communications offerings - entertainment, information and services and occupy leading positions in its respective markets. The foundation of Bertelsmann's success is a corporate culture based on partnership, entrepreneurial spirit, creativity, and corporate responsibility. The company strives to bring creative new ideas to market and create value.[137]

The Walt Disney Company is the leading teen entertainment company in the world. It is divided into four business segments, (a) it's media networks including the *Disney Channel, ABC-network, the ESPN* sports networks, and a radio network consisting of about 25 radio stations in major markets; (b) Theme parks including *Disneyland and DisneyWorld; (c) Studio Entertainment including the Disney, MGM, and Pixar film studios, and the Lyric Street and Hollywood Records labels;* and (d) consumer products tied to almost all of the manufactured entertainment products and artists they have created. In the music industry, Disney has scored the nation's number one album of 2007 with *High School Musical*. Disney is unique in that it does not own it own music distribution. Instead it uses UNI (Universal) for music platform distribution.[138]

---

135 "The Entertainment Glut" by unknown author, Business Week Magazine (09/11/98).
136 Bertelsmann A.G. CarI-Bertelsmann-Strasse, 270, D-333111 Gutersloh, Germany Phone:+49-52-41-80-1362, http://www.bertelsmann.com
137 MarketWatch 2008.
138 www.disneygo.com from the Forbes.com 2000 list.

EMI Group, PLC of England is the world's leading music publisher with over one million titles in its publishing catalogs. It celebrated its first 100 years in business in 1997. EMI was started in 1898, as the Gramophone Company. It and the Columbia Graphophone Company merged in 1931 to form Electric and Musical Industries, now better known as EMI. EMI has acquired many labels including Capitol Records, United Artists Records, The Sparrow Corporation, Charisma Records and Priority Records. It bought Richard Branson's Virgin Music Group in 1992 for $834 million dollars. In 1962, EMI made history with The Beatles and in 1998, EMI succeeded again with Garth Brooks who had sold 67 million albums worldwide.[139]

> *CREATIVE DIRECTION*
>
> *Artists want to play music, sing, sometimes become rich and famous. The problem is often they need help. Nobody is coming to discover you-the unknown artist. Instead, the artists have to present an image and talent (great demo recording and career breaking song) that labels can perceive as saleable. That is how they make their money by selling your creativity. Producers, audio engineers, union musicians, Bgv's are all used to help embellish new recordings.*

"Music has been a vital and vibrant part of Sony's culture for over twenty years. This acquisition will allow us to achieve a deeper and more robust integration between the wide-ranging global assets of the music company and Sony's products, operating companies and affiliates. It enables us to offer a total entertainment experience to consumers,"

—**Sir Howard Stringer, Chairman and CEO, Sony Corporation. (On the purchase of BMG for $1.2 billion, August 4th, 2008).**[140]

Sony Entertainment is a wholly owned subsidiary of the Sony Corporation, a $50 plus billion a year electronic software, entertainment, and hardware producer and manufacturer. Founder and Chief Advisor, *Masaru Ibuka* and Founder and Honorary Chairman, *Akio Morita* founded Sony on the concept of "The establishment of an ideal factory, free, dynamic, and pleasant, where technical personnel of sincere motivation can exercise their technological skills to the highest levels."[141] The company has fostered a culture of curiosity in science tied to leading edge technologies, entrepreneurship, development, and the commercialization of fun and profits through the sale of consumer products.

Sony believes that content that originates from dreams should be enjoyed on hardware conceived from dreams, and that tools, which originate in dreams, should have creativity as well as offer a variety of elements such as superior sound and picture quality, easy operationand portability, and an innovative design and pleasing feeling.[142] It bought *CBS Records* in 1988 for $3.5 billion and the film division (*Columbia and Tri-Star Pictures*) in 1989 for $4.5 billion. Consolidated under *Sony Pictures Entertainment* (SPE) are sub-groups of companies including: *Columbia Tri-Star Motion Picture Group (Columbia Pictures, Sony Pictures Classics, Sony Pictures Releasing, Columbia Tri-Star Film Distributors International); Columbia Tri-Star Television Group (Columbia Tri-Star Television, Columbia Tri-Star Television Distribution, Columbia Tri-Star International Television); Columbia Tri-Star Home Video, the Digital Studios Division; Sony Pictures Studios and the Culver Studios in California.*

---

139 www. EMI History from corporate Internet web page www.emigroup.com, (1998)& Hoovers.
140 MarketWatch, Inc 2008
141 "Remembering Masaru Ibuka', Sony CorporateInfo/Annual Report 98, as issued over the Internet, httni/sony.com. (1998).
142 "Digital Dream", feature section of CorporateInfo/AnnualReport 98, as issued over the Internet, http://sonv.com. (1998)

> **TALENT SCOUTS DISCOVERING A NEW ARTIST**
>
> Sometimes, a label will "buy out" the publisher's interest in an artist with a one-time lump sum of money. The publisher (or managers, producers, etc., who discovered and helped develop the act) relinquishes all future rights to the artist and their image in exchange for the negotiated amount of money. Self-proclaimed talent agents work the same way. They find and develop talent and then are "bought out" by the label. However, talent agents who pressure artists to invest their own money are often not considered legitimate by the industry.
>
> **KNOW THE BUSINESS**
>
> You can do it yourself only if your talent is awesome and starts a huge response in the city you live in Local-getting a buzz, Regionally (creating momentum) or nationally on one of the social networks or www.youtube.com. Other then that, to move past the local market you'll need a label and their creative and business support.

Sony makes both Sega and Nintendo video games and owns *Merv Griffin's Enterprises*, which produces the *Jeopardy* and *Wheel of Fortune* TV shows.[143] The music business was directed through Sony Music Entertainment (Japan) and *Sony Music Entertainment International* (SMEI) in the rest of the world until the *Sony/BMG* merger.[144] In August of 2008, Sony bought BMG's half of the music company for $1.2 billion. *Sony Corporation* is a leading manufacturer of audio, video, game, communications, key device and information technology products for the consumer and professional markets. With its music, pictures, computer entertainment and on-line businesses, *Sony* is uniquely positioned to be the leading personal broadband entertainment company in the world. Sony recorded consolidated annual sales of approximately $70 billion for the fiscal year ended March 31, 2007.[145] [146]

Time Warner was created in 1989 when *Time Publications and Warner Communications International* exchanged stock and money to merge into *TimeWarner, Inc*. Later the company approved a friendly takeover by *America Online* (AOL), at the time the leading Internet provider, which turned out to be a negative collaboration.[147] Time, Inc. was started in 1922 by *Briton Hadden and Henry Luce*. In addition to Time Magazine, it published Life and other social and business periodicals. *Harry, Jack and Sam Warner founded Warner Bros. in the late 1920's*. Classic movies produced included *Casablanca* and *Rebel Without a Cause*.[148] In the 1989 merger, Time Publications received 17.3 million shares of Warner Communication International stock. Time also purchased another 100 million shares.

Warner Communication received 7 million shares of Time stock. The total cost of the merger was $14.3 billion of which $8.3 billion were loans. In 1995, *Ted Turner* became a 10% owner of Time Warner, Inc., by selling his *Turner Broadcasting, Inc*. (*TBS Superstation, TNT cable network, the Cartoon Network, New Line and Castle Rock movie production studios, Hanna-Barbera Cartoons, Headline News, plus the Atlanta Braves baseball franchise*), to Time Warner for $8 billion.[149] Time Warner was divided into five segments: Cable Networks which includes *Home Box Office* and its many film and international companies, and all of the *Turner Broadcasting Companies*, such as *CNN, TNT,* etc; the Publishing division includes 40 top national magazines such as *People, Sports Illustrated, Fortune, Book-of the Month Club,* etc.; *Warner Music Group's record labels included Atlantic, Elektra, Rhino, Sire, Warner Bros. Records* and many affiliate labels until it was sold to Edgar Bronfman. The film entertainment segment is divided into *Warner Bros. Films* and Television consisting of approximately fourteen supportive companies (examples include *Warner Bros. Pictures, Warner Bros. Television, Looney Tunes, Hanna-Barbera, and Castle Rock Entertainment*. The Time Warner film library has more than 5,700

---

143 Ibid.
144 SONY, 7-35, Kitashinagawa, 6-chome, Shinagawa-ku, Tokyo 141, Japan+81-3-5448-2111, www.world.sony.com.
145 Sony to Purchase Bertelsmann's 50% Stake in Sony BMG; Music Company to Become Wholly Owned Subsidiary of Sony Corporation of America, JCN Newswire via COMTEX, 2008.
146 It Takes a Crisis by Adam Roundtree, Bloomingberg New-Forbes 2008.
147 "America Online and Time Warner Shareholders Approve Companies "Merger", press release, www.aol.com, (08/08/2000).
148 Sony Corporate Reports.
149 37 "Dream deal still faces many hurdles," Skip Wollenberg Associated Press as reported in The Tennessean, "Business" page IE, (September 23, 1995).

feature films, 32,500 television titles and 13,500 animated titles.[150][151]

Vivendi/Universal owned by *Vivendi of Paris*, France shocked the entertainment business by purchasing all of *Seagram Inc.* including both the liquor and entertainment companies in June of 2000. Seagram was one of the world's leading distributors of spirits (scotch and cognac), and wine. It had recently sold its interest in fruit juices and soft drinks to another distributor in order to purchase PolyGram which was mainly owned by the world's third largest electronics company, Philips Electronics of Holland.[152] It manufactured x-ray and radio tubes in the early 1900's and invented today's compact disc, and the digital compact cassette.[153][154] The purchase of Seagram Inc. gave Vivendi $34 billion in equity, $25 billion in debt and an estimated combined gross annual income of about $55 billion.[155] The combined company brought content from the world's largest music company, second largest film library, major film production studio, second largest destination theme park company, and global leader in reference, consumer and PC-based software game publishing. In 2005, Vivendi sold most of its old and worthy film and movie copyrights to NBC of the United States.[156]

MEGA'S OPERATIONS-DIVISIONS

The megas are divided into divisions that allow them to operate successfully by creating entertainment products, marketing them through promotion and publicity campaigns in their own media and popular press publications, distribute the entertainment products through their own world-wide distribution networks and in some cases, even create the electronic devices and products consumers use to listen to (mp3 music players), watch (LCD/Plasma TV's), or play (computer games).

---

150 Hoovers Online Company Capsule (1998).
151 TimeWarner, 75 Rockefeller Center Plaza, New York, NY 10019, 212-484-8000, www.timewarner.com.
152 Philips decided to drop out of the entertainment production business and focus aggressively on research and development.
153 The Music Business Handbook & Career Guide, Baskerville (1990).
154 In the summer of 1998, Philips stunned the entertainment industry by announcing the sale of its Polygram Entertainment Division to Seagram Company Ltd. of Canada. It took only 2 1/2 years for Seagram to surprise us again by selling itself to Vivendi Chanal + of Paris.
155 "Vivendi, Seagram and Chanal + to Merge, creating fully Integrated Global Media and Communications Company for the Wired and Wireless, World Group News, www.vivendi.com, (08//04/2000).
156 Vivendi/Universal, 42, Avenue de Friedland, 75380 Paris Tel: 33 1 71 7110 00, Fax: 33 1 71 7111 79, www.vivendi.com

---

SONY REINVENTS SONY

Sony is once again becoming a huge player in the entertainment business. They bought out BMG from the Sony/BMG merger to gain all rights to Bertelsmann's music copyrights. Three years ago, Sony was in financial trouble (as are all the mega's) caused somewhat by the stealing of entertainment product over the Internet and in-house problems. They hired Howard Stringer to correct the problems. He used a great business book called Who Says Elephants Can't Dance by Louis V. Gerstner Jr., to reinvent the company. His efforts have paid off by making the different Sony divisions work together. By using the PlayStation 3 division he was to launch the Blu-ray disc format and have it accepted by all the major film studios. Some of the Sony flat screen LCD TV's may be hooked directly to the internet, by-passing cable. The goal is to connect all the devices – Televisions, music players, PlayStation machines to one another and to a new Sony Network for downloading movies, TV shows, games and other digital content such as music. If he can do it... Sony defines the 360 full entertainment company that not only supply the entertainment products, but all the devices through it's own distribution systems.

QUESTION
WHAT HAPPENED TO POLYGRAM?

In the summer of 1998, Philips stunned the entertainment industry by announcing the sale of its Polygram Entertainment Division to Seagram Company Ltd. of Canada. It took only 2 1/2 years for Seagram to surprise us again by selling itself to Vivendi Chanal + of Paris. What Philips (one of the worlds largest electronic companies) had discovered was that the use of the Internet by music lovers would lead to people stealing music digitally. It was shortly after that Napster was launched and validated the theory. Thus, Universal is the combination of two of the most powerful entertainment companies ever, MCA/Universal and Polygram.

MEDIA-ENTERTAINMENT DISTRIBUTION CORPORATIONS

Some media companies are evolving into entertainment corporations. Most take advantage of digital production, creative operations, promotion, publicity, and several forms of product distribution including radio, TV, cable, satellite, internet social websites and cellphone companies to grow their audience. By using music artists (streaming and download sales) to attract viewers to their multiple outlets they are able to charge higher advertisement fees to advertisers (based on the number of impressions/viewers per thousand). In addition, sales of music downloads and advertisement supporting legal downloads increase the companies profit and loss statements. Examples include;

- *News Corp.* Rupert Murdock's News Corp. includes all of the Fox network shows and productions, Blue Sky, Dow Jones, Harper Collins Publications, The National Geographic, The Weekly Standard, The New York Post, and outside the United States the BSkyB satellite network, The News Digital Media and STAR cable networks. In addition, Murdock purchased myspace.com for about half a billion dollars to boost and facilitate a younger generation's web hits to his corporation's media holdings. His myspacemusic.com is now being supported by all the major labels as a media promotion and publicity outlet, that also offers digital streaming and downloads.[157]

- *Comcast*-Comcast Corporation is the nation's leading provider of cable, entertainment and communication products and services, with 24.7 million cable customers, 14.1 million high-speed Internet customers and 5.2 million voice customers. Comcast is principally involved in the development, management and operation of broadband cable networks and in the delivery of programming content.[158]

- *Viacom*-separated from CBS-TV networks in 2005. Its key to the music industry is the MTV and VH-1 worldwide music networks. In addition, Viacom owns the BET networks, CMT, the Comedy Central channel, Nickelodeon, Rhapsody Music Networks, Shockwave, and the Paramount and Dreamworks studios and film production companies.[159]

To proponents, though, 360 deals represent a necessary rebalancing of the industry's economics. Record companies, they note, are the ones that pay to sign artists, groom them and then use their corporate marketing clout to get them on the radio. Nine times out of 10 they fail. So, runs the rationale, they should be entitled to a share of all the bounty on the occasion when one of their bets pays off.
— Joshua Chaffin, The Financial Times [160]

360-MUSIC-ENTERTAINMENT CORPORATIONS

More than record labels yet less than mega entertainment corporations, 360 music entertainment companies provide a one-stop business that merge all three music industry revenue streams together. Of course there are many different types of *360 deals* being developed, however it is clear that labels are moving quickly toward these types of music entertainment umbrella companies that support and profit from all three revenue streams in an effort to survive the creative destruction of the traditional industry. Established artist are safe in their current recoupable deals, yet almost all new artists signed to labels are offered only some type of 360 deal.

---

157 www.newscorp.com 2008
158   www.comcast.com 2008
159   www.viacom.com
160 Ibid.

- *LiveNation* is a spin off concert promotion company from the radio moguls at *Clear Channel*. It has signed *U2, Madonna* and other major artists to long-term deals that will supply everything from music publishing, recordings, (labels), concert promotional tours, branding offers to corporate sponsorships and merchandise sales. These 360-Music Entertainment Corporations appear to be the future business model of the industry.

LABELS

Major labels have been a vital part of their parent mega entertainment corporations' strategic business plan, method of operation, and bottom-line financial success. The megas had provided the annual budget to finance the label's operation and album projects. Once artists were signed and recorded the mega distribution system, mass media and print media were used to promote and sell the albums worldwide to consumers through traditional and digital retail outlets. Due to peer-to-peer file sharing (consumer's illegal downloading of music free) many major record labels have either merged together or been sold. Only four exist today where there were six just a few years ago. They are:

- *EMI of England*
- *Universal of France*
- *Warner Music of The United States*
- *Sony Music Entertainment of Japan* (Sony/BMG)

"We ultimately will become the fifth member of each band,"

— **Monte Lipman, President of Universal Republic Records (on 360 deals)**[161]

Their business model is still the same, to create profits from the creation, manufacturing, distribution, promotion, publicity, and marketing of recorded musical products. However, consumers' continuous use of P2P has reduced their economies of scale to the point where it is difficult to break-even financially even with reduced budgets and limited artist rosters. Thus, most major labels are morphing into 360 Music Entertainment Corporations by signing new artists to 360 deals that combine all three revenue streams in order to reduce the cost and risk of doing business. Most labels are divided into functional departments that have their own autonomy, yet interlinking responsibilities. They must accomplish their individual missions, additionally working together with the other label departments to accomplish the strategic mission of the label, which is, of course, to create and sell recorded music in this very difficult digital market.

---

161 Chaffiin, Joshua, By Promoting Gigs, Record Labels Get in on Bigger Acts, www.The Financial Times.com, 2008.

NARAS

The National Academy of Record Arts and Science is the organization that represents the music business from awarding Grammy's to Music Cares, which is a program to help provide music in schools. NARAS has several chapters in local music cities such as Los Angeles, New York, Memphis and Nashville. NARAS often has GRAMMY in the schools day where local producers, musicians, audio engineers and singers talk to students about possible careers in the industry.

www.naras.org

TYPES OF LABELS

- Most *Major Labels* have the larger budgets, world distribution, promotion, and publicity to launch an act. In the past, they often signed, recorded, and distributed American artists and culture for profits. Now, they are also trying to develop territory markets by signing and exploiting (in a positive business

- way) local acts such as Chinese rock bands, Japanese acts to the Asian markets, Eastern European acts to Europe and so on. At the same time, P2P has cut the financial profits of the major labels because, according to the *RIAA, (Recording Industry Association of America)*, 51% of all releases are stolen (acquired without being paid for) which makes it difficult for the labels to stay in business.[162]

- *Affiliate Labels* are connected financially and through distribution deals with the major labels that provide unit sales through traditional retail outlets and promotion and publicity through the labels' established media connections.

- *Independent Labels* are usually controlled, owned, and established by major industry personalities, such as record producers Sam Phillips (Sun Records) or artists such as Madonna (Maverick Records). Producers use their own labels to land distribution deals with major labels and established artists often use their labels for tax write-offs and to record their friends and newly discovered talents.

- *Vanity Labels* are created by unsigned artists to sell their own recordings or to provide additional revenues.

- *Specialty and Virtual Reality Labels* focus on a genre niche, such as children's music or comedy albums, or a type of unique distribution such as Internet digital download, cell phones or websites such as www.myspace.com and www.facebook.com. The virtual reality labels do not often press CD's as they keep expenses low by providing digital downloads to the Internet users, cell phones and PDA's.

- *Promotion Branding Labels* (PBL's) have recently emerged as marketing tools for other products. Starbucks formed its own label and signed Sir Paul McCartney. Many companies are signing artists in an attempt to sell other products. Others form labels to support manufactured artists such as dolls, cartoons, or children/teenage stars on TV shows and even movies.

IMPORTANT HISTORICAL RECORD LABELS

- *Columbia Records* was the granddaddy of record labels dating from its start with the invention of the Graphophone in 1886 to its purchase by Sony in 1988. Marconi created an indestructible "Velvet Tone" disc that boosted sales for the label to an unheard of $150 million a year in 1919. In 1948, the now CBS owned label introduced the $33^{1/3}$ LP (long play) album on a vinyl disc, which became the industry standard. In the 1960's, the label introduced Columbia House direct mail order record club (after the Bertelsmann A. G. model) to the public.[163]

---

162 Reported by the Director of the RIAA at the Digital Summit program at Belmont University, April 2007.
163 "The History of the Major Labels" by Bill Damain, Performing Songwriter Magazine July/August, 2003.

- *RCA Records* (Recording Corporation of America) started as a by-product label from the establishment of the Victor Talking Machine Company in 1901 by Emile Berliner and Eldridge Johnson. The company label under the name Victor connected to HMV (the English label-His Master's Voice) and grew into a very successful label with recording artists Enrico Caruso, Al Jolson, and then later under the RCA label with Tommy Dorsey, Glenn Miller, Perry Como, Dinah Shore, Dolly Parton, DavidBowie and Elvis Presley.[164]

- *Capitol Records* was founded in 1942 by songwriter Johnny Mercer, movie producer and songwriter Buddy Desylva and retail record store owner Glenn Walichs. Capitol Records' major success came after it was purchased by EMI (Electrical Music Industries) in 1956 and its release of very successful albums by the Beach Boys and The Beatles.[165]

- Movie mogul Jack Warner founded **Warner Bros. Records** in 1958. He used many of Warner Bros.'s TV shows and movies to sell music by connecting the two in cross marketing efforts using artists in hit shows such as Kookie, Edd Byrnes in (77 Sunset Strip) and comedian Bob Newhart to sell recorded products. Neither could sing very well, yet their recordings outsold many established acts signed to other labels. Later, the very talented Everly Brothers and Frank Sinatra joined the roster along with Dean Martin and Sammy Davis Jr. Other great acts who recorded for the label under the supervision of Mo Ostin including The Kinks, The Grateful Dead, Joni Mitchell, The Doobie Brothers and Fleetwood Mac.[166]

- "Hitsville, USA" was the sign in front of *Berry Gordy Jr's* house in Detroit when he started his label **Motown Records** in 1959. A songwriter himself ("Lonely Teardrops"), Gordy used $800.00 of borrowed family money to start his company. Within just a few years the label crossed over into top 40 radio with such acts as Smokey Robinson & The Miracles, The Temptations, Diana Ross, Marvin Gaye, The Commodores, the Jackson 5 (starring a very young Michael Jackson) and Stevie Wonder.[167]

- *Herb Alpert and Jerry Moss* started *Carnival Records* in 1962 with $200. Later, they found out the name Carnival was already being used so they changed the name of their label to **A&M Records**. Using their experience from viewing a bullfight in Tijuana, Mexico, Alpert and Moss recorded a brassy sounding instrumental titled *The Lonely Bull* in their garage. It sold over 700,000 copies, which they also packed and shipped from the same garage. Additional artists such as the *Carpenters, Joe Cocker, Humble Pie, Cat Stevens, the Police, Janet Jackson, and Alpert's own album "Whipped Cream"*, with the hit *"A Taste of Honey"* made *A&M* one of the most successful independent labels ever launched. In 1989, *Alpert and Moss* sold their $200 investment label to PolyGram (owned at that time by Philips Electronic of Holland) for half a billion dollars.[168]

CREATIVE/BUSINESS MILIEU

There are constant underlying philosophical conflicts between the creative and business sides of the industry. Successful industry professionals accept the interface of creativity and structured global businesses as the key to success. Yet, when large sums of money are involved, adversarial attitudes often develop between the values of art versus the profits of business. Disagreements range from friendly discussions to lawsuits, which sometimes define the boundaries of the conversations and solutions to personal and financial conflicts. In recording, most artists want to control their own sound and performances and yet at the same time, the labels want to control their costs as much as possible. Producers hold the line on budgets. Therefore, during the recording of an album, the creative control and financial control of the

---

164 Ibid.
165 Ibid.
166 Ibid.
167 Ibid.
168 Ibid.

budget is the producer's responsibility.

WHY DO ARTISTS NEED RECORD LABELS?

MONEY!

1. It costs a lot of money to move past the local gigs to become a regional or nationally known act. Radio tours where artists visit stations, promotion with music videos, paid advertisements in the popular press and trade magazines (Billboard, PollStar) are expensive. However, the best way for an act to become successful based on their talent is to get the show started yourself locally. Local fame (word of mouth) brings regional and then national fame if you are good enough. Use other people's money to pay for the recordings, promotion, publicity and distribution (record labels). Then, while they are paying themselves back (out of your royalties) use the fame they paid for to make tons of money in concerts, merchandise, and corporate sponsorship. At this point your are a business person and hopefully a very smart entrepreneur.

2. Distribution! Once you have a saleable product, labels have the power to distribute it world-wide. However, so do you now over the Internet. The problem of course, is that there are lots of good acts and recordings on the net, very few GREAT ones. (Labels actually have people searching for acts to sign from Internet social websites).

3. Promotion and publicity work with distribution to give consumers a chance to "discover" your talents. Labels still have the power to accomplish the launching of an act. Setting up a website doesn't get it done. Word of mouth (excitement of consumers) does and that is usually accomplished by labels if the act is good enough.

FIVE FUNCTIONS OF SUCCESSFUL LABELS

In the past, labels were in the business of selling discs to wholesalers to create a profit. They worked on a 40/20/40% split of the suggested retail list price (SRLP), paying their bills and hopefully creating low financial breakeven points based on unit sales figures. The traditional business model has five FUNCTIONS OR STEPS including:

- *Find and sign* great potential sellable talent and songs.

- *Create a sellable product* (recording) in major recording studios using AF of M musicians and AFTRA vocalists.

- *Distribute* the recordings to wholesale and retail outlets using worldwide mega entertainment distribution channels.

- *Promote* the product through radio, music videos, the Internet, cell phones and paid advertisements on the Internet, in the trade magazines (<u>Billboard</u>, <u>Radio and Records</u>, <u>Gavin</u>) and popular press (as an example, People Magazine).

- *Publicity* is publicizing the act on talk shows (Letterman as example), the placement of stories in trade magazines and the popular press, the use of in-store end caps, images on the Internet, concert tours, and even paparazzi photos placed in print, broadcast news, and digital click media.[169]

---

[169] Ibid.

FOUR P'S OF MARKETING

Other than the first step of finding and signing talent the functions of a successful label (steps 2-5) consist of the four "P's" of marketing. They are product (step 2), placement (step 3 or distribution), Promotion (which includes steps 4 and 5 (Publicity), and Price which is a combination of steps 2-5 that allows the label to bring the album to market to a specific demographic and psychographic consumer base at the right price for maximum profit levels.

"A career is wonderful, but you can't curl up with it on a cold night."
—**Marilyn Monroe**[170]

WHAT ARTISTS LOOK FOR IN LABELS
(MONEY)

Prospective recording artists rarely enter into a recording deal with any real understanding of how labels work. They are often on an ego trip dreaming of becoming rich and famous from the deal. Instead, artists need to consider what the label can and will do for them to launch their career. Each of the five functions of a label should be evaluated on how much they will help an artist build a lifelong career. During the negotiations in the contract the label should put all points verbally promised in writing. Budgets should be established for recording expenses, promotion, distribution, and publicity. Financial advances must include tour support and basic living expenses while you are a work-for-hire completing the recordings. The deal will probably be for seven years with an album release in the first initial year. The following six years will be options based on album sales. Thus, you want to make sure the deal from the label will give you an opportunity to successfully record, distribute, promote and publicize your recordings and image so that the label will pick up the option for the next album. After the label has found and signed a sellable talent (they hope) and recorded them (recording budget) then the last three steps of distribution, promotion, and publicity take place at the same time launched as a marketing plan.

WHAT LABELS LOOK FOR IN ARTISTS

I have talked to many artists who have never received any royalties from their recordings. The bottom line is simple: the record labels are not in the business of making artists rich, they are in the business of selling discs and digital downloads that will make the label rich. Thus talent, as defined by the labels, is related to the amount of money they can make from an artist's recordings. This is the merger of the creative system and business system where in the past neither could accomplish much in the worldwide market without the other. The creative system provides the songs, vocalists, musicians, audio engineers and producers. The business system, consisting of labels, provides the money to create the recordings, promotion, publicity, and distribution. On the front end, labels treat artists with great respect. On the back end, in closed meetings, it is the number of units moved, break-even points achieved, and the financial bottom line that determines the respect the label has for an artist. This sounds harsh of course, yet this is a business and who else would spend millions on an unknown artist and additional money for the promotion, publicity and distribution of artistic products?

As a result, labels seek recording artists who are able to capture the imagination of the human spirit and of the current popular culture themes and beliefs. New artists who have an established image, a fan base and a successful number of units sold (even in small numbers), are seen as having more potential as they may have already developed a meaningful image that communicates some emotional message to consumers. Labels view small successes in local markets as an indication that if the act is developed, recorded and exploited (marketed) they may become very profitable.

---

170 http://www.artquotes.net/entertainment-quotes/famous-actresses/marilyn-monroe.htm

GETTING NOTICED BY A LABEL

Acts and bands are still discovered through local personalities (radio station DJ's, local promoters and record store owners who tell regional label distribution and promotions about the "local buzz" an act is creating. Without the band's knowledge, labels have personalities or regional employees attend a live performance to determine the act's potential. Often the response of the audience is seen as just as important as the band's actual quality of performance. The band's originality, uniqueness, age, industry knowledge, and sellable image are also evaluated to determine if they can be molded or developed into a major recording act.

DIGITAL DISCOVERY

Acts today are often first noticed on websites such as *www.facebook.com, www.myspace.com or www.youtube.com* or some other Internet related site. The odds are a million to one of being discovered, as most of the artists posted do not have the potential to develop into major recording acts. Recordings with the use of Pro-Tools and other improvement software do not give an act the talent and personality needed to be able to record for major labels and to perform live before huge audiences. However, developing a huge following on an Internet site tied to a local or regional buzz based on live performances, sales of digital downloads or retail CD's and some airplay will significantly put the odds of being "noticed" in your favor.[171]

SHOWCASES

Live performances before a small invited group of guests including music industry A&R personnel, managers, media, and concert promoters are sometimes used to introduce an act to powerful established industry personalities. Of course, we are assuming a certain level of success before you offer the showcase opportunity to labels.

PITCH MEMO

Pitch memos are used by acts or their legal representation to contact labels and other industry personalities to invite them to listen to demos, and attend concerts or showcases. *Electronic Bio's* consisting of

---

[171] Labels are aware of the software programs that add significant and fake numbers of views to your www.myspace.com webpages.

Labels Grabbing Artist's Concert Tour Profits

However, this is where people stealing music over the Internet has hurt your chances of making lots of money as a known artist. Record labels are having a very hard time competing with free (P2P). Thus, as soon as your music is recorded and released, it is also being downloaded by consumers who have discovered you. Record labels, to recoup their investments in the recordings, distribution and promotion (that may have cost them $800,000.00 to a million dollars) are now starting to require the artist to give them a percentage or all of the outside money gained based on your/their fame (which they helped to create and financially support) not on your music which is yours (unless you give up all your publishing rights). Therefore, revenue gained from music publishing, concert tours, merchandise sales are going to the record labels first in the newly offered 360 deals. Corporate sponsorships are still the remaining property of the artists and controlled by the manager.

recordings, videos of concerts and copies of any press articles and advertisements should be included in the pitch memos.

DEAL MEMO

The first stage of negotiation between a label interested in an act and the attorney who represents an act is covered in a three to four page deal memo. The basic points of the contract are detailed such as royalty points for the artist, options, advances, number of recordings, tour advances and other significant relevant issues. Deal memos allow each party to determine if and where there is common ground and to establish how close they are to an actual agreement.

TYPES OF DEALS

The business of record labels starts with a great recording of a great song tied to a sellable artist. The business of artist management and the corresponding corporate sponsorships, concert tours, merchandise sales, TV roles and film careers usually begins after the release of a sellable recording and after the corresponding branding and fame. Therefore, having some type of label deal is extremely important for the ultimate success of most artists. Actual record label deals are very specific and often cover many legal points not discussed in the deal memo. Therefore, do not be surprised to find actual contracts 75 to 125 pages in length. It is also very important to read and understand what you are signing as most contracts can tie up an artist's career for at least seven years.

"360 deals" have become the principal survival strategy for many music companies at a time when compact disc sales are grinding towards extinction.
— Joshua Chaffin, The Financial Times[172]

"If you look around, I don't know how much additional expertise has been added at various record companies to justify why they should be participating in all these other areas (360 deals)."
—Rick Dobbis, Business Manager for the Rolling Stones [173]

- *The 360 Deals*-The negative shift in the traditional label's economics of scale due to P2P file sharing is destroying the foundation of the music industry. It is very difficult for traditional labels to fund new artists (often at $800,000 to $1.2 million) when more than half of the new music/recordings being acquired by consumers is not being purchased. Thus, labels breakeven points have dramatically increased to a degree where it is very difficult to make a profit on most of their artists. Therefore, much of the previous items posted in the example deal in this text are now used as a basic foundation for 360 deals that require artists to repay the labels' investments with all or a percentage (usually more than 40%) of the music publishing and tours/management revenue streams. This includes song copyrights, merchandise, ticket sales, and corporate sponsorships revenues that were previously the artists/songwriters. As negative as this may sound for traditional music business models, this creative destruction of the business is also leading to many new entrepreneurial business opportunities in the industry. Note: see section 23 of the following recording contract as an example of some of the elements of a typical 360 deal.

---

172 Ibid.
173 Ibid.

- *Traditional Major deals* are high exposure, large budget agreements between artists and labels that are either part of or formerly owned by a mega entertainment corporation such as Sony/BMG, EMI, TimeWarner or Universal. There are no standard recording agreements offered by major labels. Attorneys who represent the artists and label negotiate deals. Each agreement is unique and tailored to the specific requirements of the label and artists. Terms may vary from a single, one-time release to a multiple album, several-year obligation for both parties. Exclusive recording agreements between artists and record labels are often complex, lengthy and confusing.

- *Development Deals* are offered to talented vocalists, groups, and bands perceived as having the potential to develop into major recording acts. It's a chance for the artists to professionally develop their talent at the label's expense. The label pays for extra musicians, studio time, audio engineers, tapes, computers and effects equipment, and the producer. If the final master tape is accepted, the act is offered a recording contract. The cost of the recording is recouped through record sales. If it is rejected, the recording is routinely defined as a tax write-off. Some music publishers also offer promising vocalists development deals. The publishers pitch the demo to record labels in exchange for a percentage of the artist' points if and when an artist is signed by a label.[174]

- *Indie Label Deals* range from the major personality driven labels (*Mike Curb/Curb Records, David Geffen/Geffen Records*, as examples), to artist's labels (*Madonna/Maverick Records*) to novice recording artists and musicians. It is another opportunity for many niche artists to be recorded and distributed. Amateur recording artists, musicians, and producers often work together (and share the expenses) to record albums that can be used to promote a band, generate a local buzz, and sell off the bandstand at a live performance. Former major label artists usually retain the names and addresses of their fan club members and then use the lists to sell their self-produced tapes, CDs and digital downloads. Alternative music formats are frequently self-produced on computers and sold at conventions, festivals, church services, digital downloads and concerts. Regional and genre independent record labels sign recording artists who may only have a niche client base in a specific region of the country or genre of music. Examples include Jerry Jeff Walker of Texas, artists on the formerly independent Windham Hill label and bands specializing in Latino music or Carolina Beach music. Major labels offer successful regional and genre labels affiliate status or often buy out the labels to gain the successful recording artists' contracts.[175]

- *Vanity Label (Deals)* are artists who start their own labels, pay all expenses or find an investor to pay for the studio musicians, rental, audio engineer, producer, mastering, marketing, promotion, and pressings and/or downloads. Most vanity recordings lose money because they fail to receive radio station airplay and cannot generate enough sales to cover the production costs. In addition, most are of poor quality and lack promotion, publicity and distribution. However, once and a while, a successful vanity label may become an independent label once consumers "discover" them and start to purchase their recordings over websites or local retail outlets.

---

174 Sometimes, a label will "buy out" the publisher's interest in an artist with a one-time lump sum of money. The publisher (or managers, producers, etc. who discovered and helped develop the act) relinquishes all future rights to the artists and their image in exchange for the negotiated amount of money. Self-proclaimed talent agents work the same way. They find and develop talent and then are "bought out" by the label. However, talent agents who pressure artists to invest their own money are often not considered legitimate by the industry.
175 This happened with GRP Records, Jive Records, Reunion, Rhino, Sparrow, and Windham Hill Records.

- *The Shark Deals*, similar to the song shark deal, are considered a rip-offs. Recording artists should never pay money for a recording contract or deal unless the artist continues to own the master recordings. In addition, if an indie does approach you (the artist) should always confirm that the indie label has distribution set up through a major label or mega entertainment company (Sony Red, as an example) and that it has a budget for promotion (radio airplay) and publicity (trade and popular press publication). If not, pass on the deal, since all they want is your money and they do not have a business model that will allow actual unit sales. Remember, it is the record label that pays the bills, takes the risks and provides tour support money. A legitimate label will cover the cost of recording, pressing of the CDs, etc., and market, promote, and advertise the artists and recordings.[176]

ROYALTY POINTS AND PACKAGING FEES

In the old days a certain percentage of the records would frequently break inside the packages when delivered to the retail outlets. Labels would tell the retail outlets to throw the broken records away and replace them. However, artists were "charged" for the broken records by taking a percentage off of the Suggested Retail List Price used as a royalty base to determine actual royalties. The unscrupulous thing about all of this, of course, is that CDs and digital downloads almost never have any "breakage" problems, yet the labels still use this practice in contracts. Now they simply call it a "packaging fee." As an example, let's say that an artist's royalties are established as 15% of the SRLP of $16.95. The artist would expect to receive about $2.54 for every unit sold. Yet, the breakage or packaging fee reduces that royalty by taking a percentage of between 10-25% off of the SRLP. As an example, let's say the packaging fee is 20%, so the label takes 20% off of the SRLP of $16.95 or (the SRLP of $16.95 minus $3.39). This determines the new royalty base of $13.56, ($16.95-$3.39=$13.56). Then, the label takes 15% (points determined in the contract) of the new adjusted royalty base $13.56 to determine the actual artist's royalties at $2.03. But wait, we are not done yet because most producers are paid producer royalties out of the artist's royalties for producing the album. So, let's say the producer receives 2% (usually between 1-3%), of the artist's royalties, so that reduces the artist's royalty points from 15% to 13%. Thus, the adjusted artist's royalty points of 13% of the adjusted royalty base of $13.56 is really $1.76 per unit sold. The artist thought he/she would receive $2.54 per unit sold, but in reality received $1.76 per unit sold. Also, from an accounting perspective, labels still credit all royalty points to the artist until directed (by the artist) to pay the producer points out of their royalty points.

RECORDING LABEL-RECOUPMENT

The labels use the artist's negotiated royalties to pay the debt of the recording costs, advances, marketing, tour support, and other expenses. A traditional deal calls for the label to pay 50% of music videos and marketing expenses. However, if the label determines these expenses as "tour support" then all bills are 100% recoupable. Sadly, the current business model attempts to pay the entire debt before the artists receive any royalties. Thus, most artists never break-even or receive any royalties. On average, it takes between 75,000 and 200,000 units sold before the labels break-even and about 500,000 (a gold record) units sold before the artist breaks-even. The debt to the labels (say $1,000,000) is paid off by the labels using the full artist's royalties, minus the packaging fee, as in our previous example of $2.03 per unit sold (the figure after the packaging fee and before the producer points have been subtracted). Divide the artist's royalties ($2.03) into the million-dollar debt and you can see that it will take approximately 492,610 units sold before the artist makes his/her first royalties. Then, since the producer points have been directed by the artist to be paid by the label out of the artist royalties, (2% of the new royalty base of $13.56 in our previous example, which totals 27 cents per unit sold), the debt in this case is increased another $133,004.00 (27 cents times the break-even point of 492,610 units).

---

176 Distribution is important for the success of an album. If a label isn't affiliated or connected with a mega entertainment corporation or a major record label, it will have a very hard time placing recordings into retail outlets.

Thus, the label will have to sell about 65,519 additional albums ($2.03 into $133,004.00) before the label has really recouped the total debt. In addition, some labels will use the full artist royalties, (the figure before the packaging fee and producer points are subtracted or $2.54 in our example), and then subtract the packaging fees and producer points later if (and it is a big if), the break-even points are ever reached. It just depends on how the label is running their accounting as determined in the regular and small print of the contact. However, in reality, artists do not owe the label any money (unlike a bank loan) because it is the label that pays off its own debt by applying the artist's royalties to the debt.

MATH FOR ARTIST ROYALTY POINTS

Let us say an artist has 14 points (meaning 14% of the suggested retail list price of $16.95).

Ok, that is $16.95
(Times)   x .14 equals
                 $2.37 on every CD album sold ... Correct? NO!

We forgot the packaging fee which is somewhere in the small print, a packaging fee of 15%.
                 OK, that is $16.95
                 (Times)   x .15 Packaging fee
                 Equals $2.54 (so we have to subtract that from the SRLP of $16.95)

         $16.95 Suggest Retail List Price (SRLP)
         (-)2.54 (Packaging Fee)
Equal $14.41 (which is the new royalty base)

Now things get easy, right! $14.41 (new royalty base)
         (Times the Artist Points)   .14
                 Equal $2.01 on every CD album sold ... Correct? NO!

We forgot the producer points which are also somewhere in the small print (usually 1-3%) which come out of the artist royalties since the artist hired the producer! So
                                 $14.41 New royalty base
                 (Times   x .11 (artist points minus producer points)
                 Equals $1.58 on every CD albums sold... Correct!

Thus, the label will recoup $1.58 per unit sold (apply it to the artist's account).
When the label breaks even then (and only then),
will the artist be paid for each unit sold.

RECORDING LABEL-BREAKEVEN POINTS

The record labels' break-even points are much quicker than the artists. The label receives about 40% of the SRLP from the distribution (minus the artists royalties) or in our example, $6.78 minus the artist's royalties of $1.76 for a total of $5.02. Divide the label's share of $5.02 into the million-dollar debt it created for the artist and you will see that it only takes about 199,000 units sold before it breaks even.

RECORDING LABEL-PROFITS

How much money do record labels make before artists receive any royalties? This is where artists (who do not understand how the business works) go ballistic. Take our example described above with the number of units needed to be sold before our artist would break even (568,000) units. Subtract the number of units the label has to sell before it breaks even (199,000) and the difference is 369,000 units. Take the 369,000 extra units times the record label's income of $5.02 and you can see that if the label sells the extra units it will profit about $1,852,380 before our artist make his/her first dime.

Marketing is the process of planning and executing the development, pricing, promotion and distribution goods and services to achieve organizational goals. Marketing directs the flow of products within an economy from producer to consumer by anticipating and satisfying the wants and needs of the market through the exchange process.

—James E. Finch, Ph.D. author of The Essentials of Marketing Principles[177]

MARKETING PLANS

There are four variables to the marketing mix of most labels which are product, price, promotion/publicity and physical distribution. Finding an artist and the songs that can satisfy the wants and needs of the typical music consumer is the job of the A&R department. Delivering a master recording to the label that will satisfy those consumers emotional wants is the job of the recording team (headed by the producer). Retail is the selling of the recordings (product) to consumers so that the label may make a profit on its financial investments. The Marketing Plan includes the job of the marketing and sales department to expose the right product to the right demographic and psychographic consumer base.

MARKETING PLAN-PRODUCT PLATFORMS

The products that make the labels' money are the recordings they place into retail for sale to the general public. In the past, their business model was limited to the creation and selling of recorded music. However, as the financial world has changed for the label due to P2P (consumers acquiring music without paying for it) the labels are attempting to reinvent their business models to include other revenue streams such as the artist management, concert promotion, merchandise, and corporate sponsorships. Some industry experts claim the CD is dead or quickly dieing in favor of digital downloads as consumers purchase singles instead of albums, in their homes, at a reduced price.

MARKETING PLAN-PRICE

The cost of creating, promoting and marketing recordings seldom determines the suggested retail list or selling price of an album. Consumer demand and profit levels are more important. Wholesale and retail markups between retail outlets and distribution depends on: (a) the type of distribution (retail, department stores/racks, or one-stops); (b) the type of platform the music is recorded on (CDs, DVDs) and (c) the sales propensity of the artists (a hot superstar, a high-ticket item or known artist with current radio airplay) or title albums with recurrent radio station airplay. Record labels determine the suggested retail list price (SRLP), of the CDs, etc., that are placed for sale in various retail outlets. Retailers often ignore the suggested retail list price in favor of their own marketing strategies by offering discounts on some items and raising prices on hot selling, hard-to-find recordings. However, the suggested retail list price is used to determine the wholesale price. Retail outlets use the range (difference) between wholesale (what they paid for the product) and retail (the price they sell for to the public) to generate profits. Accordingly, retail outlets that sell CD's for $16.95 more than likely paid about 60% or approximately $10.17 for the CD. The distributors are paid about 20% or $3.39 and the labels recoup the remaining 40%, or around $6.78 per album.

---

[177] CLEP Principles of Marketing.

INTERNET DIGITAL DOWNLOADS

The Internet has changed the rules of the game when it comes to the music business. Labels actually make more money per unit from digital download than CD sales. Labels make about 70¢ on every 99¢ download, plus they do not have to press CDs, ship them and administrate their Internet website marketing. The downside is that they also sell more singles than albums and therefore the industry is starting to appear much like the entrepreneurial singles businesses of the 1950's and early 60's. However, labels have somehow survived in a market where 51% of their products are acquired without being paid for and they have also had to adapt to new technology, unique delivery systems (iPods and cell phones), and consumer purchasing habits.[178]

MARKETING PLAN-PROMOTION/PUBLICITY

Record promotion is handled as a "campaign" with most of the label's efforts being focused on breaking a new release to radio stations and Internet sites. In addition, the labels often hire independent promoters to motivate local radio station airplay and retail sales. Publicity, which helps drive promotion, is often thought of as free promotion because the artists do not have to pay for the stories, pictures, and articles used in the mass media. Nevertheless, professional publicists who are paid by the label or artist's manager supply most stories to the mass media. The three levels of promotion are national, regional, and local, all of which have their advantages and disadvantages. National ads are expensive and targeted toward several demographic and psychographic types of consumers. Regional ads build support in only a section of the country and the label may therefore miss its true market. Local ads (from the free press to posters on local telephone poles) are usually poorly produced and sometimes do not generate an increase in consumers' purchases, yet they can start word-of-mouth conversations leading to a buzz about a new act. Labels also provide tour support through financial advances in order to place the act on the road (shows) which are considered events that provide endless opportunities to create radio airplay, fan hype/conversations, and word of mouth publicity that is all tied to the artist's shameless self promotion. Of course, this is the label's effort to increase consumer excitement and bottom-line product/album and digital profits by raising the level of consumer awareness and motivation to purchase products. Before 360 deals, labels would rarely receive any money from the merchandise purchased by fans at the concert. Now, it is almost always part of the recording deal and will probably soon include other event sources of income such as ticket sale profits and corporate sponsorship endorsements. Note that product distribution, promotion and publicity usually occur at the same time as the street release of the recording or album which is designed into the label's marketing plan.

Promotion in the music business is about providing a "sample" of the recordings that are for sale. Thus, it usually includes the following:

- *Radio*-According to **Billboard Magazine** and **Cable Yearbook** there are about 90 radio formats on the 12,000 plus, AM and FM radio stations in the United States. **Billboard Magazine** charts the 17 most popular which includes every type of format from top 40 to rap/hip-hop to country. Each format is charted and then the various charts are combined into the two main charts which are (a), The Hot 100, which ranks the top selling singles and radio airplay songs in the nation (based on soundscan for retail sales and BDS-Broadcast Data Systems for airplay), and (b), The Billboard 200 which lists the top 200 selling albums nationally based on actual soundscan and other reporting methods.

---

178 According to the RIAA, Digital Summit, Belmont University Spring 2007.

> **OUCH!!!!!!!**
> There are more than 20 billion illegal downloads annually or about 55 million per day or over 2 million per hour. Just think if you where the label, artist, music publisher or songwriter and you had lost all those royalties!

Radio stations and networks are not in the music business, indeed, they are in the advertisement business, so they program whatever they think will draw an audience in order to charge for the airtime (advertisements). Companies purchase advertisement airtime based on the demographics and psychograpics of cumulative audiences tied to the their lifestyles (62 nationally) and the products or services advertisers are trying to sell them. Radio is still important to labels as a method to break new artists and new releases from established acts. Of course, internet social websites and samples on iTunes and other download sites are also important. Labels have downsized their radio promotion departments and increased the emphasis on internet and cell phone promotions which is where many in the Y generation discover their new favorite acts. In addition, many consumers now discover their new acts and releases from illegal p2p downloading sites instead of radio.

Labels still have national radio promotion positions that control local and territorial (streets) promotion whose job is to increase radio station airplay of the latest releases. However, many stations are now owned by one of three conglomerates that control and program stations from a national broadcast location. Thus, it has become much more difficult to break new acts and place established acts on major radio station chains unless a certain amount of corresponding advertisements are purchased. Just as the music and entertainment industry are changing so is radio. Automation of programing is now commonplace, however stations are developing HD-radio, more internet transmission options and cellphone delivery systems in addition to the merger of XM and Sirius Satellite digital radio. Examples of radio chains include:

- *Clear Channel Radio* has more than 110 million listeners each week in all the nation's major radio markets. Its programming is available on AM/FM stations, HD digital radio channels, the Internet, via iPods and cell phones and is used via navigation systems on cars and location systems such as TomTom, and Garmin. The company's operations include radio broadcasting, syndication and independent media representation. Clear Channel Radio is a division of Clear Channel Communications, Inc. (NYSE:CCU), a leading global media and entertainment company.[179]

- *Cox Radio* is one of the largest radio companies in the United States based on revenues. Upon the completion of all announced transactions, Cox Radio will own, operate or provide sales or marketing services for 86 stations (71 FM and 15 AM) clustered in 19 markets, including major markets such as Atlanta, Houston, Miami, Orlando, San Antonio and Tampa.[180]

- *NPR (National Public Radio)* is an internationally acclaimed producer and distributor of noncommercial news, talk, and entertainment programming. A privately supported, not-for-profit membership organization, NPR serves a growing audience of 26 million Americans each week in partnership with more than 860 independently operated, noncommercial public radio stations. Each NPR Member Station serves local listeners with a distinctive combination of national and local programming.[181]

---

179 http://nab365.bdmetrics.com/NST-9-50080117/Clear-Channel-Radio-s-Total-Traffic-Network-Continues-to-Be-Real-Time-Traffic-Provider-of-Choice-in-Navigation-Devices.aspx
180 http://nab365.bdmetrics.com/NST-9-50080118/Cox-Radio-Reports-Second-Quarter-2008-Financial-Results.aspx
181 http://www.npr.org/about/

- *Advertisements* in the trade magazines (Billboard, Gavin, Variety, and others), and the popular press consisting of popular magazines (People Magazine as an example), national and local newspapers (USA-Today), and various web sites.
- *Music Videos*-MTV (MTV1, 2, etc.,), and VH-1, are worldwide brand names that still have a problem getting consumers to watch videos. However, videos are still a very quick way to break new acts into the market. Music videos used to account for about 14% of sales many years ago, now it is questionable if any additional units are sold because of the corresponding video.
- *Internet and Cell Phones*-Radio streaming and downloads are quickly becoming a new distribution method for labels and artists promotions. Most labels are also using the social websites to promote and sell established and new artists.

Publicity is about telling consumers the story behind the artist(s) and their image. While promotion provides a sample of what the labels have for sale (recordings), publicity tells the consumers why they should like and enjoy the artists and their corresponding recordings. The hope is that consumers will see the artists as a hero, villain, good old boy, sexy) and use the images for their own self-enjoyment based on sub-conscience self-definition or self-elaboration. Therefore, publicity from the labels' perspective includes:

- *Stories and interviews*-planted in the trades, popular press, mass and click media.
- *Appearances*-on TV talk shows (i.e., Jay Leno, David Letterman, Good Morning America, etc.) and the stories, pictures, and articles publicists provide the click media, local newspapers, national trade and consumer magazines.
- *Tour Support*-by the labels provide the artists with an opportunity to conduct a national tour of concerts (events). The concerts or events provide radio stations, promotions, the mass media and click media to talk about the act and the tour which tends to reinforce the mouth to mouth buzz by consumers (fans) and the end result of increased record sales.
- *Internet and Cell Phones*-are used for providing the backfill stories of the acts' image tied to their career events (success) tied to the latest recording releases and tours. The key is to provide the promotion, publicity, and distribution to retail at the same time so that the act can be discovered, heard and seen by consumers who will hopefully purchase the recordings (and tour tickets, merchandise, etc.,) based on an increased awareness of an emotional excitement and connection to the artists.

MARKETING PLAN-PLACEMENT/DISTRIBUTION

Once the master tapes have been accepted and pressed into consumer products, the distribution division ships the CDs, to wholesalers, including rack jobbers, one-stops, mass merchandisers, chain stores, and TV packagers. Label distribution provides products directly to record clubs. iTunes.com and musicnet.com are the plumbers that connect the label's digital products to Internet websites and consumers. Mega distributors include *Sony/BMG, CEMA (EMI products), UNI (Vivendi/Universal), and WEA (TimeWarner)*.[182] In the past, the traditional retail outlets for the recording business have been the following:

- *One-Stops* are the brick and mortar stores and the Mom and Pop record stores that are now mostly out of business or bankrupted. They simply cannot compete with the much lower economies of scale of digital downloads.[183]

---

182 Warner Music is not part of TimeWarner.
183 Examples include Tower Records and Sam Goodies.

- *Mass Merchandisers* which are for example, Best Buy and Circuit City that place the CDs and DVDs in the middle of the store and price them low in order to draw in customers and then encourage them to purchase a large ticket item such as a computer, LCD Television or home appliance.

- *Rack Jobbers* such as *Anderson* supply *Wal-Mart*, *K-Mart* and *Target* with CDs, racks in the stores, rent the floor space and pay a small commission on each unit sold. Unlike the One-Stops with their large inventory and slow turnover (and therefore higher prices), rack jobbers have a smaller inventory of mostly hits and fast moving recordings that will sell quickly at a lower price.

- *Record Clubs* have been one of the best kept secrets in the business as they have often been used to unload overstocked items. The CDs are sold at higher prices, (after the discounted membership units which are used as a tax write-off by the labels), the customer pays the distribution cost (shipping and handling) and artists usually only receive 50% of their royalties which is an industry standard. Columbia House and BMG Direct which are owned by the megas have quickly moved into digital downloads.

- Marketers attempt to sell the unsaleable late at night through advertisements using *Television PI Advertising*. Older consumers who do not shop in record stores or on-line still buy old recordings that seem to stimulate fond memories of their youth. Television and cable systems play the advertisements when they have unsold air or broadcast time available. They are then paid a small percent of the money consumers send in when they buy the products.

DIGITAL MUSIC DISTRIBUTION
Click media retail outlets are quickly gaining more of the retail sales through digital distribution.

- *Internet websites* such as *iTunes.com, Amazon.com, AOL.com, etc.*, and most of the record labels' supportive websites are quickly becoming the place for consumers to download music. As the Internet sites increase sales quickly, the older brick and mortar chain stores are financially failing and the mass merchandisers are using recorded music as a way to draw customers into their stores.

- *Cell Phones* are quickly adding to digital downloads, as they do not require the device to be hooked to a computer. The iPhone is the future of cell phones as it merges the iPod to the cell phone and Internet.

- *Satellite Direct Distribution* to TVs, the Internet, and G3 phone systems was launched in 2008 by *BskyB* in England. The company offers streaming music, plus downloads for a monthly subscription fee.

The Entertainment Business is a Business!

Many famous people in the music and entertainment industry have gotten into financial trouble and had to file for bankruptcy. It can happen to anyone, yet having the understanding of business concepts may help you avoid what others have created for themselves. Famous entertainment personalities who have had to file include; P.T. Barnum (circus owner), John Barrymore (actor), Kim Basinger (actress), Frank Baum (author of the Wizard of Oz), Mick Fleetwood ("Fleetwood Mac"), Toni Braxton (recording artists), David Crosby (singer and songwriter), Samuel L. Clemens (better known as author Mark Twain), and Walt Disney (film producer and theme park creator/owner).

Source-The Law Offices of R.J.Atkinson,LLC-

TOP RETAIL OUTLETS

Retail outlets are quickly changing as brick and motors are disappearing. Thus, iTunes is now the leading retail outlet for all purchased music. Wal-Mart follows with Best Buy coming in third. However, more change is on the way as digital downloads of singles are replacing the CD albums. Consumers want singles while labels want to sell albums as they are more profitable. Therefore, we are headed back to the future as the business in the 1950's was about selling singles instead of albums to teenagers who for the first time in history had free time and money.

"DRM's haven't worked, and may never work."
—**Steve Jobs**[184]

DIGITAL RIGHTS MANAGEMENT (DRM)

DRM is a copyright lock technology that has been used by the major record labels on CDs and digital download platforms to restrict the use of and copying of downloaded music to specific types of players. As an example, iTunes downloads could only be used on iPods, not on PC players and SanDisks. However, Apple dropped DRM years ago and now all of the major labels are dropping it in order to offer recordings for sale through digital distributors such as Amazon.com, Musicnet.com, and Realnetwork's Rhapsody.com. This allows purchased MP3 downloads to be played on any type of player.

"The rapid pace of our growth is humbling and exciting for us." "As we celebrate our 250 millionth user, we are continuing to develop Facebook to serve as many people in the world in the most effective way possible. This means reaching out to everyone across the world."
—**Mark Zuckerberg, founder of Facebook.com**[185]

SYNERGY OF INTERNET SOCIAL WEBSITE DISTRIBUTION

Internet social clubs/websites such as *www.myspace.com, www.facebook.com, www.ilike.com, www.bebo.com, www.twitter.com* and many others are becoming one of the main avenues for major labels as well as independent artists to sell their products. Members are allowed to sample and purchase the products bypassing *Amazon.com* and the other sites. In June of 2009, *Facebook* had 250 million unique visitors and 50.6 billion page views worldwide, according to the research firm *ComScore*. *MySpace*, meanwhile, has almost 250 million unique visitors and 45.4 billion page views. *Facebook.com*, founded in California in 2004 by *Mark Zuckerberg*, is the most popular online social networking service. Investors include *Microsoft* (a deal valued at $15 billion), venture capitalist *Peter Thiel*, and *Digital Sky Technologies* a Russian company. *Facebook* has its growing popularity outside the country. In the United States, however, *MySpace* is still on top and pulls in twice as many visitors as its main competition on a monthly basis. *MySpace* gets more than 70 million visits from U.S. Web surfers in a typical month.[186] *Twitter* has about 23 million users according to *Forrester Research* who also claims that there is about 1.5 billion internet users today and which should increase to about 2.2 billion by 2013.[187]

SYNERGY OF DIGITAL DISTRIBUTION-CELL PHONES

The combination of Internet technology to cell phones is creating a new distribution business model for music and entertainment products. *Apple's iPhone* with *AT&T* links the *iTunes store* to the digital distribution of music, movies, TV shows, radio broadcast and other forms of entertainment. Apple has sold over 6 billion songs since its kickoff in 2003.[188] In addition, *Rhapsody* has signed an MP3 distribution deal with Verizon that links *Rhapsody's* 5 million songs per day sales to all 3-G, V-Cast cell

---

184 Pugatch, M., The Economics of DRM in Capitalist Markets, Intellectual Property, Vol. 3, Issue 2 - February 2007
185 www.Telegraph.uk June 2009
186 WashingtonPost.com 2008.
187 Tweetering all the way to the bank, Economists.com July 2009.
188 Taking Wraps of the New Rhapsody, BusinessWeek.com June 30, 2008.

phone downloads.[189]

SYNERGY OF LEGAL AND FREE DIGITAL DISTRIBUTION

Advertisement based websites are attempting to offer free downloads in exchange for advertisement's mental impressions. *SpiralFrog.com* and *Qtrax.com* are two sites striving to establish legal and free music download based on advertising hits (viewers/impressions) per thousand. Advertisers pay for the site expenses, profit, and downloads based on the number of viewers who use the site for music downloads. We7 (and others like it) offer multiple distribution options and methods of purchase. Downloads are free if you accept the advertisements that terminate after a 30-60 day period. You may also purchase the music downloads without the advertisements. Several additional websites are offering free TV shows and movies with very limited advertisement interruptions. *Hulu.com* is a joint venture between *NBC-TV* and the *Fox Network*. *Discovery.com, Cartoonnetwork.com, ABC.com,* and *Joost.com* also offer free programs through advertisement impressions.

LABEL-ADMINISTRATION

The ***Chairperson of the Board or Chief Executive Officer*** commonly heads the label, provides and meets with external business opportunities and contacts, and reports earnings figures and strategic management decisions to the parenting mega executive board (of which they are a member). The President generally provides a vision of operation to the label and oversees the internal daily operations of the label. Vice-Presidents supervise their departments and are responsible for individual area employees and the successful completion of departmental tasks and goals.

The label ***CEO, President, and Vice Presidents*** work together, after the initial signing of an act, to suggest a producer, establish a budget, and develop a marketing plan for the act. A strategic allegiance is usually established with the artist's manager. It is notable that the manager must be careful not to let his or her associations with the label's executives become a conflict of interest with the recording artists they represent.[119] Upper level administrators are responsible for the development and implementation of a strategic management plan. This includes the development of a vision and mission statement, short and long-term personal and financial goals, the organization's internal policies and objectives, and the responsibility of a continuous internal and external analysis.[120]

Administrators review the sales projections and accomplishments of each of the labels' recording artists and personnel. Artists failing to achieve profitable unit sales are customarily dropped from the label after the first few poor selling record releases. The label fulfills their contractual obligations for the commitment albums and then simply does not pick up the artist's option. Artists who are not satisfied with a label may in rare cases "buyout" of their contract by mutual agreement, in one lump sum payment, or future artist royalties generated from projected album sales. However, successful artists often find it very difficult to terminate a current agreement. Court action is often required and rarely approved. Obviously, major labels have spent millions to make an artist successful and they do not appreciate an artist who wants to jump to another label after the hard work and money has been invested to make the artist famous.

DEPARTMENTS

In addition, *label employees* who fail to sign or generate profitable products or sales are encouraged to improve or leave. After continued declines in profits, both productive and non-productive employees are usually dismissed. It is not uncommon for the entire staff of a major label to be replaced for not producing profitable acts and recordings.

189 Ibid, and 3-G being a advanced download digital technology.

- ***The Legal Department*** is responsible for writing, negotiating, and (a) signing songwriters or their songs, (b) signing co-publishing deals, (c) signing new and returning recording artists, (d) signing label employees' government forms, (e) negotiating mechanical, performance, sync, and other licenses with domestic and foreign agencies, and (f) representing the label in legal actions. Accordingly, attorneys negotiate the "terms of agreement" between the creative and business sub-system players of this creative business. Once again it is creativity battling business principles. Most labels have one or more attorneys on retainer, which is a monthly stipend for their part-time employment.

- ***Royalty/Payroll Department*** pays the bills and royalties, accepts sales payments, and reviews artist's recoupment. Financial experts control the flow of money in the labels' and artists' accounts. Most expenses are billed to the artists' accounts and are recouped through album sales. This concept called recoupment is a standard practice in the business that helps the label make millions before the average artist makes their first royalties. Accountants add the recording costs and label expenses (artist development, photography, tour support, and most of the marketing, promotion, etc.) to the recording artist's ledger. Artist royalties are paid only after the negotiated label expenses for the recording, marketing of the album, and all additional expenses (tour support, etc.) have been repaid from unit sales. Artists are regularly supplied quarterly or semi-annual profit and loss statements through their manager.

- ***Artists and Repertoire*** (better known as A&R) is the communicative link between the label's creative and business sub-systems. It brings the acts to the label and administers the paperwork of an album project. Accordingly, A&R is often divided into two sections, creative and administrative. Creative A&R is the "ears" of the label, always searching for a new act or song that will help make the label (and themselves) more profitable. It is not an easy job. Between a half million to one million dollars are spent on "breaking" a new recording artist, however, the actual cost generally depends on the type of artist, the genre of music, and the type and size of the target audience. Label decisions about which acts and songs to sign are often based on research, past experiences, gut instincts, and consumer reaction. The profitability and survival of the label depends on their decisions. To avoid being a casualty of a poor decision, many labels make their "final" signing decision by committee consensus. The committee consists of the label vice presidents of each department, an A&R person presenting the act and the label's president and/or chairman of the board. The purpose is to involve everyone as a team to campaign for the signing of the artist and then to work together for the successful selling of their respective recordings. Thus, the final decision to sign an act is generally a "company decision" with the final decision being made by the CEO, President, and Vice Presidents based on the recommendation of the committee and support from all of the label employees.

A&R departments also act as an administrative facilitator between the creative and business sub-systems of the label. Songwriters create songs, musicians and vocalist record demos, and then writers pitch the tapes to music publishers. Publishers pitch the songs to A&R. Songs selected by A&R are evaluated for album projects and pitched to the recording production team, consisting of the producer, artist, and artist's manager. In pre-production, the recording artist, producer, artist's manager, and A&R representative determine which songs, musicians, and recording studio to use. After the final master recording, the accepted master tapes are converted into consumer products (platforms) such as CDs and digital downloads and distributed, marketed, and promoted through the mass media, cell phones and Internet sites to generate sales.

A typical label's ***Development Department*** is often divided into three sections: ***Creative, Artist***, and ***Product Development***:

- ***Creative Development*** activates the executive's choice of which songs will be used on videos (by commissioning video storyboards), supervises the label's marketing plan and scripts for the artist. They supervise the script treatments, budgets, production, and provide the finished videos to the marketing department for promotion.

- ***Artist Development's*** task is to help or hire specialists to improve the artist's image, appearance, demeanor, and public personality. A sellable product (a recording) has to be created and the artist's image frequently has to be enhanced. Trainers are hired to help the artist control a weight and/or drug problem, dentists to improve the smile, and stylists to suggest various types of cosmetics, clothing, and hairstyles for concert, stage, TV, and/or movie appearances. Image consultants are hired to suggest methods to help the act appear comfortable and confident on stage and with the news media.

- ***Product Development*** supervises and coordinates the development of the label's actual album projects through each department and each stage of the marketing, promotion, publicity, and distribution process.

- ***Sales Department*** totals weekly sales figures and also places co-op adds (advertisements) and *end caps* with products at retail. The ***marketing and sales*** department makes sure that CDs are placed into retail stores and Internet websites (street date), and that point-of-purchase promotions are available.

- ***Free goods*** to the retail outlets (distribution) are used to stimulate rack stocking and potential sales of new artists and releases.

- ***Promotional copies*** are different as they are not to be sold and are used by the marketing and promotion departments to provide a "sample" of the releases that are for sale at retail. Thus, promotional copies are provided free to radio stations, TV interview shows such as *Lettermen* and *Leno*, and are used to encourage and fill the local papers and magazines with stories about the label's artists (publicity).

THE RECORDING INDUSTRY ASSOCIATION OF AMERICA (RIAA)
www.riaa.org

The *RIAA* is the trade group that represents the U.S. recording industry. Its mission is to foster a business and legal climate that supports and promotes its members' creative and financial vitality. Its members are the record companies that comprise the most vibrant national music industry in the world. RIAA members create, manufacture and/or distribute approximately 90% of all legitimate sound recordings produced and sold in the United States. In support of this mission, the RIAA works to protect intellectual property rights worldwide and the First Amendment rights of artists; conducts consumer, industry and technical research; and monitors and reviews state and federal laws, regulations and policies. The RIAA® also certifies Gold®, Platinum®, Multi-Platinum™, and Diamond sales awards, as well as Los Premios De Oro y Platino™, an award celebrating Latin music sales.[190]

---

190 www.RIAA.com

THE INTERNATIONAL FEDERATION OF THE PHONOGRAPHIC INDUSTRY (IFPI)
www.ifpi.org

The *IFPI* represents the recording industry worldwide, with a membership comprising some 1400 record companies in 73 countries and affiliated industry associations in 48 countries. IFPI's mission is to promote the value of recorded music, safeguard the rights of record producers and expand the commercial uses of recorded music in all markets where its members operate.[191]

PIRACY
Both the RIAA and the IFPI work daily on the problems of piracy in the world music market. Examples of the problem include:

- 1 in 3 pre-recorded CD's sold are illegal or pirated copies.

- 4.5 billion dollars lost to labels, publishers, songwriters, and creative artists.

- There are more than 20 billion illegal downloads annually or about 55 million per day or over 2 million per hour.[192]

---

191 http://www.ifpi.org/
192 Ibid.

SUMMARY

Mega entertainment companies have controlled most of the world's film and music industry for the past 50 years. TimeWarner, Sony, EMI, Bertelsmann, and Universal are the current megas after many years of mergers and buyouts. The Walt Disney Company is now also considered a mega by landing the number one album in 2007, (High School Musical) and by its promotion of music and film promotion through its in-house TV and radio networks. Megas' business models are in house controlled financial structures from the creation of entertainment products to the distribution, promotion, and publicity and unit sales figures. The megas' have division where as the labels' financial and administrative structures are divided into departments.

However, because of P2P file sharing most of the mega's have sold or downsized their music business publishing and labels to individual investors or companies. Warner Music, Universal, Sony/BMG, and EMI and their hundreds of worldwide labels are considers major record labels. Other types of labels include affiliates, independents, vanity, internet-based labels, and product branding labels. There are several types of deals depending on the types of labels and of course, the 360 deals which combine all three industry revenue streams in order to help the label counter financial losses from illegal peer to peer file sharing.

Having musical and vocal talent does not guarantee a hit recording. Consequently, A &R directors seek the types of acts who not only have talent, but who can also sell records through a clearly defined image. There is a difference, and record labels make and lose millions of dollars each year on which acts connect with the music-buying public. Recordings are actually packages consisting of great songs that fit the image and persona of the artists supported by an excellent vocal and musical performance by the artists and musicians. Accordingly, A&R employees often risk their careers on the acts and songs they sign. Successful acts establish the credibility of the A&R person who signed them. Failures can cost them their jobs. Successful signing provides additional record producing opportunities. Album productions enhance an A&R person's status as a record producer within the company and industry. Multiple successful deals and session productions (with the corresponding gold and platinum records) make the A&R producer a powerful, very rich individual, often famous within the industry.

Labels create recordings they hope to sell to the public. Major labels use their own music publishing companies to promote and place their own songs with their signed artists. Most songs selected for album projects are funneled through the label's A&R department. Mechanical royalties are paid at the controlled composition rate of 75% of the statutory rate and are literary paid from one pocket of the company (label) to another pocket (publishing) keeping all expenses in-house. Foreign performance royalties are collected by world situated performance rights organizations and shared internally by patriarchal labels and music publishing companies. Sync rights are often reduced or paid between the TV and movie production companies within the same mega entertainment corporation, once again keeping expenses within the same corporate organization and profits higher.[193]

Of course, non-mega/major label published songs are often accepted. Songs are first considered on their "hit potential qualities," not on who owns the copyright. However, most record labels apply "pressure" to the non-major label or non-mega-affiliated publishing company to accept the controlled composition clause. If accepted, the label saves money by paying only 75% of the statutory rate and the writers or

---

[193] Foreign countries have their own performance rights organizations that collect blanket royalties such as SOCAN in Canada.

publishers often are faced with reduced royalties. It is a hard decision as a major artist may sell millions and spark performance royalties in radio airplay compared to the song not being recorded at all or by a lesser known artist who will accept the full statutory rate per unit, yet not generate as much money due to less airplay and fewer album sales. After the master tape is recorded and accepted by the label, a marketing plan that coordinates publicity, promotion, distribution, and sales is activated. The sales and marketing department coordinates the label's efforts to assure a successful launch of the product in retail markets.

The Promotion and Publicity Department coordinates the label's promotion efforts for radio airplay, free 30-second clips on iTunes and other websites and advertisements in the trade and popular press. At the same time, Publicity works on placement of stories in the trades and popular press, scheduled TV and radio talk show appearances, website homepages on www.myspace.com and www.facebook.com and co-op ads and stories in approved tour dates media.

Digital music sold on-line to consumers is creating huge profits for the music industry. It has added a new and exciting method for consumers to acquire music quickly. Record labels actually make more money from each song/album sold because they are cutting out the distribution and retail outlets, record stores, TV outlets, and record clubs' percentage of the purchasing price. Thus, the industry allows consumers to acquire their music the same way they have at traditional retail outlets, plus through the Internet music web sites (iTunes as an example) so consumers can purchase music in a quicker, less expensive, more convenient manner. Cell phones are adding to the mix by providing music download capabilities along with TV shows and movies.

STUDY GUIDE-LABELS

1. Explain why Courtney Love was so upset with her label. Do you think the label was wrong? Does she understand how labels make their money based on providing money to creative artists? Does she understand the business? Explain.

2. List the six mega entertainment corporations and there "host" countries.

   (a)

   (b)

   (c)

   (d)

   (e)

   (f)

3. Describe three *Entertainment Distribution Corporations* that control much of the world's distribution of entertainment products.

   (a)

   (b)

   (c)

4. What are the differences between a *360 Music Entertainment Corporation* and a typical record label?

5. List and explain the six different types of record labels.

   (a)

   (b)

   (c)

   (d)

   (e)

   (f)

6. What are five things typical record labels must do to have a shot at being successful? Explain each.

   (a)

   (b)

   (c)

   (d)

   (e)

7. What should recording artists look for in a label?

8. Write the formula for determining an artist true royalties per unit sold.

9. Determine the actual royalty figure (amount of money an artist will receive per unit sold) on a $18.95 SRLP album released through traditional distribution, with the artist receiving 16 points, with a 15% packaging fee, and the producer receives 3 royalties points.

10. Determine the amount of money a label will receive (minus the artists royalties) per unit sold on a $18.95 SRLP album released through traditional distribution (a 40/20/40 percent split)?

11. What are the break-even points for the artist (question 9) and the label (question 10), if the total debt in the artists' recoupable account is $1,000,000?

  (a) Artist

  (b) Label

12. Using the math from question 11, how much money did the label make before the artist's breaks-even (recoups)?

13. Define the four types of label promotions
  (a)

  (b)

  (c)

  (d)

14. Define the four types of publicity used by labels.
  (a)

  (b)

  (c)

  (d)

15. List the five types of traditional record labels' retail distribution.

   (a)

   (b)

   (c)

   (d)

   (e)

16. List the three types of digital retail distribution.

   (a)

   (b)

   (c)

17. List the top 4 retail outlets for recorded music.

   (a)

   (b)

   (c)

   (d)

18. What is *digital rights management* and who is beginning to drop their usage?

19. Explain the synergy of digital music distribution through social websites, cell phones, and advertisement sponsored/free sites.

20. List and explain the four P's of marketing related to the record label business.

   (a)

   (b)

   (c)

   (d)

21. Explain the administrative structure of a typical record label.

22. Explain the function of the following typical label departments:

   (a) Legal

   (b) Royalty/Payroll

   (c) Artists and Repertoire (A&R)

   (d) Development

       Creative

       Artists

       Product

   (e) Marketing and Sales

23. What is the difference between free goods and promotional copies?

24. Who are the RIAA and the IFPI? Whom do they represent?

25. Why is radio still important to the music business?

Lecture Points
Chapter Seven

CORPORATE STRUCTURE

STOCKHOLDERS OF THE LABEL'S PARENT COMPANY

CHAIRMAN AND THE BOARD OF PARENT COMPANY

PRESIDENT OF THE RECORD COMPANY

LABEL PRESIDENT

DEPARTMENT VICE-PRESIDENTS

LABEL DEPARTMENTS

INTERNAL OPERATIONS

FINANCE

DISTRIBUTION

MANUFACTURING

Lecture Points
Chapter Seven

SALES

INTERNATIONAL

PUBLISHING

PRODUCTION

VIDEO

MERCHANDISING AND MARKETING

PROMOTION

ADVERTISING

PUBLICITY

172

ARTIST DEVELOPMENT

Lecture Points
Chapter Seven

A&R - ARTISTS AND REPERTOIRE - Administrative & Creative

LEGAL AFFAIRS

BUSINESS AFFAIRS

MAJOR LABELS VERSES INDEPENDENTS

MAJOR LABELS

INDEPENDENT LABELS

A & R, Record deals,

A&R - ARTISTS AND REPERTOIRE

Lecture Points
Chapter Seven

ADMINISTRATIVE - CREATIVE

TRADITIONAL RECORD DEALS

RECORDING DEVELOPMENT DEAL

PUBLISHING DEVELOPMENT DEAL

MAJOR RECORD DEAL

INDEPENDENT LABEL DEAL

VANITY LABEL DEAL

THE SHARK DEAL

Lecture Points
Chapter Seven

THE SIX NEW TYPES OF DEALS

THE 360-DEAL

STANDARD DISTRIBUTION DEAL

LICENSE DEAL

PROFIT-SHARING DEAL

MANUFACTURING AND DISTRIBUTION DEAL

SELF-DISTRIBUTION

Lecture Points
Chapter Seven

HOW TO PRESENT YOUR DEMO TAPE

WHY DEMOS GET REJECTED

HOW MANY SHOULD I SEND

WHICH GOES FIRST

WHAT NOT TO SEND

CUE IT UP

LYRIC SHEET

GIVE EM' NOTICE

THE COVER LETTER

Lecture Points
Chapter Seven

STARTING YOUR OWN INDEPENDENT LABEL

SMALL IS BEAUTIFUL

DIVERSITY

DISTRIBUTION IS CONSOLIDATING

TECHNOLOGY

NEW LABEL CHECKLIST

GREAT MUSIC

BUSINESS SMARTS

PERSEVERANCE

Chapter Seven Notes

Chapter Seven Notes

Chapter Seven Notes

THE RECORDING DEAL

SAMPLE RECORDING CONTRACT

The following is a sample recording contract provided by entertainment attorney *Rush Hicks*. After reading it, you will understand why it is important to review any contract offered with an attorney before you sign.

> *EXCLUSIVE means that you can record for this label only. If you want to make a guest appearance with another artist on their label, you have to get permission from your label.*

EXCLUSIVE RECORDING ARTIST AGREEMENT

This EXCLUSIVE RECORDING ARTIST AGREEMENT (this "Agreement") is made and entered into as of _____, by and between _____, whose address is _____ ___ _____ ("Company") and _____ ("you"), whose address is _____.

1. EXCLUSIVE SERVICES.

Company hereby engages your exclusive personal services as a recording artist in connection with the production of Records and you hereby accept such engagement and agree to exclusively render such services for Company in the Territory during the Term and all extensions and renewals thereof. (You are sometimes called "Artist" below).

> *TERM is how long the contract is for. It consists of the initial period (which is usually one year or one album), followed by 4-6 option periods for a total of 7 albums. The artist grants the label the right to exercise the option periods (see section C), however, if the label declines, then the artist is dropped from the label.*

2. TERM.

(a) The term of this Agreement shall consist of an "Initial Period" and the "Option Periods" set forth below as may be exercised by Company pursuant hereto.

(b) The "Initial Period" shall commence on the date hereof and shall end on the date that is twelve (12) months after Delivery and acceptance by Company of the Recording Commitment (as defined below) for the Initial Period.

(c) You hereby grant to us four (4) separate, consecutive and irrevocable options, each to extend the Term

for additional contract periods (each herein called an "Option Period") upon the same terms and conditions applicable to the Initial Period, except as otherwise provided herein. Each such Option Period shall run consecutively beginning on the expiration of the Initial Period or the previous Option Period, as the case may be, and shall end on the date twelve (12) months after Delivery and acceptance by Company of the Recording Commitment for such Option Period. The Initial Period and the Option Periods are sometimes referred to herein as "Contract Periods", as the same may be suspended or extended as provided herein. Company shall exercise each such option by notice to you at any time prior to the expiration of the then current Contract Period.
(d) Notwithstanding anything to the contrary contained in paragraph 2(a)-(c), if, as of the date when the current Contract Period would otherwise have expired, Company has neither exercised its option to extend the Term for a further Contract Period nor notified you that Company does not wish to exercise such option, then: (i) you shall immediately notify Company that its option has not yet been exercised (an "Option Warning"); (ii) Company shall be entitled to exercise its option at any time before receiving the Option Warning or within ten (10) business days thereafter; and (iii) the current Contract Period shall be deemed to have continued until Company exercises its option or until the end of such ten business day period (whichever shall occur first).

3. RECORDING COMMITMENT/DELIVERY.
(a) During each Contract Period you shall record and Deliver to Company sufficient Masters to constitute the Record specified in the following schedule (the "Recording Commitment"):

> *THE RECORDING COMMITMENT is what the label is really agreeing to pay for. Thus, this may be a five year deal with 5 albums, but what the label is really committed to fund is the first album which is only offered during the initial period and then each option if and when the label decides to pick them up. Therefore, the publicity in the trades and newspapers may have a story about an act signing a multi-million dollar deal over several years, but what it really means is a one year or one album deal with the possibility of additional albums (one at a time) and years (one at a time) if (and that is a big if) sales are profitable for the label to pick up the option.*

CONTRACT PERIOD	RECORDING COMMITMENT
Initial Period	One Album (the "First Album")
First Option Period	One Album (the "Second Album")
Second Option Period	One Album (the "Third Album")
Third Option Period	One Album (the "Fourth Album")
Fourth Option Period	One Album (the "Fifth Album")

(b) (i) The First Album shall be Delivered to Company within ninety (90) days following commencement of the Initial Period; (ii) the Recording Commitment in respect of each Option Period shall be Delivered to Company within ninety (90) days following commencement of the applicable Option Period; and (iii) unless an authorized officer of Company shall otherwise agree in writing, and without limiting any of the other provisions herein, you shall not Deliver any Album within nine (9) months following the date of the initial commercial release of the immediately preceding Album in the United States. If any Recording Commitment is Delivered between October 15th and December 31st of a particular year, then Delivery of the Recording Commitment concerned will be deemed to have occurred on January 2nd of the succeeding year.
(c) No multiple Albums, "theme" Masters (e.g., Christmas Masters), "live" performances, instrumental-Masters, joint recordings or spoken-word Masters shall be recorded or Delivered hereunder in satisfaction of the Recording Commitment without Company's prior written consent, which may be withheld in Company's sole discretion; provided however, if Company consents to the Delivery of a multiple Album

hereunder, then such multiple Album shall be deemed a single Album for the purposes of Artist's Delivery obligations under this Agreement. If Artist Delivers and Company accepts Masters consisting of "theme", "live", instrumental, joint or spoken-word recordings, then such Masters shall not be deemed to be in partial or complete fulfillment of any of Artist's obligations hereunder.

(d) During the Term, Company shall have one (1) option ("Greatest Hits Sides Option"), to require Artist to record and Deliver up to two (2) Sides recorded after Company's exercise of such Greatest Hits Sides Option (the "New Greatest Hits Masters"). Each such New Greatest Hits Master shall embody a Composition not previously recorded by Artist and shall be intended for initial release on a "Greatest Hits" or "Best Of" Album (a "Greatest Hits Album"). Artist shall Deliver such New Greatest Hits Masters no later than sixty (60) days after Company's exercise of the Greatest Hits Sides Option. New Greatest Hits Masters shall not be deemed to fulfill any of Artist's obligations hereunder with respect to Recording Commitments.

> *THE RECORDING PROCEDURE describes the process step by step of what the artist is expected to accomplish so that master tapes can be created and delivered to the label. Many artists today are being asked to develop a sample budget, assist the label in hiring a producer, acquiring licenses approvals and clearances for songs (mechanicals) and union artists (AF of M musicians and AFTRA singers), for the recording sessions. The label has final approval of all budgets, hiring, studio rentals, dates, and expenses. This is a great example of when the artist must understand business and money.*

4. RECORDING PROCEDURE.

(a) Prior to the commencement of recording any Recording(s), you and Company shall mutually agree on each of the following, in order, before you proceed further: (i) selection of, and compensation for, individual producer(s) (including, without limitation any producer advance [or fee] and producer royalty, if any); (ii) selection of material, including the Compositions to be recorded; and (iii) the dates of recording and mixing and studios where recording and mixing are to take place. Artist shall be responsible for engaging and paying all producers of each Master ("Producer") (except that Company may engage Producer(s) at its election and deduct any sums paid to such Producer(s) from any sums payable hereunder). Company shall have the right to have a representative attend each recording session. For the first album, ------------- is approved as record producer.

(b) Upon the reasonable request of Company, Artist shall re-record any selection until a Master commercially and technically satisfactory to Company has been obtained. Company may refuse to accept, and may require Artist to deliver substitute Masters for, compositions Company deems patently offensive or which, in its judgment, violates any law, violates the rights of any person, or subjects Company to material liability for any reason.

(c) It is of the essence of this Agreement that Artist timely supply Company with all of the information Company needs in order: (i) to make payments due or required in connection with the Masters; (ii) to comply with any and all other obligations Company may have in connection with recording the Masters, and (iii) to release Records embodying the Masters. Subject to the provisions of this Agreement, Company will pay Recording Costs incurred in connection with any Master(s) Delivered hereunder not to exceed the applicable Recording Fund with respect to such Master(s). Without limiting the foregoing, Artist shall deliver to Company within forty-eight hours after each recording session the following documents pertaining to such session: all union contract forms or report forms and all necessary payroll forms (including without limitation all I-9 forms and related documentation and all W-4 forms). Artist shall deliver all other invoices, receipts, vouchers and documents within one week after the related expense is incurred. Artist shall be solely responsible for and shall pay any penalties and/or interest charges incurred by Company for late payments by reason of Artist's failure to comply with the terms of this paragraph (or Company may deduct any resulting penalty or interest charges from any and all monies payable under this Agreement or any other agreement between you or Artist and Company or its affiliates). In addition, Artist shall deliver promptly complete label copy, any liner credits and any information required to be submitted to unions, guilds or other third parties.

(d) Your submission of Masters to Company shall constitute your representation and warranty that you have obtained all necessary licenses, approvals, consents and permissions including, without limitation, written clearance(s) from the copyright owner(s)/publisher(s) for any and all "first use" compositions, licenses for sampled material, etc.; provided that, unless Company has specifically requested that Artist do so, Company will secure the actual Mechanical Licenses for compositions recorded hereunder; provided that you are solely responsible for obtaining and you hereby represent, warrant and covenant that you will obtain written clearance(s) from the copyright owner(s)/publisher(s) for any and all "first use" compositions prior to recording any such composition and promptly provide Company with copies of all such clearances. You shall be solely responsible for and pay any and all costs, fees, and expenses in connection with any and all sample licensing and authorization, and all such sums (including, without limitation, royalties and any "rollover" payments) to the extent not paid by you, shall be deducted from any and all monies payable under this Agreement or any other agreement between you or Artist and Company or its affiliates. Company shall have the right to approve or disapprove (in its unrestricted discretion) all terms and conditions of any such sample license prior to embodiment on any Master. Notwithstanding the foregoing, Company may elect to arrange directly for such authorization and licensing in which event, you shall nevertheless be solely responsible for and pay any and all costs, fees and expenses in connection with such sample licensing and all such sums (including, without limitation, royalties and any "rollover" payments) to the extent not paid by you, shall be deducted from any and all monies payable under this Agreement or any other agreement between you or Artist and Company or its affiliates.

(e) Nothing in this Agreement shall obligate Company to continue or permit the continuation of any recording session, even if previously approved hereunder, if Company reasonably anticipates that the Recording Costs attributable to the recording session shall exceed the Advances/Recording Fund for that Album or other applicable Recording Commitment or that the Recordings being produced will not be technically and commercially satisfactory in accordance with the provisions of this Agreement.

(f) Unless Company requests or approves otherwise, your performances hereunder shall be reasonably consistent in concept and style, and the Masters will be similar in general artistic concept and style, to Masters recorded and accepted by Company as satisfying your Recording Commitment for the Initial Period hereof. You will obtain Company's written consent prior to performing in any new concept or style.

> *SECTION 5-GRANT OF RIGHTS says it all! Here the artist is giving the label the right to press and manufacture the recordings throughout the world (remember the six exclusive rights)! The artist's performance is a work-for-hire which mean that they are not a full time employee of the label and thus, the copyright for the recordings will remain with the label and cannot be recaptured (35-40 years). The artist is also giving the label the right to use their likenesses (voice, photos, image, stage name, biographical information) for publicity, distribution, and promotion purposes such as in a marketing plan, videos (MTV), websites, etc. Some labels will also take care of the artist's websites. All of these expenses are usually charged back to the artist's account generally at a rate of fifty percent. However, the rate may be as high as 100% if run through tour support. Courtney Love may not understand recoupment, yet here the labels should be praised for putting their money where their mouths are. Labels fund the artist's creativity when nobody (including banks) will even consider it. This is also why you should have a very good lawyer review all of this information with you before you sign so that you will know what you are signing. Please, please, please see an entertainment attorney and ask all the right questions.*

5. GRANT OF RIGHTS.

(a) All Masters, Video Masters and other Recordings embodying Artist's performances made during the Term from the inception of the recording thereof and all reproductions derived therefrom, together with the performances embodied thereon (but excluding musical compositions embodied therein), shall be the property of Company, free from any claims whatsoever by Artist or any person deriving rights or interests from or through Artist. Without limiting the generality of the foregoing, Company shall have the exclusive and unlimited right to all the results and proceeds of Artist's recording services rendered during the Term, including, without limitation, the exclusive, unlimited and perpetual right throughout the Territory: (i) to manufacture, advertise, sell, lease, license, distribute or otherwise use or dispose of, in any or all fields of use by any method now or hereafter known (including but not limited to any form of digital or electronic transmissions as well as sales through Company's website), Records embodying Masters (including accompaniment tracks without the vocal tracks), or to refrain therefrom; (ii) to use and publish and to permit others to use and publish Artist's name (including any professional name currently utilized or hereafter adopted by Artist), approved photographs and likenesses, and approved biographical material concerning Artist for advertising and trade purposes in connection with the sale of Artist's Recordings and the exploitation, in accordance with the terms hereof, of all Masters and Video Masters produced during the Term. The materials approved by Artist that contain the Artist's name or likeness or photograph or biography may also be used by Company's foreign affiliates and licensees; (iii) to obtain copyrights and renewals thereof in sound Recordings and Video Masters (as distinguished from the musical compositions embodied thereon) recorded by Artist during the Term, in Company's name as owner and "employer-for-hire" of such sound recordings and Video Masters. Artist acknowledges that Artist's services hereunder are rendered as Company's employee-for hire for the purposes of copyright ownership of the sound Recordings and Video Masters and any related artwork made hereunder. If any such Recording or artwork is determined not to be a "work made for hire", it will be deemed transferred and assigned to Company by this Agreement, together with all rights in it, including without limitation the worldwide copyright therein and all renewals and extensions thereof. You and Artist hereby irrevocably and unconditionally waive any and all moral and like rights (including, droit morale) that you and Artist have in such Recordings and in the performances embodied therein and related artwork and hereby agree not to make any claim against Company or any party authorized by Company to exploit such Recordings or artwork based on such moral or like rights; (iv) to release Records derived from Masters recorded during the Term by Artist under any name, trademark or label which Company may from time to time elect; and (v) to perform such Records and to permit performances thereof by means of radio broadcast, television, Internet or any other method or medium now or hereafter known or devised.

(b) Company shall have the perpetual right, without any liability to any party, to use and to authorize others to use your name and the names (including any professional names heretofore or hereafter adopted), and any likenesses (including photographs, portraits, caricatures

and stills from any Videos made hereunder) and biographical material relating to Artist and any producer of Masters hereunder, on and in the packaging of Records hereunder, for purposes of advertising, promotion and trade and in connection with the making, exploitation, promotion, marketing and publicity of Records hereunder, the writing and publishing of articles by Company or third parties, in general goodwill advertising (advertising designed to create goodwill and prestige for Company and not for the purpose of selling any specific product or service), and including, without limitation, purposes collateral to such permitted purposes (e.g., MTV's advertising and promotion), without payment of additional compensation to Artist or any other person. You warrant and represent that you own the exclusive right to so use such names, likenesses and biographical materials and that the use of same will not infringe upon the rights of any third party. If any third party challenges Artist's right to use a professional name, Company may, at its election and without limiting Company's rights, require Artist to adopt another professional name approved by Company without awaiting the determination of the validity of such challenge. During the Term, Artist will not change the name by which Artist is professionally known without Company's prior written approval.

(c) Company shall have the right to maintain an artist website (including the right to incorporate Artist's name, likeness, photographs and biographical material therein) in accordance with Company's standard policies (including, without limitation, incorporating links to other sites). Artist may also maintain his/her own website; provided that (i) during the Term of this Agreement, Company shall have approval rights regarding all aspects of such website and (ii) Artist may not sell recorded product on such website. No Person other than Company and Artist shall have the right to maintain an artist website regarding Artist during the Term hereof.

> *IN THE MARKETING RESTRICTIONS, the Rush Hicks (who wrote the contract) has provided his client with protection from the label going straight to budgeting discount if the recording is not selling at a specific level. The advantage is that artist royalties are usually 50% of the established rate. So, this is an excellent move by a very good entertainment attorney that is not often seen in contracts.*

6. MARKETING RESTRICTIONS.

Company agrees that it will not release any Album delivered in fulfillment of the Recording Commitment as a Budget Record in less than twelve (12) months; or as a Mid-Price Record in less than six (6) months after initial release of the Album in the United States. If Company releases any such Album that is a Mid-Price Record or Budget Record, as applicable, prior to the expiration of the applicable time period without your consent, your sole remedy shall be that Company shall not reduce your royalty rate pursuant to paragraph 8(i) below for sales of such Album made during such period.

> *THE RECORDING FUND includes advances made to the artist at the time they sign the contract and deliver the master tapes. THE RECORDING BUDGET is the actual budget for the recording of the master tape which the label will turn around, master and sell as CDs and digital downloads. The fund increases as each option is picked up. However, the total cost is also 100% recoupable. This is an opportunity for the artist to deliver a wonderful master tape and at the same time try to save some money in order to recoup (break even) faster.*

7. ADVANCES/RECORDING FUNDS.

Company shall pay to Artist the following sums as Advances:

(a) In connection with Artist's Delivery to Company of the applicable Album(s) hereunder, Company will pay Artist an Advance in the amount by which the applicable sum below (each herein called a "Recording Fund"), as reduced pursuant to paragraph (b) below, exceeds all Recording Costs paid or incurred by Company for such Album(s). Such Advance shall be payable to Artist promptly following the Delivery of the applicable Album(s). (i) With respect to the First Album, the Recording Fund shall be $_____, payable as follows:

    (A) The sum of $_____ shall be payable to the Artist upon the execution of this Agreement.

    (B) The balance shall be payable upon Delivery of the Master Recordings. (ii) With respect to each of the Second Album through the Fifth Album, if any, the Recording Fund shall be an amount equal to sixty-six (66%) percent of the royalties earned by Artist under paragraph 8 hereof on paid Net Sales through United States normal retail distribution channels of the previously released Recording Commitment Album for twelve (12) months from USA release of such previously released Recording Commitment Album. In no event shall any such Recording Fund be less than the "Minimum" or more than the "Maximum" set forth below for the Album in question:

Applicable Album/Recording Commitment

	Minimum	Maximum
Second Album	$150,000	$250,000
Third Album	$200,000	$300,000
Fourth Album	$250,000	$400,000
Fifth Album	$300,000	$500,000

(iii) Any monies paid by Company to third parties for independent record promotion and marketing shall constitute an Advance to Artist.

(b) In calculating each Advance hereunder, the applicable Recording Fund shall be reduced by all Anticipated Costs, partial payments of such Recording Fund, and all charges and other Advances deductible therefrom (each such Recording Fund, as so reduced, is sometimes referred to herein as the "Available Fund"). As used herein, "Anticipated Costs" means any costs Company reasonably anticipates will be paid or incurred by Company for recording, mastering, mixing or re-mixing the Masters concerned and all costs which Company reasonably anticipates are necessary to clear "samples" on such Masters. Any Anticipated Costs which are deducted from a Recording Fund but are not paid or incurred by Company as set forth in the previous sentence shall be remitted to Artist. Artist agrees that the Recording Fund includes the prepayment of session union scale to Artist as provided in the applicable union codes and Artist shall complete any documentation required by the applicable union to implement this sentence. It is understood and agreed that Company shall not be responsible for paying any charges or fees for arrangements or orchestrations supplied by Artist.

(c) Each Recording Fund set forth in paragraph 7(a) above is inclusive of all Recording Costs for the production of the Masters comprising the applicable Album. All Recording Costs incurred by Company with your approval and/or all Recording Costs incurred by you or your representatives which are in excess of the aforementioned Recording Funds shall be your sole responsibility, and you hereby agree to forthwith pay and discharge all such excess Recording Costs. In the event Company elects to pay any such excess Recording Costs on your behalf (which Company shall have the right but not the obligation to do), you shall, upon demand, reimburse Company for such excess Recording Costs or, in lieu of requesting reimbursement: (i) with respect to excess Recording Costs incurred by Company (with your approval), Company shall have the right to deduct such excess Recording Costs from any monies otherwise due you under this Agreement except for Mechanical Royalties and (ii) with respect to excess Recording Costs incurred by you or your representatives, Company shall have the right to deduct such excess Recording Costs from any monies otherwise due you under this Agreement, including without limitation Mechanical Royalties.

(d) (i) All sums paid to you or Artist or on your or Artist's behalf, or at your written request to anyone on your or Artist's behalf, or to or on behalf of any person, firm or corporation representing you or Artist, other than royalties payable hereunder and (ii) any and all Recording Costs paid or incurred by Company hereunder, shall constitute Advances. Company may recoup Advances from any and all royalties (excluding Mechanical Royalties, except as otherwise specified herein) accruing hereunder.

(e) If any Album is not Delivered within ninety (90) days following its due date, Artist shall, upon Company's written demand, repay Company any amounts previously paid by Company for or in connection with such Album.

ROYALTIES are used to recoup the "all in's" (artist and producer royalties) and the full artist's debt to the label. Royalties are a percentage of the SRLP, minus the package fee, times the royalty rate (adjusted for/minus the producer's points). The points (royalties) increase per option album and also escalate per sales level (reaching gold or platinum). However, it is a usual practice to pay only 50%-75% of the royalty rate on discounted sales and digital transmissions which of course means that it will take longer to recoup the label's advances. Also, royalties are reduced for non-USA sales (foreign sales at different rates and money exchange rates) and no royalties are usually paid on promotional copies and free goods.

8. ROYALTIES.

Company shall credit to your royalty account royalties as described below. Royalties shall be computed by applying the applicable royalty percentage rate specified below to the applicable Royalty Base Price in respect of top-line Net Sales of the Record concerned:

(a) (i) The royalty rate (the "Basic U.S. Rate") in respect of Net Sales of Records (other than Audiovisual Records) consisting entirely of Masters made hereunder during the respective Contract Periods specified below and sold by Company through Normal Retail Channels in the United States ("USNRC Net Sales") shall be as follows:

TYPE OF RECORD	BASIC U.S. RATES
First Album	12%
Second and Third Albums	13%
Fourth Album and Fifth Albums	14%
Singles, EPs and Twelve-Inch Singles	10%

(ii) Notwithstanding anything to the contrary, a sale of a Digital Download shall result in Company crediting to your royalty account a royalty rate of 10% prorated based upon the number of downloads. By way of example, should Company sell an Album via Digital Download and the retail price to the consumer is $9.99, you will receive 10% or 99.9 cents per album download.

(b) The Basic U.S. Rate will escalate prospectively solely in respect of USNRC Net Sales of any particular Album constituting your Recording Commitment in excess of the following number of units: 1% at 500,000 USA Soundscan units, and an additional 1% at 1,000,000 USA Soundscan units.

(c) The royalty rate on Records sold for distribution through normal retail distribution channels outside of the United States shall be the following percentages of the Basic U.S. Rate, applied to the applicable Royalty Base Price, and, if sold by a licensee not owned or controlled by Company, shall be paid to Artist upon the same number of Records for which Company is paid:

TERRITORIES	PERCENTAGE OF BASIC U.S. RATE
Canada	75%
EU, Australia, New Zealand, & Japan	66.67%
Rest of the World	50%

(d) With respect to Records sold by Company through mail order or a record club or in conjunction with a television advertising campaign, and for Records sold other than through normal retail distribution channels, Artist's royalties shall be computed at fifty percent (50%) of the applicable rate set forth above. With respect to Records licensed by Company for sale through mail order or a record club or licensed by Company for sale in conjunction with a television advertising campaign, and with respect to Company's licenses of the Masters or Video Masters, Company shall credit Artist's royalty account with fifty percent (50%) of Company's Net Royalty Receipts, or fifty percent (50%) of the Net Amount Received by Company, as applicable, from such sales and licenses. No royalties shall be payable with respect to Records received by members of any Club Operation in an introductory offer in connection with joining it or as a result of the purchase of a required number of Records including, without limitation, Records distributed as "bonus" or "free" Records, or Records for which the Club Operation is not paid.

(e) On Records sold as premium merchandise, Artist's royalties shall be computed at fifty percent (50%) of the applicable rate and the Royalty Base Price shall be the price the distributing record company receives for the premium Record.

(f) Notwithstanding any provision to the contrary herein contained and without limiting any of Company's rights hereunder, Company shall have the right to license Masters for all types of use (visual and non-visual) on a flat fee or royalty basis, in Company's discretion, for any uses referred to in this subparagraph, and as to any such license Company may credit to Artist's royalty account, in lieu of any other royalty, fifty percent (50%) of the Net Royalty Receipts from that license.

(g) Notwithstanding anything to the contrary contained herein, the royalty rate on any Record in a New Technology Configuration shall be seventy-five percent (75%) of the otherwise applicable royalty rate. Audio-only compact discs are not a New Technology Configuration. It is specifically acknowledged that Company's actual out-of-pocket costs incurred directly in connection with the development and production (but not the manufacturing) of Records hereunder in any New Technology Configuration shall constitute Recording Costs.

(h) With respect to Records sold directly to consumers by Company in the United States or by a Principal Licensee outside the United States, other than by the methods described in subparagraph 8(d) (e.g., without limitation, telephone, satellite, cable, direct transmission over wire or through the air, and on-line computer sales) (collectively, "Direct Transmissions"), the royalty rate shall be seventy-five percent (75%) of the royalty rate that would otherwise apply if the Record concerned was sold through Normal Retail Channels. With respect to Records licensed by Company for sale directly to consumers by means of a Direct Transmission, Company shall credit Artist's royalty account with fifty percent (50%) of Company's Net Royalty Receipts, or fifty percent (50%) of the Net Amount Received by Company, as applicable, from such licenses.

(i) The royalty rate on a Budget Record or on any Record sold to the United States government, its subdivisions, departments or agencies, through military exchange channels, or to educational institutions or libraries shall be fifty percent (50%) of the applicable royalty rate set forth above; on a Mid-Price Record, seventy-five percent (75%) of the applicable royalty rate set forth above.

(j) No royalties shall be payable to Artist in respect of Records sold or distributed for promotional purposes; as surplus, overstock or scrap; as cutouts after the listing of such Records has been deleted from the catalog; as "free," "no charge" or "bonus" Records other than Albums; for Records distributed to radio stations; or for Records distributed for use on transportation carriers or for use in juke boxes. As to Records sold at a discount to "one-stops", rack jobbers, distributors or dealers, whether or not affiliated with Company, in lieu of the Records given away or furnished on a "no-charge" basis as provided above, the applicable royalty rate otherwise payable hereunder with respect to such Records shall be reduced in the proportion that said discount wholesale price bears to the usual stated wholesale price.

(k) If any Master is recorded by Artist jointly with another artist or musician to whom Company is obligated to pay a royalty for the Master, Artist's applicable royalty rate therefor shall be divided by the number of persons (including Artist) to whom Company is obligated to pay a royalty in respect of the Master. For purposes of the immediately preceding sentence, a group of artists to whom Company is obligated to pay one "all-in" royalty shall constitute one person.

(l) The royalties provided for in this Agreement are inclusive of all royalties payable to producers and all third parties (other than Mechanical Royalties) for sale of Records and use of the Masters.

(m) As to a Record not consisting entirely of Recordings delivered hereunder, the royalty to be paid hereunder shall be prorated in the proportion the Masters (or Video Masters, as applicable) that are embodied on the Record bear to the total number of royalty-bearing master recordings (or Video Masters, as applicable) embodied on that Record.

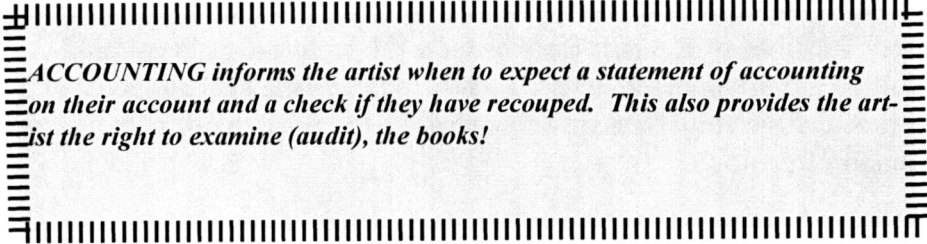

ACCOUNTING informs the artist when to expect a statement of accounting on their account and a check if they have recouped. This also provides the artist the right to examine (audit), the books!

9. ACCOUNTING.

(a) Statements as to royalties payable hereunder shall be sent by Company to Artist on or before the September 30th and March 31st for the respective semi-annual period ending the preceding June 30th and December 31st, together with payment of accrued royalties due to Artist, if any, on sales and licenses for which Company has received payment by the end of the semi-annual accounting period involved. No statements need be rendered by Company for any such accounting period after the expiration of the Term for which there are no sales or other exploitations of Records derived from Masters hereunder. Company may withhold from Artist's royalty account a reasonable reserve against anticipated returns, rebates and credits. With respect to sales of singles and other Record configurations, such reserves shall be held in accordance with Company's reasonable business judgment. Company will liquidate such reserves within four (4) accounting periods following the period in which such reserves were initially established.

(b) Artist shall be deemed to have consented to all royalty statements rendered by Company to Artist, and they shall not be subject to any objection by Artist for any reason, unless specific objection in writing, stating the basis thereof, is given by Artist to Company within two (2) years from the date the statement is rendered to Artist (the "Objection Period"). Any action, suit or proceeding relating to any royalty statement rendered hereunder must be commenced by Artist within one (1) year after expiration of the Objection Period for that statement.

(c) Company shall maintain books of account concerning the sale, distribution and exploitation of Records and Masters made hereunder. A certified public accountant or attorney on Artist's behalf may, at Artist's expense, once per calendar year, examine Company's books as same pertain to the sale, distribution and other exploitation of Records hereunder, at Company's office, during usual business hours and upon no less than thirty (30) days prior written notice. Company's books relating to activities during any accounting period may only be examined as aforesaid during the Objection Period.

(d) Royalties hereunder for sales and licenses derived from sources outside the United States shall be computed in the national currency in which Company is paid therefor, shall be credited to Artist's royalty account hereunder at the same rate of exchange as Company is paid or credited, and shall be proportionately subject to any foreign income, withholding, added value, transfer or comparable taxes which may be imposed upon Company's royalties for those sales and licenses. If Company cannot collect payment in the United States in U.S. Dollars, Company shall not be required to account to you for the sale, except as provided in the next sentence. Company shall, at your request and at your expense, deduct from the monies so blocked, and deposit in a foreign depository, the equivalent in local currency of the royalties which would be payable to you on the foreign sales concerned, to the extent such monies are available for that purpose, and only to the extent to which your royalty account is then in a fully recouped position. All such deposits shall constitute royalty payments to you for accounting purposes. To the extent possible, Company will allow you to select the foreign depository referred to in this paragraph (d).

(e) Company shall have the right to deduct from any amounts payable to Artist hereunder (1) such portion thereof as may be required to be deducted by any governmental authority, and (2) any amount payable by Company with respect to Artist's royalties under any union or guild agreement applicable to the Records and Masters hereunder. Artist agrees to execute and deliver promptly to Company such forms and other documents that may be required in connection with this paragraph.

(f) In the event Company makes any claim, or brings any action, suit or proceeding, that recovers any sums with respect to any Master, and in the event royalties are payable to Artist under this Agreement from such sums received by Company, all costs and expenses of such recovery (including, without limitation, reasonable attorneys', accounting and auditing fees and expenses) shall be deducted from the gross sums so recovered.

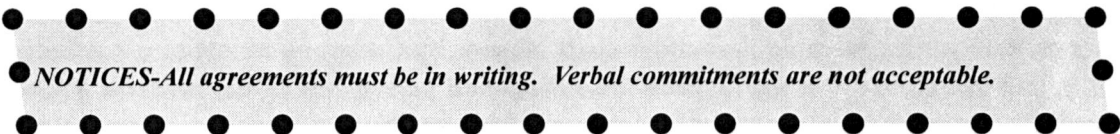
NOTICES-All agreements must be in writing. Verbal commitments are not acceptable.

10. NOTICES.

Except as otherwise specifically provided herein, all notices under this Agreement shall be in writing and shall be given by courier or other personal delivery, by overnight delivery by an established overnight delivery service (e.g., Federal Express, Airborne Express, DHL or United Parcel Service), or by registered or certified mail, return receipt requested, at the applicable address below, or at a substitute address designated by written notice by the party concerned,

    TO YOU AT:

    WITH A COURTESY COPY TO:

    TO COMPANY AT:

    WITH A COURTESY COPY TO:

Notices shall be deemed given when mailed or deposited into the custody of an overnight delivery service for overnight delivery, or, if personally delivered, when so delivered, except that a notice of change of address shall be effective only from the date of its receipt.

LICENSES FOR MUSICAL COMPOSITION-means that the label will only pay the controlled Composition Clause (CCC), usually 75% of the current statutory rate on mechanicals.

11. LICENSES FOR MUSICAL COMPOSITIONS.

(a) Artist hereby grants to Company an irrevocable license under copyright to reproduce each Controlled Composition for uses as contemplated hereunder. Company shall pay Mechanical Royalties on Controlled Compositions at 100% of the respective minimum statutory rates (without regard to playing time) for the United States and Canada, determined at the date effective on the earlier of (i) the date such Masters are Delivered to Company hereunder or (ii) the date such Masters are required to be Delivered to Company hereunder, as applicable.

(b) There shall be an aggregate Mechanical Royalty cap of twelve (12) times such rate per Album; two (2) times such rate per Single; three (3) times such rate per Twelve-inch Single; and five (5) times such rate per EP. To the extent that the aggregate Mechanical Royalty rate would exceed the cap in any Record, the excess will be deducted from any and all monies payable hereunder including without limitation, the Mechanical Royalties payable for the Controlled Compositions recorded under this Agreement. If a Composition recorded hereunder is embodied more than once on a particular Record, Company shall pay Mechanical Royalties in connection therewith at the applicable rate for such Composition as though the Composition were embodied thereon only once. All Mechanical Royalties payable hereunder shall be paid on the basis of Net Sales of Records hereunder for which royalties are payable pursuant to this Agreement. No Mechanical Royalties shall be paid on Records described in subparagraph 8(j). Company may maintain reasonable reserves with respect to payment of Mechanical Royalties. Notwithstanding anything to the contrary contained herein, Mechanical Royalties payable in respect of Controlled Compositions for sales of Records for any use described in subparagraphs 8(d), 8(e) and 8(i) shall be seventy-five percent (75%) of the otherwise applicable rate in the United States or Canada, as the case may be. Any assignment of the ownership or administration of copyright in any Controlled

Composition shall be made subject to the provisions hereof and any inconsistencies between the terms of this Agreement and mechanical licenses issued to and accepted by Company shall be determined by the terms of this Agreement. If any Single, Maxi-Single, EP or Album contains Compositions which are not Controlled Compositions, you will obtain for Company's benefit mechanical licenses covering such Compositions on the same terms and conditions applicable to Controlled Compositions pursuant to this paragraph 11.

(c) In respect of all Controlled Compositions, Company is hereby granted the irrevocable perpetual worldwide right to reprint the lyrics on the jackets, sleeves and other packaging of Records derived from Masters hereunder. Company is hereby granted the irrevocable right throughout the Territory to recreate the title and/or lyrics to any Composition embodied in a Recording delivered hereunder in the so-called "text mode" of digital compact cassettes, interactive compact discs or any other New Technology Configuration embodying such Recording, without payment to any person or entity. If Company is required to pay any monies for the exercise of any of the rights granted to it under this subparagraph 11(c), then Company shall have the right to demand reimbursement, therefore from you and Artist (and you and/or Artist shall immediately make such reimbursement) and/or the right to deduct such costs from any monies payable under this Agreement or any other agreement for Artist's services.

(d) In respect of all Controlled Compositions performed in Videos, Company is hereby granted an irrevocable perpetual worldwide license to record, synchronize and reproduce such Compositions in such Videos and to distribute and perform such Videos including, without limitation, all Audiovisual Records thereof, and to authorize others to do so. In addition, in respect of all Controlled Compositions performed in Webcasts, Company is hereby granted an irrevocable perpetual worldwide license to record, synchronize and reproduce such Compositions in such Webcasts, and to distribute and perform such Webcasts and to authorize others to do so. Company will not be required to make any payment in connection with the uses referred to in the immediately preceding two sentences, and those licenses shall apply whether or not Company receives any payment in connection with those uses. Notwithstanding the immediately preceding sentence, following Company's full recoupment of all costs in connection with a Video, Company shall negotiate in good faith with you regarding a royalty to be paid prospectively with respect to Controlled Compositions embodied in such Video in connection with the commercial exploitation of such Video. Simultaneously with your and Company's selection of creative elements of each Video produced hereunder, you shall furnish Company with a written acknowledgment from the person(s) or entity(ies) controlling the copyright in each non-Controlled Composition to be embodied in any Video confirming the terms upon which said person(s) or entity(ies) shall issue licenses in respect thereof and in respect of Webcasts. Upon Company's request therefor, you shall cause said person(s) or entity(ies) to forthwith issue to Company (and its designees) licenses containing said terms and such other terms and conditions as Company (or its designees) may require. Royalties in connection with licenses for the use of non-Controlled Compositions pertaining to Videos and Audiovisual Records are included in the royalties set forth in paragraph 17 hereof. If the copyright in any Controlled Composition is owned or controlled by anyone else, you will cause that person, firm or corporation to grant Company the same rights described in this paragraph 11, on the same terms.

EVENT OF DEFAULT is the process that will be taken by the company if the artist fails to deliver acceptable master tapes on time or if the company cannot fulfill its obligations.

12. EVENTS OF DEFAULT.

(a) In the event Artist fails to fulfill any of Artist's recording commitments hereunder in accordance with all of the material terms and conditions of this Agreement, then, in addition to any other rights or remedies available to Company, Company shall have the right, upon notice to Artist at any time prior to the expiration of the then current Contract Period (i) to terminate this Agreement without further obligation to Artist as to unrecorded or unfinished Masters or Video Masters, or (ii) to extend the then current

Contract Period for the duration of such default plus one hundred and fifty (150) days, with the times for the exercise by Company of its options to extend the Term and the dates of commencement of subsequent Option Periods deemed extended accordingly. Company's obligations hereunder, other than the obligation to pay earned royalties to Artist, shall be suspended for the duration of any such default. The provisions of this subparagraph shall not result in an extension of the Term for a period in excess of the period permitted by applicable law, if any, for the enforcement of personal service contracts.

(b) Company reserves the right, at its election, to suspend the operation of this Agreement for the duration of any of the following contingencies, if, by reason of any such contingency, Company is materially hampered in the performance of its obligations under this Agreement or its normal business operations are delayed or become impossible or commercially impracticable: Act of God, fire, catastrophe, labor disagreement, acts of government, its agencies or officers, any order, regulation, ruling or action of any labor union or association of artists, musicians, composers or employees affecting Company or the industry in which it is engaged, delays in the delivery of materials and supplies, or any other cause beyond Company's control. No suspension under this subparagraph shall exceed six (6) months during any Contract Period unless such contingency is industry-wide, in which event Company shall have the right to suspend the applicable Contract Period for the duration of such contingency.

(c) If Company refuses without cause to allow you to fulfill your Recording Commitment for any Contract Period and if, not later than sixty (60) days after that refusal takes place, you notify Company of your desire to fulfill such Recording Commitment, then Company shall permit you to fulfill said Recording Commitment by notice to you to such effect, such notice to be given, if at all, within forty-five (45) days of Company's receipt of your notice. Should Company fail to give such notice as aforesaid, you shall have the option to terminate the Term by notice given to Company within thirty (30) days after the expiration of the forty-five (45) day period; on receipt by Company of such notice, the Term shall terminate and all parties will be deemed to have fulfilled all of their obligations hereunder except those obligations that survive the end of the Term (e.g., warranties, Re-Recording Restrictions, rights of approval, and obligation to pay royalties), and you shall have no other remedy for such refusal without cause by Company to allow you to fulfill your Recording Commitment.

13. INJUNCTIVE RELIEF.

Artist expressly acknowledges that Artist's services hereunder are of a special, unique and intellectual character which gives them a peculiar value, and that in the event of a breach or threatened breach by Artist of any term, condition or covenant hereof, Company shall incur immediate irreparable injury. Artist expressly agrees that Company shall be entitled to injunctive and other equitable relief, as permitted by law, to prevent a breach or threatened breach of this Agreement by Artist, which relief shall be in addition to any other rights or remedies, for damages or otherwise, available to Company.

> *COLLECTIVE BARGAINING AGREEMENTS means that the artist will become and remain a member of the respective unions (Af of M and AFTRA/SAG) during the term of the contract. Since the labels have signed (signatory members) the union agreements and the artist is under contract, they are also required to be members. Unions in this case are a positive thing for the artist as they will represent the artist in recordings, touring, etc., and make sure they are being represented properly and paid at least union scale.*

14. COLLECTIVE BARGAINING AGREEMENTS.

During the Term, Artist warrants and represents that, if Company so requests, Artist shall become and remain a member in good standing of any labor unions with which Company may have agreements lawfully requiring such union membership, including, but not limited to, the American Federation of Musicians and the American Federation of Television and Radio Artists.

> *WARRANTIES AND REPRESENTATIONS means that you have the ability to enter into an agreement (as example, your not signed to another label, your an American citizen of legal age-18 or older, and that you have a work visa if your not a citizen of the United States).*

15. WARRANTIES AND REPRESENTATIONS; INDEMNITIES.

(a) You and Artist warrant and represent that: (i) Artist is over the age of eighteen (18) and neither you nor Artist is under any disability, restriction or prohibition, whether contractual or otherwise, with respect to your right to execute this Agreement or your and Artist's rights to perform its terms and conditions. Without limiting the foregoing, you specifically warrant and represent that no prior obligations, contracts or agreements of any kind undertaken or entered into by Artist, will interfere in any manner with the complete performance of this Agreement by Artist or with Artist's right to record any and all compositions hereunder. You further warrant and represent that Company shall not be required to make any payments of any nature for, or in connection with, the rendition of your or Artist's services or the acquisition, exercise or exploitation of rights by Company pursuant to this Agreement, except as specifically provided herein. As of the date hereof, Artist is not a resident of the State of California. Artist shall notify Company immediately in the event that Artist becomes a resident of the State of California. (ii) (1) Artist shall enter into a valid and binding contract with each producer (each, a "Producer Contract") prior to the rendering of each such producer's services hereunder. Each Producer Contract shall grant to Artist all rights necessary for Artist to fulfill all of Artist's obligations hereunder. Artist will fully and promptly perform its obligations under the Producer Contracts. Without limitation of the foregoing, Artist shall cause each producer to execute and deliver a document in the form of Exhibit A prior to commencement of recording of the applicable Master. If Artist does not enforce any of Artist's rights under a Producer Contract, Company may without limitation of Company's rights enforce such rights in Artist's name and/or the name of Company. If Artist breaches any Producer Contract, then Company may cure such breach on Artist's behalf and at Artist's expense. No modification of or amendment to a Producer Contract will be made which would directly or indirectly diminish any of Company's rights hereunder. Artist will upon Company's request furnish Company with a complete copy of any or all Producer Contracts and/or any modification of the Producer Contracts.

(2) You shall be solely responsible for and shall pay promptly all monies becoming payable to Artist, each individual producer of Recordings hereunder and all other parties rendering services on or in connection with such Recordings, both in connection with such individuals' services and also the exploitation by Company and its designees of the results of such services; provided that Company shall, in accordance with all of the terms hereof, pay Mechanical Royalties becoming payable to the copyright proprietors of Compositions embodied on Masters and monies required to be paid to the A.F. of M. Music Performance Trust Fund and Phonograph Record Manufacturers Special Payments Fund in connection with the manufacture and sale of Records derived from Masters.

(iii) No materials, or any use thereof, will violate any law or infringe upon or violate the rights of any third party. "Material," as used herein, includes:

> (i) all musical compositions and other intellectual property, embodied in the Masters,
> (ii) the name -----------as used in connection with the Masters, and (
> iii) all other ideas, other intellectual property or elements contained in or used in connection with the Masters or the packaging, sale, distribution, advertising, publicizing or other exploitation of Records embodying the Masters.
> (iv) No changes in the individuals comprising Artist will be made without Company's prior written consent. Neither you nor Artist shall have the right, so long as this Agreement is in effect, to assign Artist's professional name as mentioned on page 1 hereof or any other name(s) utilized by Artist in connection with Masters or to permit the use of said name(s) by any other individual or group of individuals without Company's prior written consent, and any attempt to do so shall be null and

void and shall convey no right or title. You hereby warrant and represent that you are and shall be the sole owner of all such professional name(s), and that no other person, firm or corporation has the right to use said name(s) or to permit said name(s) to be used in connection with Records, and that you have the authority to grant Company the exclusive right to use said name(s) in the Territory in accordance with all of the terms and conditions of this Agreement, and Company shall have the exclusive right to use said professional name as aforesaid.

(v) Except as otherwise specifically set forth in this Agreement, during the Term, Artist shall not perform for the purpose of making Records for anyone other than Company for use in the Territory and neither you nor Artist shall authorize the use of Artist's name, likeness, or other identification for the purpose of distributing, selling, advertising or exploiting Records for anyone other than Company in the Territory.

(vi) Artist shall not perform any Composition recorded hereunder for anyone other than Company for use in the Territory on Records for a period of (i) five (5) years after the initial date of release of the respective Record containing such selection or (ii) two (2) years after the expiration or other termination of the Term, whichever is later ("Re-recording Restriction").

(vii) The Masters made and/or Delivered hereunder shall be produced in accordance with the rules and regulations of the American Federation of Musicians, the American Federation of Television and Radio Artists and all other unions having jurisdiction. All persons rendering services in connection with such Masters shall fully comply with the provisions of the Immigration Reform Control Act of 1986 and any other applicable laws.

(viii) There exist no previously recorded Recordings embodying Artist's performances except those that have been sold, transferred or otherwise assigned to Company.

(b) (i) Artist agrees to and does hereby indemnify, save and hold Company harmless of and from any and all liability, loss, damage, cost or expense (including without limitation reasonable attorneys' fees) arising out of or connected with any breach, threatened breach or alleged breach of this Agreement or any claim which is inconsistent with any of the warranties or representations made by you or Artist in this Agreement, provided that such claim has been settled with Artist's consent, or has been reduced to final judgment. Artist agrees to reimburse Company on demand for any payment made or incurred by Company with respect to any liability or claim to which the foregoing indemnity applies. Pending final determination of any claim involving such alleged breach or failure, Company may withhold sums due Artist hereunder in an amount reasonably related to the amount of such claim.

If no action is filed within one (1) year following the date on which such claim was first received by Company, Company shall release all sums withheld in connection with such claim, unless Company, in its reasonable business judgment, believes an action will be filed thereafter. Notwithstanding the foregoing, if, after such release by Company of sums withheld in connection with a particular claim, such claim is reasserted, then Company's rights under this paragraph will apply ab initio in full force and effect. Artist shall have the right to participate in the defense of any action instituted on a claim for which Artist is responsible to indemnify Company, with counsel of Artist's choice and at Artist's expense; however, Company shall have the right at all times to maintain control of the conduct of the defense.

(ii) Notwithstanding anything to the contrary contained herein, Company shall have the right to settle without your consent any claim involving sums of Seven Thousand Five Hundred Dollars ($7,500) or less, and this indemnity shall apply in full to any claim so settled; if you do not consent to any settlement proposed by Company for an amount in excess of Seven Thousand Five Hundred Dollars ($7,500), Company shall have the right to settle such claim without your consent, and this indemnity shall apply in full to any claim so settled, unless you post a surety bond with a surety acceptable to Company in its sole discretion. The surety bond must name Company as the beneficiary and assure prompt, unconditional payment to Company of all expenses, losses and damages (including without limitation costs and reasonable attorneys' fees) that Company may incur in connection with said claim.

> **APPROVALS**
> *When the label needs the approval of the artist for something, they will send it to him/her in writing. The artist has five days to respond or the label will consider the matter approved.*

16. APPROVALS.

Whenever in this Agreement Artist's approval is required, it shall not be unreasonably withheld or delayed. Artist must send written notice of approval or disapproval within five (5) days after Artist receives Company's request for the approval. Failure to give due notice of approval or disapproval shall be deemed to be approval.

17. VIDEOS.

(a) Company shall have the right to require Artist to perform at such reasonable times and places as Company designates for the production of Video Masters featuring Artist's performances of Compositions embodied in the Masters and Artist agrees to perform to the best of Artist's ability thereon. Company shall be the exclusive owner throughout the Territory in perpetuity of such Video Masters and all rights therein, including, without limitation, all copyrights and renewal of copyrights with respect thereto, and the right to use and exploit such Video Masters in any and all forms and media. Company will consult with Artist with respect to the budget, producer, director and storyboard for each Video Master produced hereunder, but Company shall make the final decisions thereon.

(b) Company shall pay all Video production costs incurred in connection with the Videos consistent with the approved production budget. All sums paid by Company in connection with the production of the Video Masters shall constitute Advances to be charged against and recouped from Artist's royalties (excluding Mechanical Royalties) under this Agreement, subject to the following sentence. Fifty percent (50%) of the aggregate amount of Video production costs shall not be recoupablefrom royalties payable pursuant to paragraph 8 above, but shall nevertheless be one hundred percent (100%) recoupable from Video royalties hereunder. All Video production costs in excess of the approved budget that have been incurred due to your or Artist's acts or omissions shall be your sole responsibility, and you hereby agree to forthwith pay and discharge all such excess costs. In the event that Company agrees to pay any such excess costs on your behalf, you shall, upon demand, reimburse Company for such excess costs or in lieu of requesting reimbursement, Company may deduct such excess costs from any monies otherwise due you under this Agreement or any other agreement between you or Artist and Company or its affiliates (including without limitation Mechanical Royalties). In the event that Artist fails to appear at locations and/or on dates which have been mutually approved by you and Company, without reasonable excuse, the costs of cancellation of the shoot shall be fully deductible from all monies payable to you under this or any other agreement between you or Artist and Company or its affiliates (including without limitation Mechanical Royalties).

(c) In the event that Company decides to commercially release any Video Masters produced hereunder for sale, Company and Artist shall negotiate in good faith an artist royalty payable to Artist hereunder in connection with such sales of such Video Masters. Any such artist royalty negotiated with respect to sales of Video Masters hereunder is inclusive of any third party payments (including without limitation any payments to music publishers with respect to non-Controlled Compositions) required to be made by Company in connection with the manufacture and commercial exploitation of Video Masters hereunder.

> *MARKETING AND PUBLICITY-Although the artist's performance is a work-for-hire, the label needs them to support the MARKETING PLAN by being available for photography shoots, interviews and other promotional and publicity opportunities. This is when the artist should use SHAMELESS SELF-PROMOTION to their advantage. As an example, when a label or manager arranges the artist an appearance on Letterman, the artist's job is to get viewers excited about them, their latest record, tour, book, and TV show. That is why they are on the show, to sell themselves, their image, and all of the corresponding products.*

18. MARKETING & PUBLICITY.

(a) Artist shall be available from time to time to appear for photography, poster, and cover art, and the like, under the direction of Company or its nominees and to appear for interviews with representatives of the communications media and Company's publicity personnel.

(b) Artist shall be available from time to time at Company's request to perform for the purpose of recording for promotional purposes by means of film, videotape, or other audiovisual media performances of Compositions embodied on Masters.

> *GROUP PROVISION is simply a method to replace a leaving member. Most contracts have this even when they are signing a single artist. In addition, most labels like to sign a single artist over a group as the personality differences in a band can cause acts to disband (the Beatles). When that happens the label's future possible revenues are lost.*

19. GROUP PROVISIONS.

Artist's obligations under this Agreement are joint and several. All references in this Agreement to "Artist" include all members of the Group, inclusively, and each member individually, unless otherwise specified. If any member of the Group ceases to perform as a member of the Group, that member will be deemed to be a "Leaving Member" and the following shall apply in that circumstance:

(a) The remaining members of Artist will notify Company within thirty (30) days after a member has left, that a member has left, and the Leaving Member will be replaced by a new member, if Artist and Company so agree, to be substituted as a party to this Agreement in the place and stead of the Leaving Member. Artist agrees to cause the new member (and any new member joining the Group after the date hereof, even if not

replacing a Leaving Member) to execute and deliver to Company such instruments as Company may require to accomplish that substitution (hereinafter collectively referred to as the "Substitution Instruments"). Thereafter, the Leaving Member will have no further obligation to perform under this Agreement but will continue to be bound by the other provisions of this Agreement, and Company will continue to have the right to use the name of the Group (and any other name hereafter used for the Group) pursuant to this Agreement. Artist agrees that no person will be permitted to perform in place of the Leaving Member under this Agreement unless that performer has executed and delivered to Company his/her Substitution Instruments. Company will continue to have the right to use the name of the Group (and any other name hereafter used for the Group). No Leaving Member will make any use of the Group's name in any circumstances, nor authorize or permit anyone other than Company to use or trade upon the Group's name for any purpose. For the avoidance of doubt, it is specifically agreed that the Leaving Member shall not make or authorize any reference to the Group's name for or in connection with the Leaving Member's performances, live or recorded or taped or filmed, nor make or authorize any reference in any packaging of phonorecords or videograms, any artwork or stickers used in connection with phonorecords or videograms, or any advertising, marketing, promotion or publicity in connection with phonorecords or videograms.

(b) Company will have the right to terminate the Term with respect to the remaining members of the Group by notice to be given to Artist at any time before expiration of ninety (90) days after Company's receipt of the notice referred to in sub-paragraph (a) above. In the event of such termination, all members of the Group will be deemed to be Leaving Members as of the date of such termination notice, and sub-paragraph (c) will apply to all of them, collectively or individually as Company may elect.

(c) Artist grants to Company an option to engage the exclusive recording services of each Leaving Member (hereinafter referred to as a "Leaving Member Option"). Each Leaving Member Option may be exercised by Company at any time within ninety (90) days after Company's receipt of notice under subparagraph (a), or within ninety (90) days after the date of Company's termination notice pursuant to subparagraph (b) above, whichever shall be later. If Company exercises a Leaving Member Option, the Leaving Member concerned will be deemed to have entered into a new agreement with Company containing the same provisions as this Agreement, except as follows:

> (i) The new agreement will apply only to that Leaving Member, and all references to "Artist" in that new agreement will be deemed to refer to the Leaving Member;
>
> (ii) The term of the new agreement will commence on the date Company exercises that Leaving Member Option and may be extended by Company (exercisable in the same manner as provided in paragraph 2 above) for the same number of Option Periods that remained under paragraph 2 hereof at the time Company exercises that Leaving Member Option (but Company shall have at least 2 such Option Periods in any event);
>
> (iii) The Recording Commitment for each Contract Period of such Term shall be one (1) Album;
>
> (iv) If Artist's royalty account under this Agreement in an unrecouped position at the date Company exercises a Leaving Member Option, a pro-rata portion of the amount of that unrecouped balance will be recoupable from the royalties payable by Company under the new agreement. That portion shall be determined by a fraction, the numerator being one and the denominator being the number of members constituting the Artist prior to Company's receipt of the notice referred to in subparagraph (a) above. (e.g. 25% of that unrecouped balance if there are 4 members of Artist and one of them becomes a Leaving Member for whom Company has exercised a Leaving Member Option.) To the extent that unrecouped portion is recouped under the new agreement, it shall be credited toward recoupment under this Agreement, and to the extent that unrecouped portion is recouped under this Agreement it shall be credited toward recoupment of charges against royalties under the new agreement.
>
> (v) As to any Leaving Member who has a songwriter's agreement or copublishing agreement with Company or any of Company's affiliates, the term of that agreement shall be coterminous with the new recording agreement, as same shall be substituted for, extended and renewed.

DEFINITIONS.

For the purposes of this Agreement, the following definitions and terms shall be:

(a) "Advance" -A prepayment of royalties. Company may recoup Advances from all royalties to be paid or accrued to or on behalf of Artist pursuant to this Agreement. Mechanical Royalties shall not be chargeable in recoupment of any Advances unless otherwise expressly provided.

(b) "Album" -One (1) or more audio-only Records, at least forty-five (45) minutes in playing time and embodying at least ten (10) Masters of different compositions sold in a single package.

- "Mid-Price" Album or Record" -A Record which is sold by Company or its Principal Licensee(s) at a price that is below Company's or the applicable Principal Licensee's then-prevailing top-line suggested retail list price, which price is consistently applied by Company to such Records and which Records are sold by Company or its Principal Licensee(s) as mid-priced Records.
- "Multiple Record Set": Two or more Records packaged and/or marketed as a single unit.
- "Budget" Album or Record" -A Record which is sold by Company or its Principal Licensee(s) at a price which is below Company's or the applicable Principal Licensee's then-prevailing top-line suggested retail list price, which price is consistently applied by Company to such Records and which Records are sold by Company or its Principal Licensee(s) as budget Records.

- "Single" -A vinyl, audio-only Record not more than seven (7) inches in diameter, or the equivalent in non-vinyl configurations.
- "Twelve-inch Single" -An audio-only Record which contains not more than four (4) Recordings of different compositions.
- "Extended Play Record" or "EP" -An audio-only Record embodying thereon either five (5) Masters or six (6) Masters, but does not constitute an Album.
- "Audiovisual Record" -A Record which embodies, reproduces, transmits or otherwise communicates visual images, whether or not the interaction of a consumer is possible or necessary for the visual images to be utilized or viewed.

(c) "Base Price"-For Records and Audiovisual Records, the Suggested Retail List Price. "Royalty Base Price" -The Base Price less all excise, sales and similar taxes included in the Base Price and less the applicable Container Charges and less distributors' discounts and rebates, if any.

(d) "Container Charge" -The applicable percentages of the Base Price specified below for sales by Company:
- (i) Analog cassette Records -twenty percent (20%);
- (ii) Compact disc Records and Records in all other configurations twenty-five percent (25%);
- (iii) Analog vinyl Records -twenty-five percent (25%); and
- (iv) Electronic phonorecord delivery -no deductions

(e) "Controlled Composition" -a composition wholly or partly written, or directly or indirectly owned or controlled, by Artist or a producer of Masters or by any representative of Artist or a producer hereunder.

(f) "Digital Download" -a type of record by which a Master is transmitted or otherwise communicated to a consumer on demand via digital distribution over the internet which results in that particular Record being placed in storage on that consumer's computer or other device such that the consumer owns the Record in perpetuity (as opposed to a limited rental or license). Company will not deduct a Container Charge from your portion of Digital Download royalties.

(g) "Delivery," "deliver" or "Delivered" -The actual receipt by Company of completed, fully mixed, leadered and edited Masters comprising the applicable Recording Commitment, technically and commercially satisfactory in Company's opinion and ready for the manufacture of Records, together with all materials, consents, approvals, licenses, and permissions Artist is required to supply to Company hereunder.

(h) "Master" -An individual sound Recording recorded hereunder that embodies Artist's performance(s) as the featured recording artist(s).

"Video" or "Video Masters" -Videocassettes, Videodiscs or any other devices, now or hereafter known or developed (including, without limitation, any visual and/or audiovisual work using digital technology), that enable motion pictures and other audiovisual works that have a soundtrack substantially featuring the
performances of Artist to be perceived visually, with sound, when used in combination with or as part of a piece of electronic, mechanical or other apparatus.

(i) "Mechanical Royalties" -Royalties payable to any person for the right to reproduce and distribute copyrighted compositions on Records, including, without limitation, Audiovisual Records.

(j) "Merchandise Rights" -any use, reproduction or other exploitation in any manner, media or formats of the name, photographs, likenesses, biographical material, trademarks and/or any other identification utilized by you (other than in connection with Records hereunder), including, without limitation "fan clubs", any products, endorsements, sponsorships and/or the sale of merchandise (i.e., t-shirts and other apparel, caps, posters, biographical books, etc).

(k) "Net Amount Received" -The gross, earned, non-returnable amount received by Company (excluding royalties that are based upon a percentage of a retail or wholesale or other price and excluding advances against such royalties), less any out-of-pocket costs or expenses which Company is contractually required to make to third parties, including, but not limited to, payments to a trustee or fund to the extent required by any agreement between Company and any labor organization or trustee, and less Mechanical Royalty payments. An example of a Net Amount Received is an earned payment (not an advance) under a flat fee license or flat rate license.

(l) "Net Royalty Receipts" -Company's gross, earned royalty receipts less any out-of-pocket costs or expenses which Company is contractually required to make to third parties, and less any amounts included in the receipts that are for payments to a trustee or fund required by any agreement between Company or Artist and any labor organization or trustee, and less Mechanical Royalty payments.

(m) "Net Sales" -Eighty-five (85%) percent of Gross Sales of Albums, and seventy (70%) percent of Gross Sales of Singles and EPs, sold, paid for and not returned. "Free goods" that are given by Company or Company's distributor in lieu of discounts shall be included in "Gross Sales" under this paragraph, except for additional free goods given by Company or its distributor pursuant to special "impact" marketing programs of limited duration.

(n) "New Technology Configurations" shall mean Records in the following configurations: mini-discs, digital compact cassettes, digital audio tapes, DVD, laser discs, CD-ROM and other Records embodying, employing or otherwise utilizing any non-analog technology (whether or not presently existing or hereafter created or developed), but specifically excluding audio-only compact discs.

(o) "Record" -Any form of reproduction, transmission or communication of Recordings, now or hereafter known, manufactured, distributed, transmitted or communicated primarily for home use, school use, juke box use or use in means of transportation, including, without limitation, Records embodying or reproducing sound alone and Audiovisual Records.

(p) "Recording" -Every recording of sound, whether or not coupled with a visual image, by any method and on any substance or material, or in any other form or format, whether now or hereafter known, which is used or useful in the recording, production and/or manufacture of Records or for any other commercial exploitation.

(q) "Recording Costs" -All amounts paid or incurred in connection with the production of Masters hereunder. Recording Costs include, without limitation, all union scale payments required to be made to the Artist in connection with Masters recorded hereunder, all costs of instrumental, vocal and other personnel in connection with the recording of the Masters, travel, rehearsal, and equipment rental expenses, per diems, advances to producers, studio and engineering charges and personnel, all other amounts required to be paid pursuant to any applicable law or any collective bargaining agreement between Company and any union representing persons who render services in connection with the Masters, and all costs of mixing, remixing, mastering and re-mastering. Recording Costs do not include the costs of producing metal parts, but include all studio and engineering charges or other costs incurred in preparing Masters for the production of metal parts and/or final production Masters. (Metal parts include lacquer, copper, and other equivalent masters.)

(r) "Suggested Retail List Price" means (i) with respect to Records sold for distribution in the United States, Company's suggested retail list price in the United States during the applicable accounting period for the computation of royalties to be made hereunder, it being understood that a separate calculation of the suggested retail list price shall be made for each price configuration of Phonograph Records manufactured and sold by Company; and (ii) with respect to Records sold hereunder for distribution outside the United States, Company's or its licensees' suggested or applicable retail price in the country of manufacture or sale, as Company is paid, or, in the absence in a particular country of such suggested retail list price, the price as may be established by Company or its licensee(s) in conformity with the general practice of the recording industry in such country, provided that Company shall not be obligated to utilize the price adopted by the local mechanical copyright collection agency for the collection of Mechanical Royalties. Notwithstanding anything to the contrary contained herein, (A) the Suggested Retail List Price for premium Records shall be Company's actual sales price of such Records and (B) the Suggested Retail List Price with respect to Videos manufactured and distributed by Company shall be Company's published wholesale price as of the commencement of the accounting period in question.

(s) "Territory" -the Universe

(t) Sales "through normal retail distribution channels" means sales made to retail stores, or for re-sale to retail stores, through Company's record distributors, or, outside the United States, through Company's foreign licensees, or by Company itself, to retail stores or for re-sale to retail stores.

21. ASSIGNMENT.

Company shall have the right to assign this Agreement in whole or in part to any subsidiary, parent company or affiliate of Company or to any third party acquiring all or a substantial portion of Company's assets or equity interests or pursuant to an initial public offering. Neither you nor Artist shall have the right to assign this Agreement.

> *ASSIGNMENT OF PUBLISHING INTEREST IN RECORDED SONGS-If the artist has written any of the material that is to be recorded on their album, then they are granting two things to the label and publishing company. The two issues involved are (a) royalty splits which appear to be 50-50% as in the usual single-song contract and then (b) a 50/50% split of the copyright ownership making this a sub-publishing deal. This is usually fair as most labels want it all! The attorney once again has supported his clients in providing a very fair publishing deal in a time when most labels want a 360 deal with all publishing rights and royalties. In addition, the label has agreed to administer and license 100% of the administrative (paperwork) which is a benefit to the artists/writers.*

22. ASSIGNMENT OF PUBLISHING INTEREST IN RECORDED SONGS.

With respect to any and all musical compositions written in whole or in part by any or all members of Artist which is recorded and commercially released on any Master or Album recorded hereunder (a "Recorded Composition"), each such member of Artist hereby assigns and transfers to Company or its publishing designee, its successors and assigns, fifty percent (50%) of all of such Artist member's right, title and interest in and to each and every Recorded Composition, or portion thereof, as described above, for the entire Universe, including but not limited to such Artist member's interest in the copyrights therein and any renewals or extensions thereof. Each Artist member agrees, upon Company's request, to execute a publishing agreement with Company's affiliated publishing company with respect to each such Recorded Composition, promptly following the recording thereof by Artist and commercial release of same on any Master or Album hereunder. The parties agree that Company's affiliated publishing entity will administer and license 100% of such Recorded Composition.

> *MERCHANDISING-The company is direct in stating that "in consideration for company's development of your name, image, brand" (you need to give us sole-exclusive-rights to your merchandising). Thus, the true beginning of a 360 deal with the label trying to find an honest and fair way to spend tons of money on an act and being able to recoup their investment on more than just record sales. It is only fair as more than half of the recorded music acquired by consumers is not paid for, yet labels have to find a way to recoup their investment.*

23. MERCHANDISING.

In consideration for Company's development of your name, brand, identity and services as a recording and touring artist, you grant Company exclusive Merchandise Rights during the term of this Agreement. After deducting from gross income received from the sale of merchandise, the costs of manufacturing, shipping and fulfillment, costs associated with a merchandise salesperson (if required) such as per diems, salary, transportation and lodging, insurance, venue or hall fees, product design fees and other costs customarily associated with selling artist merchandise, the parties shall equally divide all net receipts. Company shall account to you monthly for your portion of net receipts which shall not be subject to recoupment of Advances hereunder, other than advances that specifically constitute prepayment to you of a portion of your merchandise net receipts. Company, or its designee, shall maintain books and records for the purpose of verifying the accuracy of statements rendered by Company pursuant to this paragraph, which books and records are available for your examination upon reasonable notice and at Company's principal office.

24. CONFIDENTIALITY.

Each of Artist and Company agree to keep strictly confidential the monetary terms of this Agreement; provided however that this restriction shall not apply to information which:

- (a) is required to be disclosed by law or by any order, rule or regulation of any court or governmental agency; or. 25.
- (b) is disclosed to Artist's or Company's attorney(s) or manager(s) in the ordinary course of business so long as such persons have agreed to be subject to restrictions identical to those imposed upon Company and Artist under this provision.

25. MISCELLANEOUS.

(a) This Agreement sets forth the entire agreement between the parties with respect to the subject matter hereof. No modification, amendment, waiver, termination or discharge of this Agreement shall be binding upon Artist or Company unless confirmed by a written instrument signed by an authorized person of Company and Artist. A waiver by either party of any term or condition of this Agreement in any instance shall not be deemed or construed as a waiver of such term or condition for the future, or of any subsequent breach thereof. All of Company and Artist's rights, options and remedies in this Agreement shall be cumulative and none of them shall be in limitation of any other remedy, option or right available to Company. Wherever possible, each provision hereof shall be interpreted in such manner as to be effective and valid under applicable law, but in case any one or more of the provisions of this Agreement shall, for any reason, be held to be invalid, illegal or unenforceable in any respect, that provision shall be ineffective to the extent, but only to the extent, of such invalidity, illegality or unenforceability without invalidating the remainder of that provision or any other provisions of this Agreement. It is agreed that all accountings and royalty payments required herein, and all grants made herein, shall survive and continue beyond the expiration or earlier termination of this Agreement. No breach of this Agreement by Company or Artist (except for Artist's breach of the exclusivity provisions hereof) shall be deemed material unless notice is given specifying the nature of the breach and the recipient of the notice fails to cure such breach, if any, within thirty (30) days after receipt of the notice; notwithstanding the foregoing, Artist expressly acknowledges that Company may obtain injunctive relief hereunder immediately, and Company is not required to delay for thirty (30) days or any other period.

(b) This Agreement is made in the State of Tennessee and its validity, construction and performance shall be governed by the laws of the State of Tennessee applicable to agreements made and to be entirely performed in Tennessee, without regard to any conflicts of laws principles. The Federal and State courts in Davidson County shall have exclusive jurisdiction of any dispute arising under or concerning this Agreement. Service of process pursuant to this paragraph may be made, among other methods, by delivering the same via overnight mail or mailing by certified air mail, return receipt requested, in the same manner as giving other notices under this Agreement, and shall be effective upon sending the process. Such service is deemed to have the same force and effect as personal service within the State of Tennessee.

(c) This Agreement has binding legal effect, and grants certain exclusive rights to Company for Artist's services. Artist acknowledges that Company has requested Artist to consult with and be represented by an attorney who is knowledgeable about the subject of this Agreement and the record and music and entertainment industries, to be advised about the content and effect of the provisions of this Agreement, and to follow Artist's attorney's advice about entering into this Agreement.

(d) This Agreement shall not become effective until it is executed by all parties.

IN WITNESS WHEREOF, the parties hereto have executed this Agreement on the day and year first above written.

COMPANY:
By:_____

ARTIST:
By:_____

Date:

CONTRACT TERMS

Artist Accounts: Record labels set up in-house accounts in the artist's name to fund all approved projects including recordings, advances, and tour support that are recoupable at 100%. The marketing, promotion, and publicity is recoupable at 50%, however, most labels run them through tour support so that all expenses will become 100% recoupable.

Advances: Advances are technically all monies advanced for the recordings, marketing, promotion, and publicity of an artist. However, actual money is often provided at the time an artist signs a contract to help the artist with living expenses for a short period of time (usually during sessions). The financial advances are 100% recoupable paid out of the artist's royalties (based on each unit sold) to pay the total debt to the label.

Audits: Labels hate them but they are a reality of doing business with creative artists. Labels usually grant the artist's accountant the right to audit the books (account of the artist only) to determine if the label has failed to pay any royalties received through record sales and publishing agreements. Because money is coming into the label at different times from different sources it is not unusual to find some royalties that need to be paid. A 30 to 60 day notice, in writing, is usually required before the accountant may examine the books. Audits are often allowed only once a year.

Commitment Album: Labels may offer a seven-year, seven album deal but they are only really committed to pay for the recording, marketing, and promotion of the first album during the initial period (usually one year) and then each additional album if they pick up the corresponding option (usually based on album sales figures from the previously released recording).

Controlled Composition Clause: Labels habitually want to save money on album projects and one of the ways to do this is to pay only 75% of the statutory rate for mechanical licenses. As stated earlier, if the main artist owns, controls or has written all or part of the composition, then the label can declare the song a controlled composition. Sadly, in contracts, songs that are not owned, controlled, or written by the label or recording artists are usually required to share label publishing or songwriter credits with the main recording artist. The actual songwriter(s) receives reduced songwriting share royalties, the publisher (if not part of the label) receives reduced publishing share royalties and the label's publishing company, or recording artists receive shares of royalties for songs they did not publish or write. The label also saves on the bottom line as it pays 25% less of the statutory rate for the mechanical licenses. It does not seem fair, yet it is an industry standard and it does provide a way for the label to share the fundamental financial risk of recording an unknown tune.

Copyright Owner: The record label (who pays for all the bills) is the owner of the copyright of the actual recordings. Most recording artists are signed as work-for-hire to the label so that they will not be able to recapture their copyrights between the 35th and 40th years of ownership. The value of the label's equity is tied to ownership of their very successful recording products. They can sell stock in the company based on the recordings' value (they own) and the artists they have under long-term contract.

Cross Collateralization: Labels use cross collateralization to apply the profits from a current financially successful release to pay the continuing debt of previous album releases. Most artists do not want cross-collateralization in their contracts, however, unless you are an established superstar, expect to find it in your contract.

Delivery Date: The delivery date is the actual date the artist is to present an acceptable digital master of their recording to the label (usually the Vice President of A&R).

Street Date: Actual date the recording is to be released for sale to retail outlets.

Exclusivity: Artists may only record for labels they are signed to and cannot record for any other label (during the time of the contract) without the written permission of the label. In addition, artists are not usually allowed to re-record hits created at one label for another label even after the contract has expired.

Formula: The formula is usually a pre-determined percentage of the profits or losses that will determine the artist's cash advances for the next album if the label picks up the option. If the artist is to receive an advantage of 20% of profitable sales of, lets say $1 million, then the advance would be $200,000.

Name and Likeness: Artists will need to grant to the label the rights to use their professional name, image, likeness and biographical information to market and promote their recordings.

WORLD CHARTING COMPANIES

The following are companies and their websites that chart recordings in different countries and territories.

Canada: Nielsen Canadian SoundScan
www.cria.ca / www.soundscan.com

Norway: VS Newspaper/IFPI Norway
www.ifpi.no

USA: Nielsen SoundScan
www.billboard.com / www.soundscan.com

Poland: ZPAV/Pentor Research Institute
www.zpav.pl

Austria: GfK Austrian Charts
www.autriancharts.at

Belgium: Ultratop/GfK
www.ultratop.be

Czech Republic: IFPI Czech Republic
www.ifpicr.cz

Denmark: Nielsen Music Control
www.hitlisten.nu

Finland: Finnish National Broadcasting Company
www.yle.fi/top40

France: SNEP/IFOP
www.disqueenfrance.com

Germany: Media Control
www.musicline.de

Greece: IFPI Greece/Deloitte
www.ifpi.gr

Hungary: MAHASZ
www.mahasz.hu

Portugal: AFP/AC Nielsen
Spain: PROMUSICAE/GfK/Nielsen Music Control
www.promusicae.es

Sweden: GLF/IFPI Sweden
www.hitlistan.se

Switzerland: Hit Parade
www.hitparade.ch

UK: OCC/Millward Brown
www.theofficialcharts.com

Japan: RIAJ
www.riaj.or.jp

Korea: RIAK
Australia: ARIA
www.aria.com.au

New Zealand: Media Sauce/RIANZ
www.nztop40.com

Ireland: IRMA/Chart Track
www.irma.ie

Italy: FIMI/AC Neilsen
www.fimi.it

Netherlands: GfK Austrian Charts
www.dutchcharts.nl

Brazil: ABPD
www.abpd.org.br

Mexico: Amprofon
www.amprofon.com/mx[194]

---

[194] www.IFPI.org

CONTRACT STUDY POINTS

1. What is the initial period?

2. What is an option and how many are usually offered?

3. What is the recording commitment?

4. What is the usual time period and number of albums or singles released during the initial period?

5. Explain the recording procedure.

6. Who signs the artists and who pays for the recordings?

7. Who owns the copyrights to the master recordings?

8. Explain advances to the artists.

9. Explain artist royalties.

10. What does the controlled composition clause mean (section 11 of the contract).

11. Who is responsible for the artist's responsibilities listed in the contract?

12. Explain how section 23 of the contract is something you would expect to find in a 360 deal.

13. Is the artist an employee of the label or a work for hire?

14 What is the difference to an artist if they are a work for hire?

15. What is the difference to the label?

Lecture Points
Chapter Eight

209

Band partnerships & Trademarks

BAND PARTNERSHIP AGREEMENTS

THE BAND PARTNERSHIP

SERVICES

ACTIVITIES

NAME AND LOGO

PROMISES

EARNINGS AND LOSSES

WHO OWNS WHAT

HOW THE PUBLISHING WORKS

Lecture Points
Chapter Eight

WHO IS THE PUBLISHER

VOTING RIGHTS

ACCOUNTING

ENDING THE PARTNERSHIP

WHAT HAPPENS AFTER THE BREAK-UP

ADDING A PARTNER

WHEN THEY LEAVE

BANK STUFF

ARBITRATION

GENERAL INFO

Lecture Points
Chapter Eight

SIGNATURES

TRADEMARKS

BASICS

PROTECTING THE TRADEMARK

FIRST USE

POSSIBLE CONFUSION

YOUR NAME

NAME IN SAME AREA

LOGO, DESIGN AND SLOGAN

SERVICE MARKS

DOMAIN NAMES

REGISTRATION OF YOUR NAME (Trademark)

Lecture Points
Chapter Eight

ARTISTS ACCOUNTS

ADVANCES

AUDITS

COMMITMENT ALBUMS

PACKAGING COSTS

COPYRIGHT OWNER

DEAL MEMO

DELIVERY DATE

RECORDING COMMITMENT

Chapter Eight

FORMULA

LABEL RIGHTS

MUSIC VIDEOS

NAMES AND LIKENESS

UNIONS

WORK FOR HIRE

THE RECORDING BUSINESS

Creating Recordings In Studios and at Home

"Basically, you're trying to bottle lightning all the time. There's no use putting a record out unless it's got some magic on it. And magic doesn't come easy."

—Quincy Jones, Record Producer[195]

CREATING MAGIC

Recording artists are idolized as superstars; yet, it is a very creative team of talented studio musicians, backup singers, audio engineers, and record producers that often create the recordings that lead to fame. Having the ability to sing well is one thing, getting it recorded with magic is quite another. Major label artists usually reach a level of iconic status before consumers buy (or steal) the recordings that pay for the distribution, promotion, and publicity required to launch careers.

RECORDING VARIABLES

There are three variables that determine the cost and quality of a recording:

- The recording team and studio

- The type of recording tied to union or non-union agreements

- The recording process or stages of an actual master recording session

THE RECORDING TEAM

Record/Session Producers: The session producer is the captain of the ship, directing and stimulating the creative elements of the audio engineer, studio musicians and recording artists. Suggested skills and knowledge include a passion for music, an understanding of music theory and sight-reading, and knowledge of the "number system." Producers also need to know copyright laws, music publishing, business finance and the music business sub-systems. Musicianship skills are essential for music producers. Successful producers communicate well with others, are decisive leaders, understand basic accounting skills for controlling budgets, and have strategic management skills for administration. In addition, producers commonly have a consummate understanding of the recording studio acoustics, basic electronics, and equipment capabilities and an almost magical ability to "marry" the right song to the right recording artist. The bottom line is that producers are responsible for:

- The final quality of the sound and performance on the master tape,

- The selection of songs (material) the artist sings, and recording budget.

---

[195] "The Recording Industry Career Handbook" by The NARAS Foundation (1995).

Producers know other industry professionals through networking, showcases, parties, meetings, professional organizations, industry events, award shows, etc. Successful producers know who the industry movers and shakers are (the insiders and personalities who manage and control the industry), as the majority of their work originates from those connections.[196][197]

- *Independent producers* begin their careers learning the trade by producing demo sessions for publishers and custom or vanity albums that are commonly non-label productions paid for by the recording artist or band. Some are demo recordings that showcase the recording artists or songs, which are then "pitched" to a record label. Great demo recordings often lead to the next step in the career of a producer working for a label in the A&R[198] department recording development deals.[199]

- *Record label staff producers* are hired by labels to produce development deal acts. The label pays for all expenses, including the studio, musicians, and vocalists. The producer gains additional opportunities to work with better musicians, artists, and studio equipment. If the tracks are perceived as sellable, exciting or have quality, labels may sign the act and release a single. If a label passes on the act, the cost of the development deal is commonly used as a tax write-off.[200]

- *Major independent producers* are at the top of their profession and paid handsomely. Extremely successful producers earn $1,000-5,000 per side (per song) depending on the genre of music and the financial success of the acts they are producing. In addition, they receive producer points usually 1-3% of the artist's royalties on each unit sold.[201] Major producers are highly respected for their abilities to produce hit records. Their success makes them behind the scenes stars within their own industry. Because major producers gain so much power and respect in the industry they control their destiny as clever entrepreneurs by letting different labels and artists bid for their services. Major labels often hire very successful producers as executives to run a label and use and protect their talents instead of competing with them.

Musicians change our world, life would not be the same without them. There are several types in the music industry including:

- *Garage/jam band musicians* are usually the high school students who jam in order to learn cover tunes of well-known popular acts. This often becomes their first step toward a professional career in the industry. Most musicians volunteer to perform in small clubs, coffee houses, churches and other types of gigs in order to learn the business and improve their performance skills. Many continue to improve their performance skills and knowledge during college by jamming with others who share their interests and by taking private lessons from classically trained musicians. Others simply learn how to make recordings on their computers using garage band, Pro-Tools, and logic software programs.

---

196 These include music publishers, independent producers, artist managers and others who find new talent and songs and industry insiders who are closely connected to record label operations and management executives.
197 http://www.nytimes.com/2008/08/16/arts/music/16wexler.html?_r=1&hp=&pagewanted=all
198 Department of Artists and Repertoire.
199 In the film business, *executive producers* are usually the people who finance the production of a movie project. It is rare to find an executive producer in most projects in the music industry.
200 The master tapes and thus the copyright of the recordings remain the property of the label. It is often wise for an act to buy the development tapes (if possible) as then they will not have to worry about them being released if they are signed by a different label in the future.
201 Payment of producer points is usually required on each unit sold or begun after artist recoupment expenses are paid back to the label. Very few major producers allow for the recoupment clause delay as they know that most recording artists will never sell enough product (recordings) for their labels to fully recoup expenses.

JERRY WEXLER

HOW CAN A GUY CHANGE THE WORLD?

Jerry Wexler was already in his 30s when he entered the music business, working at Billboard Magazine. He suggested they change the name of the black charts (called Race Records) to Rhythm and Blues and the name has stuck ever since. Mr. Wexler didn't care for rock 'n' roll, though he signed Led Zeppelin and eventually produced records with Bob Dylan, Carlos Santana, Dire Straits and George Michael.

His main influence came in the 1950s and '60s as a Vice President of Atlantic Records, creating new musical styles with black artists, combining elements of gospel, swing and blues. This Soul Music played a major role in bringing black music to the masses. Mr. Wexler helped the following artists record in Memphis and Muscle Shoals with white musicians, Wilson Pickett, Otis Redding, Dusty Springfield, Linda Ronstadt, Ray Charles's, Patti Page, The Drifters, The Clovers, Joe Turner, Ruth Brown, and the great hits of Aretha Franklin.

WHO RECORDS THE ALBUM?

Road and concert musicians rarely record albums in the studio with the artists. However, musicians have many career options and sources of income, including instrumentalists in rock, country, and jazz performance groups, concert bands, orchestras, other live gigs, TV, wedding and the list goes on...

- *Working musicians* receive money for their music performances. Serious musicians join unions and audition to become members of various levels of performance groups including orchestras, bands, and other types of entertainment ensembles.[202] Many use their musical skills to supplement other types of occupations. Others continue to struggle either part-time or full-time to develop a "sound" and fan-base "following" that may lead to greater financial opportunities through their creative musical performances.

- *Road musicians and event artists* are the musicians and vocalists who are on tour as an opening act or the musicians hired to perform with a recording artist. Others are often classically trained musicians who form smaller groups to perform at special social, political, or other types of events. It is very rare for the road musicians of a major recording artist to be on the actual hit recordings they are playing live. That is the job of studio musicians.

- *Studio musicians* are most often heard on major recording artists' recordings, yet very few consumers know them by their actual names. Great studio musicians can make thousands of dollars a day, charge double or triple scale for a three-hour session and often become true stars known only by the best producers and label recording artists. They are recording artists themselves, but are rarely known by the public. Studio musicians play their instruments to highlight the marriage of the song to the vocal characteristics of the recording artist. Some of the best musicians in the world are studio/session musicians and, of course, most record labels and recording artists use master session studio musicians for their album projects.[203] Recording opportunities include music soundtracks for TV shows, movies, commercials, jingles, and major artist's recordings. Possessing musical talent is imperative if you want to be a recording artist or studio musician. In addition, a music education, an understanding of copyright law, music publishing, networking, and the music business, are also important for success.

---

202 The American Federation of Musicians (AF of M) for professional musicians and The American Federation of Radio and Television Artists (AFTRA) for vocalists.

203 Road musicians or concert musicians rarely record albums in the studio with the artists. Musicians have many career options and sources of income, including as instrumentalists and or vocalists in rock, country, and jazz performance groups, concert bands, orchestras, and even in the armed forces.

Audio Engineers: Audio engineers mix the creativity of music (the song), the artistic capabilities of the artists, musicians, and BGV's (the performances) to the logical physical and technologic potentials of the studios' acoustics and equipment in order to capture (record) the best performances. Suggested skills and knowledge include a basic understanding of the business of music and entertainment, music theory, copyright laws, music publishing, marketing, management and business finance. Knowledge of computer software programs Pro-Tools, Pro-Logic, and even Garage Band is important as the industry moves toward less expensive modes of recording in order to save money and improve the bottom line on the profit and loss statement. Basic electronic, acoustics, recording equipment variables and having a continuous desire to learn the latest technical advances in recording equipment and audio production are fundamental.[204] Communication skills and the ability to work with highly creative individuals are crucial. Business courses are also helpful, as most audio engineers often become producers and both are entrepreneurs. Most will own or lease a recording studio, computer and software, a music publishing company and some, their own independent record labels. The career of the most successful audio engineers starts with basic lessons in recording or on their own computer recording themselves and others. Careers often follow a similar path including:

- ***Entry-level Audio Engineers*** are often college students who are working in a studio as an intern at the same time they are recording local musicians on the latest computer recording software. They are rarely paid for their efforts; however, they are given opportunities to learn the basics and to meet members of the creative team.

- ***Second Engineers*** are a step up in the process from entry-level engineers. They set up microphones, cables, headsets, the console, and alignment of the tape machines. Second engineers also run the tape machines and keep the log sheets during the sessions and occasionally travel with artists on the road to hone audio and mixing skills.

- ***Staff Engineers*** are sometimes employed at a recording studio. They have the ability to accomplish any level of a session, from demo to master sessions with major recording artists and triple scale musicians. Staff audio engineers' positions are commonly found in non-music recording centers where great engineers are difficult to find. Annual salaries range from $30,000 to $70,000.

- ***Major-Artist- Independent Engineers*** are at the top of their profession with a long list of hit records they helped create. They are "on-call" and most often work on master sessions for label artists and known superstars. Their pay is negotiable, ranging between $1,000 a day plus expenses to $500-$2,500 per side (per-song) which is 50% of the producers per-side rates. It is very rare for audio engineers to also receive points from the artist as producers do, however, in very special situations it has happened. Most studios located in music recording centers (Los Angeles, New York, and Nashville) have replaced staff audio engineers with independent engineers. The location for the production has become less important as many artists have studios in their homes or vacation homes and many use computers and software to record all their tracks instead of renting a major studio.

---

204 It is important to know the limits and advantages of each piece of recording equipment in order to help the artist(s) record and perform to the best of their ability and sometimes even provide musical performance assistance to improve upon what the artist is incapable of providing artistically.

> *"We all knew the scam that the record companies perpetrated."*
> —Carol Kaye, studio musician and member of the Wrecking Crew[1]

Probably the greatest records ever recorded were done in Los Angles studios by The Wrecking Crew.

WHO?

"During the sixties and seventies, perhaps the most fertile period of popular music our nation has ever produced, recording stars such as the Monkees, Carpenters, Gary Lewis and the Playboys, Jan & Dean, The Beach Boys, The Association, the Grass Roots, Simon and Garfunkel, Paul Revere & the Raiders, Kenny Rogers & the First Edition, the Mamas and the Papas, and dozens more ruled the airwaves.

However, most listeners are likely unaware that a good share of these legendary artists seldom, if ever, played any of the instruments on their own records. The musicians on the tracks were actually L.A. studio musicians who together became known as The Wrecking Crew. Thus, most of the music on the hit records were not the band musicians, it was the Wrecking Crew. The guys in the band were just the musicians on the road.

—Kent Hartman[2]

---

[1] Ibid.
[2] The Wrecking Crew by Kent Hartman, February/March 2007, American Heritage Magazine.

Signal Flow: The label business depends on the record producers and audio engineers' ability to create a sellable recording (product) that is really a one time shot based on three stages of recording including the following *signal flow* tied to stages of recordings:

- **Basic Tracks or Tracking**-Signal flowing from mics in the studio into the console, split and sent (at 186,000 miles a second), to; the 24 track tape machine or hard disk drive (computer); the monitors in the control room (speakers); the musicians headsets (ear phones); the effects (add echo, reverb, pitch control to signals); and the two-track master tape machine or computer. *Playback* of a recording reverses the signal flow from the tape machines or computer hard disk drive and allows the *producer, audio engineer, musicians and vocalists* a chance to check their creative work.

- **Overdubbing**-Is the addition of more or new recordings (tracks) to the *master tape* or computer drive. The original tracks recorded in basic tracks are saved and additional tracks are added by recording new instruments and vocals onto new tracks (*in sync*) with the previous tracks. *In-sync* means that the *record head* (on tape machines) are turned into *playback heads* so that all tracks are played back and the new tracks are recorded at the same time. Thus, the *overdub stage* is a combination of recording (tracking) and (listening) playback at the same time.

- **Mix-down**-After all tracks have been recorded the signal is played back from the 24 track tape machine or computer and the individual tracks are *mix together into a two track master* which is what consumers hear on their CDs and digital downloads.

> *"My music will go on forever. Maybe it's a fool say that, but when me know facts me can say facts. My music will go on forever."*
> **—the late Bob Marley**[205]

Recording Artist: Most people think that when labels sign vocal and musical acts to record deals *artists* are not usually considered a *work-for-hire*, but in the legal world of the music and entertainment industry, that is exactly how they are defined.[206] A *work-for-hire* is when (the artist) is hired for a specific purpose (to create recordings) and paid once for the work, losing all ownership in the property (copyright) of what has been created. Record deals are somewhat different in that a debt is created (recording, promotion, and publicity expenses) in the name of the artist. Then, as the label sells the recordings it pays back the debt it created in the name of the artist. Communication and networking skills are vital. Knowledge of a foreign language is

---

[205] http://www.artquotes.net/entertainment-quotes/bob-marley.htm
[206] Labels started placing the *work-for-hire* definition into contracts to prevent artists from recapturing their recording (copyrights) between the 35th and 40th years of ownership.

often required for traditional vocal performances and opera. A fully developed image based on the essence of the artist is important for the marketing plans of the label.

- *Royalty Artists* are rarely stellar musicians and thus labels are overjoyed when they sign an act with a great image and fan base that is also a talented musician. However, times are changing and young consumers are now demanding honest, talented musicians and artists instead of the manufactured icons their parents and grandparents admired and idolized.

- *Virtuosos* are celebrated as the best in the world based on their musical, vocal talents and fame. Examples of virtuosos are Luciano Pavarotti, Itzhak Perlman and Andrea Bocelli.

- *BGV's (background vocalists)* Publishing companies record demos of their songs to "pitch" to major record producers, artist managers, record label A&R departments, and recording artists. The assumption is the more famous the artist, the more albums will potentially be sold, resulting in greater royalty checks for the songwriters and publishers. Inexperienced singers find entry-level work at publishing companies singing demo recordings. Non-union members and college interns may earn $10.00 to $50.00 a song; not much money, but singing in a recording studio is different from performing in a choir or on stage. It provides the novice studio singer with some valuable studio experience. The acoustics, lighting, and monitoring are often complex. So, the more experience gained in the studio, the quicker one can use what was learned to become a professional recording artist. There is also another advantage: As the producers, A&R personnel, and artist managers listen to the demo tapes for a great song, they are also hearing a specific voice on the demo. Singing on demos is a great way to be heard by industry insiders who can make a singing career happen. Successful demo singers sometimes become professional singers. Job opportunities include singing for advertisements and jingle companies, as well as harmony tracks for recording sessions and television shows. Professional singers (vocalists) frequently net more money than label recording artists as they do not have to support an entourage of road musicians, managers, producers, and label marketing and promotion executives.

TYPES OF RECORDING STUDIOS

Recording Studios tend to be earmarked by their function and the equipment they have available to producers and artists. Thus, five types of studios are usually found in creative communities:

- *Master Studios*: Most large room master studios are solidly packed with the latest audio equipment and special effects toys that can be used for tracking label signed royalty artists.

- *Project Studios*: If you need a demo, low budget, limited pressing CD, or a movie soundtrack, project studios fill the gap between the very expensive master studios and the vanity, poorly insolated, horrible acoustics of a garage studio.

- *Demo Studios*: These studios are often the older analog based recording studio with minor special effects equipment. They are often used for demo, vanity and limited budget recordings.

- *Post-Production Studios*: After the overdubbing session the producer and artist often move to the special equipment post-production studio to mix the master tape computer disks.

- ***Computer based studios***: To the detriment of the recording studio business, many artists are now forgoing the cost of major recording studios in favor of computer-based software and small home based recording/acoustic rooms. Computers with Pro-tools and Pro-Logic are capable of providing recordings as good and in some cases better than the very best professional studios. Thus, even major artists are recording only basic tracks in live studios and the overdubs and mixes on computer programs at their leisure. They can even email their vocal recording to producers who can remix the final mixed tracks.

SCHEDULING SESSIONS

Sessions are "booked" in three-hour blocks scheduled from 10 a.m. to 1 p.m., 2 to 5 p.m., 6 to 9 p.m., and 10 p.m. to 1 a.m. The hour between sessions is for tearing down the current session and setting up the next session. Of course all of this is changing with the introduction of Internet recording sessions.

UNIONS
www.aftra.org
www.afm.org

A labor union is a "group of people" who band together to demand better pay and working conditions through collective bargaining. There are several unions in the music business that represent the creative artists and workers. Unions are organizations formed by individuals in the same or similar profession who band together for increased representation with employers. They bargain for wages and set scale which is the various levels of payments for different types of employment. The major unions in the music and entertainment industry are:

- ***The American Federation of Television and Radio Artists*** represents vocalists and recording artists in studio sessions, television productions, and live performances. It also represents actors, announcers, sound effects artists, and other personalities working in radio and television. Representation is focused in five areas: sound recordings, broadcast news, commercials, industries & new technologies (non-broadcast industry films), and entertainment programs (television). *The Code of Fair Practice for Phonograph Records* is the contractual agreement between AFTRA and the major record labels.[207]

- ***The American Federation of Musicians*** represents musicians for recordings and live performances in local and internationally negotiated agreements in many fields including studio and other recordings, TV, films, jingles, concerts, stage shows, symphony, opera and ballet. The AF of M has approximately 100,000 members represented by 300 plus local offices. Membership advantages include a retirement fund, health insurance and AFL-CIO benefits. The AF of M uses franchised booking agents who work on a 10-15% commission to connect union musicians with people who want to hire them. Most of the agents represent musicians and recording artists locally and nationally. Major record labels are signatories to *The American Federation of Musician's Phonograph Record Labor Agreement* that governs the wages, benefits and working conditions of all its members, including studio musicians.[208][209]

---

207 www.aftra.org
208 www.afm.org
209 The Recording Industry Music Performance Trust Fund Agreement (RIMPTF) is the largest single sponsor of live music performances in the world. Created in 1948, the fund is part of an agreement between the AF of M and the record labels. The fund is also based on record sales. The purpose of the fund is to increase the appreciation of live music performances by providing free concerts to the public.

TYPES OF SESSIONS

There are five types of actual recording sessions with the differences being based on union or non-union agreements and if you live in a right-to-work state. *The amount the money the recording recording team members receives is based on their fame, track record, contacts, and the types of sessions which are of course, based on union agreements, budgets, the purpose of the recordings and marketing plan.* Each recording session is a three-hour call with a maximum length of 15 minutes of actual saved recorded time, an unlimited number of sides (songs) and four overdubs for sweetening or corrections. Labels and recording producers have the following options when recording an act:

- *Master Sessions* (union musicians and vocalists-unlimited pressings/digital units for sale).
- *Low Budget* (union musicians and vocalists-limits the recording budget to about $100,000.00).
- *Limited Pressings* (union musicians and vocalists-limits sales to 5,000 pressings/digital units for sale with charts or airplay and 10,000 units sold without charts or airplay).
- *Demo* (union musicians and vocalists-allows pressings/digital units to be only given away for promotion and may not be sold).
- *Non-union* (no union musicians or vocalists-can't be sold by labels with union agreements).

A.F. OF M. RECORDING SCALES

www.afm.org[210]

	Leader (double Scale)	Side Musician	Health & Welfare	Pension
Master	$745.14	$372.57	$22.00	(11%)
Low Budget	$418.58	$209.99	$22.00	(11%)
Limited Pressing	$393.00	$196.50	$22.00	(11%)
Demo	$208.00	$104.00	$22.00	(11%)
Non-Union	None	None	None	None

Thus, if you hired five union musicians at master scale (meaning unlimited pressings) it will cost you $372.57, plus $22.00 (H&W), plus $40.98 (11% of basic scale for pension) or $435.55 (per player x four musicians) which equals $1,744.22. In addition, a required lead musician for the session will cost $745.14 (double scale), plus $22.00 (H&W), plus, $81.96 (11% pension) for a total of $849.10. Add the four musicians total of $1,744.22 and the leaders scale of $849.10 and the total cost to hire five union

---
210 www.afm.org/recording scales.

musicians at master scale for one three-hour session is $2,593.32. At the other end of the scale are the non-union musician sessions where you can hire anyone who wants the experience of working in the industry for free. The problem is that the difference in sound and artistic quality is everything and you get what you pay for. Great union musicians are a deal at twice the price and that is why many major labels live by the union agreements. Some other rules of the union game are that low budget sessions are for recording budgets of $99,000 or less for featured artists with a three-day union approval. Limited pressing sessions are for the pressing of 10,000 units and the promise that the label will pay the difference between master and limited pressing scale if more than the 10,000 ceiling is passed (which is good news for both the label and union members). Union demos are for demonstration purposes only, such as song plugging or potential vocal artists' pitches to label A&R departments or established artists managers, and may not be sold.

A.F.T.R.A. RECORDING SCALES

www.aftra.org

AFTRA scale is determined differently than the AF of M scale. It depends on the side or actual master takes called a side, the number of overdubs, also called a side, and the length of the actual recording in minutes and seconds, which is used as a multiplier. In addition, labels can and often do pay their royalty artist a maximum of triple scale. Thus, one side (or take) is limited to 3:30 seconds and 3:31 to 7:00 minutes is considered double or two sides and 7:31 or 10:30 is triple scale or 3 sides. Overdubbing adds sides to the total. A new recording or side in each multi-track is an additional side. So, to calculate the number of sides, take the original track, add any overdubs or additional tracks recorded and multiply by the corresponding multiplier based on the actual length of the recording. As an example, a four-minute song with two overdubs is considered six sides (the original track which is one side, plus two overdubs which is two additional sides for a total of three sides x two as the multiplier because the song is over three minutes and thirty one seconds in length).[211]

The rules of the game for AFTRA non-label royalty singers include receiving contingent scale payments for performing on recordings that sell greater than 157,500 units. As an example, AFTRA BGV's receive 50% additional scale payments on recordings that sell over 157,500 and 75% additional scale payments for recordings when 1,250,000 units are sold. For AFTRA label royalty artists the labels are required to make health and pension payments based on the royalties earned even if they are not recouped. In addition, if a recording is licensed (master licenses) by a label (copyright holder) to another medium such as a film track or visual commercial (television) then a separate payment may be provided.[212]

THE AF OF M TRUST FUND

The Recording Industry Music Performance Trust Fund Agreement is the largest single sponsor of live music performances in the world. Created in 1948, the fund is part of an agreement between the AF of M and the record labels. The fund is also based on record sales. The purpose of the fund is to increase the appreciation of live music performances by providing free concerts to the public often in the summer in the park.

---

[211] www.aftra.org
[212] Ibid.

A.F.T.R.A. RECORDING SCALES

Type of Call	Recording Scale	Recording song less than 3:31	Health & Re-tirement	Number of Overdubs	Multiplier (length of song)
Royalty Artist (single) or two vocalists. Each receive scale plus additional sides	$194.00	1 side	10% of Scale	Number of overdubs in addition to the original track/side	3:31-7:00 = 2 sides 7:01-10:30 = 3 sides
Non-Royalty Artist (single) or two vocalists. Each receive scale plus additional sides	$194.00	1 side	11.5% of Scale	Number of overdubs in addition to the original track/side	3:31-7:00 = 2 sides 7:01-10:30 = 3 sides
3-8 BGV's Each receiving scale plus one is defined as a Contractor	$87.75 Plus the contractor receives an additional $42.50	1 side	11.5% of Scale	Number of overdubs in addition to the original track/side	3:31-7:00 = 2 sides 7:01-10:30 = 3 sides

NON-UNION RECORDING SESSIONS

Enterprising recording artists, producers and musicians often cut non-union tracks. In addition, many states have right-to-work laws, as stated earlier, which allow for non-union recordings. However, most non-union recordings are used only for pitching songs and showcasing potential recording artists. If a label signs an act, it will usually re-cut the tracks with union musicians or pay the difference between what the musicians were paid and union scales. Anybody can record without using union members. Most non-union sessions are by non-professional artists, engineers, and producers who are in the process of developing their creative abilities. However, the best musicians and vocalists are usually union members and most likely will not work for less than union scale. Unions help protect their members from unscrupulous producers, scam artists, and financially shaky record labels that promise payments but rarely deliver.[213]

---

[213] Remember that major labels are signatories to the union agreements and simply cannot legally release any recordings for sale that were created without union members or musicians and vocalists who were paid less than union master scale.

STAGES OF A RECORDING SESSION

In recording studios, audio engineers typically record artists in different stages including the following:

- ***Pre-production***: Marrying the right song to the right artist is essential. The two must fit together in a way that allows the melody and lyrics to reinforce the perceptions consumers hold of the artists. Artist images are tied to the songs selected for an album. The quality of the studio musicians, the recording artist's performance, the production, and engineering all contribute to the final sound and feel of the recording.

- ***Basic Tracks***: The first stage of a recording session in the studio is called basic tracks or tracking. The rhythm instruments and scratch (rough or practice) vocals lay the foundation for the rest of the instruments and vocals, which are cut later in their final versions. Session instruments can include drums, bass guitar, piano, and electric and acoustic guitars. The recording artist adds a reference or scratch vocal for the musicians to listen to while they play. It is re-sung and rerecorded later as a finished vocal. The session process involves the musicians and vocalists listening to the demo recording of the song, tuning up, and practicing the song at least a few times to prepare for the recording. Many of the studio musicians in the music centers of Los Angeles, New York, and Nashville can learn, adapt, and contribute their musical creative talents to the essence of the song in just a few minutes.

    Basic tracks are recorded once the musicians and vocalists are ready, the audio engineer has set the microphones, monitor, and headphones, equalization and effects levels, and the producer is satisfied with the quality of the sound and musical performance during practice. Recording the right amount of signal on the tape is difficult. Too much signal will distort the tape. Too little signal will cause the playback to be noisy. Digital tape recorders and computer programs record a greater dynamic range, which solves some of the engineer's distortion and noise problems. If most of the musicians play poorly, the recording process is repeated. When the producer approves the basic musical tracks, the minor musical problems are usually fixed later. Logs are completed, which are written notes about the songs being recorded. Notes include length of the song, problems that need to be corrected in the overdub stage, and equalization and effects settings. Logs are stored in the box with the master tape. They are used in later recording sessions to alert the engineer and producers of necessary issues. Once the song has been recorded, everyone listens during tape playback for mistakes and opportunities to improve their performances. If recorded properly, the "take" becomes a "master."

- ***Overdubbing:*** Adding instrumental parts and vocals to the previously recorded master tape is called overdubbing. The prior tracks are saved and the tape machine is placed into sel-sync (short for selective synchronization). Invented by guitarist Les Paul (in 1948), sel-sync turns the record heads on the previously recorded tracks into playback heads. This allows the new instruments and vocals to be recorded in time with the instruments and vocals that were first recorded. The overdub stage is a combination of basic tracks and playback. The signal is played off the record head in playback (sel-sync) and sent to the console where it is split and sent to the monitors, effects, 2-track/DAT, and through the cue system to the musicians' and recording artists' headsets. Once the musicians and singers hear the signal (their previously recorded tracks), they play or sing their new tracks. The mics transduce the music into electrical signals, which travel back to the console at 186,000 miles per second, are split and sent to the monitors, effects, 2-track/DAT and are recorded as new tracks on the 24-or 32-track tape machine.

- *Mixdown*: The last stage in the recording process is mixdown. After all the instruments and vocals have been recorded and over-dubbed, the 24 or 32 tracks are mixed down to 2 tracks (stereo). One track of music is heard in the left ear and the other in the right. Some instruments and vocals are heard in both the left and right ears as a mono signal. Producers and audio engineers mix the tracks according to the "style" of the music; create stereo images, and 3-D depth in the mix.

- *Mastering*: If the recording team of musicians, recording artist, audio engineers, and producers have done their jobs, the creativity of the recording session has been "captured" on tape or computer disk. The 2-track tape or DAT is sent to the mastering lab to be processed, then pressed into CDs and released for digital downloads. The "spikes" make "pits" in the plastic CD during the pressing process. A laser beam scans the grooves in the CD and identifies the "pits" as 1's and the space between the "pits" as 0's. The computer chip in your CD player converts the 1's and 0's (which are the binary code) back into music.[214]

RECORDING BUDGET

Most recording contracts now call for the artist to create their own recording budget. As already provided, the three principle factors to consider are the cost of;

- *The recording team/studio.*
- *The type of session (union/non-union).*
- *The cost per each stage of the recording for one day and one song.*

Using the following matrix, you can roughly determine the cost of one song recorded in a studio and then multiply that figure by the number of songs on your album. By figuring the union scale price of the singers, royalty artists, musicians, producer, studio rental, and audio engineer for an average song, you can calculate and predict the cost of a typical 10-song album at master, limited pressing and demo rates. Select and add the expenses of renting a studio, AFTRA singers, AF of M musicians, royalty artist payments (at triple scale), a producer and audio engineer for the basic tracks, and overdubbing and mixdown stages for one song. Using average expenses for a master union recording with studio musicians and singers, major producer and audio engineer, one can see how quickly the expenses total up to a significant amount. Multiply the total cost for the master recording of one song ($18,101) by the number of songs you want to record (12 songs) for an estimated recording budget of $217,212 or about $215,000 and change.

	POPULARITY			
	Sympathetic %	Somewhat Sympathetic %	Un-Sympathetic %	Very Unsympathetic %
Paris Hilton	2	8	17	63
Britney Spears	3	15	22	51
Lindsay Lohan	3	14	21	45
Nicole Richie	3	13	20	4

Americans are generally not optimistic that any of the four will soon conquer the demons that seem to continually put them in compromising situations. No more than 1 in 3 believes any of them will overcome their problems in the next few years, while 6 in 10 believe Hilton will continue to face difficulty for the foreseeable future, and more than half say this of Spears. Close to half also believe Lohan and Richie will continue to have problems. Who cares? Their labels, movie companies, managers and all the other people who are employed by them and their entertainment corporations.
Gallup 2008

---

214 The National Association of Recording Merchandisers is a professional association that represents retailers, distributors, one stops, rack jobbers, the suppliers of the product (pressing plants, etc.,) and all non-profit organizations that are associated with the retail merchandising side of the music industry.

RECORDING BUDGET CHART

Recording Team	Responsibilities	Union	Basic Tracks 10am-1pm	Over-dubbing 2pm-5pm 6pm-9pm	Mix-down 10pm-1am	Totals
Producer	Over-all sound, performance of acts, budget	none	$5,000 per side	----------------	--------	$5,000 per side (one song)
Audio Engineer	Quality of sound and production	None-AES guild	$1,200 day rate	----------------	--------	$1,200 for the song or day
Musicians	Create great tracks	AF of M	$2,593 five musicians	$2,593 Five additional musicians	none	$5,186
Artist (vocal)	Vocally merge the emotional communicative message of the song to their personality and image	AFTRA	$640 One side triple scale, plus pension (10%)- Scratch vocal	$2,328 Four sides, plus pension (10%) 1 side, plus three overdubs times triple scale.	none	$2,968
BGV's	Support royalty artist vocals and fill harmonies	AFTRA	None	$2,047 Three Bgv's (plus conductor fee) times 6 sides	none	$2,047
Studio	Room, acoustic and equipment to fit the emotion of the act and quality of recorded sound.	None	Master studio with the day rate of $1,200	----------------	--------	$1,200
Other	Cartage Per-diem Tape/disc	None	$500 for food, limo, hotel, cartage, etc.	----------------	--------	$500
Totals	----------------	--------	$11,133	$6,968	--------	$18,101

* Rounding off all figures to dollar values.

PRODUCTION BUDGET

So, in our example the 12 song album cost $217,212.00 to record. The label now has to press CD's, (about $1.00 per CD with artwork, shrink wrap, mechanicals, and digital download storage on server sites). Of course, this is a base figure with the final cost per CD or digital download actually depending on the number of songs, complexity of the artwork, photography, booklet and other marketing concepts. The mechanicals total in this case 75% of the 9.1¢ statutory rate or $.06825 times 12 for a total of 82¢ per album. If we press 200,000 CD's and pay for the mechanicals that adds $200,000 to the budget ($164,000 for the mechanical licenses, 5 cents per CD, and about $26,000 for the jewel boxes, simple artwork, and shirkwrap or digital storage). Add the $217,212 we spent to record the album and the pressing or storage cost (plus mechanicals) and the total is $417,212. These three items, *the recording budget-including any advances), the mechanical license* (almost always at the controlled composition clause rate) and *the cost of the pressings or digital storage* are called the *all-ins*, which are recouped through artist and producer royalties.

PROMOTION AND PUBLICITY BUDGETS

Promotion budgets are based within a range of 100%-200% of the all-in's budget (recording and production pressing, etc.), depending on the act and projected units sales. Publicity is usually in a range of 50%-100% of the all-in's recording and production budget, once again depending on the act and projected sales figures. So, if the recording budget is $217,212 and the production/pressing budget is $200,000 for a total of $417,212, then, you can see that the range of total expenses for the launch of this act will be between $1,043,030 rounded down to $1 million ($417.212, the recording budget + $417,212 the promotion budget + $208,606 the publicity budget) up to a maximum launch budget of $1,668,850 rounded down to $1.5 million ($417,212 recording budget, + $834,425 the promotion budget at 200% of the all in's, + $417,212 for publicity).

BREAK-EVEN POINTS

Now that the budget for the artist has been determined (recording budget, production budget, marketing-promotion and publicity), the break-even points may be determined based on the number of units that will need to be sold at retail. Thus, the formula for the recoupment debt account of the *artist* (money loaned by the label and paid back by the label to itself) is the suggested retail list price (SRLP), minus the packaging fee (which establishes the *new royalty base*), times the artist's points (minus, the producer points), which establishes the *new artist's points base*. This determines the actual royalties the artist is to be paid per-unit sold (which for an album is usually between ($1.00-2.35) based on the original contract and the level of unit sales. Then, divide the unit royalty base (the $1.00-$2.35) into the total debt to determine the total number of units that need to be sold before the artist breaks even. In effect, the label takes the royalties that are to be paid to the artist and applies them to the recoupable debt. As an example, if the recoupable artist account is a $1.2 million dollar debt to the label and the artist royalty per-unit sold is $2.00 than you divide the $1.2 million dollar debt by the $2.00 royalty to determine that it will take 600,000 units (albums) sold before the artist will receive any money. Thus, it is easy to see why most recording artists rarely make any money from their record label deals. The record label is a different story. They receive about 40% of their SRLP or about $6.78 on a $16.95 album. Even if the album is sold for $11.95 at Target or for $9.95 as a digital download from iTunes, the original SRLP ($16.95) is still used to determine royalties and breakeven points.

The label's formula is then to subtract the artist's royalty per unit ($1.00-$2.35) from the 40% of the SRLP ($16.95 times 40%) or $6.78 minus $2.00 (using the same figure as before), thus the label receives $4.78 per unit. Divide the $4.78 into the total debt of $1.2 million dollars and you'll see that the label only has to sell 251,046 units to break even. Now lets look at the difference. Six hundred thousand units (artist breakeven point) minus the labels breakeven point of 251,046 equal a difference of 348,954 units. If the label sold them they would gain a profit of $1,668,000.00 before the artist receives any additional money.

LOWERING THE COST OF PRODUCTION

Computer software programs such as *Pro-Tools, Logic, and even Garage Band* are revolutionary to the industry's bottom line. Many albums of famous artists are created on computer-based programs. Inexpensive Mac computers and innovative PCs and software are replacing the million dollar recording studios. Computers with Pro-tools and Logic are capable of providing recordings as good and in some cases better than the very best professional studios. The saving in recording costs to the label is significant. Cost to the semi-professional artists is reduced to buying a basic computer and software. The advantage to the label is that it saves sometimes hundreds of thousands of dollars in recording costs. The advantage to the semi-professional musicians and vocalists is that they can now record demos and albums on their home computers, saving thousands in the cost of studio time, producers, union musicians, audio engineers and BGV's. This allows unknown artists a chance to break into the business by recording great tracks and then posting them on social Internet websites such as www.facebook, www.youtube, and www.myspace.com.

COMPUTER BASED RECORDING BUDGET

Recording artists who are required to create their own budgets will notice a huge difference in the cost of the recordings and the time it takes to recoup all expenses. Most consumers do not care if tracks were created in a studio or on computers. They usually can't tell the difference. As already discussed, the three principle factors to consider are the cost of (a) The recording team/studio, (b) The type of session (union/non-union), and (c) The cost per each stage of the recording for one day and one song. If you cut out the recording team players, unions, and other studio costs, the total cost of the recording will be almost nothing, and if you are talented enough, the final product sound quality will be very similar to or better than the studio generated recording that cost about $200,000. Musicians and vocalists lose opportunities; yet, for established artists, computer recordings cut costs. It is also an affordable way for new artists to break into the business.

STUDIO TERMS & EQUIPMENT

Acoustics-All the talents of the recording artist, studio musicians, audio engineer and producer are only as good as the studio's acoustics. Poor acoustics can destroy the best creative efforts of world-class musicians. Floating walls, ceilings and floors are used to isolate sound from room to room in a performance studio and control room. Grooves are cut in the floors, walls are mounted on rubber tubes, and ceilings are often spring-loaded. Windows between the performance studios and control room are made of thick, double-pane glass with 5-1/2 inches of air space between each panel. Soundproof doors complete the package.

Rooms-Recording studios are divided into rooms with different names and functions. The recording artists and musicians perform in rooms that are collectively called "the studio." Producers and audio engineers supervise and record the artists' and musicians' performances from the control room. An equipment room isolates the noise of the tape machines from the control and performance studios and a storage area is used for keeping microphones, music stands, headsets, cords, direct boxes and other recording equipment that is not in use. While the musicians and vocalists create the music in the performance studio, the audio engineer and producer enhance the quality of the sound in the control room. The studio's acoustics are used to emphasize and match the feel of the song to the image and vocal characteristics of the recording artist. Placement of the performers and their microphones add the final acoustics for the recording.

Consoles-Consoles or "boards" act as electronic traffic lights dividing and directing the microphone and electrical instrument signals to various destinations. Major components include:

Op Amps-Consoles operate off the electrical power of many small operational (op) amplifiers (amps) instead of one large, powerful amplifier. This technology was developed by the space race when it was determined that many small one-watt amplifiers were lighter to lift into outer space than one huge amp. The additional benefits to the audio/recording business include a small compact size and less noise in the final recording.

Modules-Another benefit of the space race is the design of plug-in modules that allow for quick repairs, and smaller and lighter consoles.

Effect Sends and Returns-The effect sends are controls on each module of the console that are used to send a signal to the effects equipment in order to change the quality of the sound.

Patch Bays-Patch bays allow an audio engineer to re-route the signal to a different module, special effect, or other equipment.

Multi-track Tape Recorders/Computers-Tape recorders and computers are used to store the recorded signals of the musicians, singers and vocalists. Storage devices include:

Analog Tape Machines-record both the amplitude (loudness) and frequency (number of vibrations) of the electronic signal sent by the mics through the console to the tape recorder.

Digital Machines-have a computer which converts the microphone electronic signals into the magnetic binary codes of 1's and 0's (pulses and no pulses of voltage) which are then recorded onto the computer disc or recording tape as a magnetic signal. When the codes are played back, the computer reconverts the magnetic signal or lack of signal into 1's and 0's, which are then converted back into music.

The 2-Track Tape Machines-(analog and digital) or the DAT (2-track digital audiotape machine) are used to mix the 24- or 32- track tape to 2-track stereo. Accepted master tapes are usually sent to a mastering lab to be converted into a matrix that can be used to make CDs and DVDs.

Computers-are now used to store recorded signals as often as tape machines. Software with virtual reality consoles, tape machines, 64/128 digital tracks, plus Pro-Tools with special effects allow master session quality recordings into your home as well as the best professional recording studios.

Control Room Speakers (Monitors)-In the control room, microphone signals are converted back into sound waves by monitors. To insure the speakers and control room acoustics are providing a correct sound (flat frequency response), room equalizers are used to compensate for the "hype of the sound" created by the speakers and control room acoustics. "Hype of the sound" refers to the change in the sound of the monitors caused by the acoustics of the control room. Reflective sound from the acoustics can phase add causing the speakers to sound as if they are reproducing more bass or treble.

Cue System-The cue system allows the musicians and recording artists to hear themselves in their headphones. The mic signals sent to the console are simply mixed and returned to the artists and musicians through the cue systems and their headphones. Headset boxes allow the musicians and artists to control the amplitude (loudness) of their own headphones. Most consoles have a minimum of two stereo or four mono cue systems.

Effects-Outboard equipment adds echo, reverberation, slap, gate, compression, limiting or harmonizing of the mike signal.

Compression-Used to reduce the amplitude (amount of volume) of a signal in order to record a proper signal on the tape track. Compression is also used to change the quality of the sound of an instrument or vocalist. Most have four compression ratios, various attack times, and release from compression times. It is often used to "fatten up" the sound of a kick drum or bass guitar.

Echo-Long reflections of 50 milliseconds are greater perceived as a repetition of a direct sound wave. Echo is used to make the singer or instruments sound as if they were in a different size room than the actual recording studio.

Gate-A switch (threshold) used to terminate a signal based on the amplitude. Gates are used to "block" tape hiss heard between musical notes, ambiance, rumble, and leakage from other microphones. They are regularly used on drums and overdub vocals to "tighten" the sound.

Harmonizing-Offers a variety of special effects including the doubling of an input signal, delay of signal, and changing of the pitch. Doubling allows the engineer to make one instrument or vocalist sound like two. Delay provides echo or reverberation. Changing the pitch allows the engineer to detune or tune instruments and vocalists.

Limiter-A compressor at maximum compression. The amplitude of the output is "limited" to the manually adjusted level of the threshold.

Reverberation-Sound reflections from many sources (several hard surfaces) heard more than 10 milliseconds after a direct sound wave. Reverb is used by engineers to make the vocalist or musicians sound as if they were in a large auditorium (hard surfaced, empty acoustic room) instead of the smaller, acoustically correct recording studio.

Slap-A delayed sound perceived as a distinct echo, usually a delay of 35 milliseconds or more.

Microphones-Microphones convert sound waves into electronic signals. Knowing which one to select, where to place it in the performance studio and in what proximity to the talent is extremely important. Proper selection and usage is the difference between a "great" sounding session and a mediocre one.

Dynamic Mics-have a coil of wire in the element (or top) of the mic. Sound waves vibrate a plastic diaphragm, which moves the coil in and out of a permanent magnetic field. This movement converts the sound waves into an electronic signal.

Ribbon Mics-operate on the same principle as dynamic mics, except they have flexible, metallic-ribbons. Sound waves vibrate in and out of the permanent, magnetic force field. Because the ribbon is flexible, the quality of sound generated is often considered "warmer" and "smoother."

Condenser Mics-have two plates that hold a static electronic charge; one is a permanent plate, and the other is a moveable plate. Soundwaves vibrate the moveable plate, changing the distance between the two plates which generates the electrical output of the mic. Condenser mics need batteries or phantom power supplied from the console.

Microphone Pickup Patterns-Microphones have different pickup patterns or areas where they are most sensitive to sound.

Omni-Directional Pickup Patterns-allow soundwaves to enter from all directions into the mic at approximately the same loudness level.

Cardioid Pickup Patterns-cancel the sound from the sides and rear of the mics. They sense sound waves that are only directly in front of the mic. Most mics in the recording studio use cardioid pickup patterns to avoid instruments' music from leaking into other instruments' mics.

Bi-Directional Pickup Patterns-receive sound waves from the front and back of the mic and cancel out soundwaves on the sides of the mic.

Dynamic Microphones-Use dynamic mics on high (loud) sound pressure level instruments (drums), electrical instruments (guitars, amps, electronic keyboards), and loud vocals.

Ribbon Microphones-Use ribbons mics on medium level instruments to give a bass boost or warmer sound (strings, horns, and female singers).

Condenser Microphones-Use condenser mics on low sound pressure instruments, acoustic instruments (acoustic guitar, piano), and soft whispering vocals.

Exceptions-There is, of course, an exception to the guidelines. Use condenser mics when you would normally use dynamic mics if you use a pad. A pad reduces the output of the mic and protects the inner electronics from high sound pressure levels (distortion).

Direct Boxes-Musicians sometimes connect their guitars and keyboards directly to the console. Direct boxes may be used instead of mics to convert the high impedance signal of the musical instruments into a low impedance signal acceptable to the console. Direct boxes eliminate the sound of one electrical musical instrument leaking into another open mic. However, it also limits the musicians' ability to control their own instruments' sound quality as the guitar amp's tone controls are also removed from the signal flow.

A & B Schedules-are forms filed by record labels to AFTRA detailing the total scale payments made to label recording artists (designated as "A" vocalists/artists) and to non-royalty artists (designated as "B" vocalists/artists).

Ambiance-is the "feel" or "sound" of a room that is created by its mixture of hard and soft walls, floors, ceiling, etc.

Amp or Amplifier-is an electronic piece of equipment for increasing the loudness of a soundwave or the amplitude (volume) of an electronic signal. Examples include guitar amps, monitor speakers, and operational amps inside the console.

Amplitude-is "how loud" a soundwave is or "how much" electronic signal is flowing through a circuit. Amplitude is measured in decibels (dB's).

Automated Consoles-are computer assisted by using VCA's (Voltage Control Amplifiers) to scan the settings on the console and record their positions onto one of the tape machine tracks or a computer hard disk.

Cartage-In the recording business cartage is an extra payment (paid by the session producer) for musicians (or a private company) to haul instruments and amplifiers to and from the recording sessions. Insurance coverage is provided on harps, timpani, string bass, accordions, tubas, drums, baritone saxophone, bass saxophone, cello, contra bassoon, contra bass and the clarinet.

Compressors-are outboard equipment used to reduce the amplitude (loudness) of a signal. They allow the audio engineer to record the proper amount of signal and to also change the quality of the sound. They are often used on bass guitars and kick drums to make them sound "punchier" and on singers to help the engineer "catch" increases in amplitude.

Crossover Networks-are in speakers to separate the frequencies (bass, mid-range, and treble) and send them to the proper speakers.

Contingency Scale-Payments made to AFTRA non-royalty artists members (who recorded the album) which are made by the record label after the album unit sales have reached levels of 157,000 receive payments of 50% of original scale.

Contractors-AFTRA requires the hiring of a contractor (person in charge of the AFTRA members) who is paid an additional 50%, or for one of the singers to be designated as the contractor when more than three singers are hired. The AF of M requires a contractor to be paid double scale in addition to the leader when more than 12 musicians are called for a session.

Dry/Wet-refers to recording a signal on the tape with or without reverb or "effects" while listening to the signal in the control room monitor speakers and musicians' and recording artists' headsets with the "effects" mixed in. Dry is no effect, wet is when you are recording the effect.

Dynamic Range-is the increase or decrease in amplitude of a soundwave. As an example, the dynamic range (loudness) of music is 120 dB. Editing is the process of removing unwanted sounds or musical notes by cutting the analog tape with a razor blade and then taping the parts back together, or by using a computer to electronically remove the unwanted information on digital recordings.

Effects-are outboard equipment (not located on the console) that are often "patched" into the console to change the quality of the signal. Examples include digital reverb, echo, and delay units, noise gates (which cut off the signal at various amplitude levels used to prevent noise), compressors and limiters (which reduce the amplitude or loudness of the signal), and harmonizers (which are used to change the pitch).

EQ or Equalization-refers to the bass, mid-range and treble controls on the console to change the quality of the sound. Similar examples include the tone controls on your home stereo or car radio.

Fader-is an amplitude control on the console moved up and down (instead of left to right like the volume control on your car radio). One hand can manipulate several faders at the same time. Faders control the monitor speakers, cue, the signal being sent to the recording artists' and musicians' headsets and the amount of signal being sent to the tape recorder.

Frequency-is the number of complete cycles (soundwaves or vibrations) per second, measured in "Hz" (or Hertz, after the inventor of the concept). We hear 20 to 320 Hz as bass, 320 to 5,120 Hz as midrange, and 5,120 to 20 Khz as treble. High end is treble.

In the Mud-is recording a signal too low causing the playback to have too much noise.

In the Red-is recording too much signal on the tape machine that causes distortion.

Loudspeakers-are control room and performance studio monitors. Mixer is a nickname for the console and sometimes the audio engineer who is accomplishing a mixdown.

Multiple Tracking (tracking)-The requirement of AFTRA and AF of M, musicians and singers, to be paid a new call when recording multiple parts or the same parts to additional tracks.

Oscillator-is a frequency or tone generator used to record signals on the tape, align tape machines, and provide special effects when mixed with musical instruments.

Pan Pots-are controls on the console that place a signal into the left side monitor speaker, right side monitor speaker, or center of the signal path.

SUMMARY

In the studio, teams of people work together under time and money constraints to create their final musical products. Recording artists that are also the musicians and singers, work together to create musical art with their vocals and musical instruments. Audio engineers are responsible for the quality of the technical recording. Producers are in charge of sessions, budgets, the musicians' and vocalists' performance, and the quality of the final product (master tape), which will eventually be turned into CDs and cassettes.

Recording budgets are based on three variables including (a) the recording teams consisting of the artist(s), Bgv's (background vocals), musicians, producer and audio engineer; (b) The types of sessions including union master, limited pressing, low budget, and demo and the non-union recordings which can be almost any type of session; and (c) the stage of the recording sessions which include basic tracks, overdubbing and mixdown.

No matter what kind of job you end up having in the business, everyone should understand the recording process and corresponding expenses. Studios and computer software are an integral part of the music business. When the musicians play their instruments and the recording artists sing their songs, the universal language of music is being produced and captured, generated by these recordings. Yet it takes the business side of the industry to bank and develop the act, press products, distribute CD's and digital downloads and then provide the final marketing mix of promotion and publicity. Budgets may range from hundreds of thousands of dollars to just a few dollars using various computer programs, yet the consumer response is still required to sell recordings and digital downloads.

STUDY GUIDE-
THE RECORDING BUSINESS

1. List and describe the three things (variables) that will determine the cost and quality of a recording.

    (a)

    (b)

    (c)

2. List the members of the recording team.

    (a)

    (b)

    (c)

    (d)

    (e)

3. Record producers are responsible for important issues tied to the session. Name and explain three.

    (a)

    (b)

    (c)

4. List and explain the three stages of a typical record producer's career.
    (a)

    (b)

    (c)
5. What is the difference between a garage/jam band musician and a working musician?

6. Are the road musicians for an act also the musicians used in recording sessions?

7. Who were the Wrecking Crew?

8. Describe the job of the audio engineer.

9. Explain signal flow in the three following stages of a typical recording session.
   (a) Basic tracks or tracking

   (b) Overdubbing

   (c) Mixdown

10. List the four types of audio engineers.

    (a)

    (b)

    (c)

    (d)

11. When recording artists sign their deal with a label, what type of employee are they usually considered? Why?

12. List the three types of recording artists/vocalists found in the business.

    (a)

    (b)

    (c)

13. You have to find a place to record. List and explain the five types of recording studios.

    (a)

    (b)

    (c)

    (d)

    (e)

14. In major recording centers (Los Angeles, New York, Nashville), recording sessions are scheduled together. Describe the schedule in blocks of time during a typical day.

15. Two unions represent creative artists on master recordings. List the names of the unions and name the agreement they have with the major record labels.

    (a)

    Agreement name:

    (b)

    Agreement name:

16. List the five types of recording sessions and describe the differences.

   (a)

   (b)

   (c)

   (d)

   (e)

17. List and explain the five stages of a typical master recording session.

   (a)

   (b)

   (c)

   (d)

   (e)

18. To determine a recording budget, what three issues must be considered and then placed together to reach a final figure per-song, and per-album?

   (a)

   (b)

   (c)

19. What is the master scale for a union musician?

20. Who is the lead musician and how much are they paid?

21. What level of scale is the major recording artist (vocalist) usually paid?

22. What is the range of payment for the producers.

23. Who is paid by the side?

24. Who is paid by the hour or number of songs, whichever is greater?

25. How long is a master AF of M session call?

26. Who signs the card?

27. What does the recording budget cover?

28. What does the production budget cover?
    (a)

    (b)

29. What are the all-ins?

    (a)

    (b)

    (c)

30. Once the cost of the *all-in's* are determined, how much will the cost of the following budgets add?:

    (a) Promotion

    (b) Publicity

31. What percent of the promotion and publicity budgets are recoupable?

32. What percent of the promotion and publicity budgets are recoupable if the money is part of the *tour support* offered by the label?

33. What is the math formula to determine the break-ever point for the artist?

34. What is the math formula to determine the break-ever point for the label?

35. Explain how labels often make millions before their artists make any money on royalties.

Lecture Points
Chapter Nine

TYPES OF PRODUCERS

EXECUTIVE PRODUCERS

STAFF PRODUCERS

INDEPENDENT PRODUCERS

TYPES OF ENGINEERS

INDEPENDENT ENGINEERS

STAFF ENGINEERS

SECOND ENGINEERS

ENTRY-LEVEL

KEY TERMS IN THE STUDIO

RECORDING ARTISTS

DEMO SINGERS/BACKGROUND SINGERS/GHOST SINGERS

MUSICIANS - AF of M - SAG/AFTRA

Lecture Points
Chapter Nine

THE CREATIVE BUDGET

THE UNIONS

THE STUDIO

BASIC TRACKS

OVERDUBS

MIXING

MASTERING

CONTROLLED COMPOSITION

PAYING THE SONGWRITERS

PRESSING THE PRODUCT

THE INITIAL UNITS

FREE GOODS AND PROMO COPIES

Lecture Points
Chapter Nine

THE BUSINESS BUDGET

PROMOTION

RADIO STATION AIRPLAY

FORMATS

CROSSOVERS

TRADE MAGAZINES

MUSIC VIDEO

PUBLICITY

PAYOLA

STREET PROMOTION

TRUST AND SPECIAL PAYMENT FUND

BREAKING EVEN

Lecture Points
Chapter Nine

THE BUSINESS BUDGET
Continued

DEMO DIVERSITY

VERSATILITY

PERFORMANCE

THE DIFFERENCE BETWEEN MEDIA

INDUSTRY and SONGWRITING DEMOS

MORE TIPS FOR EFFECTIVE DEMO

Lecture Points
Chapter Nine

ROOMS

CONSOLES

MULTI-TRACK TAPE RECORDERS

TAPE TO DIGITAL

MONITORS

EFFECTS

MICROPHONES

DIRECT BOXES

THE COMPLETE PRODUCER

CREATING THE CREATIVE BUDGET

CREATIVE RESPONSIBILITIES

246

**Lecture Points
Chapter Nine**

ADMINISTRATIVE RESPONSIBILITIES

PRE-PRODUCTION RESPONSIBILITIES

PRODUCTION RESPONSIBILITIES

POST PRODUCTION RESPONSIBILITIES

STAGES OF THE RECORDING SESSION

PRE-PRODUCTION

BASIC TRACKS

OVERDUBBING

MIXING

MASTERING

Lecture Points
Chapter Nine

PRODUCING A DEMO

THE STUDIO

THE PRODUCER

BUDGET

STUDIO ETIQUETTE

CONFIRM THE DATE

SET UP TIME

GUESTS IN THE STUDIO

KEEP A CLEAR HEAD

DON'T DISTRACT THE ENGINEER

Lecture Points
Chapter Nine

FOCUS

TUNING

TOO MANY COOKS

FOOD, DRINKS & SMOKING

PAYMENT

DRUMMERS

BASSISTS

GUITARISTS

KEYBOARDS

VOCALISTS

EVERYONE ELSE

Chapter Nine Notes

Chapter Nine Notes

ARTIST MANAGEMENT

Power of Attorney
The Management Team

"A live concert to me is exciting because of all the electricity that is generated in the crowd and on stage. It's my favorite part of the business."
—**Elvis Presley**[215]

"A personal manager receives a percentage of what an artist earns. If the artist makes money, so does the manager. If the artist doesn't make money, the manager can still make money. What? You must understand that as an artist you sign an exclusive personal contract, which means the artist can work with NO other manager. On the other hand, a manager has NO exclusivity to the artist. He can manage as many acts as he can sign and that is why he can be making money while you might be waiting for your royalty check to get you out of trouble. Also if one of his other acts is dong well he might be, could be, probably is spending more time with the act doing well at the time. I have heard a great manager who handled many acts say that management is like spinning plates. You try to keep them all in the air so that none of the plates slow down so much that they stop spinning, fall and break. You must keep them all spinning, albeit, some might be spinning faster than others and one might really come close to falling, you must keep them all spinning for everyone to survive."
—**Mark Volman, performer and manager of Turtles.**[216]

"Creativity is allowing yourself to make mistakes."
—**Scott Adams**[217]

"If you don't live it, it won't come out of your horn."
—**Charlie Parker**[218]

"I want to shake off the dust of this one-horse town. I want to explore the world. I want to watch TV in a different time zone. I want to visit strange, exotic malls...I want to live..."
—**Homer Simpson**[219]

---

215 http://www.artquotes.net/entertainment-quotes/famous-singers/elvis-presley/index.htm
216 Mark Volman for his Survey of Music Business packet 2008.
217 Quotations about Art, Quote Garden, www.google.com, 2007.
218 Ibid.
219 http://www.artquotes.net/entertainment-quotes/famous-actors/homer-simpson.htm

MARKETING CULTURAL ICONS

The music business is a topsy-turvy, high-pressure, competitive business where millions of dollars change hands every day based on how successful the industry's creative and business systems work together. However, most consumers are interested in the public image of the artist, not the intimate details and legalities of the business. They are most excited by the artists and their music and how it makes them feel.[220] The music industry and most of the artists themselves use their public images as marketing icons to motivate concert ticket and recorded music unit sales. Non-label artists and musicians may attain a good living from personal performances as a member of an orchestra, nightclub band or by playing at weddings and parties or by providing entertainment at a number of unique events.[221] The bottom line is having a record deal with a street release, promotion, publicity, distribution, and financial advances which places the artist into a powerful position. This allows the artist to use the notoriety from the label's marketing plan to exploit their image for profit.

Recording artists generally make the greatest share of their annual income from the billion-dollar concert industry. Even major recording/royalty artists may not sell enough CDs to cover their recording and marketing expenses. Hence, paid live appearances usually provide the cash flow most artists need to sustain the economic side of their careers. Publicity gives consumers an opportunity to like or dislike an act. No emotional connection with consumers is often considered death to a recording artist's career.[222] The labels simply cannot sell enough units to make a reasonable profit. Once again, we are faced with the reality of entertainment and music as a form of business.

NON-LABEL ARTISTS

If you just want to sing and skip the business of being a popular culture icon, then you can find employment as a soloist in choral groups, an opera singer or a BGV (background vocalists) or all the above at the same time. It is helpful to be successful even in a local market to know sight reading, have quick memorization skills, a positive personality, knowledge of the copyright law, music publishing, accounting, marketing, publicity, business management, promotion, and a basic understanding of the music business in general. Social networks such as www.myspace.com offer great opportunities for local artists to find work and other musical opportunities.

"Eighty percent of success is showing up."
—**Woody Allen**[223]

"My major (Music Business) gave me an overview of all the different aspects of the business, so when I tried to make a name for myself, I knew what questions to ask."
—**Trisha Yearwood, MCA Recording Artist**[224]

---

220 In reality, George Kelly's *Construct Theory of Personality* (Psychology) suggests that consumers choose an artist (image and their corresponding music performances and recordings) subconsciously as a way to help ourselves define our essence or personality (self-definition) or celebrate who we think we are (self-elaboration).

221 Still, you usually have to be a known personality, celebrity or unique talent to be hired to perform. Promoters need to know who you are and what you do before they will hire you. Consumers need the same information before they will listen to your records, watch your interviews, buy your books, or buy a ticket to your concert.

222 Marketing experts claim that even a negative emotional impression may be turned around with a counter public relation campaign. However, if the act does not spark a positive emotional connection then it is very difficult to change potential consumer perceptions. It would simply cost too much money, and thus the label usually drops the act.

223 http://www.artquotes.net/entertainment-quotes/woody-allen.htm

224 Yearwood is singer/businesswoman, The Tennessean, (September 16, 1994).

FAME

Moving past the local community usually requires a manager, booking agent and management team of attorneys, consultants, business accountants/business financial experts and media trainers. Building this team of experts to help exploit an artist's image through promotion, publicity, recordings, and tours is the artist's responsibility and the next step toward a successful and profitable career. In the film business, scripts have plot points where the direction of the film changes. The decision by an artist to accept creativity and artistry as a business and set up a management organization as a means for making money is a real life plot point in an act's career. The creation of an event such as a concert or nightclub appearance, gives the artists an opportunity to be paid for a performance. In addition, it gives the artist another opportunity to become an entrepreneur by selling merchandise, corporate sponsorships, endorsements, recordings, and other products to consumers.

IMAGE

What are you trying to say? It doesn't matter if you are an artist, producer, musician, or an accountant; have a professional image. If you are starting as an artist, think about what your image says about you and the songs you sing, play, produce or artist you represent. Then, try to figure out who will buy into the image you're portraying. Remember, success as an artist is based on more than the ability to sing in tune. You have to be able to find, sign great talent, control budgets, and produce great tracks if you want to be a producer. Business finance, accounting, and business plans are tied to entrepreneurship and also recommended. Listen to the artists who are not the best singers, yet have very successful careers because their image represents some emotion to consumers. Musicians, promoters, managers, booking agents, and film people, have the ability and image to accomplish for an artist what the artist cannot accomplish for themselves. Songwriters write the perfect songs for the artists who can't. Screenwriters write the story for the actors, directors and production technicians who can't. Studio musicians often play in recording sessions because they are better musicians than the actual stars. Managers manage the business of an artist who can't and booking agents acquire concert tours for the manager and the artists who either can't or don't want to. Stage managers oversee the production and presentation of the live shows and the list goes on and on. Gain experience locally and then move up to regional and then national positions working for the superstars.

"I had learned throughout my life as a composer chiefly through my mistakes and pursuits of false assumptions, not by my exposure to the founts of wisdom and knowledge."

— **Igor Stravinsky**[225]

"Don't try to explain it, just sell it."

— **Colonel Tom Parker**[226]

SHAMELESS SELF-PROMOTION

Success takes more than talent; it takes drive, passion, and the courage to achieve shameless self-promotion. In the entertainment business everyone promotes himself or herself to be hired for sessions, tours, publicity campaigns, promotion, and other industry related jobs. Students and prospective industry professionals attend professional seminars and meetings and work in jobs that will create career opportunities.

---

[225] "Can Record Labels Get Back Their Rhythm?" By Richard Sikios, Business Week, (07/2711998).
[226] http://www.barryrudolph.com/utilities/quotes.html

However, networking is a refined skill. It has to be done with confidence, humor, and a sense of respect for the boss, artists and their position in the industry. Blatantly shoving CDs at producers to prove your songwriting skills, audio engineering session work or singing ability is not advisable. If you want their help, get to know them first and learn all you can about the business. All major recording artists, producers, label executives, booking agents, and concert promoters constantly network with each other to find songs, acts, musicians, singers, and business educated executives to help their careers. It is amazing to watch a huge superstar approach an industry well-known songwriter. Both know they need each other, the artist needs a great song to sing and record in order to get airplay, sell concert tickets and record sales; the writer needs someone as famous as possible to sing and record his/her song in order to receive music publishing royalties from mechanicals, sync, and performance royalties. This same networking dance takes place everyday at all levels within the entertainment business. It's who you know and what you can contribute to the industry that will help you get your first break. Learn all you can about how to present yourself in a professional manner and how to network by using shameless self-promotion. It will put you years ahead of the competition.

"An artist in today's music business needs to have a personal manager. Maybe not in the very beginning, but I place a great amount of importance on the personal manager. I like them so much I have had 10 different personal managers. In the Turtles we had 7 managers in 5 years. If you are not strong enough to manage yourself which I believe is the case with most artists, here is an overview of what to expect from an exclusive personal manager."

—**Mark Volman, performer and manager of Turtles.**[227]

2008 TOP TOURS

Act	Total Sell Outs	Total Attendance	Total Gross Income
Bon Jovi	99	2,157,675	$210,650,974
Bruce Springsteen	46	2,181,839	$204,513,630
Madonna	38	1,357,906	$185,696,018
The Police	71	1,468,705	$149,623,800
Celine Dion	36	738,947	$91,006,221
Kenny Chesney	25	1,187,622	$86,306,618

Source-Billboard Mag. 12/12/08.

SELECTING A MANAGER

What can a manager do for you that you can't do yourself? Whoever the artist hires they better know the business, industry personalities, have major industry contacts, understand business principles, have a positive attitude and your best interest at heart. The manager is then responsible for creating a team to take advantage of every positive and possible opportunity to make money from the artist's fame, talent, and noteworthy publicity.

---

[227] Mark Volman for his Survey of Music Business packet 2008.

TYPES OF MANAGERS

Managers are hired and fired by artists. It is a relationship built on trust in an emotionally hype-filled industry. Don't hire a friend or relative because their decision will affect your career and income forever! They have to be able to say "no" to friends and family, as well as shady business offers.

- *Heavyweight/Heavy hitter*: Usually someone who represents the biggest platinum record stars who make the most money. Most of the heavyweight managers are shareholders or partners in their artist's management companies. These managers have tremendous clout in the business and when they call the president of the record company the president takes his call. This is the sure sign of a heavyweight manager in the music business. On the average they have offices in Nashville, New York, or Los Angeles.

- *Middleweight*: These are the ones working hardest at their profession. I like this type of manager the best. They have not become totally jaded with the business and they work hard at keeping up on all the possibilities and changes going on everyday. They command respect because they might not have a superstar artist yet but they always seem on the verge of having a monster act on their hands.

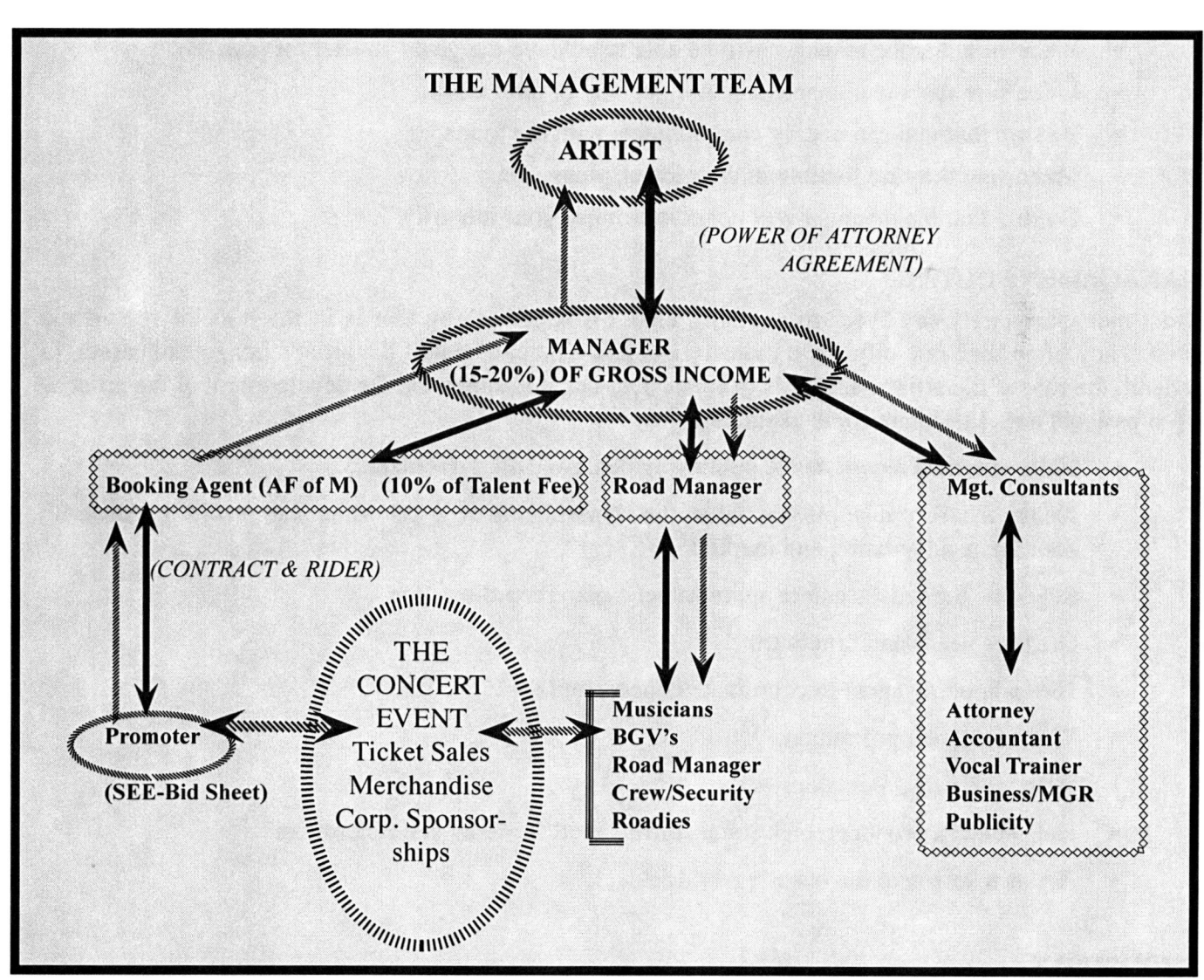

- *Lightweight* (would-be manager): This might be a good friend who has worked for the band doing everything needed. From loading the gear to loading the pipe, he sells the t-shirts, gets the towels and the drinks. He loves the music but usually doesn't know what he's talking about. They have no experience, and they make very little effort to further themselves. They call themselves a manager but they don't know the job.[228]

SELECTING A MANAGER
What do you need to know before you select a manger for your act.
- Try to be your own manager & see if you can handle it & what it involves.
- Ask them (the projected manager) what they are going to do for you.
- Make sure they behave like a professional.
- Make sure they are prepared with things you need (bio, press kits, demos, etc.).
- Develop your OWN vision.
- Select a manager who can help you achieve your vision.
- Make sure they have enthusiasm about what you are doing.
- Find out about their background.
- Don't sign anything too soon.
- Make sure that the manager will be able to achieve the goals you set for yourself.
- Make sure that the manager will not get lazy in their work.
- Be sure that you can openly communicate with the manager.
- Make sure they are flexible in their ideas, plans, etc.
- Be sure that the manager will not compromise your integrity.

MANAGEMENT DUTIES
Artist managers rarely say "yes" to anything unless it is something that is in the best interest of the artist. They often seek out only those industry insiders who can benefit the artist's image and career. In general, the role of the artist manager is to counsel, assist, and supervise the development of the artist as a professional act. Listed are some examples:
- Help negotiate record deals, publishing deals and all agreements.
- Know the record company, what the departments will do when the record is released, coordinate advertising and marketing.
- Schedule the artist's career appropriately, plan recording time.
- Creative needs and family time.
- Hire a booking agent to coordinate concert tours.
- Work on career promotion.
- Help with career decisions.
- Help select a producer, pick songs, hiring band for tours and recordings.
- Act as a liaison to the outside world.[229]

---

228 Mark Volman for his Survey of Music Business packet 2008.
229 Ibid.

NON-MANAGEMENT DUTIES

Managers are not employment agents and will ordinarily only approve of work "pitched" to them by booking agents (for concert tours), publicists (for articles and radio, personal, and TV appearances), record labels (for approval of recording issues and promotional concepts, etc.) and other business offers. Accordingly, managers are rarely songpluggers, record producers, or record label executives, yet they all know each other and often work together to create mutual success.

"On December 31, 1999, my publishing contract with Warner-Chapel expired, thus emancipating the name I was given at birth, Prince, from all long-term restrictive documents."

—The Artist formerly known as Prince

ARTIST-MANAGER RELATIONSHIP

The artist-manager relationship is built on trust. The artist has to have confidence in the manager's ability to make the decisions that will enhance his or her career opportunities. The artist is busy being an "artist" and therefore needs someone to take care of "the business" of being an artist. Good managers are plentiful, but great ones that can grow an artist's business are hard to find.

POWER OF ATTORNEY AGREEMENT

Artist managers bring order to the daily chaos caused by success in the music industry. Managers legally represent artists through a power-of-attorney agreement. It provides managers with the legal privilege and obligation of controlling the business and career decisions of the artist. Examples include: record label agreements, music publishing, and music producer selections; mass media promotion and publicity through a hired or label publicist; concert appearances supervised by the road manager and arranged by a talent agent through a concert promoter; and merchandising, corporate sponsorship, endorsements, charity and community service. The power-of-attorney agreement permits the manager to lawfully represent (to the very best of their ability) the artist(s) in business decisions.

"When I think back at The Turtles career, I can't count the Personal Managers we have signed with on my hands and feet together. Some were the biggest management stars you could ever hope for and others were trouble from the beginning. Most of those just plain didn't know what they were doing, but we signed with them anyway. During our hey-day, The Turtles actually went through seven managers in only five years and ended up signing with one of them twice. Each manager was a story unto itself. The first was a disc jockey who made his cousin the fall guy. The second kept telling us how bad the first was so we fired #1 to sign with #2. Number 2 sold fifty percent to a company in New York and so on. When I finally took the job over it was done in self-defense and probably because as a group we were more than a bit gun shy of signing any more management contracts. Making the right decision can be a lengthy bout of meetings, negotiations, re-negotiations and spiritual involvement, but making the wrong decision can wipe you out for an entire career. The time it takes deciding on a manager to work with is worth it and yet it is obvious that even after taking time, you aren't always safe. Research has been done that implies music artists will likely be with a manager longer than a spouse. This says a lot about both topics. When you do look for a manager, what is it you are looking for? What is the job of a manager when you have one and what do they earn?"

—Mark Volman, performer and manager of Turtles.[230]

---

230 Ibid.

COMMISSIONS

Managers are typically paid *15%-20%* of an artist's royalty base, such as record deals, concert tours, movie appearances and corporate sponsorships (gross income). The standard is 15% for single artist representation and 20% for groups or bands. However, the rates can be more or less depending on what is negotiated. Rarely, some managers may not receive a percentage of everything an artist is paid, only what is negotiated (called a commission base). Management fees should be based on net but are based on the gross income. However, most managers will not agree to work for net, as artists' expenses for living, touring, recording, taxes, etc., often reduce the annual take home salary to a much lower figure than most people realize. In addition, managers usually bill the artist(s) for their business related expenses.

"I would always recommend that an artist try to get an escalating contract, which involves pay raises for a manager as their artist makes more & more money. This makes a manager work harder for the artist."
—**Mark Volman, performer and manager of Turtles.**[231]

TERMINATION OF CONTRACT

Sometimes the breakup of an artist and manager is similar to a divorce as lawsuits and counter lawsuits are not uncommon with the manager claiming commissions on the artists' future royalties. Unless there has been some kind of criminal conduct by the manager he or she usually wins or gains partial royalty payment in addition to the new manager hired.

MANAGEMENT TEAM

Artist managers bring representation, administrative supervision, and surrogate control to an artist's complex image and long-term career. A strategic management plan that links the business and creative systems of the artist's career together is usually developed. Career goals are established based on the perceived commercialization of the artist's image and talents. Managers act as gatekeepers, selecting only the recording deals, concert appearances and staff members that can best enhance the artist's long-term goals. Managers supervise everything connected with the act. Booking agents establish contacts with promoters who create concert appearances. Promoters rent venues for the dates of the concerts, and then promote and advertise the event. Facility managers and their staff of event coordinators keep the arenas, theaters, and clubs in top shape for the concerts. Stagehand union members commonly provide the lighting and sound. Publicists and marketing experts provide artist interviews to retail stores and to the mass media in an effort to promote concerts. Record labels provide free recordings to radio stations and in-store promotional items (free goods) to retail outlets.

WHO ARE YOU?

In reality, George Kelly's Construct Theory of Personality (Psychology) suggests that consumers choose an artist (image and their corresponding music performances and recordings) subconsciously as a way to help define our essence or personality. Thus, we choose for ourselves a creative message that allows us to figure out who we are-(self-definition) or celebrate who we think we are (self-elaboration). So who are you? It's all in our subconscious mind and happens at 180,000 miles a second tied to a chemical reaction. Remember this is the emotion business. Consumers getting so excited about the artist, song, or image that they can relate. Now you know why fans and consumers like or dislike an act and their music and how it emotionally communicates.

---

[231] Ibid.

BOOKING AGENTS

Booking agents are licensed by the unions whose members they represent. AFTRA approves of agents who represent their members seeking employment as vocalists in recording sessions and as newscasters and TV personalities. Agents commissioned by the AF of M represent musicians employed as recording artists, session musicians, and concert or other live performers. Equity union licensed agents represent actors and actresses pursuing employment in any type of unionized live theater. Finally, SAG (Screen Actors Guild) represents actors and actresses seeking employment in any type of film media (as opposed to video which is covered by AFTRA), such as movies, TV shows and commercials. Union-franchised booking agents are ordinarily limited to 10% commission rates. The unions, of course, bring the power of collective bargaining and legally supported contracts which encourages businesses who hire union musicians and vocalists, actors and others to fulfill their financial and contractual obligations as originally stated in the deal.

TALENT BUYER

Talent Buyers are usually an independent person who doesn't work for a theatre or club but can book shows there. Often they either work for or are promoters.

ATTORNEYS

Managers hire *attorneys* to structure deals for artist tours, merchandise sales (through fulfillment companies) corporate sponsorships, label deals, appearances and any other type of business opportunity. Accordingly, some attorneys become very powerful and act as personal managers after they have established themselves in the business. Attorneys charge hourly rates ($250-$1,000 per hour) or are placed on a retainer that is a monthly minimum fee based on a negotiated number of hours of work per-month or a percentage of the artist's gross income. It is preferable to pay an attorney's hourly rate as opposed to a retainer fee in order to guarantee the productivity of the attorney.[232]

BUSINESS FINANCIAL MANAGERS

Business managers are really investment advisors. It is desirable for a business manager to have a degree in finance, plus a successful track record in investments and money market funds. Otherwise, you're turning over money to someone who only claims to know what they are doing and, unfortunately, they may blow your hard-earned commissions and royalties on thin-ice speculations. Business managers may also take care of the accounting and investment management tied to financial goals for the artist.

"It seemed when I was young, no matter how smart I became about making records and writing songs, I never became smart about my money. Ultimately all financial responsibility was my choice and I never was smart about choices. I was like most young musicians, I assumed the people handling my money did everything for you in my best interests, oh yeah, and they could be trusted. I found out quickly that I was wrong. Don't You. In today's music industry keeping track of the artist's money is a full time job. It is absolutely imperative that an artist understands that when he begins to make some significant earnings how important a business manager/accountant/bookkeeper is. Money is going to come in from many sources; tours, record royalties, publishing, merchandise and many more possible sources. Taxes are a serious issue and holding on to your hard-earned money is a specialized job. It takes people who have the knowledge to make your money grow are as important as keeping your money from risky propositions. I also have some financial suggestions for those just starting out."

—**Mark Volman, performer and manager of Turtles.**[233]

---

[232] Artists are already paying as much as 20% on average to the manager, 10% to the booking agent. Thus, paying another percentage to the attorney is not a wise economic decision.
[233] Ibid.

ROAD MANAGERS

Road managers are responsible for all the daily business decisions dealing with concerts and personal appearances on tour. As a result, road managers handle the local press, questions and concerns from promoters, local radio stations and record retail promotions. In addition, they make hotel and restaurant reservations and handle any issues of concern between the recording artist(s), band members, roadies, and tour support. Accordingly, road managers report directly to the artist and personal manager and they are the local communication link between the artist, the promoter and the manager of the venue. Great road managers often use the road and concert tours for networking, getting their industry knowledge and networking ready for starting their own artist management company.

STAGE MANAGER

The Stage Manager is in charge of details at the show. They are in charge of what happens on-stage & backstage.

PROMOTION-ARTIST PERSPECTIVE

Radio station airplay has in the past, been the most important type of exposure for new artists and their recordings. In addition, radio acted as a natural filter to expose only the potentially successful artists and recordings. However, large corporations such as *Clear Channel* (which owns close to 10% of all the radio stations in the United States) have made it very difficult to break new acts on radio. Also, *Generation Y* (the current 18-24 year old consumers), have changed the rules of the game by not reading many newspapers, watching TV, or listening to radio. Instead, they download their music and listen to what they want, when they want it through their computers, iPods, mp3 players, cell phones and iPhones. Labels are currently struggling to find ways to make consumers pay for recordings instead of illegally downloading them. Artist managers and promoters are in the same situation, as they are attempting to find better ways to exploit their acts and concert events through social networks and consumer technology.

PUBLICITY-ARTIST PERSPECTIVE

Artist managers, record labels, professional musicians and event specialists hire publicists as part-time or full-time employees from public relations firms to plant stories and articles featuring their clients (the artist) in the professional trades and consumer mass media. The publicist assimilates images that have been created, molded, or enhanced by the artist's manager and label representatives into stores, news articles, and press releases. It is always better to have an image that is true to the essence of the artist rather than a manufactured image that may be perceived as contrived. Then the publicist alerts the media to cover the events (which are often created by the management and label representatives) as news or entertainment stories. The stories are then released to the print and broadcasting mass media with the hope of stimulating a positive correlation between the artist's name and public perceptions. Increase in the public's awareness of an artist and acknowledgment of an artist's creative talents often turn into record sales and record label profits.[234]

---

[234] Thus, labels, production or film companies use publicity agents to supply photos and videos of their artists to entertainment and Hollywood gossip tv and cable shows.

PUBLIC RELATIONS

Public relations, which is usually provided by a hired publicist is the process or act of providing material (stories, press releases, etc.,) to the mass media so that once it is aired or printed consumers will develop a favorable public image for an artist. The process occurs whenever there is contact with the public or whenever an act has to counter bad publicity. Positive aspects of the act are provided to spin the truth or to let consumers choose for themselves what they want to believe about an artist. Bad publicity or negative news can hinder record and ticket sales, so management will often provide the artist's best side to enhance the artist's image with the public.

ELECTRONIC PRESS KITS AND BIO'S

Press kits help establish authenticity of new and established artists. Publicity agents assemble PR kits in an effort to alert the press and mass media of new recordings, acts, and constructed news worthy events. A press kit usually includes a black & white photograph (publicity photo), a one-page bio of demographic information, artistic and creative accomplishments, and copies of previous press releases to the trade and consumer press. Most artists are now releasing their press kits on CD-ROM and DVDs with videos and soundtracks. Some are sent by email to fans and still others are voice recordings sent as a message to consumers over cell phones. In addition, artists and their managers offer web sites and fan club home pages to keep the industry, radio and fans updated.[235]

TV APPEARANCES

Broadcast television is still used to market recording artists, musicians, and their music. Variety, late night and morning talk shows promote artists and their sellable products. Publicists are once again hired to help "place" stories about the artists in the trade and consumer press. They also help generate interest in the artist's stories and publicity that can be used by the label and the artist's manager to "book" an act on a television variety/talk show. Appearances on popular TV shows reinforce the status of the act and inform the public of new recordings being released.[236]

PUBLICITY BUDGETS

The amount of money record labels spend on publicity varies greatly. The artist manager commonly meets with label representatives to coordinate publicity. The amount of money (budget) to be spent on publicity often depends on the star factor (name and image equals the strength of the artist based on past units sold and sales projections. Maximum publicity budgets are often limited to 50-100% of the creative production budget.

WHO IS RUSH HICKS?

Thanks to Rush for providing the sample contracts in the book. Rush received his law degree from Mercer University in 1981. Since that time, he's practiced law in Nashville on historic Music Row representing artists, songwriters, artist managers, business managers, record companies, record producers, booking agencies and publishing companies.

He has taught at Middle Tennessee State University in the Recording Industry department and since 2005, has been a professor in the Mike Curb College of Entertainment and Music Business at Belmont University. He teaches such courses as Music Licensing, Artist Management, Intellectual Property and Legal Issues in the Music Industry. He is also a faculty advisor to the Showcase Council and a member of the Belmont University Faculty Senate.

---

235 The "All-In's."
236 Called the street date.

STAGE NAMES

Artists often pick a stage name other than their actual birth name with which to perform or create an image. Examples include:

Real Name	Stage Name
Robert Zimmerman	Bob Dylan
Madonna Louise Ciccone	Madonna
Marco Antonio Muniz	Marc Anthony
Victoria Caroline Adams [Beckham]	Posh Spice
John Francis Bongiovi Jr.	Jon Bon Jovi
Kenneth Brian Edmonds	Babyface
Anthony Benedetto	Tony Bennett
David Roger Jones	David Bowie
Declan Patrick McManus	Elvis Costello
Virginia Patterson Hensley	Patsy Cline
Carlos Ray	Chuck Norris
Paul David Hewson	Bono (U2)

TOUR SUPPORT

Record labels want their artists out on the road as a promotional tool to stir up record sales and profits. In addition, recording artists need to generate revenues to pay for their management team, supporting musicians, stage crew, roadies, etc. Record sales provide royalties after recoupment of all related label expenses. As a result, most active recording artists need to be on the road performing in order to pay their bills.

A career in the arts has always been difficult to establish. But in the last few years the process of breaking in has changed as digital technologies and shifting economics profoundly alter the ways in which art is made, popularized and consumed... Do-it-yourself to the extreme, the tour (F Yeah Fest) was a feat of coordination, with 28 shows in 25 cities in 27 days, and as many as four bands, three comedians and an art collective traveling together. ... (After the last show of the tour)... At 3:30 a.m., when his friends headed to a nearby bar for a final drink, Mr. Carlson stood outside the deserted bus, and took stock: he was nearly $40,000 in debt, with no real idea of how to pay off what was owed.
—**Melena Ryzik, author of the article "On the Bus and Off It: The Initiation of a Young Rock Impresario."** [237]

---

[237] Ryzik, Melena, Breaking, On the Bus, and Off It: The Initiation of a Young Rock Impresario," The New York Times 2008.

SUMMARY

It is easy to dream about someday being discovered as the next superstar artist, songwriter, producer, manager, concert promoter, scriptwriter, dancer, actor, or music video director. My point is simple; if you want to be in the business of music or entertainment you have to move past the brain rush of possibilities and take some risks. Have you got the talent, ability, personality, and business skills to make money (a career) in the business? Then, if you think you do, find out if you have what it takes to be successful by taking the first step. Start doing what you want to do even if you're dreading it! Everyone has to start somewhere and nobody starts on the top.

Create a local buzz and you'll capture the attention of someone in the business or someone who knows someone in the business. It doesn't matter if you want to produce sessions, be a session player or a touring musician. Get noticed! In other words, in the beginning your first step is to get noticed and in most cases, that means making money for someone else. Performing in a small bar or club will hopefully make the owner money and at the same time, you'll be noticed by other establishments and consumers. Build a fan base. Get their email addresses. Being able to draw a small audience is a reason for a bar or small venue to hire you to perform. Need a demo? Get on your Mac or PC or find a producer in a studio or a classmate or friend with Pro-Tools or Garage Band.

If you are a band, record an excellent demo, give it to the local radio station, put it on sale at the local record store, set up a website on one of the social networks, include a bio, files, tour dates, and create some local excitement. Develop an electronic press kit with sample songs, video interviews, news clips, and contact information. If you can get a buzz going then invite local insiders to a showcase. If you're terrific, record labels or people connected to industry personalities will help you meet the right people. A referral by a local radio personality about a band that is selling product and getting local air play will get the attention of an A&R department, as they are always looking for the next big thing. What you want and what the label desires are original acts with a great honest buzz with the potential to create great regional and then national momentum for unit sales.

Once you've created a buzz and the potential for greater success, then the right manager is someone you should consider. Many artist managers, concert promoters, know everyone you need to know. After all, they often started their career as assistants working on the road, interning with established management companies, or even in the mail room at The William Morris Agency. Most have learned the business from the bottom up. Only the smartest and best survive, the others are just full of... hot air and promises that will waste your time.

Great managers can open the doors to success in the business. Poor manager will damage any long-term career opportunities. Accordingly, the artist-manager relationship must be built on trust as the artist hires the manager, but the manager signs the act to the company. Managers supervise a management team consisting of an attorney, a talent or booking agent (who is franchised by the AF of M and commonly receives 10% of the gross income from arranged concert appearances), a business manager, (to invest and account for revenue), a publicist who will arrange opportunities for the act to use shameless self-promotion, media trainers, and of course, musicians, BGV's, road crews, and other to complete a concert tour.

STUDY GUIDE-
ARTIST MANAGEMENT

1. The most successful recording artists are usually cultural icons. Explain!

2. What do they represent to their fan base?

3. How and why does the music industry market icons?

4. Explain how an artist's image is tied to a career song, appearance, marketing plan and ultimate success.

5. When does a new artist need a manager?

6. Why does the artist need a manager?

7. List and explain three types of managers

    a.

    b.

    c.

8. Write a paragraph explaining several issues you should consider before selecting a manager?

9. An artist manager is to counsel, assist, and supervise the development of an artist's professional career. Assume you are a new artist. Write a paragraph explaining how a manager could best help you develop your career. (Look at the list of nine things they should be able to accomplish).

10. What should an artist-artist manager relationship be built on?

11. What gives the manager the power to represent an act?

12. How much should managers be paid?

13. What is a commission base?

14. What happens when an artist fires the manager?

15. Explain the management team and their responsibilities to an artist

    a. Booking agent

    b. Attorney

    c. The actual manager

    d. Road manager

    e. Road musicians, BGV's and road crew.

    f. Business manager

Lecture Points
Chapter Ten

GROSS INCOME

ARTIST EARNINGS

ARTIST EXPENSES

NET INCOME

THE MANAGEMENT TEAM

PERSONAL MANAGERS

TYPES OF MANAGERS

Lecture Points
Chapter Ten

WHAT A MANAGER EARNS

MANAGEMENT DUTIES

TIPS FOR CHOOSING A MANAGER

BUSINESS MANAGER/ACCOUNTANT

BOOKKEEPER/ACCOUNTANT

BUSINESS MANAGER

WHAT THEY DO AND WHEN TO GET ONE

HOW TO PICK ONE

HOW MUCH DO THEY MAKE

Lecture Points
Chapter Ten

BOOKING AGENT

AGENCY STRUCTURE

CONSIDERING AN AGENT

WHAT AN AGENT DOES

WHAT AN AGENT EARNS

ATTORNEY

WHAT MUSIC ATTORNEYS DO

HOW MUCH DO THEY MAKE

Lecture Points
Chapter Ten

WHEN YOU NEED AN ATTORNEY

SELF-MANAGEMENT

ORGANIZATION

OVERSIGHT

COMMUNICATION

CONTACTS

Chapter Ten Notes

Chapter Ten Notes

THE MANAGEMENT DEAL

PERSONAL MANAGEMENT AGREEMENT

This AGREEMENT (the "Agreement") made and entered into the _____ day of _____, 2008 by and between _____ (referred to as "Artist" or "your"), whose address is _____ and _____ ("Manager"), whose address is _____.

WHEREAS, Artist wishes to obtain Manager's exclusive advice, guidance, counsel, and direction in order to promote and develop Artist's Career as defined herein; and

WHEREAS, Manager wishes to provide such services on the terms and conditions set forth herein.

NOW, THEREFORE IN CONSIDERATION of the mutual covenants and agreements set forth below, and other good and valuable consideration, the receipt and sufficiency of which are hereby acknowledged, the parties agree as follows:

1. Term.

The initial term of this Agreement (the "Initial Term") shall be for a period of two (2) years commencing on the date first written above, and terminating as of the end of the last day of the second year thereafter. Artist hereby grants to Manager three (3) additional one-year option periods (each year referred to as the "Option Period") automatically exercisable by Manager unless Manager on or before the end of the preceding Initial Term and/or Option Period, whichever is applicable, notifies the Artist in writing of its desire to terminate this Agreement.

2. Manager's Services. Throughout the Term of this Agreement, Manager agrees:

To advise, guide, direct and counsel Artist in any and all matters pertaining to employment, publicity, public relations, advertising, the selection of musical material, and all other matters pertaining to Artist's Career which are not specifically excepted herein.

To advise, guide, direct and counsel Artist with relation to the adoption of the proper format for presentation of Artist's talents in the determination of proper style, mood, setting, and characterization in keeping with Artist's talent and best interest.

To advise, guide, direct and counsel Artist in the selection of artistic talents to assist, accompany, or embellish Artist's artistic presentation.

To advise, guide, direct and counsel Artist concerning compensation and privileges for his talent and similar artistic talent.

To advise, guide, direct and counsel Artist concerning the selection of booking agencies, artists' agents, artists' managers, and persons, firms and corporations who will counsel, advise, seek, and procure employment and engagements for Artist.

As pertinent to Artist's Career, to advise, guide, direct and counsel with regard to general practices in the entertainment, music and recording fields and with respect to compensation and terms of contracts related thereto.

Advise, guide, direct and counsel Artist regarding hiring publicists, marketing consultants, advertising agencies, and similar consultants and service providers hired to further Artist's Career.

To meet with Artist when reasonably requested by Artist.

For purposes of this Agreement, "Artist's Career" shall mean and refer to Artist's career worldwide in the entertainment and related businesses, including without limitation, work done by Artist in the recording, acting, literary, theatrical, music publishing, music composing, personal appearance, advertising, entertainment, amusement, music, music performance, music video, television, radio, motion picture, motion picture sound track, commercials, endorsements, video, internet and merchandising fields and otherwise related to Artist's career in the entertainment field, as now known or hereinafter devised in which Artist's artistic talents and/or name, voice, likeness, and/or public image are developed and exploited.

3. Non-Exclusivity and Territory. Manager's services under this Agreement are non-exclusive. Manager shall at all times have the right to render the same or similar services to others whose talents may be similar to or may be in competition with Artist, as well as engage in any and all other business activities, however, Manager agrees to be reasonably available to render the services to Artist hereunder. Artist's engagement of Manager under this Agreement is exclusive throughout the world.

4. Agencies and Publicity. Artist may from time to time enter into agreements with talent agencies, theatrical agencies and employment agencies whose function and obligation shall be to procure employment and engagements for Artist. Any compensation which Artist may be required to pay to these agencies shall be at the sole cost and expense of Artist. If requested by Artist, Manager agrees to supervise and screen the selection and activity of such agency. All expenses of persons of companies specifically retained by Artist to do publicity, public relations or other work on behalf of Artist shall be at the sole cost and expense of Artist.

5. Manager's Authority. Consistent with the services Manager is engaged to provide as set forth herein, and subject to any specific limitations set forth in this Agreement:

Artist hereby grants to Manager the right to approve and permit any and all publicity and advertising and to approve and permit the use of Artist's name, preapproved photograph(s), preapproved likeness(es), preapproved voice, preapproved sound effects, preapproved caricature(s), and preapproved artistic and musical materials, for purposes of advertising and publicity in the promotion and advertising of Artist's products and services. Manager agrees to consult with Artist about tour plans and other activities on a regular basis. To the extent the foregoing requires Artist's signature or written approval, Manager shall reasonably attempt to obtain Artist's signature directly or via facsimile (considering Artist's actual availabitliy and the turnaround time wih respect to the particular matter concerned), or Manager shall attempt to obtain Artist's written approval via email which, solely if granted by Artist, shall confer in Manager the limited power of attorney to render the corresponding approval on behalf of Artist in respect of the particular matter concerned. In the event Manager makes any such decision with which Artist disagrees, then Artist's decision controls and the parties agree to use their best efforts to implement Artist's preference, as may be practical and reasonable under the circumstances then existing. Notwithstanding any other provision contained in this Agreement, Manager does not have the authority to execute or approve, and shall not execute or approve (pursuant to the authority granted to Manager in this paragraph 5 or otherwise) on behalf of Artist any recording, music, or book publishing, booking agency, video, endorsement, merchandising, or any other contract or agreement of any kind whatsoever, whether written or oral.. Any such contract or agreement so executed or approved by Manager shall be null and void, and Manager indemnifies Artist with respect thereto. The authority granted to Manager pursuant to this paragraph 5 above is coupled with an interest and shall be irrevocable during the Term of this Agreement.

6. Receipt of Artist's Compensation. Artist shall engage at its expense a business manager or appropriate bookkeeping personnel to receive all Gross Income for Artist and shall account and remit to Manager in each month when there is either Compensation or expenses due Manager out of Gross Income including the period provided for in Section 7(c) below. Such business manager or bookkeeping personnel shall be available to Manager during regular business hours to confirm the receipt of monies and the payment of expenses. At the request of Artist, Manager shall assist Artist in the selection of a business manager or bookkeeping personnel. Manager and Artist (or Artist's business manager or appropriate bookkeeping personnel, as the case maybe) shall keep accurate and complete books of account and records with respect to all amounts received by Artist and Manager in connection with Artist's Career, which books may be inspected during regular business hours, by a certified public accountant designated either by Artist or Manager, upon reasonable notice to the other. Both Artist and Manager may audit up to three years at a time but may audit any given year only once. Each quarter during the Active Term and the period provided for in Section 7(c) below, Artist shall cause to be delivered to Manager a full statement of account showing the monthly Gross Income accruing to

and received by Artist and any compensation and expense reimbursement due to Manager along with a payment for any additional amount due, if any, Manager may request, during the Active Term, monthly internal statements from Artist's business manager or appropriate bookkeeping personnel and other information upon reasonable request.

7. Manager's Compensation. Since the nature and extent of the success or failure of Artist's Career cannot be predetermined the parties desire that Manager's compensation be determined in such manner as will permit Manager to accept the risk of failure and to benefit from Artist's success. Therefore, as compensation for Manager's services, Artist agrees to pay Manager during and through the Term of this Agreement (and any modifications, extensions, replacements, renewals, or substitutions of this Agreement), the following in consideration of all of Manager's services hereunder ("Fee"): a sum equal to fifteen percent (15%) of all Gross Income (as defined herein in the attached and incorporated Glossary) received or accrued (as of the last day of the Term) directly or indirectly by Artist or by any other person or entity on Artist's behalf, including without limitation, Artist's heirs, executors, administrators, and assigns, regarding Artist's Career.

(a) For purposes of this Agreement, "Gross Income" shall include, without limitation but subject to the exclusions stated in paragraph 7 of the Agreement, all of the following relating to Artist's Career: salaries, earnings, fees, royalties, advances against royalties, merchandise, gifts (excluding bona fide gifts as defined by the Internal Revenue Code), bonuses, , shares of profits, shares of stock, residuals, repeats or return fees, partnership interests, share of profits, percentages, percentages and the total amount paid for a package television or radio program (live or recorded) or other entertainment package, received directly or indirectly by Artist or by any other person or entity on Artist's behalf, including the aggregate amount paid to bands led by Artist (but only for Artist's services in connection therewith). It is understood that, for purposes hereof, no expense, cost or disbursement paid or incurred by Artist in connection with the receipt or earning of "Gross Income" (including salaries, shares of profits or other sums paid to individuals participating in Artist's presentations, recordings, videos or other forms of performances), shall be deducted therefrom prior to the calculation of Manager's compensation hereunder except only for the items excepted in paragraph 7(b) above. In the event that Artist receives, as all or part of his compensation for activities within Artist's Career, stock or other equity interests, or the right to buy stock or other equity interests, in any corporation or entity or that Artist becomes the packager or owner of all or part of an entertainment property, whether as an individual proprietor, stockholder, partner, joint venturer or otherwise, Manager's Compensation shall apply to said stock or equity, right to buy stock or equity, individual proprietorship, partnership, joint venture or other forms of interest, and Manager shall be entitled to Manager's Compensation thereof. Should Artist be required to make any payment for such interest, Manager will pay his percentage share of such payment, except if Manager does not want his Fee thereof, the reasonable value of such interest (taking into account Artist's payment therefore) shall be deemed to be Gross Income for the purposes of this Agreement.

(b) The following are specifically excluded from Gross Income: (i) tour support funds to the extent such funds cover reasonably incurred actual tour losses (or any tour support funds to the extent actually paid for or incurred on behalf of Artist by any record company or tour/live performances sponsor to cover tour/live performance losses); (ii) funds or other considerations, which are received by Artist or on Artist's behalf and which are subsequently refunded to the payee (example: deposits received by booking agencies on live engagements which are not subsequently performed by Artist, and therefore the deposit must be refunded); (iii) funds which are paid by Artist or by third parties on Artist's behalf to third parties which are expended on actual video cost, recording costs (including, but not limited to, those costs, expenditures, and advances remitted or defined as recording costs or the equivalent thereof in any recording agreement entered into by Artist), and production costs, writers and publishers, producer, mixers, engineers, studio facilities, and salaried musicians; (iv) sound and light, opening acts, support acts, each with respect

to live performances or other personal appearances by Artist, (v) actual publisher, subpublisher and administrator fees under agreements related to music publishing income; (vi) the expenses of Artist for engaging musical groups other than Artist in the entertainment industry to the extent Artist is a "packager" of an entertainment property but such expense shall not reduce Gross Income by more then the Gross Income created by such entertainment package unless Manager has approved such package arrangement in advance in writing (such approval not to be unreasonably withheld); (vii) union pension and welfare plan benefits paid to Artist and on Artist's behalf with respect to recording sessions; (ix) verifiable reimbursed expenses; (x) monies earned by Artist from passive investments; (xi) gifts received by Artist to the extent not in lieu of compensation; and (xiv) loans to Artist.

(c) After the Term, Manager shall be paid, in lieu of the Fee, a sum (the "Post-Term Commission") equal to fifteen (15%) percent of all Gross Income (except for items excluded under the paragraph 7 above) received or accrued by Artist for the first five (5) years after the Term has ended, which Post-Term Commission shall be reduced to ten (10%) percent for the five (5) years thereafter, and then further reduced to five (5%) percent for the next five years. For purposes of clarity, Manager shall not be entitled to any Post-Term Commission (or other compensation of any kind) beyond fifteen (15) years after the termination of this Agreement.

8. Manager's Expenses. In addition to the compensation provided in paragraph 7 above, Artist shall reimburse Manager for all reasonable expenses necessarily and actually incurred on Artist's behalf directly in connection with Manager's rendition of services under this Agreement during the Term including, but not limited to, overnight, certified or registered mail postage long distance telephone calls, facsimile transmissions, and travel expenses, but excluding office expenses and overhead. No Individual expense in excess of $500 shall be incurred by Manager without first having obtained Artist's prior written consent. Reimbursable expenses in any month shall not exceed an aggregate of $1,000 without Manager having first obtained Artist's prior written consent. Expenses shall only be reimbursed out of Gross Income actually earned by Artist from Artist's Career. Artist agrees that, in the event that Manager renders any services under this Agreement to Artist outside of the metropolitan area in which Manager's office is located, Manager shall be entitled to reimbursement from Artist for reasonable travel expenses (subject to applicable preapproval hereunder). In the event that Manager must travel by air, Manager agrees to purchase airline tickets at the lowest fare available at the time of booking and, when applicable, for the same "class" that Artist travels (further subject to applicable preapproval hereunder). All expenses charged or incurred by Manager shall be pro-rated with respect to Artist if Manager is simultaneously rendering services for or on behalf of other clients or parties. Subject to the foregoing, reimbursement of expenses shall be due Manager within thirty (30) days after receipt of itemized statements setting forth the nature and amount of each expense. During the Term of this Agreement and for a period of (3) years following, Manager agrees to keep and maintain reasonable documentation of each expense from which he requested reimbursement by Artist and all documentation shall be provided to Artist or his representative promptly after Artist's reasonable request.

9. **Expenses Loans and Advances.** Except as otherwise stated herein, Artist shall be solely responsible for the payment of all expenses which may arise in connection with Artist's Career, including, without limitation the cost of material, equipment, facilities, transportation, lodging and living expenses, costumes, make-up, promotion, publicity, accounting and legal fees, and Manager shall not have any liability whatsoever in such connection and therefore, such expense shall not reduce Gross Income subject to Manager's commission hereunder except only as set forth in paragraph 7 above. Manager shall not be obligated to lend to or advance money to Artist, but if it does so, Artist shall repay such amount(s) promptly from Gross Income (and only from Gross Income); Manager agrees to provide Artist a written tabulation of any such loan or advance actually made upon request by Artist. .

10. **Offers of Employment.** Artist shall advise Manager of all offers of employment related to Artist's Career submitted to Artist and will refer all inquiries concerning Artist's Career to Manager, so that Manager m ay advise Artist whether they are compatible with Artist's Career. Reciprocally, Manager shall inform Artist of any offers or prospective employment opportunities of or concerning Artist's Career which Manager receives.

11. **Career.** Artist agrees at all times to attend to Artist's Career, and to do all things reasonably necessary and desirable and consistent with this Agreement to promote Artist's Career and earnings. With Manager's advice, guidance, direction and counsel, Artist shall at all times endeavor to engage and utilize proper theatrical agents and booking agents to obtain engagements and employment for Artist.

12. **Notice of Breach.** In order to eliminate misunderstandings between the Artist and Manager, Artist and Manager agree to advise each other in writing of the specific nature of any claimed breach of this Agreement. The party receiving such notice shall have thirty (30) days after the receipt of the notice in which to cure the claimed breach. The written notice shall be deemed a condition precedent to the commencement of any arbitration and shall be sent by certified mail, return receipt requested. Notice to Artist shall be given to the address set forth in the first paragraph of this Agreement, with a copy to Artist's legal counsel, _____. Notice to Manager shall be given to the address set forth in the first paragraph of this Agreement, with a copy (which shall not constitute notice) to Manager's legal counsel, _____.

13. **Business Entities.** Artist's Career may be developed and exploited primarily through certain corporate, limited liability company or similar entities. Therefore, references herein to Artist, such as, without limitation, reference to income earned by Artist or received by Artist, shall be deemed to include the income earned or received by these entities. However, there shall be no double compensation hereunder, and therefore any distributions to Artist from such entities, including without limitation, dividends and salaries which are derived from gross revenues that have already been compensated hereunder, shall not he commissioned again upon payment to Artist.

14. Manager's Other Businesses. Artist acknowledges that from time to time during the Term, either alone or with others, Manager or individuals or entities affiliated with Manager may act as promoter of an event at which Artist shall perform. Manager agrees that in any such arrangements Artist will be compensated in the same manner as if Manager or such individuals or entities affiliated with Manager were not involved in the promotion and after full and adequate disclosure of the circumstances; however, Manager agrees to waive the Fee and Post-Term Commissions in respect of any such events to avoid a conflict of interest hereunder.

15. Parties Free to Enter into Agreement. Manager and Artist warrant that: they are under no disability restriction or prohibition with respect to their right to execute this Agreement and form its terms and conditions; no act or omission by either hereunder will violate any right or interest of any person or firm, or will subject either party to any liability, or claim of liability to any person or firm; and Artist warrants that he has the right to and shall collect any and all Gross Income derived from Artist's Career. Manager and Artist agree to indemnify the other and to hold the other harmless against any damages, cost, expenses, fees (including reasonable attorneys' fees) incurred by the other party in any third party claim, suit or proceeding instituted against the other party in which any assertion is made which is inconsistent with any warranty, representation or covenant of them provided such claim is finally adjudicated or settled with their consent (which consent shall not be unreasonably withheld).

16. Assignment. Manager shall not have the right to assign Manager's rights or responsibilities under this Agreement to any entity without Artist's prior written approval, which approval shall not be unreasonably withheld.

17. Review by Counsel. The Artist and Manager acknowledge that they have had an opportunity to retain independent counsel of their own choosing to review this Agreement and advise them regarding its terms and conditions.

18. Age. Artist represents and warrants that Artist has attained the age of eighteen (18) years.

19. Binding Effect. This Agreement shall be binding upon Artist and Manager, and, to the extent applicable, shall also be binding upon their heirs, executors, permitted successors, and permitted assigns.

20. Controlling Law. This Agreement shall be deemed to be executed in the State of Tennessee and shall be construed in accordance with the internal laws of the State of Tennessee.

21. Status of Parties. This Agreement shall not be construed to create a partnership or joint venture between Manager and Artist. Manager is an independent contractor hereunder.

22. Modification. No modification or alteration of this Agreement shall be valid unless it is made in writing and signed by both parties.

IN WITNESS WHEREOF, the parties hereto have executed this Agreement as of the day and date first written above.

ARTIST:

_____

MANAGER:

_____

ARTIST MANAGEMENT-CONTRACT TERMS

Assignment: The appointment of the manager to represent the artist.

Authority: Artists often turn over all authority for performing, interviews, etc., to the manager who will determine which offer is in the best long-term interest of the artist. This also means that the artist may not accept movies, concert opportunities, or record deals without the approval of the manager.

Audit: In contracts, artists should include the right to have an accountant audit the manager's books at least once a year.

Commission Base: The negotiated artist's revenue sources that will earn the managers a commission.

Commission Rate: The percent of the commission base that is paid to the manager for his or her service.

Creative Representation: Artists grant a power of attorney to managers, and manager accept it as a mutual agreement to exhibit common interest in the development of the artist's creative talents, recording, performing, and professional career.

Compensation: The manager's percentage of income should be stated in the contract. The percentage often ranges from 15% to 20% of all money resulting from all direct and indirect artist's activities in the entertainment industry to very specific percentages based on defined revenue sources.[238]

Employment: Managers do not act as employment agents for the acts they represent. They usually limit their role to negotiating with agents and labels for various types of deals, and consulting the artists on hiring, firing, and employment opportunities.

Exclusivity: The signed manager solely represents the artist. In addition, the artist will often be required to agree not to perform any of the legal duties assigned to the manager in the power-of- attorney agreement without any prior written consent from the manager.

Expenses: Some managers pay all the bills as stated in the contract, while others require the artists themselves to pay booking agents and personal expenses such as rental and car payments. This is also the location in the contract where the manager will state that they will not pay or loan the act any money.

Gross Monthly Earnings: The gross monthly earnings are usually the total monies made by the artists from recording royalty points, bonuses or salaries, profits from concerts and merchandise sales, music publishing and songwriting royalties, commercial endorsements, movie and television performances, and profits from shares in capital ventures.

Limitations: The power of attorney agreement is usually limited to matters reasonably related to the artist's career as a musician, songwriter, publisher, and performing artist.

Monthly Statement: Each month the manager should send the artist a copy of the financial records.

Negotiation Period: An artist may write into their management agreement a performance clause such as the requirement for the manager to secure a major recording contract for the act. If the manager fails to achieve the stated performance clause within a certain time frame (often 12 to 24 months) the artist may cancel the agreement by sending a written statement to the manager. The agreement is usually terminated within 30 days after the manager receives the cancellation notice.

---

[238] Colonel Parker received 50% of all of Elvis' income and a former Bruce Springsteen manager was at one time making 80% of Springsteen's income.

Payment of Services: All monies from the artist's performances, record sales, and commercial endorsements are paid to the manager or the artist's accountant or business manager, as approved by the manager. The manager usually collects his or her negotiated percentage of the commission base and then has the business manager invest or place the remaining portion of the monies collected into the artist's accounts or businesses.

Suspension: Artists in the music industry can be suspended from label deals and artist management agreements if they become sick, refuse to perform, breach any part of their legal contracts, or break written moral clauses or social norms by committing a criminal act.

Term: The actual length of the initial period of the agreement is usually 1 year followed by 6 options.

STUDY GUIDE-
ARTIST MANAGEMENT CONTRACT

1. The artist "hires' the manager, yet the manager "signs" the artist. Explain.

2. According to the job description in the contract, (services), what is the artist requesting from the manager?

3. Explain the "initial term" in this contract.

4. What does "advise, guide, direct, and counsel mean?

5. Who hires the booking agent?

6. Who hires the publicists, marketing consultants, and advertising agencies?

7. Who approves all publicity and advertising; the artist or the manager?

8. Who is responsible for the hiring of the business manager or accountant?

9. Explain the amount (percent) of money the manager is to be paid according to the terms of the contract?

10. Explain the term post-term commission?

11. How long does the "post term commission" last?

12. Is the manager allowed to have other businesses?

NETWORKING IN THE MUSIC BUSINESS

HOW TO NETWORK

BECOME INVOLVED IN A SCENE

READ PUBLICATIONS RELATED TO YOUR MUSIC

GO TO CLUBS AND MUSICAL EVENTS

ASK QUESTIONS

DON'T ALWAYS EXPECT TO MEET THE HEAD OF THE COMPANY

ATTEND CONVENTIONS

GIVE AND GET BUSINESS CARDS

FOLLOW UP

Lecture Points
Chapter Eleven

JOIN ASSOCIATIONS WITH PEOPLE WITH YOUR INTERESTS

INVOLVEMENT WITH MUSIC SCHOOL/COLLEGE MUSIC DEPARTMENT

ELECTRONIC NETWORKING

SETTING YOUR GOALS

YOUR DREAMS

10-YEAR GOALS

5-YEAR GOALS

2-YEAR GOALS

1-YEAR GOALS

BEING A LEADER

286

Lecture Points
Chapter Eleven

CAREER PLANNING AND DEVELOPMENT

WRITING A BUSINESS PLAN

SUMMARY STATEMENT

DESCRIPTION OF YOUR BUSINESS OR PROJECT

MARKETING PLAN

    A. Your Market's Description

    B, Your Strategic Marking Plan

OPERATIONS PLAN

PROJECT TIME LINE

FINANCIAL INFORMATION

LEGAL STRUCTURES

Lecture Points
Chapter Eleven

NETWORKING IN THE MUSIC BUSINESS

HOW TO NETWORK

BECOME INVOLVED IN A SCENE

READ PUBLICATIONS RELATED TO YOUR MUSIC

GO TO CLUBS AND MUSICAL EVENTS

ASK QUESTIONS

DON'T ALWAYS EXPECT TO MEET THE HEAD OF THE COMPANY

ATTEND CONVENTIONS

GIVE AND GET BUSINESS CARDS

Chapter Eleven Notes

Chapter Eleven Notes

CONCERT PROMOTION

PROMOTERS

Most *concert promoters* usually work independently from the record labels to create their own entrepreneurial businesses. These are the high-stakes money rollers in the music and entertainment industry as they will often make or lose hundreds of thousands of dollars in one night. They provide their expertise, money, social and business connections to stage concerts (events) that help generate the positive cash flow opportunities needed by many performing artists and labels (through increased unit sales due to the live appearance of the act). The promoters are either companies (such as LiveNation), the bands themselves (such as the Rollin' Stones) or individuals who specialize in different types of genre` of music, tours, or territories of the country or world (examples include country music or rap for types of genre`of music, the west coast, south or Europe as territories). Thus, promoters are responsible for the actual staging, marketing, and promotion of the event and the corresponding success or failure and of course, the financial profits and losses.

LIST FOR SELECTING A PROMOTER

What are the important questions the artist(s) should consider when selecting a promoter for a show or concert tour?

- Is the promoter reputable?
- Do they pay their bills?
- How do they treat their performers?
- Do they promote shows effectively?
- Do they return phone calls?
- Do they get along with other bands?
- Do they have a good reputation for accommodating bands? (parking, refreshments, etc.)
- Do they have good production values?
- Are they hospitable?
- Do they have a good reputation with the local media?[239]

LIST FOR SELECTING AN ACT

Likewise, what are the questions a promoter should ask the artist(s) before signing them (and paying at least 50% of the guarantee) for a show or concert tour? Most of these questions will be answered by the act's track record, the promoter's research on the act with contacts in the industry (people and promoters the act has worked with in the past), the information from internet sources such as www.soundscan.com, Billboard and Pollstar charts and articles, and the representative booking agent or manager.

[239] Mark Volman's Survey of Music Business Workbook 2008.

- Do they have a reputation for being on time?
- Does the artist make reasonable requests?
- Have they performed in the area before?
- How is the revenue doing on their tour?
- Can the venue handle their technical rider?
- Do they get along with their promoter?
- Does the artist have a good rep with the media?
- Will the artist relate with the venues main audience?
- How does the artist get along with your staff & crew?
- Can the promoter sell the artist in their market?[240]

TOUR QUESTION LIST

Even the simplest of questions needs to be answered before the concert tour agreement is complete. Most of the time this is accomplished in the Rider which is part of the official contract between the booking agent and the act. Some of the questions are between the act and their manager, others between the act and the booking agents (through the manager) and still others through the booking agent/manger and the promoter.

- Travel. How will the artist get to the venue?
- Will accommodations be provided?
- What percentage, if any, does the artist get for their performance?
- Will the artists pay their own expenses?
- What hospitality will be provided by the venue?
- What will he ticket prices will be?
- Will there be an opening act?
- How long will you play? Encores? Intermissions?
- Are you the only act? If not, who gets top billing?
- How much are the promoters willing to spend advertising the act?
- What technical equipment do you need to play?
- Will the artist be getting complimentary tickets?
- Will you be selling merchandise?
- How much will the venue take?
- Always get half of your deposit for playing in advance.

---

240 Ibid.

TYPES OF CONCERT PROMOTION/ARTIST DEALS

Concert promotion is a very risky business so there are many types of deals that can and are often structured. However, the following four types of deals are the basic foundations for all the various scenarios that may be negotiated.

- *Straight Guarantee*: The act receives a guaranteed amount of money regardless of the success or failure of the promoter to generate an audience. The straight guarantee deal provides the promoter with an opportunity to lock in the act as a fixed cost and therefore increase his or her potential profit based on the success of the event.

- *Guarantee Plus a Percentage of the Net (Gate)*: The act receives the guarantee plus a certain percentage of the net after the break even point (all expenses have been paid). The percentage of the net becomes a negotiation point for the band to receive additional income on a very successful event and also increases the negotiation leverage for the promoter to land or sign a more successful act for the event.

- *Guarantee Versus a Percentage of the Net*: The act receives either the fixed guarantee or a percentage of the net whichever is greater. This type of deal is a mixture of the straight guarantee deal and the guarantee plus a percentage of the net deal and provides a little more financial security to the act. If the event is poorly attended or loses money for the promoter the act is still paid the guarantee. If the event is very successful then the act is paid an amount that is more fair than just the guarantee. It also puts additional pressure on the promoter to control the bid sheet expenses and negotiate a correct percentage of the net (profit).

- *Guarantee Plus a Bonus:* The act receives a guarantee amount plus a negotiated amount or bonus based on the number of tickets sold. The bonus is a variable amount that increases as the number of seats sold hit various level. This type of deal provides more security to the promoter and act as both receive payments based on the success of the event.

CONCERT PROMOTION PROCESS

Once the promoter determines which acts to book (employ), they match the artists (who are on tour and available) with the venues that have open dates. At the same time, booking agents who represent the artists call regional promoters, corporations and venture capitalists (who may act as promoters) to generate concert dates for their artists. It's a huge gamble. Bad weather, an artist's poor health, or some other uncontrollable situation can negatively determine the final concert attendance. A low turnout may cost independent promoters thousands of dollars. Conversely, successful concerts can profit hundreds of thousands of dollars in one evening. It's easy to see why the concert promotion business is considered a very risky business.

VIRTUAL CORPORATIONS

A *virtual corporation* operated out of the top floor of hotel rooms supervised *The Rolling Stones'* recent concert tour. The company oversaw the Stones' tour, all the arrangements, its 250 employees, and its $1.5 million-a week budget. Gross income for the tour was approximately $300 million, of which the Rolling Stones collected about $100 million.[1] Virtual corporations are often established to run and supervise concert tours. They are sole-purpose companies set up to run the tour, ticketing, and merchandising. Promoters run the businesses out of their hotel rooms using multiple phone lines, cell phones, fax machines and email. These corporations often gross millions of dollars during the tour, and when the tour is finished, the companies are closed and "out-of-business."

---

1 "Top 40" Robert La Franco, Forbes (09/25/95).

DEPOSITS

The artist's manager must approve bookings (scheduling) of tour dates by the booking agent. A deposit or guarantee of 50%-100% of the agreed upon price for the act is generally required from the promoter to finalize the deal. The money is placed into an interest-bearing account. During the concert, the road manager, tour accountant, and promoter tabulate the concert receipts in the back office. The down payment is subtracted from the money owed to the band. Full payment for the band's/artist's performance is required at closing. Successful promoters are known by industry insiders and are often hired for entire national tours, regions, or clusters of cities to reduce the band's risk of working with amateur promoters.

PROFIT MARGINS

Promoters subtract their total projected expenses from their projected gross ticket sales revenues to determine their break-even points and profit margins. Knowing their profit margins helps the promoter to be familiar with how many tickets they can sell at various prices. That total becomes the projected gross ticket revenues (income). Then, using a bid sheet promoters determine their projected expenses (total cost of creating the event), subtract the projected expenses (debt) from the projected gross income (revenue), and determine profitability. Profit margins are based on how many seats must be sold to break-even or make a profit. Many concerts require 50%-80% of all tickets to be sold to break-even financially. Promoters hope the profits will be much greater than the 20% depending on the act booked, promotion, and publicity. However, other types of margins are common depending on what is negotiated on the front end and of course, the type of deal, and the number of tickets sold.

WHO IS MARK VOLMAN?

TURTLE, MANAGER, SONGWRITER, PUBLISHER, PROMOTER, PROFESSOR.

My life changed the day I signed my first record contract. I didn't know it then, but it plunged me deep into the business world of music for the next 45 years. I had no mentors, no consultants and certainly no books to offer me insights into the spiral onto which I had just embarked... a spiral through seven managers in the first five years and worse yet, signed 100% of my songwriting publishing away before I had even written my first song. The music business has changed dramatically since that first contract was signed in 1965 as a member of The Turtles, but many things still remain the same. The incredible number of stories I have personally heard, telling of lost careers and lost human beings, could fill a very large book. For every successful story, there are many more reflecting the outcomes of battered lives left to fade away in the wake of misguided musical choices and decisions Today musicians, artists and songwriters still sign agreements they do not completely understand and the results of that turn the dream of success into a battle of survival, not just as a musician, but as a battle for life.

BID SHEETS

Promoters use a bid sheet to determine their break-even points and projected expenses. The following bid sheet is based on a $200,000 projected gross event.

BID SHEET EXAMPLE

Item	Projected Cost	% of Total Projected Cost	Type of Deal Financials
Artist/Main Act Booking Agent (10%) Manager (10-20%) Tour Expenses (30-50%) • Musicians • Bgv's • Travel, Hotels, Bus & Flights • Crew/Roadies • Taxes (IRS)	**$75,000** $10-20,000 Total Projected Main Artist Cost $75,000 no gate to $95,000 Guarantee plus 50% of gate after break-even	35% 0-15% of Total	**Guarantee** A Percentage of the Gate may be part of the deal. This provides an additional 0-50% of the gross after the breakeven point ($0-20,000), which equals an additional 0%-15% to the act's total
Opening Act Booking Agent (10%) Manager (10-20%) Tour Expenses (30-50%) • Musicians • Bgv's • Travel, Hotels, Bus & Flights • Crew/Roadies • Taxes (IRS)	$10,000	5%	**Guarantee**
Venue Security • Uniform Police • T-Shirt Security • Undercover Ushers Sales Personnel Food/Commissions Tickets I.A.T.S.E. • Audio/lighting • Stage Crews-Load in/out • Constructions/stage Rider Obligations • Food/Rooms/etc.	$20,000	5-10%	**Per-day rate** which is a percent of the gross or a fixed rate which ever is higher. **Fixed Rate** The minimum fixed rate is $1.00 per seat.
TicketMaster Sales	$4,000	2% of Gross	Fixed Percent
Advertisement/Promotion • Radio • Internet • Popular press & Trades	$20,000	5-15% of Gross	Fixed Percent
Licenses • Performance Rights • Personal Bond	$2,000	1% of Gross	Blanket License (One night) determined by size/seats in venue.
Complimentary Tickets	$2,000	1% or less of Gross	Fixed Rate
Promoter • Staff • Taxes (Local & IRS)	$20,000-$40,000	10-20% of Gross	Fixed Rated over 80% Break Even Point

Clearly, the concert business is very risky. *Promoters* often negotiate a guaranteed price plus a split of the profits in order to reduce the gamble. Superstar acts may require 80-95% of tickets to be sold before profit margins are achieved or they may just produce and promote the concert tour themselves to keep all of the profits. In addition, concerts are sometimes scheduled in smaller cities between major concert venues. These concerts (called pick-ups) help pay expenses between the more profitable concerts in larger markets.

SPONSORING RADIO STATION

Labels want their artists' touring to promote their latest recordings. Promoters and labels often work together to select a local radio station to sponsor the concert. The promoter receives a break on advertisements and the station is allowed to claim it is sponsoring the concert.

RISKY BUSINESS

What if it rains or snows? What if there is another concert by another promoter the same week as yours? What if a band member gets sick? What if the artist makes a negative public statement or is caught by the press doing something illegal? The concert may still have to be played and the attendance may suffer, which means the promoter gambled and lost money.

MERCHANDISE

Merchandising is an integral part of the concert industry. Companies such as *EMI, Brockum, FMI, Nice Man and Winterland* create a huge revenue stream by providing and selling merchandise for their artist(s). The artists receive between 15-35% of the gross income from merchandise, while the providing company pays for all the merchandise, shipment, sales personnel, booths, tables, and advertisements. Artists approve the design of the merchandise and receive quarterly checks for their percentage of each piece of stock sold. In addition, the concert venue usually receives a percentage of the total merchandise profits for providing space, tables, and advertisement opportunities to the merchandising company. T-shirts, hats, records, CDs, and other types of merchandise endorsed by the artists are considered merchandise. *Soft drinks, food, and candy are considered concessions* that are sold by the venue with all profits remaining with the venue. Concession sales locations and commissions are negotiated by the booking agent and approved by the artist's manager before the final contracts are signed.

RIDER

A *rider* is an additional set of instructions for the promoter regarding specific artist's requirements. Riders usually include the size of the stage, lighting, etc., and may even include the type of food, drinks, or other necessities the artist wants supplied in their dressing room.[2]

I.A.T.S.E.

www.IATSE.org

The International Alliance of Theatrical and Stage Employees (IATSE) represents audio engineers, lighting technicians, set designers and builders, and stagehands for live shows. A union house is a venue, studio, etc., that has signed an agreement with the performance unions (AFTRA, AF of M, etc.) to allow only union members to be employed during the creation of various entertainment productions. Most Broadway venues, sports complexes, and movies made in Hollywood, are considered union jobs made or performed in union houses. Exceptions include the production facilities in right-to-work states that often allow for non-union productions.[3]

---

2 You can see some riders at www.thesmokinggun.com.
3 Several unions have also formed an alliance called the Associated Actors and Artists of America. Its union members are represented by the AFL-CIO and include Actors Equity Association (AEA), the American Guild of Variety Artists

ROADIES

The roadies are members of the touring acts who drive the trucks to each venue, load and unload and often set-up, operate, and breakdown the musical instruments, lighting, and sound equipment. The amount and type of work roadies can accomplish depends on: (a) the I.A.T.S.E union agreements with each venue, (b) the contractual agreements made with the promoter and artist's manager, and (c) specific items listed in the artist's rider.

TICKETMASTER

www.ticketmaster.com

Ticketmaster controls all tickets sold at over 3,000 U.S. venues including those of more than 50 professional sports teams. It grew its business by offering many of the venues front money (in some cases millions of dollars) for the exclusive right to sell tickets to all the events scheduled at the venues. ETM Entertainment Network is Ticketmaster's main competitor. However, Ticketmaster, in the past, has purchased most of its competitors through mergers and buyouts. In addition, Ticketmaster is currently offering services over the web and through many other ticketing venues.[4]

SERIOUS MUSIC MARKET

The serious non-profit music markets of symphony orchestras, opera, Broadway and dance companies contribute about $37 billion annually to the United States economy.[133] Many opportunities are available for classically trained, consummate musicians and vocalists. Private and public organizations, churches, universities, public and private grants, donations, businesses, and local volunteer organizations often finance orchestras and various types of choral groups. Many serious music organizations are dependent on these political, social, and music-supporting groups to provide financial support for local musicians. Local symphonies, operas, etc., are marketed through the mass media by using their public service spots on radio and TV to announce performances and provide stories and photographs to the print media.

POLLSTAR & SOUNDSCAN

www.pollstar.com

www.soundscan.com

Pollstar magazine and Soundscan data (list retail unit sales figures) are often used by industry insiders to help them make their concert business decisions. Promoters use the agency rosters to select and locate the artists they want to book. Venues use the trades to publicize their auditoriums for acts, managers and promoters. Domestic and international news stories detail the artists' lifestyles and their successful enterprises. To make business decisions, Pollstar provides a summary of radio charts, stations' play (by formats); a listing of recent concert revenues (by the average gross); the number of shows per week and per act; a summary of album sales (by artist, title, and label); and a listing of touring acts' scheduled concerts.

(AGVA), the American Guild of Musical Artists (AGMA), and the Screen Extras Guild (SEG). The AEA represents professional actors in plays and musicals; the AGVA represents live performance artists, such as singers and dancers at resorts; SEG represents extras in screen productions in Los Angeles; all other extras are covered by SAG; and the AGMA represents traditional musical artists and vocalists performing ballets, ensembles, operas, and other traditional forms of music.
4 "Will Ticketmaster Get Scalped: The Justice Dep. and Rivals Question Its Dominance", Linde Himeistein and Ronald Grover, Business Week (June 26, 1995).

BILLBOARD MAGAZINE
www.billboard.com

The most important trade publication in the business is Billboard. It covers every phase of the industry on a weekly basis and provides the most up to date news, charts, trends, and networking opportunities available.

SUMMARY

Concerts provide record labels with another way to publicize their artists and recordings. However, the concert business is really a separate industry with its own set of entrepreneurial businessmen and women. Concert promoters risk their own money on the public's interest to attend a staged event (a concert). Booking agents represent various acts. Their job is to call on the promoters to "book" the act into various tours and venues. The serious money in the industry is now in the *event* or *concert business*. While most artists never make any money from their label deals, (due to recoupment), they often become "famous" or "known" through their deals. That opens an opportunity for them to exploit their fame and talent though the third revenue stream, concerts. This is where most artists make very good to fabulous livings as performers. It also provides other opportunities including corporate sponsorships and merchandise sales to boost their bank accounts. Most *concert promoters* work independently from the record labels to create their own entrepreneurial businesses. They are the high-stakes money rollers in the music and entertainment industry as they often make or lose hundreds of thousands of dollars in one night. They provide their expertise, money, social and business connections to stage concerts (events) that help generate the positive cash flow opportunities needed by many performing artists and labels (through increased unit sales due to the live appearance of the act). Concert tours and events are very important to the artist, (don't want to disappoint the fans), thus they need to ask many questions about the type of person and deal promoters are offering.

The promoters are either companies (such as LiveNation), the bands themselves (such as the Rollin' Stones) or individuals who specialize in different types of genre` of music, tours, or territories of the country or world (examples include country music or rap for types of genre`of music, the west coast, south or Europe as territories). Thus, promoters are responsible for the actual staging, marketing, and promotion of the event and the corresponding success or failure and of course, the financial profits and losses. They usually use a bid sheet to determine all expenses for staging a concert and establish their break-even points between 50%-80% of total tickets sold. Once the deal is made with the booking agent, a deposit between 50%-100% of the bands salary is required. Booking agents are members of the AF of M licensed company that provide protection to union member band members and artists. Riders are sent to the promoters to explain very detailed artist's expectations of how the concert should be staged and administrated. Booking agents are paid 10% for acquiring concert dates for the acts they represent. Acts often share the risk with the promoter by accepting a guaranteed amount of money and then splitting the profits. The rider is an addition to the actual contract that stipulates how the act's likeness may be advertised and a detailed listing of everything that must be provided for the act, from the type of food in the dressing rooms to the size of the performance stage.

CONCERT PROMOTION TERMS

Billing: The location or placement of the act or artist's name (logo) on tickets, advertisements, and press releases. Top billing means that the name of the artist will be on top of the venue's billboard or marquee and appear in larger print than other acts' or artists' names on tickets, and first mention on radio promotion spots.

Break-Even Points: The point in financial statements where the income (monies gained) from the event (concert, recording contract, etc.) equals the cost or total expenses for the event (or cost of recording, promotion, marketing, etc. of the recording).

Comp Ticket: A complementary ticket to a concert often provided to radio stations and local important music insiders to promote an event. The number of tickets is usually supplied by the promoter and approved by the artist's manager.

Firm Offer: A firm offer is a signed contracted agreement which includes the concert dates, time of appearance, negotiated price for the act's performance, and a deposit consisting of a cashier's check or money order that will be placed into a secured account.

Four Walls: The most basic levels of service a venue has available to the concert promoter and act are listed under the term "four walls" or "four walling." The amount of electricity available (amps), heating, air conditioning, lights, and personnel, including house security, are listed on the contractual agreement between the venue and concert promoter.

Gross Potential: The GP is the maximum amount of money that will be generated by the concert if all tickets are sold.

Guarantee: A guarantee is the minimum amount of money the artist or act will earn for the performance. Often, artists will accept a guarantee plus an additional split of the profits. The bigger name acts demand a larger guarantee and a percent of the promoter's profits.

Headliner: The main attraction or most famous act to perform at the concert. Headliners are paid more money to perform than supporting acts.

Splits: A percentage (PC) of the profits or money collected from the gate (entry) after the concert expenses have reached the break-even point.

Ticket Manifest: A computerized list of every seat (and ticket price) in a venue for a specific act or artists for each concert date.

STUDY GUIDE-
THE CONCERT/EVENT BUSINESS

1. Explain the following from the artist's perspective.

    (a) Promotion

    (b) Publicity

    (c) Public Relations

2. What is the purpose of the electronic press kit?

3. Why do artists appear on TV talk shows, etc.?

4. Explain why labels provide tour support to artists.

5. Explain the role of a concert promoter.

6. Write a paragraph explaining things to consider when you (as an artist) are selecting a promoter.

7. Write a paragraph describing what a promoter should consider before selecting an act.

8. Let's assume that you are about to go out on a tour. What are some of the questions you should be asking?

9. Concert promoters use bid sheets to determine their cost of putting on a concert. Explain the cost of the following items as listed on most bid sheets.

    (a) Main act

    (b) Opening Act

    (c) Venue

(d) Ticketmaster

(e) Advertisement/promotion/sponsoring station

(f) Licenses

(g) Complimentary Tickets

(h) Promoter/staff

10. List and explain the four types of concert deals. Explain the differences of each in regards to guarantees, percent of gate, and bonuses.

(a)

(b)

(c)

(d)

11. Once the artist's manager approves a bid from a promoter, what percent of the guarantee must be paid and deposited into the artist's account?

12. What percentage of seats in a venue need to be sold for the promoter to breakeven?

13. Explain how merchandise has become an integral part of the concert business.

14. What is a rider?

15. What is I.A.T.S.E. and what do they do?

16. Define the Serious Music Market and explain why they are usually non-profit organizations.

17. Who is Pollstar? What markets and industry does it cover?

18. Why is soundscan information important to promoters?

19. Why is Billboard Magazine the most important trade in the industry? List Billboards' two most important charts.

    (a)

    (b)

Lecture Points
Chapter Twelve

TOURING

WHY TOUR?

TRAVELER'S TIPS

RESTAURANTS

HOTELS

TRAVEL

                                  FINDING GIGS

WHERE TO PLAY

GETTING READY

ASSOCIATIONS

BUSINESSES

Lecture Points
Chapter Twelve

NON-PROFIT ORGANIZATIONS

CONVENTIONS

COUNTRY CLUBS

PARK PROGRAMS

CRUISE LINES

HOTELS

PRIVATE PARTIES

PUBLIC RELATIONS FIRMS/ADVERTISING AGENCIES

SCHOOLS

Lecture Points
Chapter Twelve

THE TOURING TEAM

MUSICIANS

SINGERS

TOUR MANAGER

TOUR ACCOUNTANT

PRODUCTION MANAGER

LIGHTING DIRECTOR

SPOTLIGHT OPERATORS

FRONT OF HOUSE SOUND ENGINEER

MONITOR SOUND ENGINEER

BACKLINE AND INSTRUMENT TECHNICIANS

Lecture Points
Chapter Twelve

WARDROBE

ELECTRICIANS RIGGERS AND CARPENTERS

STEEL CREW

TRUCK AND BUS DRIVERS

GET THE MOST OUT OF YOUR SHOW

THINGS TO DO BEFORE THE SHOW

THINGS TO DO DURING THE SHOW

THINGS TO DO AFTER THE SHOW

RESOLVING THE CONTRACT

Lecture Points
Chapter Twelve

DEPOSIT

TRAVEL

ACCOMMODATIONS

PERCENTAGE POINTS

EXPENSE BUDGET

HOSPITALITY

TICKET PRICES

OPENING ACT AND PERFORMANCE TIME

MAIN ACT PERFORMANCE TIME

Lecture Points
Chapter Twelve

BILLING

ADVERTISING AND PROMOTION BUDGET

TECHNICAL REQUIREMENTS

TECHNICAL SUPPORT

PARKING

NUMBER OF COMPLIMENTARY TICKETS

MERCHANDISE PERCENTAGE

NUMBER OF STAGE OR CREW HANDS

THE ARTIST RIDER

Chapter Twelve Notes

The Rider

A *rider* is an additional set of instructions for the promoter regarding specific artist requirements. Riders usually include the size of the stage, lighting, etc., and may even include the type of food, drinks, or other necessities the artist wants supplied in their dressing room. Most riders are simple and to the point, instructions on how the artist expects the concert to be staged. Security, private phones, sound checks, hotels, color of the green room (sometimes changed to the artist's favorite color), whatever it takes. However, they can also get weird such as demanding a large bowl of m&m's with all of the brown ones removed. The following is an example of the Turtles East Coast Rider that promoters are required to complete.

Technical Rider – EastCoast

This rider attached to and made part of this contract dated _____ between **THE TURTLES featuring Flo & Eddie** (hereinafter known as the Artist/Producer) and _____ (hereinafter known as the Purchaser).

All terms and provisions in this rider and in the contract to which it is attached, are part of one and the same contract, and referred to herein as the "CONTRACT."

No part of this contract may be deleted or altered without the express written consent of PARADISE ARTISTS, Inc. and/or The Turtles.

Please read this contract and rider CAREFULLY AND THOROUGHLY. Any changes or problems MUST be made before you sign. Please return to Paradise Artists immediately.

If you have any questions regarding this rider, contact:

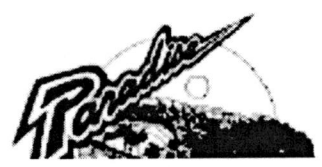

Technical Rider

A. **ACCESS TO VENUE:**

1. The Purchaser or a qualified representative of the Purchaser with full decision making power, must be in the hall and accessible and available at the time and during all phases of load-in, set-up, sound check, load-out and departure.

2. In all venues, parking close to dressing room areas must be provided. Parking spaces must be provided adjacent to the stage door for one (1) van and two (2) limousines. If in the event the Artist's entourage must use parking lot facilities, Purchaser is responsible for incurred expenses.

3. Artists and accompanying personnel should be able to pass freely to and from the backstage area and all other areas of the hall. Purchaser shall provide all passes at no cost to the Artist.

4. Artist shall be entitled to at least one (1) hour rehearsal and/or sound check time at the venue on the date of performance and the Purchaser shall ensure access to the venue for this purpose no less than four (4) hours prior to public admittance to the venue. The audience shall not be allowed to enter the venue until such time that the technical set-up and sound check are complete. Artist shall receive no less than one (1) hour sound check after all technical set-up has been completed.

B. **PERSONNEL TO BE PROVIDED BY PURCHASER:**
Purchaser shall provide, at his/her sole expense, the following for load-in, set-up, performance and load-out:

1. Two (2) truck loaders must be available for van unloading at a time to be determined by the Artist's Representative. The two (2) truck loaders must also be available

immediately after the show for loading of the van and must remain until the van is loaded.

2. A minimum of four (4) <u>experienced stage hands</u> must be available at a time to be determined by the Artist's Representative on and immediately after the performance.

3. A house electrician with a full working knowledge of the electrical facilities in the building must be available at the load-in time and during the performance.

4. Three (3) <u>experienced lighting operators</u>, one for the dimmer board and two for the follow spots, must be available at load-in time and throughout the performance.

5. Two (2) <u>experienced audio engineers</u>, one for the house and one for the monitors must be available at load-in time and throughout the performance.

6. Purchaser's production staff shall be under direction of the Artist's Representative. Also house security to be approved by Artist's Representative.

C. <u>STAGE REQUIREMENTS</u>:

1. The working stage area shall be a minimum of forty feet (40') wide and twenty-four feet (24') deep, excluding the sound wings.

2. The drum riser shall be twelve feet (12') wide and eight feet (8') deep and should be 16" or 24" in height, and carpeted.

C. <u>STAGE REQUIREMENTS (cont.)</u>

3. If Purchaser is using a portable stage, there must be skirting across all exposed areas, also all stage risers must be covered.

4. A backdrop must be used. It must be of a dark material or a black screen. A white cyclorama screen may also be used.

D. **POWER REQUIREMENTS:**

1. Four (4) 20 amp. 120 volts A.C. single phase 60 cycle circuits to be supplied, two (2) to stage left and two (2) to stage right. Each of these should have one (1) quad box on each circuits.

2. Each dressing room must have at least one (1) 20 amp. circuit.

E. **BAND GEAR REQUIREMENTS:**
The following equipment is to be provided at the **sole expense of the Purchaser** for Artist's use during sound check/rehearsal and performance(s):

1. DRUMS:
   One (1) six piece YAMAHA or equivalent kit*
   1 - 22" Kick
   1 - 14" x 5 1/2" Snare
   1 - 12" Rack Tom
   1 - 14" Rack Tom
   1 - 16" Floor Tom
   1 - 18" Floor Tom (FLOOR TOMS MUST BE FREE STD with 3" LEGS ON EACH)
   6 - **Heavy** Duty cymbal stands
   2 - **Heavy** Duty hi-hat stands
   1 - **Heavy** Duty snare stand
   1 - **Heavy** Duty drum throne

   *All drums should have NEW BLACK DOT HEADS, Rack Systems are NOT acceptable.

E. **BAND GEAR REQUIREMENTS (cont.)**

2. CYMBALS (Zildjain):
   1 - set 14" Hi-Hat
   1 - 16" Thin Crash
   1 - 18" Thin Crash
   1 - 18" Medium Crash
   1 - 20" Medium Crash
   1 - 22" Ping Ride

3. BASS RIG:
   1 - Ampeg SVT Head
   1 - 8x10 cabinet

4. **KEYBOARDS:**
   2 – Roland Juno – D synthesizers
   2 – stereo direct boxes, cables
   1 – keyboard stand that can hold two keyboards (preferably one that holds both of them flat, rather than at an angle
   Alternate keyboards (MUST BE CLEARED FIRST): Roland JP-800 or Roland D-50 or Korg M-1

5. **GUITAR AMPS:**
   2 - Fender Super Twin Reverbs. Any of these others are acceptable. Fender Twin, Fender Concert Reverb, Fender Hot Rod DeVille, Fender Hot Rod Deluxe, Fender Blues DeVille.

6. **GUITAR & ACCESSORIES:**
   1 - Fender Strat, with adjustable strap & extra strings
   1 - Fender Precision or Jazz Bass Guitar, with adjustable strap & extra strings
   3 - High Quality guitar cables
   3 - High Quality guitar stands

7. **TAMBOURINES AND COWBELL**
   2 – 12 to 15 inch Round Tambourines
   1 - Cowbell

8. Someone must be available at the time of load-in and throughout the performance with a working knowledge of the equipment.

* Any of the equipment listed above can be substituted ONLY after consultation with ▮▮▮▮▮▮▮▮▮▮▮▮▮

F. **LIGHTS:**
  1. A professional lighting system will be provided <u>at the sole expense of the Purchaser</u>. As we do not travel with a Lighting Director, one must be provided at no cost to the Artist. The system must consist of high quality components (trusses, instruments, dimmers and console.) The system also must be flown only by a highly qualified rigger, at no cost to the Artist.
     a. Main lighting system should include a minimum of 120 One (1) Kw. Instruments, 60 upstage and 60 downstage.

Colors to include are dark red, amber, mauve, med. blue, congo blue, dark green. This is a general color selection, other colors can be used.
b. Auxiliary lighting should include at least 8 One (1) Kw. instruments to used as specials on the stage itself.

2. Two (2) Super Trouper or equivalent follow spots with <u>experienced, qualified operators</u> shall be provided <u>at the sole expense of the Purchaser</u>. Each spot light shall include at least six (6) color slides in good working condition. The following ROSCOLENE color media shall be provided: flesh pink, no color pink, amber, magenta, red and blue.

3. A professional intercom system with no less than four (4) positions is also required (two at the follow spots, one at the house lighting console, one at the dimmer rack).

4. Artist reserves the right to add or delete lighting equipment as deemed necessary by Artist, in conjunction with the Purchaser's lighting company. These additions or deletions shall include, but not be limited to, the following:
a. Audience specials, Additional instruments on front end and rear truss, Floor specials, Ground row lights, Aircraft lights, Mirror ball, White Cyclorama, Black Scrim

5. Artist requires a total blackout in the house during Artist's segment of the show, unless prohibited by local fire laws or safety codes ONLY. The raising and lowering of the house lights will be at the strict instructions made by the Artist's Representative ONLY.

G. <u>SOUND SYSTEM</u>:
A sound system of the Artist's choice (based on consultation with the Artist's Representative) will be provided at no cost to the Artist. The professional and qualified house and monitor engineers will be provided at no cost to the Artist.

1. The house sound system <u>must</u> consist of high quality, professional audio components (power amps, speakers, horns, etc.) to provide clear, undistorted sound, with a distribution radius of one hundred and eighty degrees (180°) throughout the entire audience area at an evenly

distributed level of 120 db with a frequency range of 40 to 15,000 cycles per second (plus or minus 3db) at a distance of thirty feet (30') from the stage with a decrease in level of no greater than 5db per 100' thereafter.

2. A minimum 3-way stereo system is preferred: Meyer MSL-3 with subs, EAW 850 with subs, or equivalents should be used. System power amplifiers should be Crest, Crown or Carver.

3. Preferred house mixing console is Yamaha Pm400, Soundcraft Series IV, Midas XL-3 or gamble EX Series. Console should have a minimum of 32 (40 preferred) input channels. Each channel should have 4 band sweepable equalization, a minimum of 4 auxiliary sends and insert points. Console should have at least 4 (8 preferred) sub-master outputs. A desk lamp is required.

4. House signal processing rack must include:
   a. Two (2) 1/3 Octave Equalizers (Klark Teknik, Urei, White)
   b. Two (2) 3-way Active Crossovers
   c. One (1) Yamaha Rev. 5 or Rev. 7
   d. Two (2) Yamaha 900's
   e. One (1) Roland Rd 3000 Delay
   f. Eight (8) Noise Gates
   g. Eight (8) Compressors
   h. Clear-Com from F.o.h. to Monitor desk
   i. One (1) Cassette deck for recording or DAT
   j. One (1) CD player for playback

5. Preferred monitor consoles are Ramsa, Soundcraft or Yamaha, with a min. of 24 inputs and 8 discrete mixes.

6. Monitor signal rack must include at least:
   a. Eight (8) 1/3 Octave Equalizers
   b. Eight (8) Noise Gates
   c. One (10) Digital Reverb. Unit (SPX 90 or equivalent)

7. Monitors shall consist of eight (8) bi-amped wedges, two (2) 3-way side fills and one (1) 3-way drum fill. *All monitors and power amps* are to be of the highest professional standards, (JBL, Meyers, Yamaha) as Artist requires an <u>extremely loud, undistorted monitor system</u>.

8. MICROPHONES AND STANDS:
   a. Two (2) Beta 87 or Beta 58 Hand-Held, wireless (Flo & Eddie)
   b. Five (5) Shure Beta SM 58
   c. Five (5) Shure Beta SM 57
   d. Three (3) Shure SM 81
   e. Six (6) Sennheiser 409, 421 or EV 308, 309
   f. Two (2) Beyer M88
   g. Sixteen (16) AKG or Beyer boom stands
   h. Four (4) Atlas MS20, also Two (2) Atlas MS10

* Any of the equipment listed above can be substituted ONLY after consultation with ███████████████.

H. **BILLING CLAUSE**:
Billing for all forms of advertising must read as follows:

> THE TURTLES (100%)
> featuring (25%)
> FLO & EDDIE (75%)

I. **OPENING ACTS**:
Purchaser shall provide, at Purchaser's sole expense, an opening act. Said opening act to be mutually agreed upon.

J. **MERCHANDISING**:
The Artist brings along their own merchandising personnel. Please make sure they are welcomed and are put in contact with the proper people to coordinate their sales of the Artist's merchandise.

   1. The Artist reserves the sole, exclusive and irrevocable right to sell all merchandise, both inside and outside the hall. Purchaser shall have no interest in the proceeds from the Artist's sales of any and all merchandise. The Purchaser agrees that there will be no other sale or distribution at the engagement of any merchandise baring the name, logo or likeness of the Artist.

   2. The Purchaser shall be responsible for obtaining for the Artist, a "most favored nation" percentage deal with the hall, <u>without exception</u> regardless of the event in which it was given. If the Artist does not receive a "most favored

nation" percentage deal, the Purchaser will be responsible to make up the difference between the "most favored nation" percentage and the percentage actually received by the Artist.

3. Purchaser shall also make it his/her responsibility to prevent any other act(s), on the bill, from signing autographs on the premises (i.e. audience area, hall lobby, outside hall) during the Artist's performance.

K. **TAPING AND FILMING:**

1. Artist shall have, at no cost to Artist, the sole and exclusive rights to film, record or otherwise reproduce and embody any and all performance by Artist, including, without limitation, audio tapes, video tapes, radio transmission and any other audio visual process or solely visual process. No video camera or audio recording machine can be can be used by any other personnel.
NO EXCEPTIONS.

2. No recording, filming, taping, broadcasting or photography of the performance shall be permitted without written consent by the Artist.

ARTIST'S PERSONAL REQUIREMENTS

A. **DRESSING ROOMS:**

1. Purchaser shall provide two (2) properly maintained, clean, well ventilated, well lighted dressing rooms for the <u>exclusive</u> use of the Artist. Rooms must have working locks with keys (keys should be given to Artist's Representative upon request for the duration of the performance).

2. The rooms must each be equipped with hot and cold running water, adequate heating, mirrors, towels, soap, at least one (1) 20 amp circuit and comfortable seating for at least eight (8) people.

3. There must be at least two (2) clean and safe lavatory facilities accessible from the dressing rooms that are for the sole use of the Artist. **NOT FOR PUBLIC USE.**

4. Dressing rooms must be accessible to the stage without passing through any audience areas.

5. No less than twelve (12) high quality towels must be provided at the beginning of each show.

6. In the event that mobile homes are used for dressing rooms: One (1) 34 foot mobile home or Two (2) smaller mobile homes able to accommodate seven (7) people must be provided for the <u>exclusive</u> use of the Artist. Keys are to given to the Artist's Representative. Security is to be provided for the vehicle before and after the show. It must be accessible to the stage when parked. In the event that the vehicle is to be used for transportation, a driver must be provided at the discretion of the Artist's Representative. The mobile home must be properly cleaned, adequately ventilated (A/C), running water and curtains to cover windows, all prior to Artist's arrival.

B. <u>HOTEL ACCOMMODATIONS</u>:

1. Purchaser shall pay for and provide the Artist and their entourage with <u>SEVEN (7) Single Deluxe Hotel Rooms with KING size beds</u> throughout the duration of the performance(s). (PLEASE SEE ATTACHED ROOM LIST- PAGE 18)

   HOTEL MUST* BE ONE OF THE FOLLOWING:
   -Marriott/ Marriott Courtyard
   -Hilton
   -Radisson
   -Doubletree
   -Embassy Suites
   -Holiday Inn Select
   *<u>*Any other hotel must be approved by</u>
   ▮▮▮▮▮▮▮▮▮▮

2. If the engagement at which the Artist is to perform is held at a hotel or resort, the Artist's hotel rooms shall be of first class quality at the same hotel or resort.

3. At the sole discretion of the Artist, the aforementioned rooms will be provided for one (1) day <u>prior to</u> the engagement date. Due to the Artist's traveling schedule and/or rehearsal/sound check requirements, <u>early check in MUST be available</u>. This is the Purchaser's responsibility.

4. The hotel at which the Artist shall stay **MUST** have an attached restaurant or the hotel **IS NOT ACCEPTABLE** to the Artist.

5. All hotel rooms shall be paid in advance of the Artist's arrival. If the hotel rooms are not paid in advance forcing the Artist to pay for their own hotel rooms, Artist will expect full payment for the hotel rooms along with the balance of the engagement fee due in cash prior to sound check on the day of the engagement. **ARTIST WILL NOT PERFORM UNTIL THIS MATTER IS SETTLED TO THEIR COMPLETE SATISFACTION.**

C. **TRANSPORTATION:**

Purchaser shall provide, at his/her sole expense, transportation from airport(s) (at Artist's arrival time(s)) to hotel, from hotel to venue and back for sound check and/or rehearsal, from hotel and back to performance(s), and from hotel to airport(s) at Artist's departure time(s). Artist recommends a ten passenger van, instead of limousines.

D. **COMPLIMENTARY TICKETS:**

Purchaser will provide Artist with a minimum of twenty four (24) complimentary tickets for each performance. In the invent of a free show or private party, Artist shall be afforded twenty four (24) invitations or VIP section for Artist's guests.

E. **SECURITY:**

All accesses to stage will be guarded by house security at all times and only those persons designated by Artist will be allowed on stage during Artist's performance If the Artist is forced to pass through audience, a security force of four (4) security guards must be present to escort the Artist to and from the stage. There should be one (1) security guard at the backstage entrance and one (1) security guard at the dressing room entrance from the commencement of sound check until the departure of Artist at the conclusion of the performance(s).

F. **REFRESHMENTS**:

1. At sound check, soft drinks, coffee and tea should be available to the Artist and crew.

2. DINNER: Purchaser has the option of providing one of the following THREE (3) evening meal plans:

    a. A hot three (3) course sit down meal provided for Artist and Crew (approximately 7 people) by Purchaser at his sole expense; <u>A MINIMUM OF TWO (2) COMPLETELY VEGETARIAN MEALS MUST BE PROVIDED (NO MEAT, CHICKEN OR FISH!); NO FAST FOOD WILL BE ACCEPTED AT ANY TIME.</u>

    b. $30.00 per diem for dinner expense to Artist from Purchaser for seven (7) persons. ($210.00 <u>CASH</u>);

    c. Restaurant in Hotel to provide dinner for seven (7) at no expenses to Artist (i.e. Artist can sign meal to hotel room).

    <u>PLEASE ADVISE BY CIRCLING A, B or C from above.</u>

3. Purchaser will furnish, at his/her sole expense, the following items which should be available in the Artist's Dressing Room upon their arrival before performance:

    - One (1) large platter of assorted deli meats and cheeses (NO PREPACKAGED MEATS OR CHEESES will be accepted)
    - One (1) large platter of assorted fresh vegetables and dips
    - One (1) large platter of assorted fresh fruits
    - One (1) large bowl mixed nuts
    - One (1) large bag potato chips
    - One (1) large bowl plain, fresh popcorn
    - Assorted crackers, breads and rolls (white, rye, sourdough and wheat)
    - Assorted desserts
    - One (1) case of (12 oz bottles) sparkling water (Perrier)

-One (1) case (24 bottles) of BOTTLED spring water
-One (1) case of assorted fruit juices (orange, cranberry, etc)
-One (1) case BOTTLED beer (lite and regular) (Local beer acceptable)
-One (1) case assorted sodas (diet and regular)
-Hot coffee
-Hot Tea (herbal preferred)
-Fresh Milk and Powdered Cream
-Honey and Fresh Lemon
-Napkins
-Plenty of Ice
-Hot cups for Coffee and Tea
-Cold cups (16 oz.) for sodas, water, juice (at least 3 dozen as we use these on stage)
-Condiments (mustard, mayonnaise, ketchup, etc.)

G. Should inclement weather render the performance by the Artist impossible, unsafe or not feasible, Purchaser shall nevertheless pay Artist full compensation as provided herein. Artist's safety will be determined by Artist.

H. Purchaser shall pay all taxes of any kind levied against the Artist as a result of this engagement.

POSTPONEMENT/CANCELLATION

ARTIST MAY POSTPONE OR CANCEL THIS CONTRACT AND THE SERVICES TO BE RENDERED HEREUNDER, AT THE ARTIST'S SOLE DISCRETION, BY GIVING THIRTY (30) DAYS PRIOR NOTICE TO THE PURCHASER.

ALL PROVISIONS OF THIS CONTRACT AND THE RIDER ATTACHED HERETO ARE OF THE ESSENCE AND FAILURE OF THE PURCHASER TO COMPLY WITH ANY PROVISIONS WITHOUT THE PERMISSION OF THE ARTIST OR THE ARTIST'S REPRESENTATIVE SHALL CONSTITUTE A MATERIAL BREACH.

ACCEPTED & AGREED:	ACCEPTED & AGREED:
PURCHASER	████████████
DATE	**DATE**

ROOMING LIST – EASTCOAST

These rooms must all be *SINGLE ROOMS* with *KING SIZE BEDS*.

GUEST:	ROOM #
1.	_____ (NS)
2.	_____
3.	_____ (NS)
4.	_____ (NS)
5.	_____ (NS)
6.	_____ (NS)
7.	_____ (NS)

NS = Non-smoking

*Any changes, please contact:

Microphone Input List

1. OHSR
2. OHSL
3. KICK
4. SNARE
5. HH
6. RACK - I
7. RACK - II
8. FLOOR - I
9. FLOOR - II
10. BASS DI
11. BASS MIC.
12. Roland Juno 1 (Stereo)
13. Roland Juno 1 (Stereo)
14. Roland Juno 2 (Stereo)
15. Roland Juno 2 (Stereo)
16. AXE - SR
17. AXE - CENTER
18. VOX - SR
19. VOX - BASS
20. VOX - KEY
21. VOX - EDDIE
22. VOX - FLO
23. VOX - SPARE

QUESTIONS:

NOTES:

For Stage Setup
see next page.

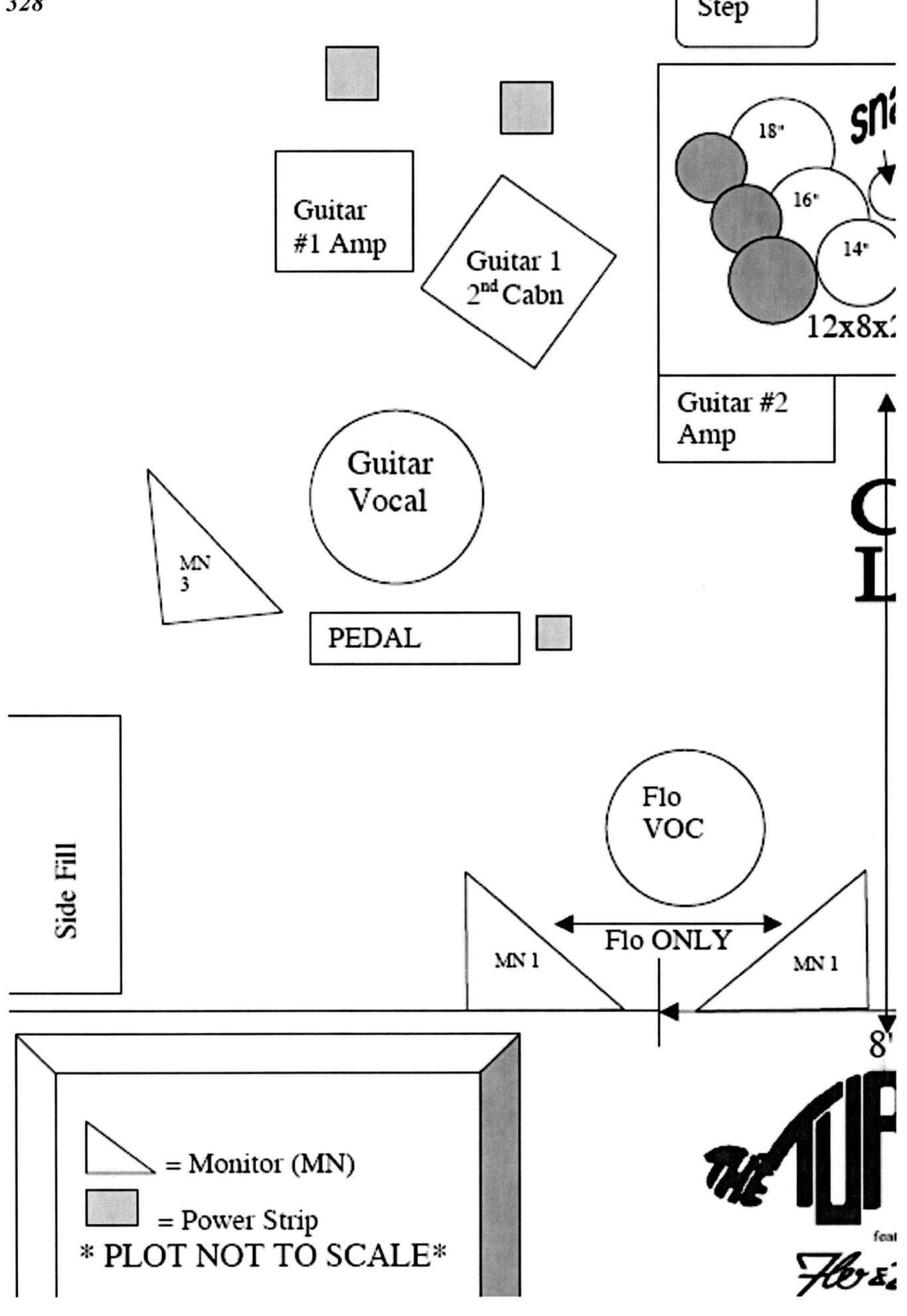

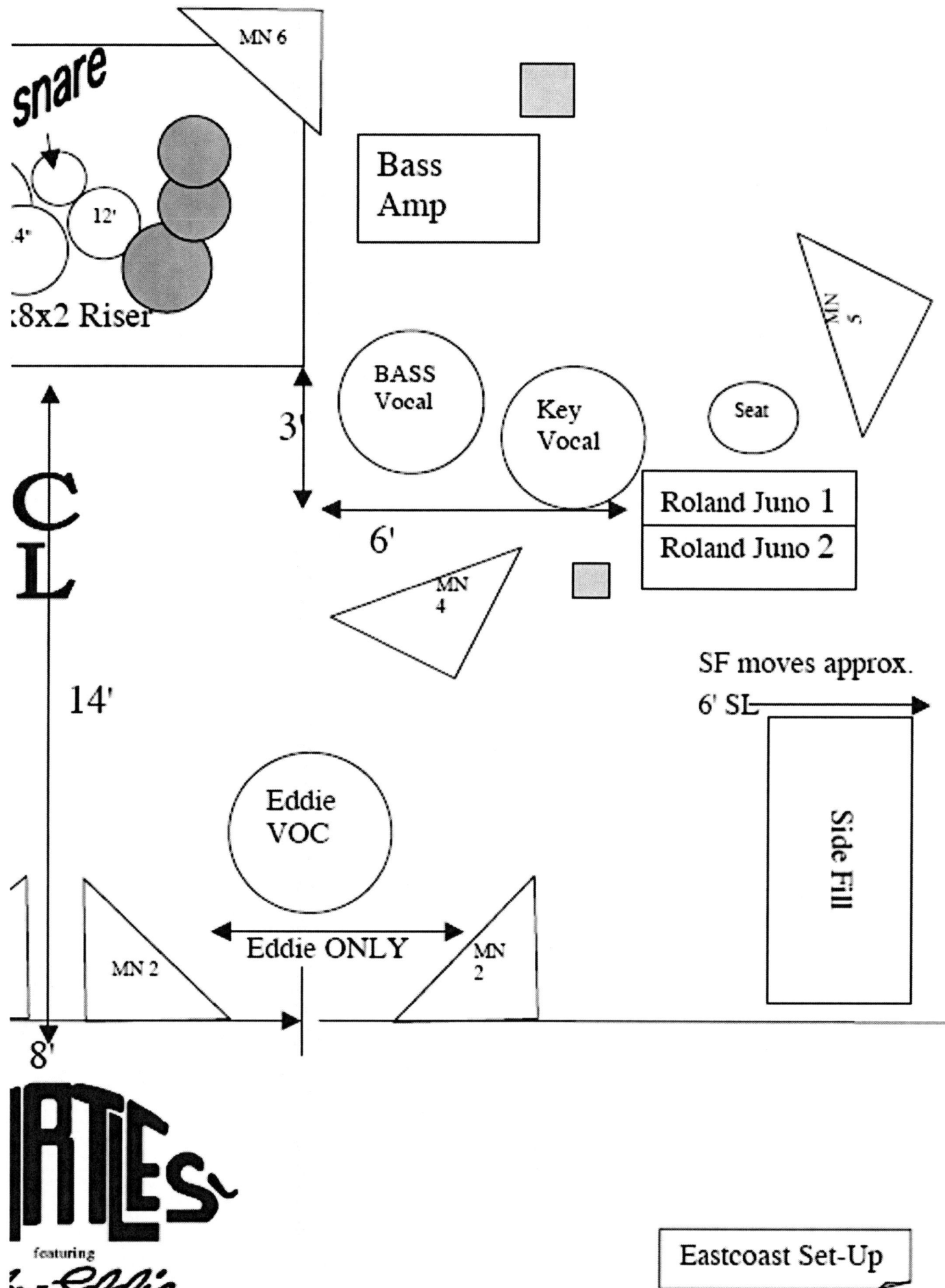

Lecture Points
Chapter Thirteen

Publicity planning, Press kits

BUILDING IMPRESSIVE PROMO KITS

MAILING ENVELOPE

FOLDER WITH STICKER LOGO

PHOTO

DEMO TAPE

COVER LETTER

ARTIST OR BAND BIO (GRAPHY)

BUSINESS CARD/ROLODEX CARD

GIG SCHEDULE

Lecture Points
Chapter Thirteen

331

RADIO AND PRESS QUOTES

SONG LIST

VIDEO (DVD)

PROMOTIONAL NOVELTIES

WHERE THE PROMO KIT GOES

ENTERTAINMENT BUYERS

MEDIA CONTACTS

INDUSTRY CONTACTS

The Creative Destruction of the Music & Entertainment Industry

CREATIVE DESTRUCTION
Joseph Schumpeter's original theory of creative destruction appears to describe the current state of the business of music and entertainment. It is clear that technology and consumer P2P file sharing is destroying the economic base of the music and film industry. However, at the same time it is providing products to new consumers worldwide. It is only a matter of time before some entrepreneur develops a new business model that will safely support the financial investments of the industry into creative artists' products. Thus, music and entertainment over the Internet is fundamentally changing the way artists, recording companies, retail channels, and end users, create, distribute, and buy music and entertainment products. The business of fame and all of the corresponding sub-businesses (recordings, touring, cell phone ditribution, merchandise, corporate sponsorships and many more) are here to stay. They will just continue to grow into an even larger entertainment based industry. The question is how?

"A process of industrial mutation that incessantly revolutionizes the economic structure from within, incessantly destroying the old one, incessantly creating a new one."
—Joseph Schumpeter [1]

A BUSINESS PERSPECTIVE
Even if the artist didn't make any money (in most cases) before their recordings sold *Gold* (500,000 units), they still did not have to fund any of the recordings, marketing plans, promotion and publicity. They have had in the past, an opportunity to become famous free on the labels dime. In addition, they could make their own money as entrepreneurs selling their live performances in concert tours, and their images through merchandise and corporate sponsorships. However, we have to remember that without the creative artist, the labels have nothing to sell. Yet, 51% of the music acquired by consumers is not paid for. Do we have a problem here? Of course, because of technology and other factors the industry is in the middle of a classic form of *creative destruction*.

"If we do our job...Music's not black or white, it's green."
—**Jim Caparro, PGD**[2]

---
[1] Joseph Schumpeter in his work entitled "Capitalism, Socialism and Democracy."
[2] http://www.barryrudolph.com/utilities/quotes.html

THE NEW DIGITAL MUSIC INDUSTRY

Many of the issues in this text describe the new digital music business and the corresponding sub-businesses created by an artist's fame. The previous quotes by many of our country's past industrial leaders illustrates their inability to accept technology and the future it may provide. Their predictions were based on holding onto the past and not accepting the process of creative destruction of the industry and thus, the future possibilities.

PREDICTING CHANGE

Many educated, very smart, well placed and well meaning people have tried to predict industry changes. Often the predictions years later are laughable. Here are some examples:

"Home Taping Is Killing Music"
— A 1980s campaign by the BPI, claiming that people recording music off the radio onto cassette would destroy the music industry.

"Television won't last. It's a flash in the pan."
— Mary Somerville, pioneer of radio educational broadcasts, 1948.

"[Television] won't be able to hold on to any market it captures after the first six months. People will soon get tired of staring at a plywood box every night."
— Darryl Zanuck, movie producer, 20th Century Fox, 1946.

"When the Paris Exhibition [of 1878] closes, electric light will close with it and no more will be heard of it."
—Oxford professor Erasmus Wilson

"The wireless music box has no imaginable commercial value. Who would pay for a message sent to no one in particular?"
— Associates of David Sarnoff responding to the latter's call for investment in the radio in 1921.

"There is no reason anyone would want a computer in their home."
— Ken Olson, president, chairman and founder of Digital Equipment Corp. (DEC), maker of big business mainframe computers, arguing against the PC in 1977.

"The cinema is little more than a fad. It's canned drama. What audiences really want to see is flesh and blood on the stage."
—Charlie Chaplin, actor, producer, director, and studio founder, 1916.

"This 'telephone' has too many shortcomings to be seriously considered as a means of communication. The device is inherently of no value to us."
— A memo at Western Union, 1878 (or 1876).

"The world potential market for copying machines is 5000 at most."
— IBM, to the eventual founders of Xerox, saying the photocopier had no market large enough to justify production, 1959.

"Dear Mr. President: The canal system of this country is being threatened by a new form of transportation known as 'railroads'... As you may well know, Mr. President, 'railroad' carriages are pulled at the enormous speed of 15 miles per hour by 'engines' which, in addition to endangering life and limb of passengers, roar and snort their way through the countryside, setting fire to crops, scaring the livestock and frightening women and children. The Almighty certainly never intended that people should travel at such breakneck speed."
— Martin Van Buren, Governor of New York, 1830.[3]

The population of the planet is continuing to increase and at the same time, computers, software, the internet, and cell phones are being purchased by more people. They are all music and entertainment consumers. Everyone of them. Thus, the market share of consumer who are able to use and enjoy music and entertainment is quickly increasing at the same time the prices of the end-users devices are falling. The songwriting/music publishing revenue stream annually grosses around $255 billion in the United States and is increasing with the continued world's support of copyright protection. Computer recordings instead of actual artist (sorry) for demo work, plus the use of email for all correspondence including song plugging will continue to save money on the front end of creating the product and business operations.

"What we are seeing now is all these new forms of life growing out of the dead body of the music business."
—**Peter Gabriel, artist, producer, entrepreneur** [4]

NEW BUSINESS MODELS
It appears that there are four new possible business models developing:
- *Music as a public utility*-all citizens would be charged a monthly fee for music supplied similar to a water or electric bill. The government would probably get involved and start taxing the system.

- *Free Music*-would give music away and recoup the expenses from other revenue streams such as concert promotion, merchandise sales and corporate sponsorship. Fulfillment of copyright obligation would be difficult to manage.

- *Artists as Free Agents*-Creative artists would sign contracts similar to sports personalities who would perform for several years and then gain their freedom to either start their own businesses or sign with another mega entertainment corporation.

- *360 Entertainment Corporations*-With the industry business model broken, and at this point, with DRM being dropped by the megas, it appears that a change and an opportunity for entrepreneurship is developing. Labels may stop being called labels as they may develop into 360 companies that will still launch acts on the front end and recoup their investment on the back end by controlling all three revenue streams.

---
3 wrong predictions, www.google.com
4 On Hollywood video interview, 2008, http://www.youtube.com/watch?v=scB41mWVs-I&eurl=http://www.mediafuturist.com/2008/07/peter-gabriel-v.html

SUMMARY

Most of the changes in the business are related to digital production (being able to record excellent quality songs by computer and software programs) and digital distribution of the recordings through P2P networks, subscription services, and downloads websites such as itunes. The P2P networks or the acquiring of music/recordings without paying for it, (which of course is not legal), has also caused financial economic of scale problems for record labels. They are struggling to make a profit as in the old days by selling their recordings. At the same time, artists and musicians need the profession recordings, money, guidance, marketing, tour support and potential exposure (of their images and recordings) the label's provide. Sadly, due to P2P use by consumers, much of the labels' cost for their recordings is not recoupable. Thus, as record sales decrease, labels are making less money on their investment in signed artists. What a catch 22, the artists usually need the labels support and marketing in order for consumers to discover them. And the labels need the artists to record and consumers to buy their products.

This is the creative destruction of the industry that will bring many new opportunities for everyone in the business. The music is still the bell ringer. It can just be created, distributed, and discovered by consumers, in new and exciting ways. Thus, even if you are using a computer program to create the product and websites and cell phones to distribute the recordings, the experts at the label are still a vital part of the puzzle. They know and understand how the business works. The professionals in the business are still going to be the power players the creative community will need for success. However, 360 deals will need to become a standard in the industry as the label will have to receive some of the artists profits from the tours merchandise sales to recoup their investments on the recordings and signed artists. Some of the labels may move toward 360 companies where all industry services (including management), are under one roof.

Consumers may change their purchasing habits more toward listening to music streaming services instead of buying or even stealing the recordings they love. This is still the emotion business based on a creative systems of writers, musicians, performing artists and other and a business systems based on the labels' money, production, publicity, distribution, sales and marketing. How the two systems work together and share the profits may be changing and evolving, yet the consumers desire to be entertainment will always remain a growing profitable business. This is the best time in many years to become a part of the industry. Go for it.

Index

Symbols

360 7, 8, 24, 142, 143, 149, 154, 163, 165, 208, 334

A

A&R 83, 148, 153, 160, 163, 203, 215, 219, 222
AF of M 18, 19, 107, 146, 216, 220, 222, 225, 226, 232, 233, 259, 295
AFTRA 11, 146, 216, 220, 222, 223, 225, 226, 231, 232, 233, 259, 295
Agents 18, 259
Article 1, Section 8 40, 53
Artist Managers 3, 18, 29
Artists 3, 8, 9, 10, 11, 14, 15, 20, 27, 29, 116, 139, 147, 159, 160, 169, 192, 194, 204, 215, 216, 219, 220, 252, 259, 262, 280, 281, 295, 296
ASCAP 7, 46, 67, 70, 81, 99, 107, 109, 118, 122, 123, 124, 126
attorneys 18, 20, 160, 253, 259
Audio Engineers 3, 10, 16, 29, 216, 217
Authorship 41, 61, 98

B

BDS system 124
Berne Convention 48, 49, 55
Bertelsmann 22, 38, 108, 137, 138, 163
BGV's 11, 16, 22, 217, 219, 222, 223, 226, 228
Bid Sheets 13, 319
Billboard 26, 42, 44, 45, 49, 121, 146, 297
Billboard Magazine 26, 154, 303
Billy Rose 82
Bing Crosby 82
bio 261
blanket license 123, 124, 125, 126
BMI 7, 67, 70, 81, 99, 100, 107, 109, 118, 122, 123, 124, 126
booking agent. 259, 293, 329
Booking agents 18, 258, 259, 298
Branford Marsalis 14
break-even 18, 151, 152, 293, 293, 299, 329
Broadway and Vaudeville 80
business managers 26
business model 38, 146, 151, 153
business plan 18
business side 15, 17, 18, 80, 234
business system 15, 17, 19, 28, 29, 80, 147

C

Career plans 18
Career Song 82
Carl Perkins 82
Carol Kaye 218
CARP 44, 48
cash flow 252, 290, 298
Cell Phones 8, 9, 156, 157, 158
cell phones 14, 18, 26, 39, 144, 146, 154, 157, 160, 260, 261, 292, 319
claim of a copyright 40, 61, 62
Clear Channel Radio 155
Click Media 18

click media 14, 17, 19, 26, 28, 146, 156
Co-publishing 113, 114, 115
co-publishing 111, 113, 126, 160
Collective Works 41
Colonel Tom Parker 253
Comcast 142
Compulsory License 68, 119
Compulsory Licenses 69
compulsory performance license 44
Computer graphic artists 19
Concert Promoters 18
consumers 15, 17, 18, 19, 20, 22, 28, 37, 46, 50, 77, 79, 80, 81, 98, 110, 147, 153, 154, 156, 157, 164, 214, 216, 219, 224, 228, 252, 252, 253, 258, 260, 261
Consumers, 19
Copyright Act 40, 42, 45, 68
Copyright laws 38
copyright notice 43, 48, 49
Copyright Office 38, 40, 44, 45, 48, 62, 63, 69, 109, 116, 126
copyright owner 41, 44, 46, 48, 62, 68, 69, 123
Copyrights 4, 5, 20, 37, 38, 42, 43, 45, 46, 47, 49, 50, 52, 62, 69, 71, 116
Corporate sponsors 19
Corporations 19
Courtney Love 137, 165
Cox Radio 155
creative destruction 24, 142, 149, 332, 333
creative risks 19
creative side 15, 17
creative system 15, 19, 147
Creativity 2, 3, 4, 5, 37, 119, 124, 251
Cross Collateralization 98, 203

D

deal 43, 81, 99, 100, 111, 113, 126, 137, 140, 147, 149, 151, 203, 215, 222, 252, 259, 293, 329
Deals 111, 149, 150
departments 108, 109, 126, 159, 160, 161, 163, 219, 222
Desmond Child 77
digital transmission 45, 69, 118
distribute 17, 27, 41, 44, 46, 47, 48, 62, 119, 138, 147, 161, 234
DMC 45, 122

E

Edgar Leslie 82
Elton John 131, 137
Elvis Presley 20, 77, 145, 251
EMI 38, 108, 137, 139, 150, 156, 163, 295
Engineers 3, 10, 16, 29, 217
entrepreneurial 20, 27, 39, 80, 138, 154, 290, 298
entrepreneurs 15, 17, 20, 28, 215, 217
Entrepreneurship 3, 20, 28
Equity 6, 111, 259, 295
equity 83, 110, 111, 113, 115, 126, 203
event 18, 26, 216, 253, 258, 260, 293, 298, 299, 329
Exclusive Rights 40, 42, 53, 118
exploit 62, 80, 98, 99, 111, 115, 118, 123, 138, 252, 253, 260

F

Fair Use Rights 68
First Use Rights 118
fixed 38, 40, 41, 43, 50, 51, 61, 69, 138, 224
formula 138, 204

Free Goods 98
Free goods 98, 161, 199

G

Garage Band 217, 228
George Kelly 79, 252, 258
George M. Meyer 82
George Porter 80
Gershwins 67
Guarantee 13, 292, 294, 299, 319, 319
guarantee 163, 259, 293, 299, 329

H

Herb Alpert and Jerry Moss 145
HFA 118
hold 48, 78, 98, 118, 125, 145, 224, 231
Homer Simpson 251
Hulu.com 159

I

I-phones 14, 260
I-Pods 14
IATSE , 295
icons 38, 219, 252
Ideas 50
IFPI 9, 24, 37, 162, 169, 205, 206
Igor Stravinsky 253
Image 12, 161
image 14, 15, 17, 18, 22, 39, 69, 77, 140, 147, 148, 150, 161, 163, 204, 219, 226, 229, 252, 253, 256, 258, 261, 262
INDEX 336–372
international copyright treaties 49
Internet 8, 9, 15, 18, 19, 22, 24, 26, 27, 39, 42, 45, 47, 62, 63, 98, 107, 109, 118, 126, 139, 140, 142, 144, 146, 148, 154, 155, 156, 157, 158, 160, 161, 164, 184, 220, 228, 294, 332
iPhones 14, 260
iPods 14
Irving Berlin 43
iTunes 17, 19, 27, 47, 156, 157, 158, 164, 227

J

James Bramston 79
James Hetfield of Metallica 14
Jay Livingston and Ray Evans 67
joint work 70, 99
JUSTICE SOUTER 48

K

Kent Hartman 218
Kurt Cobain 14

L

Labels 7, 8, 17, 22, 26, 29, 31, 38, 119, 143, 144, 146, 147, 148, 151, 154, 155, 163, 165, 203, 218, 221, 253, 260, 295
Led Zeppelin 82
letter of termination 125
Library of Congress 2, 38, 42, 43, 44, 62, 69, 116, 126
limited times 40

M

Made for Hire 41

Major Labels 144
management 15, 18, 26, 50, 99, 149, 153, 159, 214, 215, 217, 252, 253, 258, 259, 260, 261, 262, 280, 281
Managers 3, 12, 18, 28, 29, 253, 255, 257, 258, 259, 260, 280
managers 16, 17, 18, 20, 26, 82, 98, 109, 118, 140, 148, 150, 160, 215, 219, 222, 253, 256, 257, 258, 259, 260, 261, 280, 296
marketing and sales 153, 161
Mark Voleman 12, 13, 251, 254, 256, 257, 258, 259, 290
Mass Media 7, 18, 30
mass media 14, 15, 18, 19, 26, 38, 43, 49, 77, 99, 100, 126, 138, 154, 160, 257, 258, 260, 261, 296
Mechanical 5, 6, 68, 118, 119, 120, 121, 126, 131, 163, 183, 186, 188, 190, 193, 195, 197, 198, 199
Mechanical License 119
Mega Entertainment Corporations 137
megas 157, 163
Melena Ryzik 262
Merchandising 10, 295
Mike Curb 150
Monte Lipman 143
Musicians 3, 10, 11, 16, 18, 19, 29, 125, 192, 194, 215, 216, 220, 226, 228, 231, 253, 294
Music producers 68
Music Publishers 3, 6, 17, 29, 37, 107, 108, 109, 118
Music video 19

N

Neighboring Rights 48
NET Act 45
News Corp. 142
NMPA 6, 37, 109, 118, 127
Notice of Intention 48
NPR 155
NSAI 82

P

P2P 144, 153
p2p 27, 55, 155
Partnerships 3, 19
Patents 38
Peer-to-peer 46
Performance Rights Organizations 81, 122
performance rights organizations 67, 99, 115, 122, 123, 124, 126, 129, 163
Phonorecords 41
Plato 15
points 83, 98, 146, 147, 149, 150, 151, 152, 215, 217, 253, 280, 293, 329
Pollstar , 296
power-of-attorney 257
Press kits 261
Pro-Tools 17, 217, 228
Producers 3, 10, 16, 29, 49, 144, 145, 214, 225, 229, 234
Profit Margins 13, 293, 329
Promoters , 3, 13, 18, 26, 30, 252, 258, 292, 293, 295, 296, 319, 329
promoters 18, 148, 154, 253, 254, 258, 260, 290, 292, 293, 296, 298, 319, 329
Promotion 7, 8, 11, 12, 13, 17, 24, 29, 137, 144, 154, 164, 227, 240, 253, 260, 292, 294, 299, 300, 319
Promotional copies 161
Publicists 3, 17, 26, 29, 258, 261
Publicity 8, 10, 11, 12, 137, 146, 154, 164, 227, 240, 252, 260, 261, 300
Publishers 3, 5, 6, 17, 29, 37, 70, 82, 83, 107, 108, 109, 111, 115, 117, 118, 121, 122, 125, 126, 160
publishers 22, 39, 42, 44, 46, 67, 77, 80, 81, 82, 83, 98, 99, 100, 107, 108, 109, 110, 111, 113, 115, 116, 118, 119, 120, 121, 122, 123, 124, 125, 126, 150, 160, 164, 215, 219
publishing deal 62

Q

Qtrax.com 159

R

Radio 8, 11, 13, 17, 18, 24, 68, 146, 154, 155, 156, 192, 194, 216, 220, 260, 294, 295
Recording Artist 14, 80, 137, 252
recording contracts 225
Recording Studios 3, 11, 17, 29, 219
record label 68, 108, 125, 149, 151, 152, 203, 215, 219, 232, 257, 260
RECORD LABEL REVENUE STREAM 22
record labels 15, 17, 18, 19, 22, 27, 40, 44, 82, 83, 98, 108, 125, 126, 140, 142, 143, 144, 147, 149, 150, 152, 157, 158, 163, 166, 216, 217, 220, 223, 231, 237, 257, 260, 261, 290, 298
Record Producers 3, 16, 29
recoup 112, 113, 121, 126, 153, 186, 197, 215, 228, 334
Recoupment 8, 151
registration 42, 61, 62, 63, 99, 116
Retail outlets 19, 153
RIAA 9, 46, 121, 144, 154, 161, 162, 169
rider 18, 295, 296, 298, 311
Ringtones 121
Rodgers and Hammerstein 67
royalties 17, 26, 40, 44, 46, 47, 48, 68, 83, 98, 99, 108, 109, 111, 112, 113, 115, 116, 117, 118, 119, 120, 121, 122, 123, 124, 125, 126, 137, 147, 151, 152, 157, 159, 160, 163, 164, 203, 215, 222, 254, 258, 259, 262, 280
Royalty Artists 219
royalty base 151, 258
Royalty Points 8
Rupert Murdock' 142
Rush Limbaugh 38

S

SAG 259, 296
scale 156, 216, 217, 220, 221, 222, 223, 225, 226, 231, 232
Serious Music Market 13, 296, 303
SESAC 7, 67, 70, 81, 99, 107, 109, 118, 121, 122, 123, 124, 126
SGA 82
shameless self-promotion. 28, 253, 254
shark 111, 116, 126, 151
Single song contracts 111
sole proprietorship 19
Songcasting 109
Songwriters 3, 5, 15, 29, 51, 61, 67, 82, 83, 116, 117, 120, 123, 160, 253
SONGWRITING/MUSIC PUBLISHING REVENUE STREAM 20
Sonny Bono 4, 46, 55, 111
Sony 22, 38, 108, 137, 139, 150, 151, 156, 163
Sound recordings 39, 42, 70
SoundScan 121
Soundscan 187, 296
SpiralFrog.com 159
SRLP 146, 151, 152, 153
Staff writer 112, 117
Stage Manager 260
Statute of Anne 39, 40
Statutory Rate 119
Steve Jobs 158
Studio musicians 216, 253
studio musicians 16, 19, 150, 214, 216, 220, 224, 225, 229
Sub-publishing 115

Supreme Court 37, 47, 48, 124
Sync Licenses 121, 126

T

Talent 3, 8, 12, 14, 15, 18, 29, 30, 259
THE MANAGEMENT/TOURING REVENUE STREAM 24, 25
The Turtles 257
The Walt Disney Company 7, 137, 138, 163
Thomas Edison 43
Ticketmaster , 296
Time Warner 7, 22, 38, 108, 137, 138, 140, 141, 150, 156, 163
Tin Pan Alley 80, 111
Tom Whalley 14
Trademarks 38
Trade secrets 38
Trisha Yearwood 252

U

Unions 220, 223
United States Constitution 40
Universal 22, 38, 49, 108, 137, 141, 150, 156, 163

V

Van Morrlson 37
Viacom 142
virtual corporation 292, 319
Vocalists 3, 15, 29

W

Warner Music 140, 143, 156, 163
WIPO 4, 45, 50
Woody Allen 252
work-for-hire 61, 68, 98, 111, 147, 218
works-for-hire 218
World Intellectual Property Organization 45, 50
Wrecking Crew 218
WTO 4, 50
www.facebook.com, 27, 148, 158
www.myspace.com 9, 27, 144, 148, 158, 164, 252
www.youtube.com 27, 148, 334

LaVergne, TN USA
06 January 2010
169033LV00001B/96/P